SOURCE READINGS IN *Music* HISTORY

Also available in a one-volume composite edition.

SOURCE READINGS IN *M*USIC HISTORY

OLIVER STRUNK

EDITOR

Revised Edition

LEO TREITLER GENERAL EDITOR

VOLUME 5

The Late Eighteenth Century

Edited by WYE JAMISON ALLANBROOK

 W·W·NORTON & COMPANY
New York · London

The text of this book is composed in Caledonia
with the display set in Bauer Bodoni and Optima.
Composition by the Maple-Vail Book Manufacturing Group
Manufacturing by Maple-Vail Book Manufacturing Group
Book design by Jack Meserole
Cover illustration by Mary Frank

The Library of Congress has cataloged the one-volume edition as follows:

Source readings in music history / Oliver Strunk, editor. — Rev. ed.
    / Leo Treitler, general editor.
        p.   cm.
    Also published in a 7 v. ed.
    Includes bibliographical references and index.
    ISBN 0-393-03752-5
    1. Music—History and criticism—Sources.   I. Strunk, W. Oliver
(William Oliver), 1901–   .   II. Treitler, Leo, 1931–   .
ML160.S89   1998
780′.9—dc20   94-34569
                                                       MN

ISBN 0-393-96698-4 (pbk.)

W. W. Norton & Company, Inc., 500 Fifth Avenue, New York, N.Y. 10110
http://www.wwnorton.com

W. W. Norton & Company Ltd., 10 Coptic Street, London WC1A 1PU

2 3 4 5 6 7 8 9 0

FROM THE FOREWORD TO THE FIRST EDITION OF *SOURCE READINGS IN MUSIC HISTORY*

*T*his book began as an attempt to carry out a suggestion made in 1929 by Carl Engel in his "Views and Reviews"—to fulfil his wish for "a living record of musical personalities, events, conditions, tastes . . . a history of music faithfully and entirely carved from contemporary accounts."[1] It owes something, too, to the well-known compilations of Kinsky[2] and Schering[3] and rather more, perhaps, to Andrea della Corte's *Antologia della storia della musica*[4] and to an evaluation of this, its first model, by Alfred Einstein.

In its present form, however, it is neither the book that Engel asked for nor a literary anthology precisely comparable to the pictorial and musical ones of Kinsky and Schering, still less an English version of its Italian predecessor, with which it no longer has much in common. It departs from Engel's ideal scheme in that it has, at bottom, a practical purpose—to make conveniently accessible to the teacher or student of the history of music those things which he must eventually read. Historical documents being what they are, it inevitably lacks the seemingly unbroken continuity of Kinsky and Schering; at the same time, and for the same reason, it contains far more that is unique and irreplaceable than either of these. Unlike della Corte's book it restricts itself to historical documents as such, excluding the writing of present-day historians; aside from this, it naturally includes more translations, fewer original documents, and while recognizing that the somewhat limited scope of the *Antologia* was wholly appropriate in a book on music addressed to Italian readers, it seeks to take a broader view.

That, at certain moments in its development, music has been a subject of widespread and lively contemporary interest, calling forth a flood of documentation, while at other moments, perhaps not less critical, the records are either silent or unrevealing—this is in no way remarkable, for it is inherent in the very nature of music, of letters, and of history. The beginnings of the Classical

---

1. *The Musical Quarterly* 15, no. 2 (April 1929): 301.
2. *Geschichte der Musik in Bildern* (Leipzig, 1929; English edition by E. Blom, London, 1930).
3. *Geschichte der Musik in Beispielen* (Leipzig, 1931; English edition New York, 1950).
4. Two volumes (Torino, 1929). Under the title *Antologia della storia della musica della Grecia antica al' ottocento*, one volume (Torino, 1945).

symphony and string quartet passed virtually unnoticed as developments without interest for the literary man; the beginnings of the opera and cantata, developments which concerned him immediately and deeply, were heralded and reviewed in documents so numerous that, even in a book of this size, it has been possible to include only the most significant. Thus, as already suggested, a documentary history of music cannot properly exhibit even the degree of continuity that is possible for an iconographic one or a collection of musical monuments, still less the degree expected of an interpretation. For this reason, too, I have rejected the simple chronological arrangement as inappropriate and misleading and have preferred to allow the documents to arrange themselves naturally under the various topics chronologically ordered in the table of contents and the book itself, some of these admirably precise, others perhaps rather too inclusive. As Engel shrewdly anticipated, the frieze has turned out to be incomplete, and I have left the gaps unfilled, as he wished.

For much the same reason, I have not sought to give the book a spurious unity by imposing upon it a particular point of view. At one time it is the musician himself who has the most revealing thing to say; at another time he lets someone else do the talking for him. And even when the musician speaks it is not always the composer who speaks most clearly; sometimes it is the theorist, at other times the performer. If this means that few readers will find the book uniformly interesting, it ought also to mean that "the changing patterns of life," as Engel called them, will be the more fully and the more faithfully reflected. . . . In general, the aim has been to do justice to every age without giving to any a disproportionate share of the space.

It was never my intention to compile a musical Bartlett, and I have accordingly sought, wherever possible, to include the complete text of the selection chosen, or—failing this—the complete text of a continuous, self-contained, and independently intelligible passage or series of passages, with or without regard for the chapter divisions of the original. But in a few cases I have made cuts to eliminate digressions or to avoid needless repetitions of things equally well said by earlier writers; in other cases the excessive length and involved construction of the original has forced me to abridge, reducing the scale of the whole while retaining the essential continuity of the argument. All cuts are clearly indicated, either by a row of dots or in annotations.

Often, in the course of my reading, I have run across memorable things said by writers on music which, for one reason or another, were not suited for inclusion in the body of this book. One of these, however, is eminently suited for inclusion here. It is by Thomas Morley, and it reads as follows:

> But as concerning the book itself, if I had, before I began it, imagined half the pains and labor which it cost me, I would sooner have been persuaded to anything than to have taken in hand such a tedious piece of work, like unto a great sea, which the further I entered into, the more I saw before me unpassed; so that at length, despairing ever to make an end (seeing that grow so big in mine hands which I thought to have shut up in two or three sheets of paper), I laid it aside, in full determination to

have proceeded no further but to have left it off as shamefully as it was foolishly begun. But then being admonished by some of my friends that it were pity to lose the fruits of the employment of so many good hours, and how justly I should be condemned of ignorant presumption—in taking that in hand which I could not perform—if I did not go forward, I resolved to endure whatsoever pain, labor, loss of time and expense, and what not, rather than to leave that unbrought to an end in the which I was so far engulfed.[5]

OLIVER STRUNK
The American Academy in Rome

5. Thomas Morley, *A Plain and Easy Introduction to Practical Music,* ed. R. Alec Harman (New York: Norton, 1966), p. 5.

FOREWORD TO THE REVISED EDITION

> *Hiding in the peace of these deserts*
> *with few but wise books bound together*
> *I live in conversation with the departed,*
> *and listen with my eyes to the dead.*
> *—Francisco Gómez de Quevedo*
> *(1580–1645)*

*T*he inclusion here of portions of Oliver Strunk's foreword to the original edition of this classic work (to which he habitually referred ironically as his *opus unicum*) is already a kind of exception to his own stricture to collect in it only "historical documents as such, excluding the writing of present-day historians." For his foreword itself, together with the book whose purpose and principles it enunciates and the readings it introduces, comes down to us as a historical document with which this revision is in a conversation—one that ranges over many subjects, even the very nature of music history.

This principle of exclusion worked for Strunk because he stopped his gathering short of the twentieth century, which has been characterized—as Robert Morgan observes in his introduction to the twentieth-century readings in this series—by "a deep-seated self-consciousness about what music is, to whom it should be addressed, and its proper role within the contemporary world." It is hardly possible to segregate historian from historical actor in our century.

For the collection in each of the seven volumes in this series the conversation begins explicitly with an introductory essay by its editor and continues with the readings themselves. The essays provide occasions for the authors to describe the considerations that guide their choices and to reflect on the character of the age in each instance, on the regard in which that age has been held in music-historical tradition, on its place in the panorama of music history as we construct and continually reconstruct it, and on the significance of the readings themselves. These essays constitute in each case the only substantial explicit interventions by the editors. We have otherwise sought to follow Strunk's own essentially conservative guidelines for annotations.

The essays present new perspectives on music history that have much in common, whatever their differences, and they present new perspectives on the music that is associated with the readings. They have implications, therefore, for those concerned with the analysis and theory of music as well as for students of music history. It is recommended that even readers whose interest is focused on one particular age acquaint themselves with all of these essays.

The opportunity presented by this revision to enlarge the book has, of course, made it possible to extend the reach of its contents. Its broader scope reflects achievement since 1950 in research and publication. But it reflects, as well, shifts in the interests and attitudes that guide music scholarship, even changes in intellectual mood in general. That is most immediately evident in the revised taxonomy of musical periods manifest in the new titles for some of the volumes, and it becomes still more evident in the introductory essays. The collections for "Antiquity and the Middle Ages" have been separated and enlarged. What was "The Greek View of Music" has become *Greek Views of Music* (eight of them, writes Thomas J. Mathiesen), and "The Middle Ages" is now, as James McKinnon articulates it, *The Early Christian Period and the Latin Middle Ages*. There is no longer a collection for "The Classical Era" but one for *The Late Eighteenth Century*, and in place of the epithet "The Romantic Era" Ruth Solie has chosen *The Nineteenth Century*. The replacements in the latter two cases represent a questioning of the labels "Classic" and "Romantic," long familiar as tokens for the phases of an era of "common practice" that has been held to constitute the musical present. The historiographic issues that are entailed here are clarified in Solie's and Wye Jamison Allanbrook's introductory essays. And the habit of thought that is in question is, of course, directly challenged as well by the very addition of a collection of readings from the twentieth century, which makes its own claims to speak for the present. Only the labels "Renaissance" and "Baroque" have been retained as period designations. But the former is represented by Gary Tomlinson as an age in fragmentation, for which "Renaissance" is retained only *faute de mieux,* and as to the latter, Margaret Murata places new emphasis on the indeterminate state of its music.

These new vantage points honor—perhaps more sharply than he would have expected—Strunk's own wish "to do justice to every age," to eschew the "spurious unity" of a "particular point of view" and the representation of history as a succession of uniform periods, allowing the music and music-directed thought of *each* age to appear as an "independent phenomenon," as Allanbrook would have us regard the late eighteenth century.

The possibility of including a larger number of readings in this revision might have been thought to hold out the promise of our achieving greater familiarity with each age. But several of the editors have made clear—explicitly or implicitly through their selections—that as we learn more about a culture it seems "more, not less distant and estranged from ours," as Tomlinson writes of the Renaissance. That is hardly surprising. If the appearance of familiarity has arisen out of a tendency to represent the past in our own image, we should hardly wonder that the past sounds foreign to us—at least initially—as we allow it to speak to us more directly in its own voice.

But these words are written as though we would have a clear vision of our image in the late twentieth century, something that hardly takes account of the link, to which Tomlinson draws attention, between the decline of our confidence about historical certainties and the loss of certainty about our own identities. Standing neck deep in the twentieth century, surrounded by uncountable numbers of voices all speaking at once, the editor of this newest selection of source readings may, ironically, have the most difficult time of any in arriving at a selection that will make a recognizable portrait of the age, as Morgan confesses.

Confronted with a present and past more strange and uncertain than what we have been pleased to think, the editors have not been able to carry on quite in the spirit of Strunk's assuredness about making accessible "those things which [the student] must eventually read." Accordingly, this revision is put forward with no claim for the canonical status of its contents. That aim has necessarily yielded some ground to a wish to bring into the conversation what has heretofore been marginal or altogether silent in accounts of music history.

The sceptical tract *Against the Professors* by Sextus Empiricus, among the readings from ancient Greece, is the first of numerous readings that run against a "mainstream," with the readings gathered under the heading "Music, Magic, Gnosis" in the Renaissance section being perhaps the most striking. The passage from Hildegard's *Epistle* to the prelates of Mainz in the medieval collection is the first of many selections written by women. The readings grouped under the reading "European Awareness of Other Musical Worlds" in the Renaissance collection evince the earliest attention paid to that subject. A new prominence is given to performance and to the reactions of listeners in the collection from the Baroque. And the voices of North American writers and writers of color begin to be heard in the collection from the nineteenth century.

There is need to develop further these once-marginal strands in the representation of Western music history, and to draw in still others, perhaps in some future version of this series, and elsewhere—the musical cultures of Latin America for one example, whose absence is lamented by Murata, and the representation of the Middle Ages in their truly cosmopolitan aspect, for another.

This series of books remains at its core the conception and the work of Oliver Strunk. Its revision is the achievement of the editors of the individual volumes, most of whom have in turn benefited from the advice of numerous colleagues working in their fields of specialization. Participating in such a broadly collaborative venture has been a most gratifying experience, and an encouraging one in a time that is sometimes marked by a certain agonistic temper.

The initiative for this revision came in 1988 from Claire Brook, who was then music editor of W. W. Norton. I am indebted to her for granting me the privilege of organizing it and for our fruitful planning discussions at the outset. Her thoughts about the project are manifested in the outcome in too many ways to enumerate. Her successor Michael Ochs has been a dedicated and active editor, aiming always for the highest standards and expediting with expertise the complex tasks that such a project entails.

Leo Treitler
Lake Hill, New York

CONTENTS

NOTES AND ABBREVIATIONS

Footnotes originating with the authors of the texts are marked [Au.], those with the translators [Tr.].

References to other volumes in this series are indicated as follows:

SR   Oliver Strunk, ed., *Source Readings in Music History*, rev. ed., Leo Treitler, ed. (New York: W. W. Norton, 1997)

SR 2   Oliver Strunk, ed., *Sources Readings in Music History*, rev. ed., Leo Treitler, ed., vol. 2: *The Early Christian Period and the Latin Middle Ages*, James McKinnon, ed. (New York, Norton, 1997)

SR 4   Oliver Strunk, ed., *Source Readings in Music History*, rev. ed., Leo Treitler, ed., vol. 4: *The Baroque Era*, Margaret Murata, ed. (New York: W. W. Norton, 1997)

SR 6   Oliver Strunk, ed., *Source Readings in Music History*, rev. ed., Leo Treitler, ed., vol. 6: *The Nineteenth Century*, Ruth A. Solie, ed. (New York: Norton, 1997)

Years in the common era (A.D.) are indicated as C.E. and those before the common era as B.C.E.

THE LATE
EIGHTEENTH
CENTURY

INTRODUCTION

*W*hen the first edition of *Source Readings in Music History* was reissued in 1965 in five separate volumes devoted to the five canonical periods of music history, the documents from the latter half of the eighteenth century were collected under the customary heading "The Classic Era." In the years since, however, there has been a growing recognition that period labels are vexed, each in its own way, and perhaps none more than this one. Like most period labels in music history ("Romantic" being a notable exception), "Classic" or "Classical" is a designation applied only in retrospect; it is not to be found anywhere in the pages of the method books and essays from which these selections are drawn. Such designations nevertheless offer a taxonomic power and convenience of reference that are considered by the user to outweigh the dangers of the procrustean bed they provide for the time period in question. In this particular case, however, the label bespeaks an act of appropriation that long posed a serious barrier to our coming to understand late eighteenth-century music as an independent phenomenon. In at least two of the word's accepted senses—"model of excellence" and "that which is distinguished from Romantic"—"Classic" is a designation given by writers whose gaze is turned back to the past, in a spirit either of self-congratulation or of conservative dismay: they think to find there the source of what is best in the writer's present, or to divine a benchmark against which to measure modern decline. Behind either search lies a tacit confidence about continuity between the present and its recent past: if one claims a work or a style as a model, there is a presumption that one knows how to use it, and hence what it is. The process of appropriation began in the early nineteenth century when E. T. A. Hoffmann declared the music of the preceding decades truly romantic—of a piece with his musical present. In an 1813 article titled "Beethoven's Instrumental Music,"[1] Hoffmann pronounced instrumental music to be the "only genuinely romantic art," because "its sole subject is the infinite." Beethoven, of course, he judged to be the most profound practitioner of this new and transcendent music, in which "the lyre of Orpheus opened the portals of Orcus" to "disclose . . . an unknown realm." But he also swept Mozart and Haydn into the charmed circle, styling them as the originators of the Romantic spirit, and in so doing he fixed them firmly on this side of the boundary between the musical past and present. Although a later generation reclassified

1. See *SR6*.

these first two Romantics as Classic prototypes for the Romantic canon, they never lost their claim to kinship, but were treated as familial and hence familiar—as composers whose stylistic premises were transparent, presenting no obscurity to the critical eye.

This assumption endured with remarkable persistence in one form or another for almost 150 years. Since in the late 1940s, when the original version of this anthology was being assembled, the music of the late eighteenth century was still considered continuous with "our music," there seemed to be little point in seriously examining the premises of its composition. The great pedagogical treatises of the mid-eighteenth century—of Leopold Mozart and Carl Philipp Emanuel Bach, for example—were just beginning to appear in English editions as Oliver Strunk was preparing translations from them for the first edition of *Source Readings*. The notion of instrumental music's "transcendence" and the formalist attitudes that it implied were common currency. The vocabulary of analysis was still that imposed by nineteenth-century theorists of "sonata form." Standard teaching editions of Mozart piano sonatas still came with a critical apparatus at the top of the page identifying Exposition, Development, Recapitulation, and Principal and Secondary Theme; these instructions seemed as indisputable as the directions for rendering ornaments which appeared at the foot of the page. It is not surprising that the only real intellectual matter of the period seemed to reside in quasi-literary issues such as the "Querelle des bouffons" (the "Quarrel of the Comedians," the Parisian pamphlet war over the merits of French and Italian music that raged in the early 1750s), the virtues of "reform" (Gluckian) opera, and, in performance practice, the correct rendering of the trill.

Only recently have musicologists, in part through investigations of some of the texts newly included in this volume, begun to realize that this utterly familiar music was nonetheless written under premises more remote from us than could previously have been conceived. The late eighteenth century was an era of practical pedagogues in the Capellmeister tradition, "compleat" musicians trained to competence in every aspect of composition and performance, sacred and secular, in a court's music "chapel," and prepared to instruct their successors in similar skills. They wrote composition method books much as they did instrument tutors—in the conviction that composition is a craft (rather than an unconscious creative act), and thus teachable to the pliant student. They started their musical apprentices off with small pieces, teaching them rules of thumb that led seamlessly to the composition of larger works. Joseph Riepel's *praeceptor* states with playful clarity twice in nine pages, in graphic outsize fonts, a principle that will have its final working-out in the *Versuch einer Anleitung zur Composition*, the composition treatise of Heinrich Christoph Koch: A MINUET IS NOTHING OTHER THAN A CONCERTO, AN ARIA, OR A SYMPHONY. "Minuet" in this sentence translates into the minimal version of what today is often called "rounded binary form"—a sixteen-measure piece organized in units of four measures (subdividable into two-measure units) that makes a full circuit harmonically, and achieves rhetorical completeness through an increasingly emphatic degree of punctuation at the ends of its articulating cuts or phrase lengths. Symphony and sonata movements, as both Riepel and Koch go on to show, are simply expanded versions of the basic minuet syntax; *galant* dance rhetoric provides the skeleton for composition.

Dice games for composing minuets were a parlor commonplace, and a spirit of gamesmanship suffuses these expansions, which are achieved by paraphrase and parody, by combination and permutation, in short, by an understanding of "the mechanical rules of melody," in Koch's own formulation. The teaching of classical rhetoric that was crucial for Riepel and Koch—and to the music of their contemporaries—was not the doctrine of figures or local embellishments, but the more basic one of prosodic lengths. Essentially Koch's "mechanical rules" show the composer how to invent articulated segments that are intrinsically musical, yet have the conviction of good verbal rhetoric—the equivalent in music of ancient rhetoric's *kommata* ("coins" or "chips"), *kola* ("members"), and *periodoi* ("circuits" or "cycles")—commas, colons, and periods.[2] Koch calls them incises *(Einschnitte)*, phrases *(Sätze)*, and periods *(Perioden)*. These names were originally coined to refer to the lengths themselves, not to the signs that designate the ends of the lengths; the marks of punctuation took their names from the cuts they punctuate. Koch's teachings of "melodic punctuation" (again his own formulation) are not in fact rules but the enunciation of syntactical paths with subsidiary options. The thrust of the Ciceronian period lies behind them: expansion is not symmetrical (architectonic) but linear or dynamic. More and greater lengths are required toward the end of a section or movement, where persuasion naturally concentrates its efforts. An architecture that was "frozen music," as Goethe famously declared, would have resulted in startlingly misshapen buildings.

Rather than a prefabricated vessel filled with striking musical ideas (a description more appropriate to Romantic sonata form), a movement of a musical work was to these teachers a canny manipulation of these musical lengths or phrases, conceived in rhetoric, as it were, and generated in dance. Koch's definition of the composition of movements and works as "the connection of melodic sections into periods of greater length" is not the same as "form"; the emphasis is on process—construction—rather than structure, the fluid over the frozen. Later in the *Versuch*, Koch extends a simple eight-measure bourrée tune to thirty-two measures to become a section of a sonata movement by means of his expansion techniques. As commas and colons are joined in periods, periods joined to make the larger whole, and these shapes find differentiation according to medium and occasion—symphony, quartet, concerto. The essential shape for the larger works, like that of the smaller ones, is binary: one massive period with "appendices," closing on the key of the fifth degree,

2. See, for example, Johann Mattheson, *Der vollkommene Capellmeister*, trans. Ernest C. Harriss (Ann Arbor, Michigan: UMI Press, 1981), pt. II, chap. 9.

comprises the first part, while the second is divided into two, with anticipatory and recapitulatory functions. Like Koch, Francesco Galeazzi and Jérôme-Joseph de Momigny see a movement as essentially created of periods; they take a step beyond Koch, however, in classifying periods by affect and function. Galeazzi articulates the frequent habit of the cantabile period, which he calls the *passo caratteristico* or "characteristic passage," and Momigny in 1806 differentiates periods even more narrowly, inventing an analytical vocabulary—"opening," "spirited," and "connective" periods, for example—that reflects their functions as dynamic rather than architectonic entities. Discussions of instrumental genres by Johann Joachim Quantz in the 1750s and Koch in the 1790s provide a gauge of instrumental music's gradual advance toward independence and individuation. For Quantz a symphony is still a *sinfonia*—an opera prelude (he complains that it is chronically unsuitable to the ensuing action). Koch, on the other hand, is describing fully independent symphony, quartet, and concerto movements, and has obviously been moved by the newly achieved grandeur of these genres. He compares the concerto to a Greek tragedy in its passionate dialogue between actors and chorus.

In this comparison of Koch's, as well as in the preceding discussion of instrumental music, speech and voice are fundamental reference points. The word *melody*—*Melodie, chant, cantilena*—has a remarkable prominence in most of the texts included here, in discussions of compositional techniques as well as in those of expression. This focus on the leading line in preference to the supporting harmony—either that of contrapuntal parts or of the *basse fondamentale*—is a significant compositional premise, which had been urged previously by Johann Mattheson in the earlier part of the century.[3] The operative metaphor is not the Romantic "song without words," but a precise and articulate melos. Jean-Jacques Rousseau, in his *Essay on the Origins of Language*, considers melody to be the equivalent of design or line in painting, and in his *Letter on French Music* he stresses the importance of the "unity of melody," that is, music in which all parts function as support for the cantilena. Galeazzi defines and discusses a movement as a "well-conducted melody." It is in this understanding of melody that the mechanical and the expressive meet. "After all," writes Vincenzo Manfredini, "music is only singing," or, in other commonplaces of the day, a melody that must "speak to the heart" (again Rousseau) through a "language of feelings" (Daniel Gottlob Türk).[4] The human voice implies expressive intent, and the cantilena leads the listener through a movement. One can learn to deploy the instrumental cantilena as mechanical figures, but once in place it is expressive as the human voice is expressive—a leading edge that controls the design with a projection of one or another pas-

---

3. Mattheson, pt. II, chaps. 1–41.
4. Hester Piozzi draws an analogy between melody and harmony, innocence and virtue, and comes down on the side of virtue (that is, complexity—"worked-outness"). But it was precisely the quality of "innocence"—a simple directness that "moves the heart"—that the composers of the late 1700s set as their goal.

sion. Hoffmann had speculated that Beethoven was less successful in writing vocal music because that medium "excludes the character of indefinite longing"; since words must always signify, vocal music is too precise. That very precision of reference was the virtue that had moved eighteenth-century writers to hold up the vocal as their paradigm: reference to a shared world of human experience was the means by which music moved its auditors. Momigny reflects this idea when he supplies the cantilena of the first movement of Mozart's String Quartet in D Minor, K. 421, with an imagined text that conveys the affect of noble pathos embodied in the music by personifying it in the figure of *Didone abbandonata*. Here the instrumental is not the ineffable, as it later becomes; explanation of its nonsemantic reference takes the form of translating its commas, colons, and periods into the signifying lengths of speech. Momigny's dramatic text is a "program," perhaps, but an analytical one, reflecting his confidence that one can articulate the "precise" (his word) intentions of the composer.

Momigny's immediate predecessors, however, did not need to illustrate the dominant expression of a piece by crafting a parallel poem. Expression could still be objectified into affects or stances, and the means of its communication—for both composer and performer—were a matter of instruction. What makes this possible is the connection of expression with gesture; oft quoted is Cicero's statement in *De oratore*: "Every motion of the soul has by nature its own look and sound and gesture; one's whole frame and countenance and all the sounds one utters resound like strings in a lyre as they are struck by a motion of the soul."[5] Each affect has a characteristic motion, which can be given musical shape to a great extent—as Johann Philipp Kirnberger points out—by the proper choice of meter. Kirnberger urges the performer to internalize these gestures by assiduous practice in the rhythms of social dance music. All pedagogues worth their salt include a discussion that resembles Kirnberger's anatomy of meters, though not as tirelessly complete. Although Kirnberger was considered old-fashioned because of his focus on the music of J. S. Bach, Türk echoes many of Kirnberger's prescriptions at the end of the century, turning them into finely detailed instructions to the amateur keyboard player for the performance of music expressing various affects. Türk also includes the ubiquitous discussion on the taxonomy of style—high, middle, low; church, chamber, theater; French, German, Italian; strict, free:[6] shared human venues as well as shared human passions dictate the shape and texture

5. See, for example, Charles Batteux, *The Fine Arts Reduced to a Single Principle* (Paris, 1747), trans. Edward A. Lippman, in *Musical Aesthetics: A Historical Reader, Volume I: Antiquity to the Eighteenth Century* (New York: Pendragon Press, 1986), p. 266; Daniel Webb, *Observations on the Correspondence between Poetry and Music* (London, 1769), in Lippman, vol. 1, p. 202; Johann Nikolaus Forkel, *Allgemeine Geschichte der Musik* (Leipzig, 1788), p. 282, n. 5.
6. See, for example, Mattheson, pt. 1, chap. 10; Johann Adolf Scheibe, *Der critische Musikus* (Leipzig, 1745), vol. 1, chaps 13–15, 23–24; Koch, *Musikalisches Lexikon* (Frankfurt, 1802), "Styl, Schreibart." Hester Lynch Piozzi's account of various countries' predilections in music, heavily colored with *sensibilité*, is an idiosyncratic version of the taxonomy of national styles.

of a work. On the other hand, personal style—that most remarked on and remarkable characteristic of Romantic composers—merits only a passing mention in Türk's discussion, just as Koch cites Mozart and Haydn not as world-historical figures but as composers who excelled in meeting the requirements of a particular genre. Only Johann Friedrich Reichardt's whimsical imagining that Haydn, Mozart, and Beethoven built themselves distinctive styles as snails construct their shells—a summerhouse, a palace, and a cathedral respectively—foreshadows later attitudes, both in its stress on individual stylistic differences and in its choice of the architectural metaphor.

Among those who wrote more generally about style and expression there is little disagreement yet—with the possible exception of Michel-Paul-Guy de Chabanon—about the existence of a codifiable relation between expression and gesture, or expression and motion. Some balk at the use of the traditional word "imitation" to describe music's depiction of the motions of the soul, preferring to limit the term's significance to the representation of natural phenomena and calling any other use "expression." But they all take for granted an external referent for the act: it is not "self-expression." Often, taking their cue from Cicero, they elaborate an actual physiology for the relation—a theory of sympathetic vibrations in which the impression of the passion is communicated to the soul via the effect of the tones on the nerves. Johann Jakob Engel is impressed by the phenomenon of the musical glasses, an instrument whose eerie tones were said to be capable of sending the average person into a deep melancholy: "man is only an instrument," writes Chabanon. This doctrine leads Engel to a psychophysiological theory of music as an imitation that "paints" not an external object, but the impression the object makes on the soul. Because its objects are human passions, which can be represented by certain codifiable note patterns, Engel's remains a theory of affect, but one that by internalizing expression confirms with a new certainty that mere natural phenomena are not a proper object of imitation. Chabanon, on the other hand, is a maverick who takes a strong stand against imitation, preferring to think of music as direct, unmediated sensation, with no capacity for reference. But even in his writings the prevailing teachings are deep-seated: he still assumes a natural connection between the motion of tones and states of the soul. He is, perhaps unwittingly, one of the few writers to articulate and give grudging approval to the kind of mediated or topical imitation that was so central to the expressive vocabulary of late eighteenth-century compositions. In his formulation, imitation is plausible when the composer "gives one melody the character of another," that is, when serious music imitates occasional music, and the common coin of popular song and dance becomes the expressive vocabulary of symphonies and sonatas. Mozart stands somewhere between Engel and Chabanon, taking what could be characterized as a more "composerly" view. To him music both is and is not the things it imitates: it can paint a throbbing heart, but it also has forms and syntactical properties that are irreducibly its own, and not to be exceeded. Two currents seem to flow together in his opinion—an assumption that music is not entirely a mimetic art, because at some level its materials are distinguished as well by a purely internal consistency of relation, and a conviction reflecting the widespread notion that the more violent and base passions are not appropriate subjects for music: the art should edify, not introduce degraded motions into the soul. As music comes to be considered at once more private and more transcendental, such seemingly conservative opinions will become a staple of the new aesthetic.

Vocal music being the eighteenth century's dominant paradigm, opera may seem to come late to this essay, but with good reason. While *opera buffa* was the operatic genre that exerted the most pressure on the development of late eighteenth-century style, as a popular form it had developed no real critical or pedagogical texts of its own. Opera was, of course, at the forefront of critical debate throughout the century. A prodigious amount of ink was expended in discussions of the relative merits of French and Italian opera in the three famous literary duels of the eighteenth century: the first revolved around the opera of Lully, a second—the notorious "Querelle des bouffons"—was sparked by the 1752 appearance in Paris of a troupe of Italian *buffi*, or comedians, and the third pitted the operas of Christoph Willibald Gluck against those of the Italian Niccolò Piccinni. In addition to the question of music and national character, there were several other axes to this famous debate, only roughly coincident: old versus new-fangled, words versus music, serious versus comic, and reform versus unreconstructed, or "whatever will sell." Mozart and Francesco Algarotti could be seen as staking out opposing extremes in the words and music debate: Algarotti (seconded by the reform-minded Gluck) described the composer as a tyrannical sovereign, while Mozart, in a letter to his father, playfully compared the poet to a trumpet player, a mere purveyor of professional tricks. Although not an essay on musical comedy *per se*, Rousseau's famous *Letter on French Music* was occasioned by comic opera, in the form of Giovanni Battista Pergolesi's intermezzo *La serva padrona* (in his lamentably short life, this Neapolitan composer managed to create two cultural icons—this intermezzo and his *Stabat mater*, the most frequently published work in the latter half of the century). Rousseau's bellicose declaration that "the French have no music and cannot have any; or . . . if they ever have, it will be so much the worse for them" was quoted persistently in essays throughout the rest of the century, and *buffa* arias were praised for their simplicity and clarity of motive, the propulsive power and expressive flexibility of their rhythms, and the aptness of their language for musical setting; the Chevalier Chastellux credited the Italians with having invented the musical period (drawing his paradigm not from *opera buffa* but from *opera seria*—his idol was the poet Pietro Metastasio).[7] The reverence that Charles Burney expressed upon entering the

---

7. F-J. de Chastellux, *Essai sur l'union de la poésie et de la musique* (Paris, 1765), p. 17.

city of Naples, "impressed with the highest of ideas of the perfect state in which I should find practical music," is a tribute to the extraordinary influence that city had had in Europe as the birthplace of *opera buffa*.

While all the programs of earnest reformers could not make the operas of Gluck any more than a memorable cul-de-sac in operatic history, *buffa* not only defined three of the greatest operas that hold the stage today—*Le nozze di Figaro, Don Giovanni,* and *Così fan tutte*—but also played a significant role in the shaping of late eighteenth-century style, one that even today is incompletely articulated. In addition to the considerable impact of its simplicity and popular spirit, *buffa* made a critical contribution to the development of contrast as a compositional premise through the witty economy of comic representation that enabled characteristic styles or *topoi* to bump up against one another while remaining recognizable entities. Yet *buffa* had no Tosi, no Manicini.[8] Scrambling to get the next new work on the boards, its composers did not take the time to frame statements of intent in the form of dedicatory epistles, and the art was too much of a popular form to encourage systematizers. Praise of *buffa*'s power came from some unlikely quarters: Algarotti admired its direct expressiveness, which he claimed occurred *faute de mieux*, as a result of the limited abilities of its singers, and Mancini expressed admiration for its actors, the like of which were unfortunately no longer to be found on the *seria* stage. But Vincenzo Manfredini's rather chaotic polemic—an attempt to define an eighteenth-century *seconda prattica*—is as close as we come to a description of the aria styles of Mozart and his colleagues, and it does not offer much in the way of definition.

There is, however, an extraordinary and baffling work of the imagination that enacts *buffa*'s power in an unforgettable but unsettling way: Denis Diderot's *Rameau's Nephew*. Left unpublished until 1804, it could be said to a point a way—a *via negativa*—to the aesthetic conversion that occurred at the beginning of the nineteenth century. Halfway through the dialogue, the Nephew, that brilliantly abject changeling and court jester, delivers a pedantic lecture on the Rousseauian view of melody as an imitation of the cry of passion, in which he compares *buffa*'s Parisian triumph to an act of religious subversion (the bloodless *coup d'état* of the foreign god). Then he is off into a manic display—a performance of a performance, affecting all the styles, playing all the parts, working himself into an inspired frenzy. But this time when the lyre of Orpheus opens the portals of Orcus, all that happens is that gibbering ghosts fly forth, brushing past the faces of the astonished spectators. In the hands of this imitator, the kaleidoscopic *buffa* style—the style of styles—suddenly seems morally bankrupt. Lacking a moral self, the Nephew is caught in an infinite

8. Pier Francesco Tosi (c. 1653–1732) and Giambattista Mancini (1714–1800), both eminent castrati who wre also singing teachers, wrote the definitive texts on vocal practice in *opera seria* for the early and later halves of the eighteenth century. For Tosi's treatise see SR4; for Mancini's see this volume, pp. 131–41.

regress, standing ever outside of the things he imitates with such devilish clarity. One thinks of Don Giovanni and Leporello expressing exaggerated comic
pity at the antics of the fulminating Elvira. Until now we have been tacitly
viewing the imitator as a benevolent deity, arranging his representations on the
magic-lantern screen for our pleasure and edification. In this account he
becomes a fractured soul, a madman, a demon perhaps. Perhaps the escape
from this dark side of comedy lies in E. T. A. Hoffmann's "music of indefinite
longing"—a longing for a lost innocence. Germaine de Staël gives a positive
face to this nostalgia in her brief essay on Rousseau. The metaphysics of sensibility transforms the characteristic style—in this case the Swiss herdsman's
song, the *ranz des vaches*—from a representation among representations into
a Proustian object that provides a window into a lost past, where women are
young again and men are moral. Wrenched from the context of the variegated
mimetic discourse shaped by *buffa,* the musical *topos* has become a signifier of
our separation from Arcadia, and a stimulus to the state of yearning melancholy
that seems to offer to lead us back. There would be no recrossing this deep
aesthetic divide.

•   •   •

It is in the very nature of this project that the following list of acknowledgments
is long. It was clear from the start that a satisfactory completion would depend
on extensive consultation with my colleagues in the field. Consult I did, and
was overwhelmed by the volume and generosity of the replies. An extraordinary number of people took time away from their work to reflect on what texts
they would like to see represented in an anthology of this sort. If there are
significant omissions in this selection—and there certainly are—my consultants
bear no blame for my idiosyncrasies. But from them I derived a rich list of
suggestions and, more important, a valuable perspective against which to make
my final choices. I owe particular thanks in this regard to Katherine Bergeron,
Bruce Alan Brown, Scott Burnham, Floyd K. Grave, Deborah Hayes, Eugene
Helm, Jan LaRue, Janet M. Levy, Justin London, Frederick Neumann, William
S. Newman, Ruth Halle Rowen, Susan Snook-Luther, Jane R. Stevens, Cynthia
Verba, and Neal Zaslaw. Special gratitude is due to Leonard G. Ratner, who
consulted with me at length; to Mary Hunter, whose guidance was critical in
the selection of new texts concerning opera; to Stefan Eckert and Ingeborg
Ratner for their help on the Riepel translation; and to Curtis Price and his
colleagues Robert Hume and Judith Milhous, who generously prepared a
selection from the diaries of Susanna Burney that they are just now bringing
to light. I am grateful to all those who allowed me to reprint their translations,
and especially to Nancy K. Baker, Bathia Churgin, and Raymond Haggh,
who worked closely with me in preparing the final selection from their work.
Jeanne Pang Goyal of Stanford University, Wallace Plourde at the St. John's
College Library, and Judy Tsou at the UC Berkeley Music Library tracked

down elusive texts. Consultations with my Strunk coworkers Ruth Solie and Margaret Murata were informative and consoling, Michael Ochs was forbearing beyond my deserts in the final stages of the process, and Leo Treitler has been the consummate editor, whose intelligence and tact have made a pleasure out of hard work.

THE PRACTICE OF COMPOSITION: MEASURE AND PHRASE

1 Joseph Riepel

Joseph Riepel was born in Austria in 1709 and schooled in Linz and Graz, where he studied philosophy and music. After some years of study in Dresden with a pupil of Johann Joseph Fux, he moved to Regensburg in 1751, where he pursued a career as a composer, violinist, and theorist in the chapel of the Count of Thurn and Taxis until his death in 1782.

Riepel's major theoretical work was *Anfangsgründe zur musicalischen Setzkunst (Fundamentals of Musical Composition)* a work published in five chapters over a period of sixteen years, from 1752 till 1768. It is cast as a dialogue between a pupil and a teacher, probably in imitation of the *Gradus ad Parnassum* of Fux, to whom Riepel pays tribute in his first chapter. In the same section he seeks to regularize the study of melody, a concern relatively new to eighteenth-century theory and probably activated by the growing popularity of the *galant* style, with its emphasis on short phrases organized into clear and symmetrical periods. The first book of its kind to appear, Riepel's treatise may not have the lucidity of organization attained by his successor, Heinrich Christoph Koch, but his influence on Koch was considerable. Koch praises Riepel as one who "shed the first rays of light" over "matters that were then still completely hidden in darkness."

FROM *Fundamentals of Musical Composition*

(1752)

CHAPTER ONE. DE RHYTHMOPOEÏA, OR ABOUT RHYTHMIC ORDERING[1]

Pupil. My honorable schoolmaster in Monsberg sends friendly greetings to your honor, and asks whether you might teach me a little something in composition.

Master. I am glad the schoolmaster has so much confidence in me.

Pupil. He thinks very highly of your honor, that much I know.

TEXT: The original edition (Frankfurt and Leipzig, 1752), pp. 1–9. Translation by Wye J. Allanbrook.

1. *De metro.* Although often, even among the most trustworthy writers, foot, meter, and rhythm are absolutely the same. So says Vossius, *De poematum cantu et viribus rhythmi*, p. 11. [Au.] Isaac Vossius was a Netherlands scholar whose treatise *On the Song of Poetry and the Powers of Rhythm*, delivered as lectures at Oxford in 1673, concerned the expressive powers of meter and rhythm.

Master. I am obliged to him. But excessive ceremony could possibly just get in our way. Never in my life have I been able to tolerate these titles. If it's all right with you, let us say *du* to one another.

Pupil. With the greatest of pleasure; this way I know that we are dealing with each other sincerely. As you can see, my teacher has supplied me with a few sheets of paper, so that you can write down the fundamental rules for me.

Master. Given the inexhaustible sea of music, it is less feasible to contain all the rules of composition on a few sheets of paper than it is to squeeze the Danube through a narrow fountain.[2]

Pupil. But my master says that I should try to be finished with you soon. He himself wants to take me under his wing afterwards, and make a complete man out of me.

Master. I believe that. I know many schoolmasters who are always ready to give advice to any would-be Capellmeister. I hope your master is not the worst of them. But I will say this to you—We won't be finished with our writing in two or three days, especially since I at any rate do not have the time to be brief as well as clear. So I'll be direct at some times, circuitous at others, and I'll write down only a little something about all these rules. But it's better to write extensively about this little something than nothing at all. In short: in fourteen days you should learn from me what it took me more than fourteen years to learn from others. But *nota bene:* only in so far as you grasp everything well. Now tell me if you have good notions and thoughts in your head to put on paper.

Pupil. Oh yes, if I can only compose the bass for them.

Master. That you should learn from me in a single day. But first I want to know whether you have an adequate knowledge of the proper arrangement of the melody. For he who wishes to build houses must have the proper materials.

Pupil. Then I'll quickly compose some French dances, or so-called minuets, to prove my capability.

Master. It is certainly no great glory to compose minuets, but on the other hand it is very exacting. For a *minuet,* as far as its working-out is concerned, is *nothing other than a concerto, an aria, or a symphony.* You'll see this clearly in a few days. So we'll tend to begin in a wholly small and insignificant fashion, but with the aim of achieving from that something greater and more praiseworthy.

Pupil. In my opinion there is nothing in the world easier to compose than a minuet. I've actually ventured to write down a whole dozen quickly, one after another. Just look, for example, at one in C. (I just want to see what fault will be found with it.)

---

2. *Verum gutta cavat lapidem* [But a drop will hollow out a stone]. And I make this remark just as a pastime; I'm not willingly idle when I can have something to make sport with. [Au.].

I have written in numbers above the measures so that if, contrary to all expectation, there should be any error you can point it out more clearly. I certainly don't mean to boast.

Master. Good heavens! You don't yet know one note from another. I will extract from this minuet—if I must call it that—some singing or cantabile measures. Otherwise, please whom it will, I myself wouldn't give you good pipe tobacco for it.

Pupil. I couldn't have dreamt this. What's the reason?

Master. No. 1. I say that *an even number of measures is pleasing to the ear in all compositions,* and is especially required in a minuet. But in the second part you composed an uneven number of measures, namely thirteen.

No. 2. Each part generally should contain no more than eight measures. It's true you haven't made this error in the first part, but you have in the second; probably because you don't yet know how to distinguish among a *Zweyer,* a *Dreyer,* and a *Vierer.*[3] Therefore you have

No. 3. not really separated off the opening, or *theme,* and articulated it fully with distinct *Zweyer* or *Vierer.*

No. 4. I see some measures that are without motion, and some where the notes run too much by step. But until the cadence a minuet requires notes that move either perfectly or imperfectly.[4]

No. 5. I don't see a single measure in the second part that resembles one in the first. But one must take particular care with that, since a minuet *must be as coherent as a concerto, an aria, or a symphony,* etc. Consequently I could make at least a half dozen minuets out of yours, because it contains so many different kinds of notes and measures.

No. 6. An experienced natural scientist once confided in me that a minuet

---

3. By *Zweyer, Dreyer,* and *Vierer* Riepel means "two-measure unit," "three-measure unit," and "four-measure unit." Since there is no satisfactory English equivalent, the terms and their plurals (identical to the singulars) have been left untranslated in the text.

4. By "perfect" motion Riepel means at least quarter-note motion on every beat in a measure; by "imperfect" motion he means a motion of a half note and a quarter note. The third alternative— a dotted half note—he calls "dead." See p. 23, where he explains the term.

will succeed without much effort, and advance with unfailing propriety, if it rises in the first part and falls back again in the second. But I see just the opposite in yours.

No. 7. Keen connoisseurs of minuets require the fourth and fifth measures to be clearly distinguished, especially in the first part. That is, if the fourth measure has notes that move perfectly, then the fifth should consist of notes that move imperfectly; or the opposite.

Pupil. This is dreadful! If I just knew right now what a *Zweyer* and a *Dreyer* were, or a moving or running note, I would begin to make changes immediately.

Master. A *Zweyer*[5] consists of two measures that are generally similar in motion to the two measures following them:

first *Zweyer*   second *Zweyer*

But in these neighboring *Zweyer* the notes shouldn't all move exactly alike. You can also do the following:

or

Now a *Dreyer*[6] consists of three such measures:

first *Dreyer*   second *Dreyer*

or

5. *Binarius.* [Au.]
6. *Ternarius.* [Au.]

Pupil. I understand that very well now, for you can see it and hear it. But which ones are better for a minuet—the *Zweyer* or the *Dreyer?*

Master. The *Zweyer;* the *Dreyer* aren't of any use here. But I'll tell you today when and where these can be put to good use.

Pupil. Then you can make a *Dreyer* out of a *Zweyer,* and vice versa, by cutting a measure off, for example, or adding one.

Master. Absolutely. Now a *Vierer*[7] consists of four measures:

This kind of *Vierer* can always have a seat and a vote in a minuet.

Pupil. I can see that, because it is not very different from two *Zweyer:*

Master. If a *Vierer* doesn't follow, then in a pinch I wouldn't finally dispute your opinion. But the *Zweyer* look clearer in the following version than in yours:

Pupil. This is true, but how does it happen?

Master. Because here the second *Zweyer* ends a tone higher. Your *Zweyer,* on the other hand, both end on the tone F.

Pupil. Now I see that too. But tell me which ones are better, the *Zweyer* or the *Vierer?*

Master. I don't know of any difference between the two.

Pupil. But I am surprised my teacher never said anything to me about such useful and necessary things. Perhaps he doesn't even know what a *Zweyer,* a *Dreyer,* and a *Vierer* are.

Master. Hush! That would be astonishing. Then how could he pass himself off as a composer? For that means having perfect mastery of *rhythmic ordering,* which among other things is *a major part of the composition of all works of music;* and fugues are not completely excluded from this. How this is we will see further on.[8]

---

7. *Quaternarius.* [Au.]
8. One or another old-fashioned quibbler may certainly be very surprised about this, especially one who does not want to understand what is newfangled. But we are talking here about people like me, since I have very often had to hear the word *newfangled* [*neugebacken*]. [Au.] Riepel

Pupil. Then we'll let it go in the meantime. First I'll improve my minuet with regard to No. 1, and just cut out the third measure ✠ in the second part to make a *Zweyer* out of a *Dreyer:*

Menuet

This way the second part contains exactly twelve measures.

And this correction was made according to precept No. 1.

Now just tell me quickly, what are notes that run stepwise?

Master. This sort of thing, for example:

They precede or follow one another without jumping a line or a space.[9] On the other hand the following are notes that move disjunctly:

For some jump from line to line, and some from space to space.

Pupil. Excellent! You mentioned in No. 2 that in each section there should only be eight measures. So I'll omit the extra stepwise notes, namely measures 5 through 8 in the second part:

---

seems to be saying that composers who persist in writing in the old-fashioned fugal style, of whom the pupil's first teacher must be one, will be surprised to discover that fugues should also be governed by modern metrical practices. He sees himself here as a man of reason and moderation caught between pedants and facile innovators—a familiar modern dilemma.

9. *Intervallum.* [Au.]

and make quarter notes out of the ninth and tenth measures, which are now measures 5 ✠ 6:

Menuet

In all there are just sixteen measures.

And this correction was made according to precept No. 2.

But why are notes running stepwise not desirable?

Master. Oh, they are perfectly desirable, and certainly in an *Allegro assai* or a *Tempo presto* and *prestissimo* of a symphony, a concerto or solo, and so forth, they are the best notes of all, because they are flowing and light, and don't hinder the quick strokes of the bow. Moreover, singers like them as well as instrumentalists do, although *they prefer ascending to descending ones:*

Allegro   or Presto   etc.

as being *easier* than the following:

Allegro   or Presto   etc.

Pupil. And probably also easier for flutes, oboes, horns, and trumpets?

Master. Absolutely; particularly for them.

Pupil. I must make a note of this *wonder of nature.* I think that hundreds of compositional decisions rest on this point.

Master. But a minuet always requires notes that move perfectly, namely quarter notes:

They can also be varied or altered:

But in a minuet I can't tolerate the following variation, where the full quarter note stands last:

not good

Pupil. Then it probably wouldn't be desirable in the following version, would it?

Master. Finally, a single such ✠ measure can slip through. Now I would also prefer to let the last four measures of your minuet stay as they are:

running stepwise

Pupil. And why these precisely?

Master. Because the minuet strains to make its cadence or rest just as a hungry man wants supper after work, or—You shouldn't laugh; for *a beginner* in particular *must conceive of this and a thousand other similes if he doesn't want to fill his compositions with* empty, silly, and *pedantic notes.*

Pupil. Now don't take me wrong, but on account of precept No. 3 I would rather lay out the entire minuet with clear *Zweyer* and *Vierer:*

Menuet

And that was according to precept No. 3.

Master. Before you turn to No. 4, I must tell you that a motionless note should never be used in the middle of such a short or dance-style minuet except at the end of the first and second parts. But you can bring this kind of motionless or dead note to life in the following way:

These measures move imperfectly:

Now two measures of this type are quite useless in a minuet. You should always precede or follow one of them with a measure of perfect motion:

Pupil. Fine. Now I'll alter the minuet again, and also make the fifth measure ✠ of the first part a little more alive:

And that was according to precept No. 4.

Now I know that I can use measures with perfect motion throughout (with the exception of the last notes of both sections):

Master. This one is more lively; the previous one, on the other hand, was more singing, and that *cantabile* is produced by measures with imperfect motion.

Pupil. I already know that. I just need to ask whether I can also use dotted notes:

Master. No. I don't think these are at all desirable in a minuet—unless the dancing-master has gone lame. I like the following type about two-thirds better:

Pupil. Fine. I'll be guided accordingly. And concerning No. 5, I think that in the minuet that I corrected before there is enough similarity. I will set out the minuet once again and indicate the similarity with the sign ✠:

And that was according to precept No. 5.

Pay close attention! In the first section the notes marked ✠ go down, in the second, up. So I think that one hears enough similarity or coherence.

Master. Who told you this? Listen, the inversion of the notes marked ✠ is taken by many to be a mere ornament. People often make use of this device in other compositions; indeed sometimes you're forced to it. But I probably wouldn't have noticed it immediately in your minuet if I hadn't seen the explanatory sign ✠ by it.

Pupil. Then I certainly could have done it this way:

or this way:

or with a double correspondence:

If I had time, I would want to bring out still more correspondences. But I would rather ask you concerning No. 6, what rising and falling are?

Master. Isn't this very easy to understand?

rising   falling

Pupil. Good. I'll make my minuet rise and fall too:

And that was according to precept No. 6.

Master. Wait a minute! You're climbing too high. Let me put it this way: in this version the minuet is too youthful, since its melody loses its *seriousness and maturity.*

Pupil. I could certainly just begin lower:

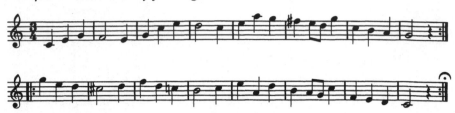

Master. That's very good. But you don't need to rise or fall in every *Zweyer.* Even the cadences are not completely bound to this rule. Hence the cadence of the second part can often by itself express the fall, just as in the first part a single note (marked ✠) can express the rise:

Pupil. Excuse me, but it still doesn't please me nearly as well as an orderly rise and fall. I hope to do better.

Master. As for No. 7, in the fourth and fifth measures I'll mark with larger numbers both the imperfect and the perfect motion:

or the opposite:

Pupil. What does the second part say to that?

Master. It could also behave this way if it wanted to. But it is often so undisciplined that it will not follow any rule. Moreover, the first part can captivate the amateur listener so quickly that he won't fret much about the second part, especially since it is only considered to be a close for the first part.

Pupil. I will compose yet another one, and introduce the same movements into the second part also:

or the opposite:

And finally that was according to No. 7.

So now can I boast that I know how to compose an orderly minuet?

Master. You must never boast.[10] Also, the rules by themselves do not amount to so much. For someone else might compose a minuet whose arrangement was not so orderly as yours, but whose melody[11] was more lively. And that minuet would probably find much more approval among the dilettantes than yours would, after all the rules and measurements we have researched together.

Pupil. Well do I know that one must always and above all look for a good melody.

10. *Propria laus olfacit male* [Self-praise has a bad smell]: we are speaking Latin. But a touch of self-love and a desire for honor are certainly as little harmful to the student as they are to all honorable men in the world. [Au.]
11. *Il cantabile.* [Au.]

2 Johann Philipp Kirnberger

Johann Philipp Kirnberger (1721–1783) was a member of a distinguished group of musical pedagogues in Berlin in the latter half of the eighteenth century, along with Friedrich Wilhelm Marpurg, Carl Philipp Emanuel Bach, Johann Joachim Quantz, Johann Georg Sulzer, and Johann Abraham Peter Schulz. It is likely that Kirnberger studied with Johann Sebastian Bach in Leipzig sometime in 1741. He revered Bach as a composer and teacher, and saw himself as propagating Bach's teaching methods in his principal treatise, *Die Kunst des reinen Satzes in der Musik* (*The Art of Strict Musical Composition*). This work, along with most of Kirnberger's other writings and compositions, was written in the service of Princess Anna Amalia of Prussia; he held this position from 1758 until his death.

Kirnberger's reverence for Bach has caused him to be considered conservative for his time, but he is actually more a transitional figure. He composed in the *galant* as well as the strict style, and urged social dance pieces as models for the study of meter and rhythm in performance. *Die Kunst des reinen Satzes in der Musik* is known principally for its harmonic teachings: it synthesizes the principles of Rameau with figured-bass practice, and the study of counterpoint with a harmonic orientation. The section on tempo and meter also reflects a time of transition: the connection Kirnberger makes between musical movement and the passions was still operative at the time, and while he discusses some time signatures that were no longer in use, their vestiges survived in the more limited spectrum of meters used by *galant* composers.

FROM *The Art of Strict Musical Composition*
(1776)

VOLUME 2, PART 1, CHAPTER 4
TEMPO, METER, AND RHYTHM

A succession of notes that mean nothing by themselves and are differentiated from one another only by pitch can be transformed into a real melody— one that has a definite character and depicts a passion or a particular sentiment—by means of tempo, meter, and rhythm, which give the melody its character and expression. It is immediately apparent to everyone that the most moving melody would be completely stripped of all its power and expression if

TEXT: As translated by David Beach and Jurgen Thym in J. P. Kirnberger, *The Art of Strict Musical Composition* (New Haven: Yale University Press, 1982), pp. 375–77; 380–82; 384–88; 390–92; 394–98; 399–400. The music examples have been renumbered.

one note after another were performed without precise regulation of speed, without accents, and without rest points, even if performed with the strictest observance of pitch. Even common speech would become partly incomprehensible and completely disagreeable if a proper measure of speed were not observed in the delivery, if the words were not separated from one another by the accents associated with the length and brevity of the syllables, and finally if the phrases and sentences were not differentiated by rest points. Such a lifeless delivery would make the most beautiful speech sound no better than the letter-by-letter reading of children.

Thus tempo, meter, and rhythm give melody its life and power. *Tempo* defines the rate of speed, which by itself is already important since it designates a lively or quiet character. *Meter* determines the accents in addition to the length and brevity of the notes and the lighter or more emphatic delivery; and it shapes the notes into words, so to speak. But *rhythm* establishes for the ear the individual phrases formed by the words and the periods composed of several phrases. Melody is transformed into a comprehensible and stimulating speech by the proper combination of these three things.

But it must be kept in mind that none of these elements is sufficient by itself to give the melody a precise character; the true expression of the melody is determined only by their synthesis and their interaction. Two compositions may have the same rate of *allegro* or *largo*, yet still have an entirely different effect; according to the type of meter, the motion is more hurried or emphatic, lighter or heavier, even while the speed remains the same. From this it is clear that tempo and meter must combine their forces. The same is also true of rhythm: the components from which a melody is formed can assume an entirely different expression depending on meter and tempo.

Thus, whoever wants to write a melody must pay attention to the combined effect of tempo, meter, and rhythm and must consider none of these without regard to the other two. Nevertheless, it is unavoidable for me to discuss each of them separately here and to tell the aspiring composer what he needs to know about each individual point.

I. TEMPO

The composer must never forget that every melody is supposed to be a natural and faithful illustration or portrayal of a mood or sentiment, insofar as it can be represented by a succession of notes. The term *Gemüthsbewegung*, which we Germans give to passions or affections, already indicates their analogy to tempo.[1] In fact, every passion and every sentiment—in its intrinsic effect as well as in the words by which it is expressed—has its faster or slower, more violent or more passive tempo. This tempo must be correctly captured by the composer to conform with the type of sentiment he has to express.

1. The German words used by Kirnberger for tempo are *Bewegung* and *Taktbewegung*. The former also has a more general meaning that has been translated throughout as "motion." [Tr.]

Thus I must admonish the aspiring composer above all that he study diligently the nature of every passion and sentiment with regard to tempo, so that he does not make the terrible mistake of giving the melody a slow tempo where it should be fast, or a fast tempo where it should be slow. However, this is a field that is not limited to music, and that the composer has in common with the orator and poet.

Furthermore, he must have acquired a correct feeling for the natural tempo of every meter, or for what is called *tempo giusto*. This is attained by diligent study of all kinds of dance pieces. Every dance piece has its definite tempo, determined by the meter and the note values that are employed in it. Regarding meter, those having larger values, like alla breve, $\frac{3}{2}$, and $\frac{3}{4}$ meter, have a heavier and slower tempo than those of smaller values, like $\frac{2}{4}$, $\frac{3}{4}$, and $\frac{6}{8}$ meter, and these in turn are less lively than $\frac{3}{8}$ or $\frac{6}{16}$ meter. Thus, for example, a loure in $\frac{3}{2}$ meter has a slower tempo than a minuet in $\frac{3}{4}$ meter, and the latter is in turn slower than a passepied in $\frac{3}{8}$. Regarding note values, dance pieces involving sixteenth and thirty-second notes have a slower tempo than those that tolerate only eighth and at most sixteenth notes as the fastest note values in the same meter. Thus, for example, a sarabande in $\frac{3}{4}$ meter has a slower tempo than a minuet, even though both are written in the same meter.

Thus the *tempo giusto* is determined by the meter and by the longer and shorter note values of a composition. Once the young composer has a feeling for this, he will soon understand to what degree the adjectives *largo, adagio, andante, allegro, presto,* and their modifications *larghetto, andantino, allegretto,* and *prestissimo* add to or take away from the fast or slow motion of the natural tempo. He will soon be able not only to write in every type of tempo, but also in such a way that this tempo is captured quickly and correctly by the performers.

However, tempo in music is not limited just to the different degrees of slow and fast motion. There are passions "in which the images flow monotonously like a gentle brook; others where they flow faster with a moderate stir, but without delay; some in which the succession of images is similar to wild brooks swollen by heavy rains, which rush violently along and sweep with them everything that stands in their way; and again others in which the images are similar to the wild sea, which violently beats against the shore and then recedes to crash again with new force."[2] Similarly, tempo in melody can also be violent or tender, skipping or monotonous, fiery or bland even when the degree of fast or slow motion is the same, depending upon the type of note values chosen for the melody.

•   •   •   •   •

Thus the composer, in constructing a piece, has to consider two things regarding tempo: (1) the slow or fast pace of the tempo; and (2) the characteris-

2. See the article "Ausdruck" in Sulzer's [*Allgemeine*] *Theorie der schönen Künste* [Leipzig, 1771–74]. [Au.].

tic motion of the parts of the measure, or the type of rhythmic changes. Lively sentiments generally require a fast tempo; but the expression can become playful, or flirtatious, or happy, or tender, or pathetic by means of the type of characteristic motion of the parts of the measure, or the rhythmic steps. Likewise, a slower tempo generally is appropriate to the expression of sad sentiments, but through the second type of motion the expression can become more or less agitated, tender or violent, gentle or painful. Of course, it is not the motion alone that has this effect; the remaining good qualities of an expressive melody must be united with it, but then it contributes most forcefully to the expression.

This may be sufficient to draw the prospective composer's attention to the effect of motion in general. In the following two sections of this chapter we will have the opportunity to discuss in greater detail the particular effects of metric and rhythmic motion. Therefore, it may suffice here to add a couple of remarks for the young composer regarding motion in general.

He must be careful in writing a piece not to make it hurry or drag. Although these words are common only in the theory of performance, they can also be applied to composition. It can easily happen that a composer, without noticing it, rushes the tempo in writing a fiery Allegro, or lets it drag in a sad Largo; or, out of fondness for a phrase, he may unwittingly become lax about the tempo, so that the phrase becomes vague because of its fast rate of rhythmic motion or dull because of its slowness. The composer suffers in the performance of such pieces, but through his own fault.

He must not overstep the limits of fast or slow tempo. What is too fast cannot be performed clearly, and what is too slow cannot be comprehended. This applies mainly to pieces where the composer himself indicates the tempo.

Because of the long period of vibration of low notes, all short note values must be avoided in the low register; but in the high register they are more effective than long sustained notes. The progression of the bass generally relates to that of the highest part like the walk of a mature man to that of a young girl. Where she takes two or three steps, he takes only one, yet both cover the same distance. Not that a young girl could not go slowly and a mature man quickly, but it is not as natural. Similarly, the voices in the middle registers can be considered as gaits of boys and young adults by analogy to the shorter or longer note values of their rhythmic steps.

Finally, the composer must not neglect to designate the tempo of his piece as precisely as possible whenever it cannot be determined from the features given above. He must use the terms *allegro assai, allegro moderato, poco allegro*, etc., wherever the word *allegro* would indicate a tempo that is too fast or not fast enough. The same is true of slow pieces. The words that refer to characteristic motion, such as *maestoso, scherzando, vivo, mesto*, etc., are often of the greatest significance in expressive pieces, and not meaningless for those who want to perform a piece well. Hasse is so precise in the designation of his tempi that he often makes lengthy descriptions of how the piece is to be performed: *Andantino grazioso, ma non patetico, non languente; Allegro vivo, e con spirito,* or *allegro vivo, che arrivi quasi all'allegro intiero; un poco lento, e maestoso, ma che non languisca, e abbia il dovuto suo moto.*[3]

II. METER

If one imagines a melody in which all the notes are presented with the same intensity or stress, and in which they have the same length or duration (as if, for example, the melody were to consist only of whole notes), it would be comparable to a monotonously flowing stream. What distinguishes one melody from another is the faster or slower current: one is comparable to a thundering stream, another to a gentle, somewhat faster or slower flowing river, and a third to a gently rippling brook. If a more or less full and consonant harmony is imagined along with such a melody, one has everything that could distinguish one melody from another.

The entire power or expression of such a melody would consist only of a gentle and light or a lively and strong current, which would lull us to sleep or wake us up. If melody is to become similar to speech and adapted to the expression of various emotions and sentiments, individual notes must be turned into meaningful words and several words into comprehensible phrases. This transformation of a mere stream of notes into a melody resembling speech is accomplished in part by accents that are given to a few notes, and partly by the difference in their durations. It is just the same as with common speech, where we distinguish words and sentences only by means of the accents and durations of syllables.

Meter actually consists of the precise uniformity of accents that are given to a few notes and of the completely regular distribution of long and short syllables. That is, when these heavier or lighter accents recur at regular intervals, the melody acquires a meter or a measure. If these accents were not distributed regularly, so that no precise periodic recurrence occurred, the melody would be similar only to common prosaic speech; but with this periodic return it is comparable to poetic speech, which has its precise meter.

This matter can also be conceived by picturing a simple motion. A melody that just flows along without accents resembles a continuous motion, like that created when a body falls or is thrown through the air; but an accented melody is similar to a motion divided into steps or to walking. Just as walking receives its particular character from the type as well as the speed of the steps, melody receives its character and expression in quite a similar way.

A regular walk has steps of equal length, each of which represents a measure of the melody. However, the steps can consist of more or fewer little movements or *beats,* and these movements or beats, all of which are of the same

3. "A little Andante that is graceful, but not pathetic or languishing; an Allegro that is lively and spirited; a lively Allegro that is almost a full Allegro; rather slow and majestic, but without languishing, and with its own proper motion."

duration, can have smaller divisions or parts; they can also be distinguished by other modifications—by gradations of heavy and light, flowing or leaping, etc. If a precise uniformity is observed in the steps and small movements, this results in the measured walk which we call dance, and this is precisely analogous to measured melody. In just the same way as dance expresses or portrays various sentiments merely by motion, melody does it merely by notes.

Whoever considers this closely will easily understand how much the character of a melody depends on tempo and meter. The clearest examples of this can be found in the various dance melodies. However, it is not possible to give definite rules that would specify the most suitable tempo and meter for every type of sentiment. For the most part, it depends on a refined and accurate sensitivity.

Everything that can be said to a composer about this subject beyond what I have already stated about tempo is contained in the following main topics: (1) that all types of meters invented and in use up to now be described to him, each according to its true structure and its precise execution; (2) that the spirit or character of each meter be defined as precisely as possible; (3) finally, for the situation where the melody is to be written to a given text, that directions be given how the best or at least a suitable type of meter is to be chosen for it. I will have to discuss these three points here.

•　•　•　•　•

The measure consists of two, three, or four equal beats; besides these, there is no other natural type of measure.

To all appearances, only three time signatures would be required to indicate these meters, namely, one that indicates a measure of two, another that indicates a measure of three, and a third that indicates a measure of four beats. However, from what we have stated already in the preceding section of this chapter about *tempo giusto* and the natural motion of longer and shorter note values, it becomes clear, for example, that a measure of two quarter notes and another of two half notes, and likewise a measure of three quarter notes and another of three eighth notes, indicate a different tempo, even though they have the same number of beats. In addition, longer note values are always performed with more weight and emphasis than shorter ones; consequently a composition that is to be performed with weight and emphasis can only be notated with long note values, and another that is to be performed in a light and playful manner can only be notated with short note values.

From this the necessity of different meters with the same number of beats becomes apparent, which we shall now consider in greater detail. In general, meters are divided into even and odd; *even* are those of two and four beats; and *odd*, those of three beats, which are also called triple meters. Furthermore, a distinction is made between simple and compound meters: *simple* meters are constituted in such a way that each measure amounts to only one foot, which cannot be divided in the middle; however, *compound* meters can be divided in the middle of each measure, since they are composed of two simple meters, as will be shown in greater detail below.

Before we list the meters in order, it must still be noted that it is just as easy to divide each beat of a meter into three parts or to triple it as it is to perceive triple meter; this is already obvious from the existence of triplets. This gives rise to meters of *triple beats*, where three pulses fall on one beat. We shall indicate these now, along with the meters from which they are derived, and shall note what is necessary regarding their true structure, their usefulness or unusefulness, and their exact execution. [See Table 1.[4]]

TABLE 1

SIMPLE EVEN METERS OF TWO BEATS

1. $\frac{2}{1}$ meter or ϕ: tripled—$\frac{6}{2}$ meter.
2. $\frac{2}{2}$ meter or ¢:   tripled—$\frac{6}{4}$ meter.
3. $\frac{2}{4}$ meter: tripled—$\frac{6}{8}$ meter.
4. $\frac{2}{8}$ meter: tripled—$\frac{6}{16}$ meter.

SIMPLE EVEN METERS OF FOUR BEATS

1. $\frac{4}{2}$ meter or O: tripled—$\frac{12}{4}$ meter.
2. $\frac{4}{4}$ meter or C: tripled—$\frac{12}{8}$ meter.
3. $\frac{4}{8}$ meter: tripled—$\frac{12}{16}$ meter.

SIMPLE ODD METERS OF THREE BEATS

1. $\frac{3}{1}$ meter or 3:   tripled—$\frac{9}{2}$ meter.
2. $\frac{3}{2}$ meter: tripled—$\frac{9}{4}$ meter.
3. $\frac{3}{4}$ meter: tripled—$\frac{9}{8}$ meter.
4. $\frac{3}{8}$ meter: tripled—$\frac{9}{16}$ meter.
5. $\frac{3}{16}$ meter: tripled—$\frac{9}{32}$ meter.

4. It is clear from this table that Kirnberger's conception of the distinction between simple and compound meter is not consistent with the commonly accepted definition of these terms. The meters listed in the right column, those that are derived from the simple meters in the left column by multiples of three, are normally considered as compound meters; Kirnberger, however, considers them among the simple meters. According to Kirnberger, compound meters, the most useful of which are listed in Table 4.2, are derived from simple meters by multiples of two. This definition leads to certain inconsistencies; no meter of nine (three triple beats), for example, can be considered as compound, since it cannot be divided in the middle. Other meters, like $\frac{6}{8}$, can be simple (derived from $\frac{3}{4}$) or compound (derived from $\frac{3}{8}$); but in both cases, the measure is divided into two triple beats. [Tr.]

OBSERVATIONS ABOUT SIMPLE EVEN METERS OF TWO BEATS

(A) $\frac{2}{1}$ meter, which is also called *large alla breve* by some, consists of two whole notes or semibreves per measure. However, as is the case with the $\frac{6}{2}$ meter of two triple beats that is derived from it, it is no longer used because of the confusion caused by the rests, since the same rest has a value of half a measure at one time and a whole measure at another. In place of these, it is better to use $\frac{2}{2}$ and $\frac{6}{4}$ with the adjective *grave* to indicate the emphatic and weighty performance required by these meters. I know of only one Credo by the elder Bach in the large alla breve meter of two beats, which he designated, however, with C to show that the rests have the same value as in ordinary alla breve time.[5] Telemann, however, has even written church pieces in $\frac{6}{1}$ and other similar meters; one can easily see that these are only eccentricities.

(B) $\frac{2}{2}$ meter, or rather *alla breve*, which is always designated by ¢ or ₵, is most often used in church pieces, fugues, and elaborate choruses. It is to be noted about this meter that it is very serious and emphatic, yet is performed twice as fast as its note values indicate, unless a slower tempo is specified by the adjectives *grave, adagio,* etc. The same is true of the $\frac{6}{4}$ meter of two triple beats that is derived from $\frac{2}{2}$ meter, but the *tempo giusto* of this meter is somewhat more moderate. Both meters tolerate no shorter notes values than eighths.

(C) $\frac{2}{4}$ meter has the same tempo as alla breve but is performed much more lightly. The difference in performance between the two meters is too noticeable for anyone to believe that it makes no difference whether a piece is written in C or in $\frac{2}{4}$. Consider, for example, the following melodic phrase in both meters:

Example 1

If this phrase is performed correctly, everyone will notice that it is much more serious and emphatic in *alla breve* (A) than in $\frac{2}{4}$ (B) meter, where it comes close to being playful. This is the difference between meters having the same number of beats, as was noted above.

$\frac{2}{4}$ meter as well as the $\frac{6}{8}$ meter that is derived from it are most often used in chamber and theater pieces. In their natural tempi, sixteenth notes and a few thirty-second notes in succession are their shortest note values. But if the tempo is modified by the adjectives *andante, largo, allegro,* etc., more or none of these note values can be used, depending on the rate of speed.

5. The work to which Kirnberger refers is the Credo from the *Mass in B Minor* (BWV 232). [Tr.]

(D) $\frac{2}{8}$ meter would be appropriate only for short amusing dance pieces because of its fast tempo and its all too great lightness of execution. However, it is not in use, and we would not have mentioned it if $\frac{6}{16}$ meter—which is derived from it and in which many pieces have been written—did not have to be listed. It differs greatly from $\frac{6}{8}$ meter in the hurried nature of its tempo and the lightness of its execution. J. S. Bach and Couperin[6] have written some of their pieces in $\frac{6}{16}$ meter, not without good reason. Who does not know the Bach fugue at (A) in Example 2?[7]

Example 2

If this theme is rewritten as at (B), the tempo is no longer the same, the gait is much more ponderous, and the notes, particularly the passing notes, are emphasized too much; in short, the expression of the piece as a whole suffers and is no longer the one given to it by Bach. If this fugue is to be performed correctly on the keyboard, the notes must be played lightly and without the least pressure in a fast tempo; this is what $\frac{6}{16}$ meter requires. On the violin, pieces in this and other similarly light meters are to be played just with the point of the bow; however, weightier meters require a longer stroke and more bow pressure. The fact that these and several other meters that we shall list are considered superfluous and obsolete today indicates either that good and correct execution has been lost or that an aspect of expression which is easy to obtain only in these meters is entirely unknown to us. Both of these conclusions do little credit to the art, which supposedly has reached its peak in our time.

•   •   •   •   •

OBSERVATIONS ABOUT SIMPLE EVEN METERS OF FOUR BEATS

(A) $\frac{4}{2}$ meter, or **O**, like $\frac{2}{1}$ time, is no longer in use; it also is objectionable because of the confusion caused by its rests, as is the $\frac{12}{3}$ meter of four triple beats derived from it. They are mentioned here only because one now and then comes across old pieces in these meters. Instead of these, it is better to use $\frac{4}{4}$ and $\frac{12}{8}$ meter with the adjective *grave* to designate the weighty tempo and emphatic performance appropriate to the former meters. If young composers should come across church pieces in *alla breve* time where there are four half

6. Former court organist in Paris. He has published many pieces engraved in copper under the title *Pièces de Clavecin*, which in all respects are models of good keyboard pieces. [Au.]
7. Fugue in F major (BWV 880) from *Das wohltemperierte Klavier*, Part 2. [Tr.]

notes between two barlines, they must not let themselves be misled and conclude that the meter is $\frac{4}{2}$. This occurs only as a convenience for the composer to avoid an excess of barlines and ties, and he is free to do so. But this does not change the nature of the ¢ measure, which always has the same stress every other half note; and the upbeat and downbeat of the measure is fixed even when four, six, and more measures are joined without barline, as Handel, among others, has frequently done in his oratorios. Furthermore, this does not cause confusion regarding the rests, whose value always remains the same in such situations.

(B) $\frac{4}{4}$ meter, which is designated by **C**, is of two types: either it is used with the adjective *grave* in place of the $\frac{4}{2}$ meter just mentioned, in which case it is called large $\frac{4}{4}$ time; or it is the so-called common even meter, which is also called small $\frac{4}{4}$ time.

Large $\frac{4}{4}$ time is of extremely weighty tempo and execution and, because of its emphatic nature, is suited primarily to church pieces, choruses, and fugues. Eighth and a few sixteenth notes in succession are its fastest note values. To distinguish it from small $\frac{4}{4}$ time, it should be designated by $\frac{4}{4}$ instead of **C**. The two meters have nothing in common except for their signatures.

Small $\frac{4}{4}$ time has a more lively tempo and a far lighter execution. It tolerates all note values up to sixteenth notes and is used very often in all styles.

The same is true of $\frac{12}{8}$ meter of four triple beats that is derived from $\frac{4}{4}$ meter. A few older composers who were very sensitive about the manner in which their pieces were performed often designated pieces consisting only of sixteenth notes by $\frac{24}{16}$ instead of $\frac{12}{8}$ to indicate that the sixteenth notes should be performed lightly, quickly, and without the slightest pressure on the first note of each beat. Composers and performers today seem to know so little about these subtleties that they believe, on the contrary, that such meter designations were only an eccentricity of the older composers.

(C) $\frac{4}{8}$ is the lightest of the quadruple meters in execution and tempo. It is distinguished from $\frac{2}{4}$ meter by the weight of its beats, all of which are equally stressed; but in $\frac{2}{4}$ meter the first and third beats are emphasized.

Example 3

Therefore, it has a somewhat slower tempo than $\frac{2}{4}$ meter. Yet, since the liveliness of the tempo makes the stress of the beats less noticeable in both meters, the two are not as different from one another as are $\frac{4}{4}$ meter and *alla breve*. Furthermore, today's composers no longer designate pieces with $\frac{4}{8}$, but always with $\frac{2}{4}$ instead.

Although $\frac{12}{16}$ meter of four triple beats, which is derived from $\frac{4}{8}$ meter, is presently neglected and $\frac{12}{8}$ meter is always written instead, it is completely different from the latter in its greater lightness of execution. The elder Bach has certainly not written the fugue at (A) in Example 4 in $\frac{12}{8}$ and the other at (B) in $\frac{12}{16}$ without good reason.[8]

Example 4

Everyone will easily perceive the distinction between the two meters in these examples. The one at (A) designates a slower tempo and a more emphatic performance; furthermore, many sixteenth notes can be used in this meter. However, no shorter note values can be used in the one at (B), and the sixteenth notes are performed quickly and plainly, without any emphasis. Handel, Bach, and Couperin have written many pieces in $\frac{12}{16}$ meter.

In quadruple meter, the first and third beats are accented, but the second and fourth unaccented. The former are also called strong and the latter weak beats. Of the accented beats, the first is in turn stressed more than the third, as can be seen from Example 5, where ‾ means accented, and ˘ unaccented.

Example 5

Therefore the principal notes of the melody must always fall on the first beat; the other notes receive more or less weight depending on the intrinsic stress of the other beats. In these meters, the closing note always falls on the first beat and must last four beats, except in pieces where the phrase begins on the upbeat, because the cadence is felt only up to the point where a new phrase can begin.

•   •   •   •   •

OBSERVATIONS ABOUT ODD METERS OF THREE BEATS

(A) $\frac{3}{1}$ meter, which consists of three whole notes per measure, and the $\frac{9}{2}$ meter of three triple beats that is derived from it are of no use whatsoever. The weighty and emphatic performance that would be specified by both is achieved by means of the two following meters, particularly if the adjective *grave* is added; furthermore, in the latter the eye is not exhausted by the many large

8. The first is the subject of the Fughetta in C minor (BWV 961); the second is the subject of the Fugue in C-sharp Minor (BWV 873) from *Das wohltemperierte Klavier*, Part 2. [Tr.]

notes and rests that cause only ambiguity and confusion in the former meters.

(B) $\frac{3}{2}$ meter is used very often, especially in church pieces, because of the ponderous and slow performance indicated by its note values. In this style, quarter and, at most, eighth notes are its fastest note values. In the chamber style, sixteenth notes can also be used in $\frac{3}{2}$ meter; C. P. E. Bach has even begun a symphony in this meter with many thirty-second notes in a row.[9] With such note values, the three beats of this meter must be indicated most clearly in the other voices; otherwise the melody would remain fuzzy and incomprehensible to the listener.

Because of the different weights of their beats, $\frac{3}{2}$ meter has no other similarity with $\frac{6}{4}$ meter except that both contain six quarter notes. Yet it is to be noted as something special that good composers of old have treated the courante, which is generally written in $\frac{3}{2}$, in such a way that both meters were often combined in it. Consider, for example, the first part of a courante for keyboard by Couperin in Example 6.[10]

Example 6

9. Wotquenne lists a symphony in E-flat for two horns, two oboes, two violins, viola, and bass (1757) that begins with continuous sixteenth-note (but not thirty-second-note) motion in $\frac{3}{2}$ meter. See Alfred Wotquenne, *C. Ph. Em. Bach: Thematisches Verzeichnis seiner Werke* (Leipzig, 1905), no. 170 (p. 61). [Tr.]
10. François Couperin, *Pièces de Clavecin*, Book I (Paris, 1713), first order, first courante. [Tr.]

The second and sixth measures and the bass melody of the seventh measure of this courante are in $\frac{3}{2}$ meter, but the other measures are written in $\frac{6}{4}$. In the works of J. S. Bach there are a number of courantes treated in this same way.

The $\frac{9}{4}$ meter of [three] triple beats that is derived from $\frac{3}{2}$ occurs rarely, since $\frac{9}{8}$ is used instead. But it is easily understood that the two meters are very different with respect to the performance and tempo that they specify. In the church style, where a ponderous and emphatic execution is generally combined with a subdued and slow tempo, $\frac{9}{4}$ meter is preferable by far to $\frac{9}{8}$, since a melody that assumes a serious expression in the former meter can easily appear playful in the latter:

Example 7

(C) Because of its lighter execution, $\frac{3}{4}$ meter is not as common in the church style as $\frac{3}{2}$; but it is used very often in the chamber and theatrical styles.

Its natural tempo is that of a minuet, and in this tempo it does not tolerate many sixteenth notes, even less thirty-second notes, in succession. However, since it assumes all degrees of tempo from the adjectives *adagio, allegro*, etc., all note values that fit this tempo can be used, depending on the rate of speed.

The $\frac{9}{8}$ meter of three triple beats that is derived from $\frac{3}{4}$ has the same tempo as $\frac{3}{4}$, but the eighth notes are performed more lightly than in $\frac{3}{4}$.

It is a mistake to consider this meter as a $\frac{3}{4}$ meter whose beats consist of triplets. He who has only a moderate command of performance knows that triplets in $\frac{3}{4}$ meter are played differently from eighths in $\frac{9}{8}$ meter. The former are played very lightly and without the slightest pressure on the last note, but the latter heavier and with some weight on the last note. The former never or only rarely permit a harmony to be sounded with the last note, but the latter do very often. The former do not permit any arpeggiations in sixteenth notes, but the latter do very easily. If the two meters were not distinguished by special qualities, all gigues in $\frac{6}{8}$ could also be written in $\frac{2}{4}$; $\frac{12}{8}$ would be a **C** meter, and $\frac{6}{8}$ a $\frac{2}{4}$ meter. How senseless this is can easily be discovered by anyone who rewrites, for example, a gigue in $\frac{12}{8}$ or $\frac{6}{8}$ meter in **C** or $\frac{2}{4}$ meter.

$\frac{3}{4}$ and $\frac{9}{8}$ meter gave the older composers the opportunity to use an $\frac{18}{16}$ meter of three sextuplet beats when they wanted to indicate that the piece should be performed lightly, swiftly, and without the slightest pressure on the first note of each beat:

Example 8

However, since such subtleties of performance have been lost to such a degree that even many who are called virtuosos perform six beamed sixteenths like two compounded triplets, $\frac{18}{16}$ meter belongs among the meters that are lost and highly dispensable today.

(D) $\frac{3}{8}$ meter has the lively tempo of a passepied; it is performed in a light but not an entirely playful manner and is widely used in chamber and theatrical music.

$\frac{9}{16}$ meter of three triple beats that is derived from $\frac{3}{8}$ was used in many ways by the older composers for gigue-like pieces that are to be performed extremely quickly and lightly. But it no longer occurs in contemporary music; $\frac{9}{8}$ meter appears in its place.

(E) $\frac{3}{16}$ meter, which indicates the truly light performance of hasty pieces and dances that are commonly written in $\frac{3}{8}$, where only one beat can be heard for each measure because of the very fast tempo, has been used rarely. In Handel's keyboard suites there is a gigue in $\frac{3}{16}$ meter that begins as shown in Example 9.

Example 9

That this is nothing other than $\frac{3}{16}$ meter—even though the signature is $\frac{12}{8}$ instead of $\frac{3}{16}$ in the edition by John Walsh[11]—is evident from the concluding note, which falls on the downbeat and lasts for just three sixteenths. This is not possible in $\frac{12}{16}$ meter but is possible in compound $\frac{6}{16}$ meter, as will be shown in greater detail when we discuss compound meters.

$\frac{9}{32}$ meter of three triple beats that is derived from $\frac{3}{16}$ is of no use at all and, furthermore, has never been used.

These triple meters have the common element that, in each, three beats are felt per measure, the first of which is always accented, the third unaccented. The second can be accented or unaccented, depending on the nature of the piece. That is, it is usually accented in ponderous meters and in serious pieces, as in chaconnes and many sarabandes; but in light meters this second beat is weak. This two-fold treatment of the second beat in triple meter is clarified by Example 10.

11. In the Walsh edition of the second volume of these suites (London, 1736?), the meter signature is given as $\frac{12}{8}$ but the piece is notated in $\frac{12}{16}$. Kirnberger, however, insists that the meter is really $\frac{3}{16}$ but notated in $\frac{12}{16}$ to avoid writing so many barlines. [Tr.]

Example 10

In the first example, a nonessential dissonance, which can only appear on a strong beat, falls on the second quarter. In the second, the cadence falls on the same beat; consequently it is also accented here. But in the third example it is weak.

What I have stated previously about the treatment of even meters with regard to the different weights of the beats can easily be applied to triple meter as well. Suspensions or nonessential dissonances, principal notes, and cadences can fall only on accented beats. However, cadences on the second strong beat of the triple measure are less common than those on the first, or downbeat. Many English and, particularly, Scottish dances deviate from this rule and conclude on the upbeat; but in this way they acquire a somewhat strange flavor, which is noticeable even to an untrained ear.

When eighth notes occur in $\frac{3}{4}$ meter and sixteenths in $\frac{3}{8}$, the first of these eighths or sixteenths is accented.

•   •   •   •   •

Let this now suffice concerning knowledge of the mechanical nature of all common meters. . . . I now have to consider:

2. the spirit of actual character of each of these meters from the standpoint of their power to express sentiments and passions.

Here it is not so much the even or odd number of beats in a measure that matters as the slower or faster tempo and the heavier or lighter gait of the measure. One meter can be used for contrasting passions, depending upon the tempo and other factors. However, since each meter has a treatment that is most suitable and natural to it, or, if one wants, most common, then it also has to this extent a special character that can, of course, be taken away from it by a strange and unusual treatment.

Thus, what I have to say here concerns the special ease with which this or that meter can assume a certain character.

It is to be noted in general that, among the meters which have the same number of beats, the one that has larger or longer beats is naturally a bit more serious than the one of shorter beats. Thus $\frac{4}{4}$ meter is less lively than $\frac{4}{8}$ meter; $\frac{3}{2}$ meter is more ponderous than $\frac{3}{4}$, and the latter is not as lively as $\frac{3}{8}$.

For solemn and pathetic pieces, *alla breve* is especially appropriate and is therefore used in motets and other solemn church pieces. Large $\frac{4}{4}$ meter has a very emphatic and serious motion and is suited to stately choruses, to fugues in church pieces, and generally to pieces where pomp and gravity is required. $\frac{3}{2}$ meter is emphatic and very serious as long as not too many short notes are used. $\frac{4}{4}$ meter is best suited for a lively and exhilarating expression that is still somewhat emphatic. $\frac{2}{4}$ is also lively but certainly combined with more lightness and, for that reason, can be used well to express playfulness. $\frac{4}{8}$ meter is definitely totally fleeting, and its liveliness no longer contains any of the emphasis of $\frac{4}{4}$ meter. The character of $\frac{3}{4}$ appears to be gentle and noble, particularly when it consists only, or at least mostly, of quarter notes. But $\frac{3}{8}$ meter has a liveliness that is somewhat frolicsome.

These general characters are defined even more specifically by the particular note value that prevails and by rules that determine progression by larger or smaller intervals. The character of $\frac{3}{4}$ meter is entirely different when quarter notes are used almost exclusively throughout than when many eighths and even smaller notes occur, and when it progresses mostly by small intervals than when leaps occur more often. Since many dances receive their peculiar character from such special determining features within the same meter, and since I plan to discuss this matter in a special chapter, I will have the opportunity to speak there about the character of such pieces that are bound to specific rules.

From the few remarks that I have made here about the different characters of the meters, it is evident that this difference of meters is very well suited to express particular nuances of the passions.

Each passion has its own degrees of strength and, if I may say so, its own deeper or shallower character. Joy, for example, can be solemn and almost exalted; it can be overwhelming, but also leaping and frolicsome. Joy can have these and even more levels and nuances, and such is the case with the other passions as well. Above all, the composer must have a definite impression of the particular passion that he has to portray and then choose a more ponderous or lighter meter depending upon whether the affect in its particular nuance requires one or the other.

3 Heinrich Christoph Koch

Heinrich Christoph Koch was born in 1749 into a family of musicians who worked at the court of Rudolstadt, a provincial town in eastern Germany. Except for a brief period spent studying in Berlin, Dresden, and Weimar in 1773, he remained in Rudolstadt as a court violinist and composer until his death in 1816 (his compositions, unpublished except in his own treatise, were largely ceremonial cantatas and miscellaneous instrumental music). In 1792 he withdrew from the post of *Kapellmeister* to the more modest rank of *Konzertmeister* in order to concentrate on his work as a teacher. From this position of quiet seclusion he wrote two of the most important pedagogical works of the later eighteenth century: *Versuch einer Anleitung zur Composition* (*Introductory Essay on Composition;* 1782–93) and the *Musikalisches Lexikon* (*Music Lexicon;* 1802). The *Versuch* is a systematic treatise on composition for the beginner. Although it includes discussions of all the elements of music, Koch was fully aware of the central role played by melody in the *galant* aesthetic of "stirring the feelings," and placed his primary emphasis on the study of its "mechanical rules." These rules are the new teachings of melodic syntax, of the period, and of the period's extension into the full-fledged instrumental forms of the symphony and the concerto. As examples Koch cites the music of his day, of Carl Heinrich Graun, Franz Benda, and Haydn; in the third volume of the *Versuch* he praises Mozart's six quartets dedicated to Haydn.

FROM *Introductory Essay on Composition*

(1782–93)

[VOLUME 2 (1787)]

PART 2. ON THE MECHANICAL RULES OF MELODY: ON THE WAY IN WHICH MELODY IS CONNECTED WITH RESPECT TO THE MECHANICAL RULES

SECTION 3. ON THE NATURE OF MELODIC SECTIONS

§77. Certain more or less noticeable resting points for the mind are generally necessary in speech and thus also in the products of those fine arts which attain their goal through speech, namely poetry and rhetoric, if the subject that they present is to be comprehensible. Such resting points for the mind are just as necessary in melody if it is to affect our feelings. This is a fact which has never yet been called into question and therefore requires no further proof.

By means of these more or less noticeable resting points, the products of these fine arts can be broken up into larger and smaller sections. Speech, for example, breaks down into various periods or sentences through the most noticeable of these resting points; through the less noticeable the sentence, in turn, breaks down into separate phrases and parts of speech. Just as in speech, the melody of a composition can be broken up into periods by means of analogous resting points, and these, again, into single phrases and melodic segments.

In this section, we shall necessarily first become acquainted with the material nature of the sections which form the periods of melody. Then we can profitably study their formal nature, that is, the way in which the smaller melodic sections are connected into a principal section of the whole, or the construction of melodic periods.

§78. If we consider the various sections in musical works which compose

TEXT: As translated by Nancy Kovaleff Baker in *Heinrich Christoph Koch: Introductory Essay on Composition* (New Haven: Yale University Press, 1983), pp. 1–3, 6–9, 11, 13–16, 41–43, 45–46, 65–66, 85–86, 95–96, with minor alterations. The music examples have been renumbered.

their periods, then two main characteristics are found through which they distinguish themselves as divisions of the whole. The first is the type of their endings, or that which characterizes the resting points in the material aspect of the art. The second is the length of these sections, together with a certain proportion or relation between them which can be found in the number of their measures once they are reduced to their essential components.

The endings of these sections are certain formulas, which let us clearly recognize the more or less noticeable resting points. We have as yet no generally accepted technical term which would appropriately express not only the variety of these formulas in general, but also the particular order in which the different kinds and types can follow one another in the construction of melodic periods.[1] For lack of a completely suitable term and on account of its similarity to the labelling of the larger and smaller resting points in speech, we shall call this *melodic punctuation.*[2]

The length of these melodic sections, on the other hand, and the proportion or relationship which they have amongst themselves with regard to the number of measures will be called *rhythm.*

§79. Now the divisions of melody formed through resting points for the mind are of such a nature that one alone may or may not be understood as a section of a period; that is, these divisions may contain either complete or incomplete thoughts. If such a melodic section contains only an incomplete idea, another one must be added if it is to be understood or felt as a complete section; this will be called an *incise.*[3] However, if the thought is considered complete as a section, then something more may still be required to express the idea or feeling of the entire period. In other words, the complete thought is of such a kind that the period either cannot or can be closed with it. In the first case it will be called a *phrase of partial close,* and in the second case, because of its character-

---

1. The term "ordering of tones" can express neither the different kinds and types of ending formulas of melodic sections nor the manner of their connection into periods. For according to its components it can do no more than either show the propriety in the sequence of tones, which in the first section I called "melodic progression," or indicate an aspect of modulation, namely, the order in which the different subsidiary keys of a main key of a composition can be made to be heard. [Au.]
2. Even this term is not completely suitable, for the resting points are something essential not only in speech but also in melody. In the first, the distinguishing marks in their visible presentation are nothing more than an aid to discover more quickly the more or less noticeable resting points (which even without punctuation marks would still be there). In melody there is no need of this aid, because its resting points affect our feeling enough that there is no need to use special signs to indicate them. Nevertheless, these subjects have a great deal of similarity; for example, a dot ends the periods of speech in the same way as the cadence closes the periods of melody; the phrase of partial close and the incise differentiate the melodic sections of the period just as do the semicolon and comma the smaller sections of the periods in speech. It is this similarity in particular which induced me to use the term "punctuation" in connection with the differentiation of melodic sections. [Au.] "Phrase of partial close" and "incise" translate the German terms *Absatz* and *Einschnitt,* which Koch uses along with *Schlußsatz,* or "closing phrase," to designate the three types of melodic sections according to the finality of their punctuation; see §79.
3. From the Latin *incisio,* or "clause."

istic cadence formula, we shall call it a *closing phrase,* in order to distinguish it from the phrase of partial close.

From this division there result three different types of melodic sections, namely incises, phrases of partial close, and closing phrases. According to the introduction in the preceding section [§78], what is important for all of these divisions is the formula through which they become noticeable as resting points, or, to use our chosen term, their punctuation mark and also the length or number of their measures.

•   •   •   •   •

§80. Completeness in melodic phrases manifests itself in different ways. (1) A phrase may contain only as much as is absolutely necessary for it to be understood and felt as an independent section of the whole; such a phrase I shall call a *basic phrase.* Or, (2) it may also contain a clarification, a more complete definition of the feeling, and in this case the phrase is an *extended phrase.* Or, (3) two or more phrases, complete in themselves, are combined so that externally they appear in the form of a single phrase; such a phrase we wish to call a *compound phrase.*

CHAPTER 1. ON BASIC PHRASES AND THE INCISES CONTAINED IN THEM

•   •   •   •   •

§82. A basic phrase is complete when it can be understood or felt as a self-sufficient section of the whole, without a preceding or succeeding incomplete segment fortuitously connected with it. The following phrases in Examples 1 through 4, for instance, are of this type.

Example 1

Example 2

Example 3

Example 4

Allegretto

The dissimilarity among these basic, complete phrases referred to in §79 shows itself when we compare them with one another. Some are of such a nature that we necessarily expect still one or more sections to follow in the whole to which they are joined because (usually) they cannot close the whole themselves. Both phrases in Examples 1 and 2 are of this type and are called phrases of partial close because they are unable to conclude the whole. The phrases in Examples 3 and 4, on the other hand, can close the whole after other preceding sections, and because of their characteristic ending formula we call them closing phrases.

Furthermore, the essential difference between a phrase of partial close and a closing phrase depends on nothing more than the essential difference of ending formulas. Hence phrases of partial close can be transformed into closing phrases through alteration of their ending formula, and vice versa. Thus, for example, the phrases of partial close found above in Examples 1 and 2 are changed into closing phrases in Examples 5 and 6, and, conversely, the closing phrases in Examples 3 and 4 are changed into phrases of partial close in Examples 7 and 8.

Example 5

Example 6

Example 7

Example 8

§83. In complete phrases the melody may cohere so closely that no noticeable resting points can be discovered by which these complete phrases may be broken up into incomplete segments. Or the melody of these phrases may contain noticeable resting points, so that the phrases can be broken up into incomplete segments. Examples of the first category of these complete phrases are presented in the previous section [§82]; examples of the second category will be more closely examined forthwith.

§84. When we sing or play the following phrases in Examples 9 through 11, our feeling persuades us that (1) the resting points which cut up the phrase into incomplete segments are felt at the places marked Δ and that (2) when we sing or play these phrases only up to the sign Δ, they still need something more to be complete. They do not impress us as complete phrases unless we connect the segment immediately following Δ.

Example 9

Example 10

Example 11

These resting points in the complete phrases, or these still incomplete segments of a phrase, are called incises.[4] They may not be revealed through any-

---

4. Henceforth Koch uses the sign Δ to indicate incises and the sign □ to indicate complete phrases or phrases of partial close.

thing external, as in the quoted examples, or they may contain an outward sign of a short rest, as in Examples 12 through 14.

Example 12

Example 13

Example 14

•   •   •   •   •

1. *On the length of basic phrases and the incises contained in them*

§86. Complete phrases need less or more length depending on whether they are basic or somewhat extended phrases. Because in this chapter we shall first consider the nature of basic phrases so that we can later understand more clearly how and through what means they can be extended, we now deal only with the length of basic phrases.

§87. Most common, and also, on the whole, most useful and most pleasing for our feelings are those basic phrases which are completed in the fourth measure of simple meters. For that reason they are called *four-measure phrases.* They may actually appear as four measures in simple meters or in compound meters in the form of only two measures. All of the preceding examples in the chapter are of this nature.

•   •   •   •   •

§88. When four-measure phrases are broken down into smaller segments through resting points, they contain, according to §83, either complete or incomplete incises.[5] The most common incises of four-measure units are those

---

5. Koch defines a complete incise as one that "takes two or more measures of a simple meter," while an incomplete incise "fills only a single measure" (§85). Simple meters are those in which

complete incises which consist of two measures and thus divide the phrase into two segments of equal length. . . . Very unusual, on the other hand, is a complete incise of three measures *in a four-measure unit,* as in Example 15.

Example 15

If the four-measure phrase contains incomplete incises, however, then usually two incomplete incises follow one another and form a complete incise of two measures, as in Example 16. . . .

Example 16

More unusual are basic phrases of four measures in which one incomplete incise is not followed immediately by another similar one, but is closely connected with the next segment of the phrase, as in Example 17.

Example 17

§89. Not all basic phrases are complete in the fourth measure; often such a phrase becomes complete only in the fifth or sixth, occasionally not until the seventh measure. These basic phrases of more than four measures should not be confused with extended phrases of the same number of measures, because the former require a different treatment from the latter in the joining of phrases in a period.

If a phrase is complete in the fifth measure of a simple meter then it is called a *five-measure phrase.* Such a phrase can arise in three ways:

It can arise (1) from a four-measure phrase, by means of the extension of two metrical units to two measures. When, for example, the metrical units of

---

the measure has only one downbeat, or strong part ($\frac{2}{2}$, $\frac{2}{4}$, $\frac{3}{4}$, and $\frac{3}{8}$), while compound meters consist of a pair of these measures with the barline omitted ($\frac{4}{4}$, $\frac{6}{4}$, and $\frac{6}{8}$).

the first measure in the phrases of Examples 18–20 are extended to complete measures and thereby made more emphatic, this results in the five-measure phrases in Examples 21–23.[6]

Example 18

Example 19

Example 20

Example 21

Example 22

Example 23

When a four-measure unit which is to be extended to a five-measure unit contains a complete incise of two measures, as does, for instance, the phrase in Example 20, then not only the first segment can contain the extension as in Example 23, but also the second, as in Example 24.

6. Examples 22 and 23 are taken from Carl Heinrich Graun's opera *Catone in Utica*. [Tr.]

Example 24

But in practice, the extension of the first segment occurs far more often than the extension of the second one.

The five-measure unit can also arise (2) from the joining of two unequal segments, of which each is incomplete in itself and in which there is no extension. In this case, the first segment of the phrase, or the incise, is longer than the second segment, as in Example 25.

Example 25

More unusual is the case in which the second segment of a five-measure phrase not arising through extension is the longer one, as in Example 26.[7]

Example 26

• • • • •

CHAPTER 2. ON EXTENDED PHRASES

§105. A phrase is extended when it contains more than is absolutely necessary for its completeness. The extension of a phrase through which the feeling it contains is defined more precisely can be brought about by various means. The first of these means is the repetition of a segment of a phrase, and this can occur either in the same key which underlies the passage to be repeated or in another key.[8]

If the repetition of a segment of a phrase occurs in the same key, then either the repetition has the same underlying harmony, or it occurs on degrees of the scale which require a different harmony.

7. Koch discusses means of composing six- and seven-measure phrases in §90 and §91.
8. In periods often entire complete phrases are repeated, sometimes in the same key, sometimes also in another key. The discussion of such repetitions does not belong in this part, which is concerned only with the nature of melodic sections, but in the following one, where the connection of these divisions is treated. [Au.] Koch refers here to Section 4, "On the Connection of Melodic Sections, or the Construction of Periods," parts of which are excerpted on pp. 56–61 and 73–85.

The repetition is made with a segment of the phrase which either does or does not contain the ending formula of the complete phrase. In the first instance, when the punctuation figure of the phrase must also be repeated, the repetition (especially when it is varied) has the appearance of an appendix. This instance will be separately treated later, after consideration of the repetition of those segments in which the punctuation formula of the complete phrase is not repeated.

§106. When a basic phrase is extended through the repetition of only a single measure, then this repetition always occurs in the same key. The measure which is reiterated can be the first or one of the middle measures of the phrase, for instance Examples 27 and 28.

Example 27

Example 28

Composers usually tend to have this single repeated measure performed more softly or more loudly and, moreover, the repetition itself can be varied in different ways without damage, as in Examples 29 and 30.

Example 29

Example 30

In this case, the repetition of a measure is not only on the same harmonic basis, but also on the same degrees of the scale. *Such a five-measure phrase arising through the repetition of a measure retains the value of a four-measure phrase under all circumstances relating to the connection of several melodic*

sections. It is considered as a four-measure unit with regard to the rhythmic relation of phrases.

A single measure of the phrase may be repeated so that the repetition does occur on the same underlying harmony, but the upper voice is inverted with the middle voice, whether actually present or only presumed, as in Example 31.

Example 31

The perceptibility of the repetition is often lost through this inversion of voices. Such a four-measure phrase, changed into a five-measure one in which the repetition of a measure is not noticeable enough because of the inversion of the upper voices, is usually treated as a five-measure unit in the construction of periods.

§107. In practice, far more common than the repetition of a single measure is the extension of a basic phrase through the repetition of two measures which form an incise; for instance, Example 32. Both these repeated measures can be varied in all possible ways, for instance as in Example 33.

Example 32

Example 33

When in the repetition of two measures the upper voices are inverted as in Example 34, then feeling never fails to recognize this repetition.

Example 34

Thus such a four-measure phrase, which has been extended to six measures by the repetition of two, is always considered as a four-measure unit with respect to the rhythmic relations of phrases.

•   •   •   •   •

§110. The second means through which a phrase can be extended and the content of it more closely defined is the addition of an explanation, an appendix, which further clarifies the phrase. This appendix can be a section of the phrase itself, whose repetition makes the content of the phrase more emphatic, as in Examples 35 and 36, or it may be an incomplete segment which is not yet present in the phrase but which is able to define its content more closely, as in Examples 37 and 38.

Example 35

Example 36

Example 37

Example 38

[VOLUME 3 (1793)]

SECTION 4. ON THE CONNECTION OF MELODIC SECTIONS, OR THE
CONSTRUCTION OF PERIODS

• • • • •

§7. It is recognized as a general rule that with every skill to be acquired, one
must proceed gradually from the easier to the more difficult, from the simpler
to the more complicated. Likewise with the skill of joining melodic sections
into a whole, the beginning composer must follow this rule. For supposing that
at the first attempt to invent a melody he chose an elaborate composition, then
a thousand hindrances would stand in his way, partly real, partly only imaginary.
He avoids all these hindrances together with the detrimental consequences of
such a reversed procedure if he first learns to write small compositions.[9] If he
is then given instruction in how such a small composition can be given a greater
length through various means, it will not seem difficult to him to proceed by
degrees to the largest and most complex kinds of compositions.

To give the beginner opportunity for this gradual progress, I am dividing the
various ways of connecting melodic sections into different chapters. Thus the
second chapter is to treat the diverse ways of connecting melodic sections in
short compositions.

In the third, I shall attempt to show how these small compositions can be
enlarged by different means.

The subject of the following chapters, however, will be the ways of connecting several melodic sections, or the arrangement of larger compositions.[10]

In this way I hope to be able to make comprehensible to the beginner the
various methods of connecting melodic sections. Moreover, this gives me the
best opportunity to show without long-windedness the most essential matters
concerning the arrangement of each particular composition, which I promised
to do in the introduction to the first volume.

Remark
I have further divided the chapters which concern this subject into special exercises,
partly in order not to weary the beginner through the quick succession of the several
ways of connecting phrases, but especially in order to give him more opportunity to
exercise his power of invention through imitating all particular methods of connection. Nothing will be troublesome about these exercises if he is sufficiently practiced
in counterpoint and has studied the contents of the second part of the second volume
with the necessary attention.

9. Here and afterwards in this section, by "composition" I understand not the joining of several
   individual movements, for example an Allegro, Andante, and Presto, into a symphony or sonata,
   but I mean each of these individual movements separately. I will not use the customary expression "section" because I have applied it already too precisely to the parts of a whole. [Au.]
   Unlike the English word "section," the German word *Satz* is readily used to designate an entire
   movement as well as a portion of a movement. Because *Satz* is so important to Koch as
   "phrase," he wants to reserve it for that use exclusively.
10. Portions of this chapter are included on pp. 73–85.

But is not genius too greatly limited or indeed even suppressed through such imitations in which a certain form is determined? The reason for this objection is well known. From time immemorial there have been people who wished to shake off all imagined constraints of art, who chose to concede everything to genius, but nothing at all to craft. If young composers who wish to use these pages for instruction should be taken in by this prejudice, I can say nothing further here than to reassure them that their genius neither will nor can as yet show itself to its total extent, and that no other way can probably be devised to lead their genius in the right direction. If one has once used the proper ways of connecting melodic sections through imitation of the correct forms, then these fetters fall off by themselves.

•   •   •   •   •

CHAPTER 2: ON THE CONNECTION OF MELODIC SECTIONS INTO PERIODS OF SHORT LENGTH, OR THE ARRANGEMENT OF SHORT COMPOSITIONS

•   •   •   •   •

Exercise 1, in which four melodic sections are connected,
of which two contain a cadence in the main key

§24. In this case the two sections which contain the cadence are usually the second and fourth phrase; that is, they divide the whole into two small periods or sections, which are either repeated as a reprise or performed without repetition. Now with regard to both those melodic sections which close not with cadences, but merely with phrase-endings, four different situations or punctuation forms are possible here. For with our accepted condition that the second and fourth section make a cadence in the main key, either (1) the first melodic section can close with a phrase-ending on the triad of the main key, that is as a I-phrase, the third section with a phrase-ending on the triad of the fifth, that is as a V-phrase.[11] Example 39 is such a case.[12]

Example 39

11. In §93–§104 Koch discusses the "ending formulas" of melodic sections (a matter already touched on in §82). There are essentially two types, each involving closure on the strong beat of a measure on a note (often embellished) of the triad that is the goal of that particular section. If the triad is on the keynote of the composition, the phrase is called a I-phrase [*Grundabsatz*], if on the fifth degree, then a *V-phrase* [*Quintabsatz*]. In §25 Koch lists the other three possibilities for the endings of melodic sections 1 and 3 when 2 and 4 end in the main key: V and I, V and V, and I and I.
12. This minuet by Haydn is the third movement of a divertimento for two violins, flute, oboe, violoncello, and bass composed before 1766, Hoboken II:1. [Tr.]

Remark 1

In connection with the example, the opportunity immediately arises to make a remark which had occurred to me in §22.[13]

This short composition has the most perfect unity. It consists of four melodic sections and contains only a single main idea, which, however, is modified in various ways. This is the first four-measure phrase, which initially appears as a I-phrase, but immediately afterwards has been repeated and changed into a closing phrase. In the second section, the phrase which is a V-phrase and with its repetition is the closing phrase is essentially the very same phrase; it has merely been given a different turn. The phrase has been played in contrary motion and through a passing modulation has been given more variety.

From this it is apparent that a single phrase can indeed be sufficient for such a short composition if the composer knows how to give it a different direction and connection so that the whole, despite its unity, obtains nevertheless the necessary variety.

But one must not believe that in such short compositions of four phrases the three last phrases always have to arise through modification of the first. No! In most such compositions two truly different melodic sections are connected; the remaining two then arise partly through alteration and partly also through repetition of the preceding sections, as in Example 40.

Example 40

13. In §22 Koch enunciates the important late eighteenth-century principal of unity tempered by variety, explaining that using four different melodic sections in one short composition would result in too much variety, destroying the coherence of the whole.

Compositions of this kind are found in which even three different melodic sections have been connected, without the piece being deprived of all unity. But in this case the fourth phrase necessarily must be a clear repetition of the first or second phrase, otherwise the piece would lose its unity. When the second section of the preceding minuet is composed in the manner of Example 41, it is a short piece of sixteen measures which contains three different phrases.

Example 41

In most cases, however, the composition is better when the connected phrases are more similar to each other, as in Examples 39 and 40.

・　・　・　・　・

Exercise 2, in which four melodic sections are connected,
of which one contains a cadence in a secondary key

§30. Here, too, the first cadence, which closes in a secondary key, is usually made by means of the second phrase, and the whole is divided into two periods of equal size.

When the major mode is used, this secondary key in which the second phrase closes is the major key of the fifth; but when the minor mode is used, it can be either the minor key of the fifth or the major key of the third.

§31. In the major mode, when the second phrase closes with a cadence in the fifth, again four different punctuation forms arise with regard to the first and third phrases. (1) The first melodic section can be a I-phrase, the third a V-phrase. This is the most usual form for four melodic sections of which the second closes with a cadence in the fifth (Example 42).[14]

Example 42

14. In order not to give examples only in the meter and tempo of the minuet, I choose for this exercise the type of short composition described in §20, and I leave it to the beginner to practice these forms also on the minuet or other dance melodies. [Au.] Koch classifies short compositions into three types: dance melodies, melodies for songs and odes, and "short pieces of no defined character, whose meter, tempo, and arrangement of rhythm and punctuation depend entirely upon the imagination of the composer." This last is the type of composition described in §20.

(2) Both the first and the third melodic section can be a V-phrase. When the first phrase of the Allegretto of Example 42 is altered, the punctuation form shown is obtained (Example 43).[15]

Example 43

etc.

15. Koch goes on to give examples of the other two possibilities for the endings of melodic sections 1 and 3 (V and I, I and I), and closes §31 with a lengthy discussion of the various ways in which melodic section 3 can lead back into the closing section.

11

THE PRACTICE OF COMPOSITION: MOVEMENT AND WORK

4 Johann Joachim Quantz

An outstanding flute player and composer for the flute, Johann Joachim Quantz began his career as an oboist in the Dresden town band in 1716. He was born in 1697 and received his first training in counterpoint under J. D. Zelenka, a pupil of Fux, in Vienna. In 1724 he set out on a series of extended journeys. He visited Italy, where he studied in Rome with Francesco Gasparini. In 1726 he went to Paris, where he stayed seven months and published several instrumental works, and in 1727 to London, where he stayed three months. In 1728 Quantz entered into relations with Frederick the Great, who became a great admirer of his art and engaged him in 1741 as a flutist and composer to his court. He retained this position until his death in 1773.

Quantz was an extremely prolific composer: for the King alone he wrote three hundred concertos and two hundred other compositions. His best-known work, however, and the one that best testifies to the solidity of his musicianship, is his method for the flute, *Versuch einer Anweisung die Flöte traversière zu spielen* (*Essay on a Method for Playing the Transverse Flute;* 1752). The book does not confine itself to flute playing but discusses questions of general importance for the musical practice and musical aesthetics of the time.

FROM *Essay on a Method for Playing the Transverse Flute*

(1752)

CHAPTER 18. HOW A PERFORMER AND A PIECE OF MUSIC OUGHT TO BE JUDGED

28. To judge an instrumental composition properly, we must have an exact knowledge, not only of the characteristics of each type of piece which may occur, but also, as already observed, of the instruments themselves. In itself, a piece may conform both to good taste and to the rules of composition, and hence be well written, but still run counter to the instrument. On the other hand, a piece may conform to the instrument, but be in itself useless. Vocal music has certain advantages which instrumental music must do without. The words and the human voice work to the composer's greatest advantage, with regard both to invention and to characterization. Experience clearly shows this when, in the absence of voices, arias are played on an instrument. Without words and without the human voice, instrumental music, quite as much as vocal music, should express certain passions and transport the listeners from one to another. But if this is to be properly managed, to compensate for the

TEXT: The original edition (Berlin, 1752), pp. 293–305. Translation by Oliver Strunk, with minor alterations.

absence of words and of the human voice, neither the composer nor the performer may have a soul of wood.

29. The principal types of instrumental composition in which voices take no part are: the concerto, the overture, the sinfonia, the quartet, the trio, and the solo. In each of the following there are two varieties: the concerto, the trio, and the solo. We have *concerti grossi* and *concerti da camera*. The trios are, as the phrase goes, either elaborate or *galant*. With the solos the case is the same.

30. The concertos were originated by the Italians. Torelli is said to have written the first ones. A *concerto grosso* consists of a mixture of various concerted instruments wherein, as an invariable rule, two or more parts—the number may sometimes run as high as eight or even higher—concert with one another. In the *concerto da camera*, however, there is only a single concerted instrument.

31. The qualities of a *concerto grosso* require, in each of its movements: (1) a majestic ritornello at the beginning, which should be more harmonic than melodic, more serious than humorous, and relieved by unisons; (2) a skillful mixture of the imitations in the concerted parts, in order that the ear may be unexpectedly surprised, now by this instrument, now by that; (3) these imitations must be made up of short and pleasing ideas; (4) there must be a constant alternation of the brilliant and the ingratiating; (5) the inner tutti sections must be kept short; (6) the alternations of the concerted instruments must be so distributed that one is not heard too much and another too little; (7) now and then, after a trio, there must be woven in a short solo for one instrument or another; (8) before the end the solo instruments must briefly repeat what they had at the beginning; and (9) the final tutti must conclude with the loftiest and most majestic ideas of the first ritornello. Such a concerto requires numerous accompanying players, a large place, a serious performance, and a moderate tempo.

32. Of concertos with a single concerted instrument, the so-called *concerti da camera*, there are likewise two varieties. Some, like the *concerto grosso*, require many accompanying players, others a few. Unless this is observed, neither the one nor the other has its proper effect. From the first ritornello one can gather to which variety a concerto belongs. If it is serious, majestic, more harmonic than melodic, and relieved by many unisons, the harmony changing, not with eighth or quarter measures, but with half or full measures, many players must accompany. If, on the other hand, it consists in a fleeting, humorous, gay, or singing melody, the harmony changing rapidly, it will have a better effect with a few players accompanying than with many.

33. A serious concerto, that is, a simple one written for many players, requires the following in the first movement: (1) There should be a majestic ritornello, with all the parts well elaborated. (2) There should be a pleasing and intelligible melody. (3) There should be regular imitations. (4) The best ideas of the ritornello may be broken up and used for relief within or between the solos. (5) The thoroughbass should sound well and be suitable for use as a bass.

(6) The composer should write no more inner parts than the principal part permits, for it is often more effective to double the principal melody than to introduce forced inner parts. (7) The progressions of the thoroughbass and of the inner parts may neither impede the principal part in its liveliness nor drown out or stifle it. (8) A proportional length must be observed in the ritornello. It should consist of at least two main sections. The second of these, since it is to be repeated at the end of the movement as a conclusion, must be clothed with the finest and most majestic ideas. (9) Insofar as the opening idea of the ritornello is neither singing nor wholly suitable for solo use, the composer must introduce a new idea, directly contrasted with the first, but so joined to it that it is not evident whether it is introduced from necessity or after due deliberation. (10) The solo sections must be in part singing, while the ingratiating quality should be in part relieved by brilliant, melodious, harmonious passages, always suited to the instrument, and also, to maintain the fire to the end, by short, lively, majestic tutti sections. (11) The concerted or solo sections may not be too short or the inner tuttis too long. (12) The accompaniment to the solo must contain no progressions which might obscure the concerted part; on the contrary, it must be made up alternately of many parts and few, in order that the principal part may now and then have room to come to the fore with greater freedom. In general, light and shade must be maintained throughout. When the solo passages permit it, or when the composer knows how to invent such as will, it is most effective that the accompanying parts beneath them should introduce something familiar from the ritornello. (13) The modulation must always be correct and natural, not touching on any key so remote that it might offend the ear. (14) The laws of meter, to which the composer has at all times to pay strict attention, must here, too, be exactly observed. The caesuras, or divisions of the melody, may not fall on the second or fourth quarter in common duple time, or on the third or fifth beat in triple. The composer must endeavor to maintain the meter with which he begins, whether it be by whole or half measures or, in triple time, by two-, four-, or eight-measure phrases; otherwise the most artful composition becomes defective. In triple time, in an arioso, if the melody permits frequent divisions, successive caesuras after three- and two-measure phrases are permitted. (15) The composer may not follow up the solo passages with uniform transpositions *ad nauseam;* on the contrary, he must imperceptibly interrupt and shorten them at the right time. (16) The ending may not be hurried unduly or bitten off too short; on the contrary, the composer should endeavor to make it thoroughly solid. Nor may he conclude with wholly new ideas; on the contrary, the last solo section must repeat the most pleasing of those ideas that have been heard before. (17) The last tutti, finally, must conclude the Allegro, as briefly as possible, with the second section of the first ritornello.

34. Not every variety of measure is suitable for the first movement of a majestic concerto. If the movement is to be lively, the composer may employ common duple time, in which the smallest note is the sixteenth, permitting the

caesura to fall on the second half of the measure. If it is also to be majestic, he should choose a broader meter, one in which the caesura regularly occupies the full measure and falls only on the down beat. If, however, it is to be both serious and majestic, he may choose for it, in common duple time, a moderate tempo in which the smallest note is the thirty-second, the caesura falling on the second half of the measure. The dotted sixteenths will in this case contribute much to the majesty of the ritornello. The movement may be defined by the word *allegretto*. Notes of this kind can also be written in the moderate alla breve time. It is only necessary to change the eighths to quarters, the sixteenths to eighths, and the thirty-seconds to sixteenths. In this case, however, the caesura may always fall on the beginning of the measure. The ordinary alla breve time, in which the smallest note is the eighth, is to be regarded as the equivalent of two-four time and is more suited to the last movement than to the first, for, unless one writes continually in the strict style, using all the voices, it is more expressive of the pleasing than of the majestic. In general, triple time is little used for the first movement, unless in the form of three-four time with occasional sixteenths and a movement in eighths in the inner and lowest parts, the harmony changing, as a rule, only with full measures.

35. The Adagio must be distinguished from the first Allegro in every respect—in its musical rhyme-structure, its meter, and its key. If the Allegro is in one of the major keys, for example in C major, the Adagio may, as one prefers, be in C minor, E minor, A minor, F major, G major, or even G minor. If, on the other hand, the first Allegro is in one of the minor keys, for example in C minor, the Adagio may be in E-flat major, F minor, G minor, or A-flat major. These successions of keys are the most natural. The ear is never offended by them, and the same relationships apply to all keys, whatever they may be called. He who wishes to surprise the listener in a painful and disagreeable way is at liberty to choose, beyond these keys, such as may give pleasure to him alone. To say the least, considerable caution is necessary in this regard.

36. For the arousing and subsequent stilling of the passions the Adagio offers greater opportunity than the Allegro. In former times it was for the most part written in a plain dry style, more harmonic than melodic. The composers left to the performers what had been expected of themselves, namely, to make the melody singable, but this could not be well accomplished without considerable addition of embellishments. In other words, in those days it was much easier to write an Adagio than to play one. Now, as it may be readily imagined that such an Adagio did not always have the good fortune to fall into skillful hands, and since the performance was seldom as successful as the author might have wished, there has come of this evil some good, namely, that composers have for some time past begun to make their Adagios more singing. By this means the composer has more honor and the performer less of a puzzle; moreover, the Adagio itself can no longer be distorted or mutilated in such a variety of ways as was formerly often the case.

37. But since the Adagio does not usually find as many admirers as the Allegro among the musically uninstructed, the composer must endeavor in every possible way to make it pleasing even to those listeners without musical experience. To this end, he should above all strictly observe the following rules. (1) He must aim studiously at the greatest possible brevity, both in the ritornellos and in the solo sections. (2) The ritornello must be melodious, harmonious, and expressive. (3) The principal part must have a melody which, though it permits some addition of embellishments, may still please without them. (4) The melody of the principal part must alternate with the tutti sections used between for relief. (5) This melody must be just as touching and expressive as though there were words below it. (6) From time to time something from the ritornello must be introduced. (7) The composer may not wander off into too many keys, for this is the greatest impediment to brevity. (8) The accompaniment beneath the solo must be rather more plain than figured, in order that the principal part may not be prevented from making ornaments and may retain complete freedom to introduce, judiciously and reasonably, many or few embellishments. (9) The composer, finally, must endeavor to characterize the Adagio with some epithet clearly expressing the passion contained therein, in order that the required tempo may be readily determined.

38. The final Allegro of a concerto must be very different from the first movement, not only in its style and nature, but also in its meter. The last Allegro must be just as humorous and sprightly as the first is serious. To this end, the following meters will prove useful: $\frac{2}{4}$, $\frac{3}{4}$, $\frac{3}{8}$, $\frac{6}{8}$, $\frac{9}{8}$, and $\frac{12}{8}$. In no case should all three movements of a concerto be written in the same meter. But if the first movement is in duple time and the second in triple, the last may be written either in triple or in two-four time. In no case, however, may it stand in common duple time, for this would be too serious and hence as little suited to the last movement as two-four or a rapid triple time to the first. Similarly, all three movements may not begin on the same step, but, if the upper part begins on the keynote in the first movement, it may begin on the third in the second movement and on the fifth in the third. And although the last movement is in the key of the first, the composer, to avoid similarity in the modulations, must still be careful not to pass through the same succession of keys in the last movement as he did in the first.

39. Generally speaking, in the last movement (1) The ritornello must be short, lively, fiery, but at the same time somewhat playful. (2) The principal part must have a simple melody, pleasing and fleeting. (3) The solo passages should be easy, in order that the rapidity of the movement may not be impeded. They must, furthermore, bear no similarity to those in the first movement. For example, if the solos in the first movement are made up of broken notes and arpeggios, those in the last movement may proceed by step or by turn figures. Or if there are triplets in the first movement, the passages in the last movement may be made up of even notes, or vice versa. (4) The laws of

meter must be observed with the utmost severity. For the shorter and more rapid the variety of measure, the more painful it is if these laws are violated. In $\frac{2}{4}$ and in rapid $\frac{3}{4}$, $\frac{3}{8}$, and $\frac{6}{8}$ time, the caesura, then, must always fall on the beginning of every second measure, the principal divisions on the fourth and eighth measures. (5) The accompaniment may not employ too many voices or be overcrowded; on the contrary, it must be made up of such notes as the accompanying parts can produce without undue movement or effort, for the last movement is as a rule played very rapidly.

40. To insure a proportional length, even in a concerto, consult a timepiece. If the first movement takes five minutes, the Adagio five to six, and the last movement three to four, the whole is of the proper length. And it is in general more advantageous if the listeners find a piece rather too short than too long.

41. He who now understands how to make a concerto of this sort will also have no difficulty in contriving a humorous little *concerto da camera* of the playful kind. It will, then, be unnecessary to discuss this separately.

42. An overture, played before an opera, requires a majestic beginning, full of gravity, a brilliant, well-elaborated principal section, and a good combination of different instruments, such as flutes, oboes, or horns. Its origin is due to the French. Lully has provided excellent models. Some German composers, however, among them Handel and Telemann, have far surpassed him in this. Indeed, the French fare with their overtures very much as do the Italians with their concertos. Still, in view of their excellent effect, it is a pity that the overtures are not more usual in Germany.

43. The Italian sinfonias, having the same purpose as the overtures, naturally require precisely the same qualities for their majestic display. But since most of them are contrived by composers such as have exercised their genius more in vocal than in instrumental music, we have thus far only a very few sinfonias that are perfect in all respects, and thus can serve as a good model. Sometimes it seems as though the composers of opera, in contriving their sinfonias, went about it as do those painters who, in finishing a portrait, use the leftover colors to fill in the sky or the costume. In the meantime it stands to reason, as previously mentioned, that a sinfonia should have some connection with the content of its opera or at least with the first scene of it and not, as frequently occurs, conclude invariably with a gay minuet. I have no wish to propse a model in this regard, for it is impossible to bring under a single head all the circumstances that may occur at the beginning of an opera. At the same time, I believe that it should be very easy to find a mean. It is admittedly quite unnecessary that the sinfonia before an opera consist always of three movements; could the composer not conclude, perhaps, with the first or second? For example, if the first scene involved heroic or other fiery passions, he might end his sinfonia with the first movement. If mournful or amorous passions occurred in it, he might stop after the second movement. But if the first scene involved no specific passions at all, these appearing only in the course of the opera or at the end, he might close with the third movement. By so doing, he would have an

opportunity to arrange each movement in a way suitable to the matter at hand. The sinfonia, moreover, would still retain its usefulness for other purposes.

44. A quartet, that is, a sonata for three concerted instruments and a thoroughbass, is the real touchstone of the true contrapuntist, as it is also an affair wherein many a one not properly grounded in his art may come to grief. Its use has never become really common; as a result, it may not even be known to everyone. Indeed, it is to be feared that in the end this kind of music will have to suffer the fate of the lost arts. A good quartet implies: (1) pure four-part writing; (2) a good harmonious melody; (3) short, regular imitations; (4) a judicious combination of the concerted instruments; (5) a proper thoroughbass suited for use as a bass; (6) ideas of the sort that are mutually invertible, so that one may build either above or below them, the inner parts maintaining an at least tolerable and not displeasing melodic line; (7) that it must not be obvious whether this part or that one has the advantage; (8) that each part, after a rest, must reenter, not as inner part, but as principal part and with a pleasing melody (this, however, is to be understood as applying, not to the thoroughbass, but only to the three concerted parts); (9) that if there is a fugue, it must be carried out in a masterly and at the same time tasteful fashion in all four parts, observing all the rules. A certain set of six quartets for various instruments, chiefly flute, oboe, and violin, composed quite some time ago by Herr Telemann, may serve as particularly beautiful models of this kind of music.

45. A trio, while it is a task less tedious for the composer than a quartet, nevertheless requires on his part almost the same degree of artistry, if it is in its way to be of the proper sort. Yet it has the advantage that the ideas introduced may be more *galant* and pleasing than in the quartet, for there is one concerted part the less. In a trio, then, the composer must follow these rules: (1) He must invent a melody which will tolerate a singing counterpoint. (2) The subjects proposed at the beginning of each movement may not be too long, especially in the Adagio, for in the imitations which the second part makes at the fifth, fourth, and unison, an overlong subject can easily become wearisome. (3) No part may propose any subject that the other cannot answer. (4) The imitations must be brief and the passages brilliant. (5) In the repetition of the most pleasing ideas a good order must be maintained. (6) The two principal parts must be so written that the thoroughbass below may be natural and sound well. (7) If a fugue is introduced, it must be, as in the quartet, carried out in all the parts, not only correctly, observing all the rules of composition, but also tastefully. The episodes, whether they consist of passages or of other imitations, must be pleasing and brilliant. (8) While progressions of the two principal parts in parallel thirds and sixths are an ornament of the trio, they must not be overdone or run into the ground, but rather interrupted by passages or other imitations. (9) The trio, finally, must be so contrived that one can scarcely guess which of the two parts is the first.

46. To write a solo is today no longer regarded as an art. Almost every instrumentalist occupies himself in this way. If he has no ideas, he helps himself with

borrowed ones. If he is lacking in knowledge of the rules of composition, he lets someone else write the bass for him. As a result, our time brings forth, instead of good models, many monstrosities.

47. As a matter of fact, it is by no means so easy to write a good solo. There are composers who understand composition perfectly and are successful in works for many voices, but who write poor solos. On the other hand, there are composers for whom solos turn out better than pieces for many voices. He who succeeds in both is fortunate. Little need as there is to have mastered all the innermost secrets of composition in order to write a good solo, there is as little chance of accomplishing anything reasonable of this kind without having some understanding of harmony.

48. If a solo is to reflect credit on the composer and the performer, then (1) its Adagio must be in itself singing and expressive; (2) the performer must have opportunities to show his judgment, invention, and insight; (3) the delicate must be relieved from time to time by something ingenious; (4) the thoroughbass must be a natural one, above which one can build easily; (5) no idea may be too often repeated, either in the same key or in a transposition, for not only can this make difficulties for the player, but it can also become tiresome for the listeners; (6) the natural melody must be interrupted occasionally by dissonances, to arouse the passions of the listeners in a suitable manner; (7) the Adagio must not be too long.

49. The first Allegro requires: (1) a flowing, coherent, and somewhat serious melody; (2) well-connected ideas; (3) brilliant passages, well unified melodically; (4) a good order in the repetition of the ideas; (5) choice and beautiful progressions at the end of the first part, so arranged that, in a transposition, they may conclude the second part also; (6) that the first part be somewhat shorter than the second; (7) that the most brilliant passages be reserved for the second part; (8) that the thoroughbass be natural, causing such progressions as will maintain a continuous liveliness.

50. The second Allegro may be either very lively and rapid, or moderate and aria-like. In this, the composer must be guided by the first movement. If it is serious, the last movement may be lively. But if it is lively and rapid, the last movement may be moderate and aria-like. With regard to variety of meter, what was said of the concertos must also be observed here, lest one movement be like the other. In general, if a solo is to please everyone, it must be so contrived that it affords nourishment to each listener's temperamental inclinations. It must be neither purely cantabile nor purely spirited from beginning to end. And just as each movement must be very different from any other, the individual movements must be in themselves good mixtures of pleasing and brilliant ideas. For the most beautiful melody will in the end prove a soporific if it is never relieved, and continuous liveliness and unmitigated difficulty arouse astonishment but do not particularly move. Indeed, such mixtures of contrasted ideas should be the aim, not merely in the solo, but in all kinds of music. If a composer knows how to hit this off properly and thereby to set in motion the passions of his listeners, one may truly say of him that he has

attained a high degree of good taste and found, so to speak, the musical philosopher's stone.[1]

1. Compare Charles Burney's characterization of John Christian Bach (*A General History of Music*, vol. 4, p. 483): "Bach seems to have been the first composer who observed the law of *contrast* as a *principle*. Before his time, contrast there frequently was, in the works of others; but it seems to have been accidental. Bach in his symphonies and other instrumental pieces, as well as his songs, seldom failed, after a rapid and noisy passage to introduce one that was slow and soothing."

5 Heinrich Christoph Koch

FROM *Introductory Essay on Composition*
(1782–93)

[VOLUME 3 (1793)]

PART 2. ON THE MECHANICAL RULES OF MELODY: ON THE WAY IN WHICH MELODY IS CONNECTED WITH RESPECT TO THE MECHANICAL RULES

SECTION 4. ON THE CONNECTION OF MELODIC SECTIONS, OR THE CONSTRUCTION OF PERIODS

CHAPTER 4. ON THE CONNECTION OF MELODIC SECTIONS INTO PERIODS OF GREATER LENGTH, OR THE ARRANGEMENT OF LARGER COMPOSITIONS

1. On the Nature and Arrangement of the Most Common Compositions

V. *On the symphony*

§100. The symphony is an instrumental piece of many parts, of which the four main ones, namely the first and second violin, viola, and bass, are strongly reinforced. It is used not only for the introduction of a play and a cantata, but also for the opening of chamber music or concerts. In the first case, it often consists of only a single Allegro; but in the latter case, it usually contains three movements of different character. For the most part, the character of magnifi-

TEXT: *Versuch einer Anleitung zur Composition* as translated by Nancy Kovaleff Baker in *Heinrich Christoph Koch: Introductory Essay on Composition* (New Haven: Yale University Press, 1983), pp. 197–204, 207–13, with minor alterations.

cence and grandeur belongs to the first Allegro, the character of pleasantness to the Andante, and of gaiety to the last Allegro.

Because the symphony is one of the most important compositions for those composers who wish to occupy themselves only with instrumental pieces, a closer description of its characteristics is not out of place here. Thus I shall insert an extract concerning the aesthetic nature of this composition from Sulzer's *Allgemeine Theorie der schönen Künste*.[1]

> One can compare the symphony with an instrumental chorus just as the sonata with an instrumental cantata. In the latter, the melody of the main part, which is only set simply, can be composed so that it bears and often even requires decoration. In the symphony, on the other hand, where every voice is set more simply, the melody must already contain the maximum force in the notes written out, and no voice can bear the least decoration or coloratura. Because it is not an exercise like the sonata but must be sightread, there must be no difficulties which cannot be confronted and clearly played at once by many.
>
> The symphony is particularly suited for the expression of greatness, solemnity, and grandeur. Its goal is to prepare the listener for important music or, in a chamber concert, to summon all the magnificence of instrumental music. If it is to satisfy this goal completely and be an integral part of the opera or church music which it precedes, then, besides expressing greatness and solemnity, it must put the listener into the frame of mind which the following piece requires. It must distinguish itself by the distinct style proper for either church or theater.
>
> The chamber symphony, which is an independent whole, aiming at no following music, attains its purpose only through a sonorous, brilliant, and fiery style. The Allegros of the best chamber symphonies contain great and bold ideas—powerful bass melodies and unisons; concerting middle parts; free imitations; often a fugally treated theme; sudden transitions and digressions from one key to another, which are more striking the weaker the connection is; and considerable gradations of loud and soft, especially the crescendo, which is of the greatest effect when it is used together with an ascending melody which increases in expression. . . .
>
> The Andante or Largo between the first and last Allegro has, to be sure, no such closely defined character, but often is of pleasant, or somber, or melancholy expression; yet it must have a style which is in keeping with the dignity of the symphony. . . .
>
> Opera symphonies are like the chamber symphony more or less, but adapted to the character of the opera to be presented. Yet it seems that they tolerate less extravagance and need not be so elaborate, because the listener is more attentive to what follows than to the symphony itself. . . .

§101. The first Allegro of the symphony, to which the description above particularly applies, has two sections which may be performed with or without repetition. The first of these consists only of a single main period and contains

---

1. Johann Georg Sulzer, ed., *Allgemeine Theorie der schönen Künste (A General Theory of the Fine Arts)* (Leipzig, 1771–74), "Symphonie." Sulzer's was the earliest comprehensive German encyclopedia of the arts. The article on the symphony was written by Johann Abraham Peter Schulz, a German conductor and composer who was a pupil of Johann Philipp Kirnberger. Sulzer had originally assigned the articles on music to Kirnberger, who was the sole author from the start of the alphabet through "Modulation." Because of ill health, Kirnberger then enlisted Schulz's aid, and later entrusted to him the composition of the remaining articles, starting with the letter *s.* Koch made considerable use of the work, quoting it extensively both here and in his *Musikalisches Lexikon.* The ellipsis marks in the extract indicate Koch's own ellipses.

the plan of the symphony; that is, the main melodic phrases are presented in their original order and afterwards a few of them are fragmented. Following the cadence a clarifying period is often appended that continues and closes in the same key in which the preceding one also had closed. Thus it is nothing else than an appendix to the first period and both united may quite properly be considered a single main period.

The construction of this period, as also of the other periods of the symphony, differs from that of the sonata and the concerto not through modulations to other keys, nor through a specific succession or alternation of I- or V-phrases. Rather it differs in that (1) its melodic sections tend to be more extended already with their first presentation than in other compositions, and especially (2) these melodic sections usually are more attached to each other and flow more forcefully than in the periods of other pieces, that is, they are linked so that their phrase-endings are less perceptible. For the most part, a melodic section is directly connected with the caesura tone of the preceding phrase-ending. Very often no formal phrase-ending is written until the rushing and sonorous phrases are exchanged for a more singing phrase, usually to be played with less force. Thus many such periods are found in which a formal phrase-ending is not heard until there has been a modulation into the most closely related key. For the main melodic sections are all presented in the main key just as infrequently in the symphony as in other compositions. Rather, after the theme has been heard with another main phrase, the third such phrase usually modulates to the key of the fifth—in the minor mode also towards the third—in which the remaining sections are presented, because the second and larger half of this first period is devoted particularly to this key.

In the newer symphonies, the first Allegro tends to be preceded by a brief introductory passage which is slow and serious. This introduction differs from the so-called Grave of the overture in that it requires neither characteristic figures nor a special meter. Rather it can appear in all meters and use all figures which have an earnest character. Discounting passing modulations, this passage remains in the main key, in which it closes either with a V-phrase-ending or with a cadence. Often a seventh with a fermata is added to the triad ending the V-phrase, or the cadence runs over into the following Allegro; that is, the caesura tone of the cadence is at the same time the first note of the Allegro.

§102. The second section of the first Allegro consists of two main periods, of which the first tends to have greatly diverse types of construction. Nevertheless, if one discounts the smaller variations, they may be reduced to the following two main types of treatment.

The first and most usual construction of the first period of the second section begins in the key of the fifth[2] with the theme, occasionally also with another main melodic idea, either note for note, in inversion, or also with other more

2. If the composition is in a minor key and the first period has ended in the major key of the third, then it is the minor key of the fifth. But if in a minor key the first period closes in the minor key of its fifth, then there is a modulation to the major key of its third in this second period. [Au.]

or less considerable alterations. After that it either modulates back into the main key by means of another melodic idea, and from this to the minor key of the sixth, or also to the minor key of the second or third. Or it may not first return to the main key; rather the phrase that goes from the fifth into one of the keys mentioned may be led there by means of a sequence or another type of extension, with which generally one or several passing modulations are used. Then a few of those melodic sections that are best suited for presentation in one of these keys[3] are repeated or dissected in another form or combination than they had in the first period, whereupon the period ends in this key.

Usually a short phrase is connected with this second main period of the symphony, which consists of a segment of a main melodic idea drawn out in a sequential way. By this means the modulation is carried back to the main key, in which the last main period begins.

The other method of building this period frequently used in modern symphonies is to continue, dissect, or transpose a phrase contained in the first section—often only a segment of it—that is especially suitable for such treatment. This is done either in the upper part alone or also alternately in other parts. There may be passing modulations in several keys, some closely and some distantly related, before the modulation into that key in which the period is to end. Either this happens only until the ending of the V-phrase in this key, or the phrase is continued in a similar manner until the close of the entire period. An example of this latter type of treatment will be given later, when we consider the connection of periods in particular. However, if the fragmentation of such a phrase is carried only to the end of the V-phrase in that key in which this period will close, then after this V-phrase a few melodic ideas of the first period, usually changed somewhat, are presented in that closing key before the cadence arrives. Examples of this may be found in many Haydn and nearly all Dittersdorf symphonies.

In this case too the period usually acquires the appendix mentioned before, which modulates back to the main key for the beginning of the last period.

By the way, modern symphonies do not always start this second period in the key of the fifth; often it begins in an entirely unexpected key, either without any preparation or by means of only a few introductory tones that follow the cadence in the fifth.

§103. The last period of our first Allegro, which is devoted above all to the main key, most frequently begins again with the theme in this key, but occasionally may also start with another main melodic idea. The most prominent phrases are now compressed, as it were, during which the melody usually shifts to the key of the fourth, but, without making a cadence in it, soon again returns to the main key. Finally the second half of the first period, or those melodic

---

3. It should not be forgotten, however, that this matter is considered here not aesthetically, but only technically. [Au.]

ideas of the first period which followed the V-phrase in the fifth, is repeated in the main key and with this the Allegro ends.

§104. The Andante or Adagio of the symphony is found in three different forms. In the first of these, already used in the older symphonies, the Andante has two main sections, which are presented with or without repetition. The first section always consists of only one main period, as in the Allegro; when based in a major key, it modulates to the key of the fifth, but, based in a minor key, it modulates either to the major key of the third or to the minor key of the fifth, and closes therein.

With the second section, the question is whether or not the Andante is to be greatly extended. If the movement is to be very long, then it tends to have two main periods, which in their external structure are very similar to both those periods of the second section of the Allegro described above in §102. The most important external difference is that in the Andante the melodic ideas are less extended and not so often compounded; thus more formal phrase-endings are used than in the Allegro. This accords with the nature of the feelings which tend to be expressed in slow movements. . . .[4]

On the other hand, if the Andante is not to be very long, then these two periods are contracted into a single one. This happens if the working-out of the melodic ideas in the minor key of the sixth or second and the cadence in this key are omitted. After the theme has been presented in the fifth and there has been a modulation back to the main key, the minor key of the sixth, second, or third is touched either not at all or only in passing. Then the theme is repeated again or, without that repetition, those phrases which followed the V-phrase in the first period are presented again in the main key. Examples of this sort are not hard to find, for nearly every short, complete Andante or Allegretto shows the use of this form.

§105. The second form which the Andante of the symphony takes is the rondo. Nothing else important remains to be said of this here, because it already has been described above in connection with the aria.[5]

§106. The third design or form of the Andante shows the use of variations on a short *andante* or *adagio* passage. This usually consists of two sections of eight to ten measures each and often has an appendix, which is presented between every variation as a ritornello. The variations of the principal melody are performed either by the first violin alone, or in alternation with other parts. Examples of this form are found in very many symphonies by Haydn, who not only was the first one to make use of it in an Andante movement but also has produced first-rate masterpieces in it.

---

4. Koch here cites the Andantino e cantabile of Haydn's Symphony No. 42 as an example of an Andante in which the second section contains two periods.

5. In §85 and §86 Koch describes the form familiar to us today, where a simple theme (the *Rondosatz*, consisting of a V-phrase repeated to end as a I-phrase) alternates with two couplets, the first in the dominant and the second in a closely related key.

§107. According to the character which it assumes, the last Allegro of the symphony appears either in the form of the first Allegro or as a rondo. Sometimes it also contains variations on a typical dance melody or on a short *allegro* passage; these variations are, however, usually mixed with brief episodes in closely related keys, after the manner of the rondo.

Remark

Many composers like to add to the symphony a minuet with a so-called trio, which comes sometimes before, but mostly after the Andante. Because such a minuet is not intended for the dance, not only can its length be arbitrary, but it can also contain sections of an uneven number of measures.

VI. *On the sonata*

§108. The sonata, with its various species—the duet, trio, and quartet—has no definite character, but its main sections, namely its Adagio and both Allegros, can assume every character, every expression which music is capable of describing. "In a sonata," says Sulzer, "the composer can aim at expressing either a monologue in tones of sadness, lamentation, or affection, pleasure, and cheerfulness; or he can try to sustain purely in sentiment-laden tones a dialogue among similar or contrasting characters; or he may merely depict passionate, violent, contradictory, or mild and placid emotions, pleasantly flowing on."[6]

Because in the composition of sonatas the main parts are only set simply, the melody of the sonata must stand in relation to the melody of the symphony just as the melody of the aria does to the melody of the chorus. That is, because it depicts the feelings of single people, the melody of a sonata must be extremely developed and must present the finest nuances of feelings, whereas the melody of the symphony must distinguish itself not through such refinement of expression, but through force and energy. In short, the feelings must be presented and modified differently in the sonata and symphony.

§109. The *two-voice sonata* or the *solo*, because it expresses the individual feelings of a single person, necessarily requires the greatest refinement of expression and of the modifications of the feelings to be portrayed. Thus the melody must be most highly developed. Because every instrument is capable of different refinements of expression which it alone can produce, the composition of a sonata requires the most exact knowledge of that instrument for which such a piece is to be composed. Thus good sonatas can only be expected from those composers who also are virtuosi on the instrument for which they write such pieces.

Among the Germans, *C. P. E. Bach* has distinguished himself particularly in this type of composition through his clavier sonatas. Only his highly developed, personal style of playing, combined with the most profound knowledge of composition, could bring about what he has achieved in this line.

---

6. Sulzer, ed., *Allgemeine Theorie,* "Sonate" [Tr.]

For the violin and flute *Franz Benda* and *Quantz* have composed sonatas of which many completely correspond to the ideal one inevitably forms of a good sonata. It is only unfortunate that the path broken by these men was subsequently followed by far too few. Much too often a more refined and cultivated expression was replaced by empty noises with many difficulties, which left the heart the more unstirred the more the fingers moved.

Noisy, overcomplicated sonatas are, to be sure, a necessity for those soloists who wish to display mere technical skill on the instrument, and not expression of feelings. But more thought should be given to the general usefulness of sonatas designed for the public. For not only amateurs but also most artists are concerned more about expressive pieces than about difficult works of this kind. Proof of this is given by the clavier sonatas of *Türk*, which are generally loved because along with the suitable presentation of pleasant feelings they do not frighten off the amateur by too many difficulties. Moreover, they are written in a style which is very affecting for any feeling not yet overindulged—all qualities which can rightly be required of compositions of this kind which are intended for the public.

§110. The external arrangement of the sonata, namely, the different forms of both its Allegros and its Adagio, need not be examined in particular here, for the sonata assumes all the forms which already have been described before in connection with the symphony. Thus, for example, the first Allegro has two sections which are usually repeated. The first of these sections contains one main period, the second section has two, and all follow the same course of modulation as the main periods of the symphony. The last Allegro also can have either the form just indicated, or the form of the rondo, or also variations on a short passage such as has been described in §20.[7]

But as similar to one another as the forms of the sonata and the symphony may be in the number of periods and the course of modulation, as different, conversely, is the inner nature of the melody in the two. This difference, however, can be better felt than described; only the following external distinction can generally be observed: in the sonata the melodic sections are not connected as continuously as in the symphony, but more often are separated through formal phrase-endings. They are not usually extended through the continuation of a segment of this or that melodic section or through sequences, but more often by clarifying additions, defining the feeling most accurately.

• • • • •

IX. *On the quartet*

§118. The quartet, currently the favorite piece of small musical societies, is cultivated very assiduously by the more modern composers.

If it really is to consist of four obbligato voices of which none has priority over the others, then it must be treated according to fugal method.

7. See p. 60, n. 14.

But because the modern quartets are composed in the *galant* style, there are four main voices which alternately predominate and sometimes this one, sometimes that one forms the customary bass.

While one of these parts concerns itself with the delivery of the main melody, the other two melodic voices must proceed in connected melodies which promote the expression without obscuring the main melody. From this it is evident that the quartet is one of the most difficult of all kinds of compositions, which only the composer completely trained and experienced through much practice may attempt.

Among the more modern composers, *Haydn, Pleyel,* and *Hoffmeister* have enriched the public the most with this type of sonata. The late *Mozart* also had engravings made in Vienna of six quartets for two violins, viola, and violoncello with a dedication to Haydn.[8] Among all modern four-part sonatas these most closely correspond to the concept of a true quartet and are unique on account of their special mixture of the strict and free styles and the treatment of harmony.

X. *On the concerto*

§119. The *concerto,* an instrumental piece in which a main part is accompanied by an entire orchestra, also has no definite nature. But its three main sections, namely its two allegros and its adagio, can assume every mood which music is capable of expressing.

It is that piece with which the virtuosos usually may be heard on their instrument; thus there are concertos for all of the standard instruments of an orchestra.

For reasons shown in connection with the solo, the composer can, however, write a good concerto only for that instrument which he himself plays with a certain degree of skill. Not only did many a concerto player formerly lack a sufficient number of such pieces, but also he often could not use those which were obtainable because of the special way of playing which they required. Thus nothing else remained for many concerto players, especially those who played an instrument for which not many concertos had yet been composed or become known, than to compose their concerto parts and their accompaniment themselves, as best they could, or to let them be composed by others. Nowadays, since various instrumentalists of all kinds concern themselves with composition, this product of music is so assiduously cultivated that there is no reason to complain about the lack of concertos for any instrument. Nevertheless, the procedure referred to before remains the story of many a concerto which now appears in public. Moreover, there are musicians who make a commercial business of adapting concertos by once popular masters for every instrument through transpositions in other keys and through alteration of passages without compunction. Indeed it is certain that composers even write

8. Koch is referring to Mozart's "Haydn" Quartets, K. 387, 421, 428, 458, 464, and 465, which were published in 1785. [Tr.]

point of view than the solo. The expression of feeling by the solo player is like a monologue in passionate tones, in which the solo player is, as it were, communing with himself; nothing external has the slightest influence on the expression of his feeling. But consider a well-worked-out concerto in which, during the solo, the accompanying voices are not merely there to sound this or that missing interval of the chords between the soprano and bass. There is a passionate dialogue between the concerto player and the accompanying orchestra. He expresses his feelings to the orchestra, and through short interspersed phrases it signals to him sometimes approval, sometimes acceptance of his expression, as it were. Now in the Allegro it tries to stimulate his noble feelings still more; now it commiserates with him, now comforts him in the Adagio. In short, by a concerto I imagine something similar to the tragedy of the ancients, where the actor expressed his feelings not towards the pit, but to the chorus. The chorus was involved most closely with the action and was at the same time justified in participating in the expression of feelings. Then the listener, without losing anything, is just the third person, who can take part in the passionate performance of the concerto player and the accompanying orchestra. Ponder these ideas further, listen to most of *C. P. E. Bach's* concertos, which so completely correspond to this ideal, or better, from which this ideal is derived, and then judge whether the concerto is no more than mere exercise for composer and player, no more than mere pleasure for the ear, aiming at nothing else.[11]

§120. The first Allegro of the concerto contains three main periods performed by the soloist, which are enclosed by four subsidiary periods performed by the orchestra as ritornellos.

In modern concertos, the first ritornello is generally worked out at length. It consists of the principal melodic sections of the plan of the Allegro, which are brought into a different connection and extended through other means than in the solo of the concerto part.[12] With these sections a few suitable subsidiary ideas are connected in the ritornello which again lead to a main idea.

At present this ritornello takes three different forms. It either (1) makes up only one period, in which the melody stays in the main key throughout the entire passage (with the exception of short passing modulations); or (2) consists of two periods connected with one another. In this case, when it is based in a major key, there is a modulation to the key of the fifth,[13] after the V-phrase of this key a cantabile phrase from the solo is played, and then the first period of

11. Because the composition of concertos tends to be the *ne plus ultra* of most beginning composers, it is hoped one will not find this digression on the worth of this composition and the abuses to which it is subjected entirely useless and unnecessary. [Au.]
12. As has already been shown . . . the first main period of the solo part is worked out before the ritornello is arranged as the introduction to the solo part. [Au.] Koch refers here to a discussion earlier in the *Versuch* where, following Sulzer, he divides the compositional process into three phases—*plan, realization,* and *elaboration* (vol. 2, pt. 1). In the concerto, the first main period of the solo contains the plan of the work and is composed first. The opening ritornello is part of the second phase, or realization, and is composed after the first period of the solo.
13. The application to the minor mode has already been mentioned several times in discussions of the preceding types of compositions. [Au.]

concertos in advance for a possible commission without yet knowing for wl instrument the passages still lacking should be suited. But these are only s cial cases. The concerto is subject to a far more detrimental abuse, however that the expression "to play in company" all too often is understood as nothi more than to demonstrate skill in a clean and plain execution of the meloc figures and in overcoming well-chosen difficulties. Instead the skill attaine should be used only to present the expression of certain feelings through most highly refined performance appropriate to them.

If concertos were composed and performed more generally according to a better model, then many men of taste would be more satisfied with this type of composition. *Sulzer,* for example, whose judgments concerning the other kinds of compositions we so readily defer to, says of the concerto that it is basically nothing but an exercise for composer and player and an entirely inde-terminate pleasure for the ear, aiming at nothing more.[9]

But is this verdict perhaps too harsh? Should not this judgment be directed towards only such concertos as are condemned by discerning concerto players themselves?

If one disregards the abuses of the concerto, shown before, which do not yet generally prevail, why should the concerto alone be merely exercise for com-poser and player? Why should this composition alone be a mere pleasure for the ear, aiming at nothing further?

Sulzer concedes that in the sonata music can show its ability to portray feel-ings without words. Why should music have this ability less in the concerto, since the composer possesses in its richer accompaniment more means to increase the expression of the main part than he does in the sonata? What is particularly offensive to *Sulzer* seems to be the form of the concerto, for he says in the article "Sonata": "The form of a concerto appears to be intended more to give a skillful player the opportunity to be heard accompanied by many instruments than to render the passions."[10]

If one discounts the ritornellos in a concerto, which after all can be as little detrimental to the expression of feelings in this composition as they are in the aria, what difference remains then between the form of the sonata and that of the concerto which promotes the expression of feelings in the sonata but could be detrimental to it in the concerto? Perhaps *Sulzer* understands here by the form of the concerto merely that usage by which long passages are composed in certain places in the periods of a concerto which are nothing more than an exercise for the player, because in most cases they have so little in common with the expression of a definite feeling that they may be transferred to any concertos? This seems to be the most probable. But the presence of these passages is anything but essential in the form of the concerto.

It appears to me that the concerto must be judged from an entirely different

9. Sulzer, ed., *Allgemeine Theorie,* "Concert." [Tr.]
10. Ibid., "Sonate." [Tr.]

the ritornello is closed with a formal cadence in this key. With the caesura note of this cadence, a phrase begins which leads the melody back into the main key in one of those ways described in §31.[14] After the return to the main key, a melodic section of the first period is usually repeated, in order to give the entire ritornello a certain kind of completion and to maintain the unity of this passage before the close follows with the principal cadence in the main key. However the first ritornello is also formed so that (3) there is indeed a formal modulation into the key of the fifth, and after the V-phrase in it a principal melodic section is played in this key. But immediately afterwards, without a formal close in this key, there is a modulation back to the main key and the ritornello concludes. This last form is the most usual in more modern concertos.

§121. Lately a short introductory passage of slow tempo and earnest character has preceded the first Allegro of a concerto.[15] It is used in modern symphonies and has already been described above in connection with the symphony. In the concerto also, this passage usually closes with the so-called half cadence, after which the ritornello of the first Allegro begins without interruption.

§122. With the entry of the first main period, or the first solo part, the cadence of the ritornello generally comes to rest completely before the solo begins. That is, the solo does not enter with the caesura note, but first begins its period after a fully completed close of the ritornello. On the other hand, the second solo and also the entrance of the [second] ritornello do not leave the cadence completely at rest but enter with its caesura tone.

§123. Nothing remains to be noted in connection with the three main periods of the solo part, for they have the same external arrangement and the same course of modulation as the three main periods in the first Allegro of the symphony. The type of melody, on the other hand, is very similar to that of the sonata. It is just as developed as in the sonata, but usually is more protracted through the means of extension already known to us, and the melodic sections are better connected through the omission of the ending formulas of phrases. At the caesura-note of phrases or incises, the melody of the main part is sometimes interrupted by the orchestra with short passages, which consist either of repeated segments of the principal melody or of phrases which occurred only in the ritornello.

In well-composed concertos, every single part of the accompanying orchestra makes its contribution to the main part, according to the ideal described before. As a segment of the whole, it is involved in the passionate dialogue and has the right to show its feelings concerning the main part through short phrases. To this end, these voices do not always wait for the conclusion of the

14. See p. 61, n. 15.
15. C. P. E. Bach did compose slow introductions to two of his harpsichord concertos, W. 41 (1769) and W. 43, no. 5 (1772), and Anton Rosetti (c. 1750–1792), Bohemian composer, conductor, and double-bass player, wrote a Grave introduction to his Grand Concerto in F Major for two horns (c. 1785). This practice, however, was certainly not the norm. [Tr.]

incise or phrase in the principal part, but throughout its performance may be heard alternately in brief imitations; yet they must be placed and arranged so that they do not obscure the performance of the main part.

The beginning composer can get to know the treatment of the accompaniment to the concerto just described nowhere better than in the clavier concertos of *C. P. E. Bach*. In addition to the skill of forming the melody so that it permits such imitations in the accompaniment, much practical experience and artistic feeling are required not to overdo the effect and harm the main voice.

§124. At the caesura-tone of the first main period, which, as has been mentioned already, closes in the key of the fifth, the second ritornello begins again with the main phrase. It repeats a few melodic sections which already were contained in the first ritornello and closes likewise with a formal cadence in the key of the fifth. With the caesura-tone of this cadence, the second solo part begins in this key again. In fact, the second solo usually starts with a melodic section which was not contained in the first period, but is a powerful, conspicuous, yet suitable subsidiary idea, which again leads very appropriately to a main idea.

This period is treated like the second main period of the first Allegro of the symphony; therefore it is closed in the minor key of the sixth, at times also in the minor key of the second or third. With its caesura-note, a short ritornello begins which forms the subsidiary period already described in connection with the symphony. By means of a melodic section that is extended through sequence or the continuation of a metrical formula, the ritornello modulates back into the main key, in which it closes with a V-phrase; thus the third solo of the principal part can again begin in the main key.

§125. In its form the third solo part in the concerto again resembles the third main period of the first Allegro of the symphony. At the caesura-tone of this period, the ripieno parts usually introduce, by means of a few measures, a fermata on the six-four chord of the keynote. The soloist sustains this longer than the other instruments and connects with it either a free fantasy or a capriccio, which is mistakenly called a cadenza because it is made at the close of the composition. With the caesura-tone of this so-called cadenza, which always ends with a formal cadence, the last ritornello begins. This generally consists of the last melodic sections of the initial ritornello, with which the entire first Allegro concludes.

§126. The Adagio of the concerto usually takes the form already described in §84 in connection with the aria.[16] In the more modern concertos, however, instead of the customary Adagio, often a so-called romance is composed. This

---

16. In §84 Koch essentially describes the *da capo* and its modifications. In its most common form, the aria "has two main periods in the first section. . . . A short instrumental interlude separates [the first section] from the second section, which in this case is only a single period, and after the second section the first is repeated either entirely or only in part" (Baker, p. 169). The other forms of aria that Koch discusses are the Rondo (§85–§86), and one he styles a more modern form (§87), which has a section in slow tempo followed by a quicker second section.

has a definite character, which one can best get to know from Sulzer's description of the romance in poetry.

"Nowadays," says Sulzer, "the name romance is given to short narrative songs in the extremely simple and somewhat antiquated tone of the old rhymed romances. Their content may be a passionate, tragic, amorous, or even merely entertaining narrative.[17] . . . Ideas and expression must be of the utmost simplicity and very naive."[18]

This composition usually takes the form of the rondo, which already has been described at length.[19]

§127. The last section of the concerto is either an Allegro or a Presto. It may take the form of the first Allegro, or of an ordinary rondo with very amplified episodes, or of variations on a short melody consisting of two sections. The essentials of the variation form have also been mentioned in connection with the last Allegro of the symphony.

17. In music this last type of romance is not used, because now it is composed only in a slow tempo. [Au.]
18. Sulzer, ed., *Allgemeine Theorie*, "Romanze." [Tr.]
19. See above, §105 and p. 77, n. 6.

6 Francesco Galeazzi

Francesco Galeazzi's career as violinist, composer, and teacher took him from Turin, the city of his birth in 1758, to Rome where he practiced his art as music director of the Teatro Valle, and finally to Ascoli, where he resided until his death in Rome in 1819. His *Elementi teorico-pratici di musica* (*Theoretical-Practical Elements of Music*) resembles Quantz's *Versuch* in that it is no mere instrument tutor, but a comprehensive work. While it includes the expected violin tutor and a brief history of music, the fourth part is a treatise on composition that covers a wide range of topics, from harmony, counterpoint, and rhythm to the affects of keys and the invention of melodic figures through combination and permutation. Galeazzi's discussion of writing large-scale compositions occurs in the second section of the volume, headed "Melodia," in which he describes a movement of a composition as a "well-conducted melody." With remarkable clarity and detail he spells out the periods of this spun-out cantilena with their various functions, including the "Characteristic Passage," which has sometimes been interpreted as an early version of the "second theme" of nineteenth-century sonata-form theorists.

FROM *Theoretical-Practical Elements of Music*
(1796)

ARTICLE III. OF MELODY IN PARTICULAR, AND OF ITS PARTS, MEMBERS, AND RULES

23. To find a motive or to continue it even for a few measures is indeed the work of a beginner, but not that of the perfect composer. In the larger pieces of music, such as arias, or other pieces of theatrical or church music, and in instrumental music, such as symphonies, trios, quartets, concertos, etc., when the motive has been written, nothing has yet been accomplished. This much is certainly true, that the best composers do not make any distinction among motives; each one is equally good to them. But let us not anticipate something we must discuss shortly. The art, then, of the perfect composer does not consist in the discovery of *galant* motives or agreeable passages, but consists in the exact conduct of an entire piece of music. It is principally here that one recognizes the ability and knowledge of a great master, since any very mediocre motive can, if well developed, make an excellent composition.

24. Therefore, since we have to discuss here the most interesting aspect of modern music, that is, the conduct one must follow in laying out the melodies, we shall advise our reader first to learn from compositions by others how to discern and distinguish well parts and members, which we shall here enumerate and explain in all detail. Every well-conducted melody is divided into two parts, either connected, or separated in the middle by a repeat sign. The first part is usually composed of the following members: 1. Introduction, 2. Principal Motive, 3. Second Motive, 4. Departure to the most closely related keys, 5. Characteristic Passage or Intermediate Passage, 6. Cadential Period, and 7. Coda. The second part is then composed of these members: 1. Motive, 2. Modulation, 3. Reprise, 4. Repetition of the Characteristic Passage, 5. Repetition of the Cadential Period, and 6. Repetition of the Coda.

25. Now let us analyze all these members, one by one, and demonstrate their arrangement and order in the very simple little melody that we give [Example 1]. The periods and the conduct of this short melody shall serve as a model for

Example 1

[Principal Motive]

TEXT: Vol. 2, pp. 253–60, translated by Bathia Churgin, *Journal of the American Musicological Society* 21 (1968), 189–99, with minor alterations.

all the others in any other style, either vocal or mixed, and this by necessity, in order not to increase by too much the already abundant number of examples in this volume.

26. The Introduction is nothing but a preparation for the true Motive of a composition. It is not always used, and it is the composer's choice to introduce it. In the example given by us this member is lacking, but it will be observed that Example 2 is the introduction of a trio from one of my works. It is therefore sometimes possible, instead of beginning with the true motive, first to present a section of cantilena in preparation for it. If this section is suitable, and connected in a natural way to the motive, it makes an excellent effect, provided that it makes a cadence, either formal or implied, at the moment when the motive begins. It is good practice that the Introduction (if there is one) be sometimes recalled in the course of the melody, so that it should not seem to be a section that has been detached, and entirely separated from the rest. For the fundamental rule for the conduct of the composition consists in the *unity of ideas.*

Example 2

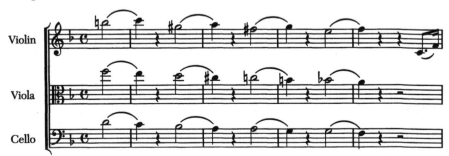

27. The Motive, then, is nothing but the principal idea of the melody—the subject or theme, one might say, of the musical discourse—and the whole composition must revolve around it. The Introduction may begin on any note, and even outside the key, but the Motive must infallibly begin with the notes constituting the key, that is, with its first, third, or fifth degree. In addition, it must be well rounded and lucid, for, being the theme of the discourse, if it is not well understood, the discourse that follows will not be understood either. The Motive should always terminate with a cadence either in the principal key, or on its fifth or fourth. In duets, terzets, and quartets, vocal as well as instrumental, the period is often repeated twice in different voices. The Motive in our example extends from measure 1 to measure 9. The Motive, then, is a most essential member of every melody. It is characteristic of beginners to rack their brains to select a beautiful Motive for their compositions without reflecting that every good composition must always grow in effect from the beginning to the end. Now, if one selects a wonderful Motive, it will be very difficult for the composition to keep growing in interest; on the contrary, indeed, it will considerably decline. This will totally discredit the composition in spite of a most beautiful Motive. If, on the contrary, one uses a mediocre Motive, well conducted according to the precepts we will now give, the composition will keep increasing its effect, which will make it more interesting and agreeable to the audience at every moment, and earn it more than the usual applause. It is precisely this that we see to be the practice of the most classical writers. Hence ordinarily an excellent Motive is in most cases the mark of a poor composition, for the merit of a composition consists, as has already been said, in the conduct and not in the Motive.

28. I call the *second Motive* what is named the countersubject in the fugue: that is, an idea which is either derived from the first motive or is entirely new, but which, well connected with the first, immediately follows the period of the Motive, and also sometimes serves to lead out of the key, terminating in the fifth of the key, or in the minor third for keys of the minor third. In most cases, if the Motive has ended its period in the fifth of the key, the Second Motive will begin in this same key; but if the Motive has cadenced in the principal key, then the Second Motive will begin in this key, leading then, as has been said, to the fifth or the fourth, etc. This period only occurs in very long pieces; in short pieces it is omitted, so that it is not essential. In the given example [Ex.

1] the Second Motive is tightly connected in measure 10 to the following period, which serves to depart from the key and go to the fifth, which is usually the first modulation to be heard.

29. The *Departure from the Key* follows either immediately after the Second Motive or with it, if there is one, or else immediately after the true Motive. In pieces of some length it is not good to leave the key too soon, in order to give the ear time to master fully the idea of the principal key; while if one leaves the key too soon, people will no longer know what key the composition is in. Then the first modulation is made to the most closely related keys, namely to the fifth or to the fourth in keys with a major third, and also to the minor third in keys of the minor third, as was stated above. This period must not be dragged on too long, but should end in the fifth of the key in which it is actually set, so that the following period may emerge with more prominence and individuality. In the example in front of us, what we have discussed here extends through measure 16, where we see the cadence in D, the fifth of the key of G, to which the modulation or Departure from the Key was made. Such a period is always necessary, and it often becomes mingled with that of the Second Motive, as happens in our example.

30. The *Characteristic Passage* or *Intermediate Passage* is a new idea, which is introduced toward the middle of the first part for the sake of greater beauty. This must be gentle, expressive, and tender in almost all kinds of compositions, and must be presented in the same key as the one to which the modulation was made. Often such a period is repeated, but only in more extended compositions; in short compositions it is very often omitted entirely. The period may be seen from measure 17 to measure 20.

31. The Cadential Period then follows. This is a new idea, but it is always dependent on previous ideas, especially on the principal Motive or the Second Motive, and in it the melody is made ready and prepared for the cadence. If the voice or instrument has shown off its gentleness and expression in the Characteristic Passage, it will display animation and skill, with agility of voice or hand, in the period we are now discussing. Consequently, this period in vocal music is a good place for figuration and brilliant passagework, and in instrumental music for the most difficult passages, which then close with a final cadence. Such a period is seen in the example from measure 21 to measure 24, where the final cadence takes place. In instrumental music very often this period is repeated twice, arranged in two different parts in order that each performer may exhibit his particular ability. In short pieces it is presented only once, and it is an essential period, since it is one that concludes the composition.

32. After making the final cadence, which concludes the last cadential period, it is not unusual that instead of ending the first part here, a new period, called a Coda, is elegantly added. It is an addition to or prolonging of the cadence, and therefore not an essential period, but it serves very well to link the ideas which end the first part with those which have begun it, or with those

with which the second part begins, as we intend to point out. And this is its principal function. It can be seen from measure 24 until the end of the first part.

33. It is well to know here that in all pieces of music, of whatever kind or style, whether divided in the middle by a repeat sign or continuous, the first part always closes in the fifth of the principal key, rarely in the fourth, and often in the minor third of keys with a minor third.

34. The second part then also begins with its Motive, which can be done in four different ways: 1. Beginning it with an Introduction, either analogous to the first part, if there is one, and transposed to the fifth of the key, or modulating in various ways. This method, however, is tedious and little practiced by good composers. 2. Beginning the second part with the same Motive as the first, transposed to the fifth of the key. This method is also in disuse, like the former, since it does not introduce any variety into the compositions, which is always the purpose of all the skills of genius. But the following two are the most commendable methods: 3. One can begin the second part with some passage freely taken from the first, and especially from the Coda (if there was one), but in the same key in which the first part ends; and this is precisely the practice in our example, from measure 29 to measure 34, where the beginning of the first part is developed out of the outline of the last two measures of the Coda. 4. Finally, the last method is to begin the second part with an idea that is quite new and foreign. In such a case, however, it is not good to present it in the key in which the first part ends, but rather, for greatest surprise, it should be in some related key, but separated and unexpected. This period is always essential.

35. Then follows the *Modulation,* which is always made using passages and ideas linked with the first or second motive, or with the motive of the second part. So it is as regards the melody, but concerning the methods and rules to follow in modulation and long modulatory progression,[1] this subject of greatest importance merits a separate article, which will follow.

36. The *Reprise* succeeds the Modulation. However remote the Modulation is from the main key of the composition, it must draw closer little by little, until the Reprise, that is, the first Motive of Part I in the proper natural key in which it was originally written, falls in quite naturally and regularly. If the piece is a long one, the true Motive in the principal key is taken up again as has been said, but if one does not want to make the composition too long, then it will be enough to repeat instead the Characteristic Passage transposed to the same fundamental key. In our example the Modulation may been seen to continue through measure 41, at which point the principal Motive is then resumed in its proper key. In such a case, the motive itself has to be conducted gradually to the fourth of the key, as can be seen here in measure 48, and it then makes a cadence on the fifth as is done in measure 52. Or if the second

---

1. Galeazzi explains this term (*circolazione*) in his article on modulation (vol. 2, pp. 264–65). [Tr.]

method has been used—that is, the reprise of the Characteristic Passage—then the Modulation ends on the fifth of the key, in order to start the Characteristic Passage next in the main key; and also in this case it is good practice for the harmony somewhere to touch, although in passing, on the fourth of the key.

37. The repetition of the last three periods of the first part is made by transposing them to the principal key and writing them one after another, in the same order they had in the first part. The Characteristic Passage must be the same as that of the first part (the key alone being changed), but the cadential period may be varied if one wishes, provided that it maintains a certain analogy with that of the first part. The Coda can even be omitted or completely changed if one does not wish to repeat it just as it was in the first part, as is done in our example. A most beautiful device is often practiced here, which is to recapitulate in the Coda the motive of the first part, or the Introduction, if there was one, or some other passage that is both remarkable and well suited to end with; this produces a wonderful effect, reviving the idea of the Theme of the composition and bringing together its parts. In this example the repetition of the Characteristic Passage can be seen from measure 53 to measure 55 [56], that of the Cadential period from measure 56 [57] to measure 59, and finally the repetition of the Coda until the end of the piece.

38. Such is, more or less, the structure and conduct of the melody generally speaking, as is the fashion according to the present style. Since, however, each kind of musical composition has its proper character, and therefore a somewhat different conduct from the others, we shall speak of this separately in the following articles.

7 Jérôme-Joseph de Momigny

Born in Belgium in 1762, Jérôme-Joseph de Momigny received his early training as an organist. He lived in Lyons during the French Revolution, and moved to Paris in 1800 to open a publishing house. A theorist of universalist ambitions, he intended to formulate a music theory based on natural principles that would replace all others, and to publish texts that would do the same. This grandiose plan failed, and he was driven into bankruptcy in 1828. His final years were marked by pronounced mental deterioration; he died in the lunatic asylum at Charenton in 1842.

The title of Momigny's 1806 treatise—*Cours complet d'harmonie et de composition* (*A Complete Course of Harmony and Composition*)—announces his fundamentalist goals, and its dedication leaves no room for doubt: his work is "based on incontestable principles drawn from nature, which are in accord with all good practical works, ancient and modern, and which because of their clarity are within the reach of all." Although Momigny's messianic certainty may strike us as naive, he was an original and independent thinker and his treatise is is a mine of interesting theories. He endeavored to expand current notions of tonality, beginning with a Rameau-like system based on the chord of nature. He also developed a detailed account of phrase structure, which he put into practice in extended musical analyses of Haydn's Symphony No. 103 and of Mozart's D-minor Quartet, K. 421, which follows here. These analyses, which wander from narrow discussions of melodic detail to the broadest considerations of the poetics of expression, consistently reveal Momigny's wide-ranging musical intelligence.

FROM *A Complete Course of Harmony and Composition*

(1806)

CHAPTER XXX. ON COMPOSITION, STRICT OR FREE, IN FOUR PARTS

ANALYSIS OF A QUARTET BY MOZART. ABOUT THE MUSICAL STYLE OF THIS PIECE.

The style of this *Allegro Moderato* is noble and pathetic. I decided that the best way to have my readers recognize its true expression was to add words to it.[1] But since these verses, if one can call them that, were improvised, as it were, they ought not to be judged in any other regard than that of their agreement with the sense of the music.

I thought I perceived that the feelings expressed by the composer were those of a lover who is on the point of being abandoned by the hero she adores: *Dido,* who had had a similar misfortune to complain of, came immediately to mind. Her noble rank, the intensity of her love, the renown of her misfortune—all this convinced me to make her the heroine of this piece. She should be made to speak in a manner worthy of herself, but this is the task of a great lyric poet. It is sufficient to my task that the feelings of this unhappy queen be recounted and carefully set to music that renders them faithfully.

•　•　•　•　•

TEXT: The original edition (Paris, 1806), vol. 1, p. 371; vol. 2, pp. 388–98, 401–403. Translation by Wye J. Allanbrook. The music example is transcribed from vol. 2 of the plates that accompany the edition; a piano reduction of the music has been omitted.

1. Momigny's text and a translation may be found on pp. 113–14.

CHAPTER XXXI

ANALYSIS OF THE SECOND REPRISE OF THE ALLEGRO MODERATO
OF THE MOZART QUARTET

It is particularly in the first part of the second reprise of a great piece that a
good composer makes himself known. It is there, above all, that genius needs
to rely on skill. It is there that one must develop all the riches of harmony, all
the depth of counterpoint—in short all the unexpected and delightful devices
that the magic art of transitions has to offer.

But it is also in the second reprise of a great piece that anyone who has not
studied music well is forced in spite of himself to reveal his poverty and impotence. He can still deceive the ignorant many with a chaotic din, or with forced
transitions. But the true connoisseur can no more be duped by this charla-
tanism, by this empty noise, by this false science, than by the bad Latin that
Molière most wittily placed in the mouth of Sganarelle.[2]

When one wishes to form an opinion about a piece of music, one must first
see if the author has depicted there what he should depict, and at what point
he has seized the truth of the expression, or to what point he could carry it,
using the means that his art affords. Then one must see if the style of the piece
is pure and correct, if each verse has a good rhythm, if each period is well
rounded, if each voice or part remains within its proper range. Finally one
must see if the ensemble makes the full impression that the subject requires;
and to assign to a composer the place that he deserves to occupy in public
opinion, one must in addition consider what degree of natural and of acquired
talent the piece supposes, in accordance with which one judges it.

Imbued with these ideas, let us go on to analyze the second reprise of the
quartet [see music example, pp. 101–13].

The beginning of this second reprise is for two measures the same as that of
the first, except that instead of *D d̄, d d, c♯ d, d d,* it is *E♭ e♭, e♭ e♭, d e♭, e♭ e♭.*[3]

Although on the keyboard the key of D minor is next to the key of E♭ major,
they are nonetheless quite distant from one another in the feeling that they
stir. Moreover, this perfect major chord *E♭ g b♭ e♭* is not that of a tonic but of
a dominant. Note that the *b♮* of the preceding measure is a *c♭*, and that this *c♭*
that *Mozart* has nevertheless written *b♮,* in order to cause more surprise, is
announced as the sixth note of the key of *E♭* minor, taken in the diminished
seventh chord of the leading-tone *d f a♭ c♭.* But as this chord is not followed by
the perfect minor chord *e♭ g♭ b♭,* but by the perfect major chord *e♭ g b♭,* that *d
f a♭ c♭* that we took first as a diminished seventh chord of the leading tone of
the key of *E♭* minor is incontestably the chord of the chromatic fourth of the

2. Sganarelle, the protagonist of Molière's farce *Le Médecin malgré lui,* spouts nonsense Latin to
convince his patients that he is a doctor.
3. The commas in these renderings represent not barlines but motivic articulations.

key of $A\flat$.[4] But are we in $A\flat$ major or $A\flat$ minor? We don't know yet, since the dominant chord is the same in minor as it is in major. But we quickly find out what to hold on to, since when the $c\flat$ appears,[5] it indicates that we are in $A\flat$ minor. But this does not last long; I see in the second part of the third measure a $g\flat$ in the cello that seems to want to lead us into $B\flat$ minor. But the $e\flat$ of the dominant seventh chord of the key of $b\flat$, f a c $e\flat$, which changes suddenly into a $d\sharp$, leads us into a minor rather than directing us into $B\flat$ minor.

By means of this $d\sharp$, substituted for $e\flat$, the dominant seventh chord f a c $e\flat$ is transformed into that of the diminished seventh and diminished third on the chromatically raised fourth degree of the key of A minor, which is $d\sharp$ f a c. It appears here under the form of the augmented sixth attached to a perfect major chord, f a c $d\sharp$. Thus the f of the cello becomes the sixth of the key of A minor, instead of remaining the dominant of the key of $B\flat$.[6]

The movement from $e\flat$ to $d\sharp$, thereby changing the key, is an *enharmonic* transition.

Although we talk a great deal about the enharmonic genre, there is still not, properly speaking, a genre of this nature in music: there are only *enharmonic transitions*. And although J. J. *Rousseau* affirms, perhaps according to serious composers, but certainly according to poor musicians, *that the enharmonic genre is the first that had been used among the Greeks*,[7] one ought to take care not to believe it. *For it is as if he were maintaining that the first objects that struck the eyes of the Athenians were those that one can only perceive with the help of a microscope*, which is to misunderstand the nature of our constitution. In short, *enharmonics* are for our ear just about what *microscopic* objects are for sight.

One could also compare enharmonics to homonyms. We know that a homonym is a word whose sound, and sometimes whose spelling, represents several different objects. For example the word *son* denotes equally the ringing of a bell or the sound of any stringed instrument, the bran one extracts from *wheat*, and the masculine possessive pronoun *son*, as in this phrase: le *son* de *son* violon ne vaut pas le *son* de ma farine.[8] Likewise on the piano the $e\flat$ and $d\sharp$ are represented by the same key. There is no transition when this key or any other is only taken under one single aspect. But when the two aspects are used consecutively, and by means of this device one changes key, this is a enhar-

---

4. Momigny makes heavy weather out of the brief inflection of the minor mode in the diminished-seventh chord that precedes the V^7 of $E\flat$ in the second ending to the first reprise (see example, p. 101, m. 1). Calling the $E\flat$ major chord a dominant needlessly complicates the analysis of an already complex passage.

5. In the second measure of the second reprise.

6. The $d\sharp$ combines with the f to form an augmented sixth, which expands to the dominant octave on e.

7. In the *Dictionnaire de musique* (Paris, 1768) Rousseau says only that the enharmonic genre was "according to some, the first of the three to be discovered" ("Enharmonique," p. 192).

8. "The *sound* of *his* violin is not worth the *bran* from my meal." The equivalent homonyms are, of course, not available in English.

monic transition whether one passes from $d\sharp$ to $e\flat$, or from $e\flat$ to $d\sharp$, and like-wise successively with regard to all the other keys.

Why, one may ask, did *Mozart* not write a $d\sharp$ in the place of $e\flat$, just as you yourself have indicated by writing $d\sharp$ over the $e\flat$ that precedes the $e\natural$ (see example, p. 102, m. 5). It is so that the performer will rest on the $e\flat$, and not go looking for a $d\sharp$ that would seem to be a dissonance and that would torment the ear rather than agreeably surprising it.

This proves to us that we should feel some regret for those pianos with quarter tones that were so complicated and difficult to make and to play. It refutes what many theorists have put forward in that regard.

Since the enharmonic is only, if I can express myself thus, a kind of marvel-ous flying bridge by means of which one passes, almost magically, from one climate into another far distant, this is reason enough for us to be very reserved in the use that one can make of it. *To abuse it is to proclaim the pretensions of a novice rather than to demonstrate the skill of a great master.* But let us go on.

Mozart, who composed almost all his first reprise in the free style, begins to make use of a subject here, after the first two measures of the second reprise.

This subject is furnished by the second measure of the beginning: $E\flat$ d $e\flat$ $e\flat$ $e\flat$.

After the first violin has played the subject twice, the cello takes hold of it, sounding it three times in its turn, but in A minor. The viola becomes the echo of the cello at the distance of a half-measure, repeating the same motive in *broken imitation* at the octave. It continues with the same subject, but shortens it and climbs diatonically, $f\sharp$ e $f\sharp f\sharp$, $g\sharp f\sharp$ $g\sharp$ $g\sharp$.

Over this cello and viola, which present only a subordinate subject, the sec-ond violin plays no. 1, the principal motive, a $g\sharp$ c b e, imitated at the second and *alla stretta*, that is to say, in rhythmic compression, by the first violin: no. 2, $b\natural$ a d c f. This is true skill. For all its merit, it is not coldly calculated, but has a somber and genuine expression that penetrates to the depths of the soul. This should be attributed equally to the rhythm, the movement, and the into-nations of the passage.

With the words *voilà le prix de tant d'amour!* ["this is my reward for such a love!"] Mozart resumes the free style exclusively until the fifth verse.

How the anger of the queen of Carthage bursts out in the music of the third musical verse! and how the last syllable of the word *amour* is felicitously placed on the $b\flat$, in order to express the grief that Dido feels at having rashly aban-doned herself to this passion for a perjurer! The second time she repeats this word she cannot finish it, because she is choked by the grief that overwhelms her. It is here that the viola part, which represents her sister or confidante, takes up the word to address to the Trojan the reproaches that *Dido* no longer has the strength to make herself.

Did *Mozart* invent a new subject for this? He refrains from displaying that barren abundance so contrary to *unity*, that reveals a student. On the contrary, as a great contrapuntalist, he brings back his first motive here—not simply and as it has already been heard, for that would only be babble, but elaborated anew, and in a manner that produces a great effect.

In the first period of this second reprise he had taken for subject only one of the measures of his first motive—the second of these two measures. Here he takes two of them, the first and the second. *A A, a a, g♯ a, a a.*

After the first measure, an imitation in stretto at the second with this same subject is heard in the second violin. The cello enters one eighth note afterward, and plays a subordinate motive as accompaniment. This cello motive is an imitation, as regards rhythm, of the accompaniment that is found in the viola and in the second violin in the first measures of the second reprise.

In the three first measures of the reprise *Mozart* could have put half notes in the second violin and viola just as he did in the cello. Probably he preferred to use an eighth-note rest and three eighth notes to keep the passage from becoming languid.

Dido, throwing an angry look at *Aeneas,* says to him: *Fuis, malheureux!* ["Fly away, you wretch!"] It is a shortened imitation of the passage in the second violin, at the second above, and *alla stretta.*

The cello, which during this time has kept to the subordinate motive, in its turn lays hold of the principal subject, and says: *D D, d d, c♯ d, d d.*

The subordinate motive in the cello then passes to the viola. The imitation in stretto at the second, or rather at the ninth above the principal subject in the cello, is reproduced in the second violin—*e♭ e♭, e♭ e♭, d e♭, e♭ e♭*—and then in the first violin one measure after—*f♯ f♯, f♯ g.*

Note the gradual rise of the subject of the fifth verse. This subject is successively carried on six consecutive degrees of the musical scale, moving from *a* up to *f♯* inclusively. The viola begins on *a,* the second violin on *b♭,* the first violin on *c♯,* the cello on *D,* the second violin on *e♭,* and the first on *f♯.*

A student would have put all these imitations of the same subject in the same part. Then we would no longer have heard anything but a kind of scale in place of this dialogue that is so compressed, so pressing, and so admirable. At the moment when *Mozart* abandons this subject, the viola catches hold of the imitation of a motive that has already been heard, both toward the end of the first reprise and in the *link* that joins this reprise with the second—*d g b♭ b♭ b♭.* This subordinate theme is immediately imitated by the second violin, while the first violin plays that other most expressive subject, that transport of the soul, *D, c b♭ a, g f e.*

In this place *Dido,* seeing that her disdain does not have a powerful enough effect on the heart of *Aeneas,* again has recourse to supplication, saying to him: *Non! reste encore.* ["No! stay here."] Easily deceived, she adds (in an aside): *Il paraît s'attendrir!* ["He seems to be moved!"]

In order to fit the words to this passage in a suitable manner, it was necessary to think the aside out carefully. Since the preceding subject has no connection with the one to which these words are set, it could have seemed to be a shortcoming, whereas it is a genuine beauty.

Mozart, who is always careful not to multiply subjects unnecessarily, uses the same subordinate theme here that he had just put in the viola and second violin. So this latter imitates the principal subject at the fifth below with these notes: *G, f e d c b♭ a.* Then *Dido* says a second time, but one degree lower than the first: *Non! reste encore* (eighth verse).

Again the second violin imitates the melody at the fifth below, with these notes: *F, e d c b♭ a g.*

Here Mozart avoids a third repetition, which would be an error, known as *Rosalie,* or a third *révérence.*[9] Without abandoning the subordinate motive in the viola, he compresses the principal subject in the two violins, which gives this passage more movement and passion.

The large intervals that the first violin covers also add much to the effect of this verse, and paint in a very sensitive manner the confusion that reigns in *Dido's* soul.

In the ninth verse *Dido,* eyes full of tears of love, addresses this prayer to *Aeneas: À l'objet qui t'adore, rends la vie et le bonheur* ["Return life and happiness to this creature who worships you"]. She breaks off suddenly in the middle of the last word, as if struck by a sudden but fatal light, which illuminates the feelings and intentions of *Anchises'* son. Then she says to him, *Non, déchire mon coeur, ingrat!* ["No, tear my heart to pieces, thankless wretch!"]

In the music of the ninth verse the harmonic cadences are compressed to the point that toward the end they are composed only of two eighth notes each. This verse itself ends with melodic cadences in sixteenth notes, which gives the style of this period an astonishing passion that transports and ravishes the soul.

The motive that *Mozart* uses in the tenth verse is the same as that which has just been heard as a subordinate motive in the course of the third period.

Note that from the seventh to the tenth verse the cello *has been controlled by a motive* composed of a quarter note and a dotted eighth—*b♭ g, b♭ c, e c, e f, a f, a b♭, d b♭, d e.* This bass line contains two voices in one: one part could do *b♭ g, b♭ c* and the other *e c, e f,* etc. But having already arranged the three upper parts, *Mozart* saw that he had to make the cello take by itself what could have been played by the viola and cello in turn.

At the notes *g d, g c♯* the harmonic cadences contract, lasting no more

---

9. Alluding to the three reverences habitual, at least in earlier times, when one arrived at a formal gathering. [Au.] *Rosalie* (or *Rosalia,* from the title of an Italian popular song, *Rosalia, mia cara*) is a pejorative term usually applied to excessive use of sequences in exact transposition up or down a whole step. The transposition here is not exact, and Momigny's concern seems to be instead with excessive repetition. His remarks in this paragraph apply ahead to the ninth verse of his text.

than a half-measure each. In the tenth verse the cello is no longer under constraint.

In the viola and above the held note in the cello is the subordinate harmonic motive *c♯ e a a a*. This motive is successively imitated by the two violins—*a c♯ e, e e e: c♯ e a, a a a a*. In this cadence the principal motive is *a b♭*, in the following one *b♭ c♯*, and then *c♯ d*. Consequently the first violin takes the subordinate motive immediately before the principal subject, doing the job of two parts.

The first part of the second reprise finishes with the complement of the fourth period, for the fifth is only a short connective period, that is, a link that joins the first part of this reprise to the second.

SECOND PART OF THE SECOND REPRISE

The second part of the *second reprise* of this movement is the exact repetition of the beginning of the first reprise up to the chord of the false fifth and major sixth *c♯ e g b♭*, on the *e* of the cello that ends the eighth period. The material from here to the end of the movement is only the remainder of the first reprise transposed from F major to D minor, but with the modifications necessitated by this change of mode, and with some other trivial differences dictated by taste or sensibility.

So just as one divides a building into three parts—the dome and two wings—and a sermon into three points, so also does a substantial movement in music fall into three *parts*. These parts subdivide into *periods,* these periods into *verses,* these verses into *phrases,* these phrases into *propositions,* and these propositions or cadences into *members.*

To speak more precisely, I will divide the periods into *principal periods* and *lesser periods.* I will allow four kinds of principal periods: *opening* periods, *spirited* periods, *melodic* periods, and *flashes.*

There are three sorts of lesser periods: *intermediary, complementary,* and connective or *linking* periods.

Opening periods are those with which one begins a movement. Ordinarily this period also begins the third part of the musical discourse.

The *spirited* period is one that ordinarily is placed after the opening period and a gentle intermediary period. This spirited period is full of vigor, and quite often closes the first large portion of the first reprise.

Melodic periods are those that are preeminently cantabile.

The periods I call *flashes* are those that serve to demonstrate the skill and competence of the performer.

Intermediary periods are all those that are placed between the principal ones, and are neither complementary nor conjunctional.

Complementary periods are those that one uses to make a meaning more complete.

The complementary period thus serves as a kind of cornice or border for the period that precedes it.

Connective periods are large *links* that serve to bind together two periods that usually could not be immediately placed one after the other without shocking the ear, or at least leaving it unsatisfied.

•   •   •   •   •

THE PERIODS OF THE SECOND REPRISE

The period that begins the second reprise is not a simple opening period in which the composer abandons himself to his genius, but one of those in which genius is controlled by a *theme*. This period, which we would expect to finish with the first verse, is augmented by a *supplement* that contains the entire second verse and a complement that only finishes when the fifth verse begins. As a result, the period is very well balanced.

The second period is of the intermediary type. But it has such skilled counterpoint that it deserves a place in the rank of the finest principal periods.

The third period has even more exaltation, yet no less depth. This intermediary period, like the preceding one, belongs in the number of those that one would search for in vain in most composers. Keep in mind that most of these composers have only a very weak tincture of the profound art of counterpoint, and seem completely alien to the inspired power that great knowledge nourishes.

The complement of this period is itself a little period, which serves as the frame to the preceding one, although not in the manner of frames of paintings, which draw their name from their squared shape[10] and surround a picture on all sides. A frame of the sort that I call a complementary period touches the period it completes only on one side, comprising what the Italians have called a *coda* (tail)—one or two periods that are added to close a movement more completely.[11]

The fifth period is connective, since it attaches the first part of the second reprise to the second.

The first reprise and the second part of the second reprise are in some way like the two wings of a building. The first part of the second reprise lies between the two other parts like a dome between two lateral pavilions. The part of this opening period to which are set the words *Ingrat! je veux me plaindre, et non pas t'attendrir* ["Thankless wretch! I want to protest, and not to relent"] seems to me sublime.[12]

10. *Cadre,* the French word for "frame," comes from the Latin *quadratum,* "four-sided thing" or "square."
11. Momigny seems to have left out a number here, labeling as the complement of the fourth period what is actually the complement of the third, and continuing in the error by calling the next period the fifth.
12. "The opening period . . . is divided into two full-scale verses, attached by a semi-harmonic link" (Momigny, *Cours complet,* vol. 2, p. 398).

There are many definitions of the sublime; it is in my view a *bon mot* of the soul. The intellect alone can in no way produce the sublime. Further, one does not say of a remark, however intelligent it may be, that it is sublime, although one says that it is acute, pointed, ingenious. In general the sublime is the expression of what a noble soul experiences in a extraordinary situation.

In a serious situation, but one that it wants to expose to humor, the intellect gives birth to an epigram. In a situation of the greatest moment, a great soul portrays itself by a sublime remark.

The seventh period responds to the second period of the first reprise,[13] but I have separated its complement here: it forms the eighth period.

The ninth period responds to the third period of the first reprise.[14] I have also separated its complement to form the tenth period.

The fourth period of the first reprise is the counterpart of the eleventh period of this one.[15]

13. "The second period is of the class of *intermediaries*. It is attached to the first period by a melodic link, *a f d a*. It is also divided into two verses [the third and fourth], attached to one another by the *melodic link a g♯ a g♯ a g♯ a*. The fifth, sixth, seventh, and eighth verses, included in this period, nevertheless form a separate little period, called a complementary period" (Momigny, vol. 2, 398–99).

14. "The third period . . . is another intermediary period. It closes with the tenth verse [the twenty-fourth in the second reprise]; the eleventh and twelfth [the twenty-fifth and twenty-sixth, or the tenth period] form a period complementary to this one" (Momigny, vol. 2, p. 399).

15. The . . . fourth period is not precisely a spirited period because it does not make enough racket. But it can still be considered as one, whether because of its imitations in stretto, because of the fervor with which the parts answer one another, or finally because of the abandon that prevails in the melody of the fourteenth [thirtieth] verse" (Momigny, vol. 2, p. 399).

Example [from Mozart, String Quartet, K. 421]

mour!   oui, voi-là   le prix de tant d'a-mour!

4th verse   5th verse

Fuis,   mal - heu-reux!   Fuis,   mal - heu-

6th verse

reux!   Non!   reste _ en - co - re.   (Il pa-rait s'at-ten-drir!)

7th verse

103

Non! reste _ en - co - re. (Il pa-rait s'at-ten-drir!)

8th verse

[4th period]

À l'ob - jet qui t'a -

9th verse

Complement of the 4th period

do-re rends la vie _ et _ le _ bon-heur. Non dé-chi-re mon coeur. In -

10th verse   11th verse

104

fais mon dé-plai-sir, in - grat! ___ je veux me plain-dre et non pas t'at - ten-drir.

Ah! quand tu fais mon dé-plai-sir, in - grat! _ je veux me plain - dre, me

16th verse

7th period

plain-dre et non pas _ t'at-ten-drir. Quoi! tu peux _me quit-ter _sans rou-gir?

17th verse

18th verse

106

8th period

Quoi! tu peux me quit - ter___ sans rou - gir? Quoi! rien ne peux te re - te -

19th verse

9th period

nir?   Fuis! non, reste, ou je vais mou-

20th verse   *21st verse*   *22nd verse*   *23rd verse*

rir___ reste, ou je vais mou - rir___ reste,_ ou je vais mou-

24th verse

10th period

- rir. Ar - rête, __ ar - rête, __ ou je vais __ mou - rir. ____   Je t'en

25th verse

11th period

pri - e!   je t'en pri - e!   Si je te perds, __ je vais mou -

f

26th verse   *f* 27th verse   28th verse

rir. _____ si je te perds, __ si __ je __ te __ perds, je vais mou -

29th verse   30th verse

108

12th period

rir.　　　Ah,　　si ja-mais pour toi ＿＿　　　j'eûs quel - ques char -

31st verse

mes, ＿　　　viens, ＿　　ta - rir, viens,　ta - rir ＿＿　　mes

pleurs.　　　Ah! ＿＿ si ja-mais Di - don ＿　　eût ＿ pour ＿ toi ＿ quel - ques

cresc.

32nd verse

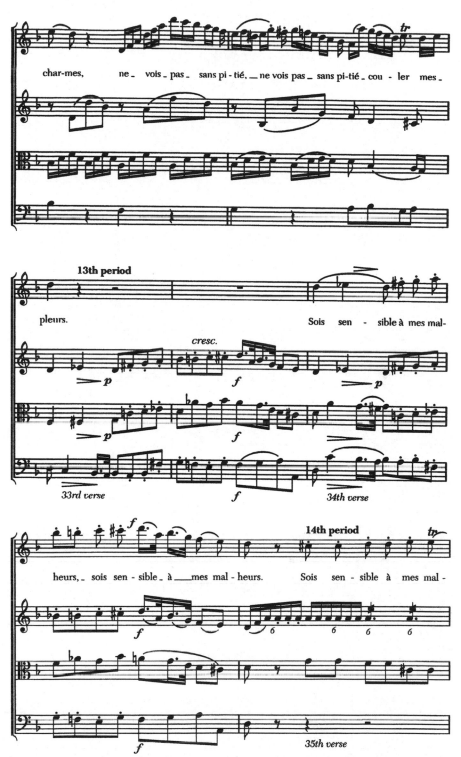

char-mes, ne _ vois _ pas _ sans pi - tié, _ ne vois pas _ sans pi-tié _ cou - ler mes _

13th period

pleurs.   Sois sen - sible à mes mal-

cresc.

33rd verse

34th verse

heurs, _ sois sen - sible à _ mes mal - heurs.   Sois sen - sible à mes mal-

14th period

35th verse

110

heurs, sois — sen - si - ble - à — mes mal - heurs.

36th verse

15th period

Quoi! tu ne ré-ponds rien?

37th verse

16th period

Quoi! tu ne ré-ponds rien?

Quoi! tu ne ré-ponds rien?

38th verse

39th verse

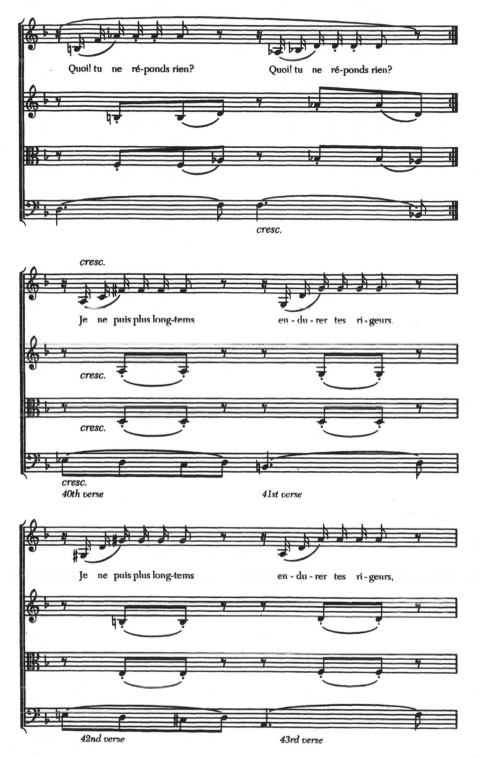

Quoi! tu ne ré-ponds rien?   Quoi! tu ne ré-ponds rien?

cresc.

cresc.

Je ne puis plus long-tems   en - du - rer tes ri - geurs.

cresc.

cresc.

cresc.
40th verse   *41st verse*

Je ne puis plus long-tems   en - du - rer tes ri - geurs,

42nd verse   *43rd verse*

112

TEXT: DIDO'S LAMENT

Reprise II, Part I

Hélas! mes larmes, mes appas,	Alas! my tears, my charms,
Ne te touchent pas.	don't touch you.
Tu veux me donner le trépas.	You want me to die.
Monstre indigne du jour,	O monster unworthy of the light,
Voilà le prix de tant d'amour!	this is my reward for such a love!
Fuis, malheureux! Non! reste encore.	Fly away, you wretch! No! stay here.

(*à part, avec espoir*) Il paraît s'atten-
    drir!
	(*Aside, hopefully*) He seems to be
	    moved!

À l'objet qui t'adore
Rends la vie et le bonheur.
Non, déchire mon coeur,
Ingrat!

To this creature who worships you,
return life and happiness.
No, tear my heart to pieces,
Thankless wretch!

Reprise II, Part II

Ah! quand tu fais mon déplaisir,
Ingrat, je veux me plaindre
Et non pas t'attendrir.
Quoi! tu peux me quitter sans
    rougir?
Quoi! rien ne peut te retenir?
Fuis! non, reste, ou je vais mourir.
Arrête, arrête, ou je vais mourir.
Je t'enprie! je t'enprie!
Si je te perds, je vais mourir.
Ah, si jamais pour toi j'eûs quelques
    charmes,
Viens, tarir mes pleurs.
Ah! si jamais Didon eût pour toi quel-
    ques charmes,
Ne vois pas sans pitié couler mes
    pleurs.
Sois sensible à mes malheurs.
Quoi! tu ne réponds rien?
Je ne puis plus longtemps endurer tes
    rigueurs.
Je le sens; je meurs.

Ah! when you cause me grief,
thankless wretch, I want to protest,
and not to relent.
What! can you leave me without
    blushing with shame?
What! can nothing restrain you?
Fly away! No, stay, or I shall die.
Stop, stop, or I shall die.
I beg you! I beg you!
If I lose you, I shall die.
Ah, if I ever had any charms for
    you,
come and dry my tears.
Ah, if Dido ever had any charms
    for you,
do not watch my tears flow without
    pity.
Be moved by my misery
What! you do not respond?
I cannot endure your cruelty any
    longer.
I feel it; I am dying.

$\mathcal{P}$ERFORMANCE PRACTICES

8 Carl Philipp Emanuel Bach

Johann Sebastian's second son, sometimes called the "Berlin" or "Hamburg" Bach, Carl Philipp Emanuel Bach was born in 1714 at Weimar. In 1738 he moved to Berlin and in 1740 became harpsichordist to Frederick the Great. In 1767 Bach gave up this position to become Telemann's successor as director of church music at Hamburg. He died there in 1788.

As a composer, Bach wrote works for clavichord and pianoforte as well as for harpsichord, and preferred the latter two instruments for the practice of improvisation. While his keyboard sonatas established him as the primary representation of the *galant* in Germany, many of them borrow features from the improvisatory mode—declamation, abrupt changes of mood, sudden modulations to remote keys—to create a powerfully emotive rhetoric often called the "sensitive" (*empfindsam*) style. He was also known for his virtuoso harpsichord concertos, chamber music, and symphonies, and he composed much sacred music during his tenure in Hamburg.

His theoretical work, the *Versuch über die wahre Art, das Clavier zu spielen* (*Essay on the Proper Manner of Playing a Keyboard Instrument*; in two parts, 1753–62) has remained to the present day a source of primary importance for the musical practice of the time.

FROM *Essay on the Proper Manner of Playing a Keyboard Instrument*

(1753)

CHAPTER 2. ABOUT EMBELLISHMENTS IN GENERAL

1. No one, perhaps, has ever questioned the necessity of embellishments. We may perceive this from our meeting them everywhere in great abundance. Indeed, when we consider the good they do, they are indispensable. They tie the notes together; they enliven them; they give them, when necessary, a special emphasis and weight; they make them pleasing and hence arouse a special attention; they help to clarify their content; whatever its nature, whether sad, gay, or of any other sort we please, they invariably contribute their share; they provide the correct manner of delivery with a considerable part of its occasion and material; a mediocre composition may be assisted by them, while without them the finest melody must seem empty and monotonous, the clearest content at all times unclear.

TEXT: As edited by Walter Niemann from the second (1759) edition of the original (5th ed., Leipzig, 1925), pp. 24–31. Translation by Oliver Strunk, with minor alterations.

2. For all the good embellishments may thus do, they may do equal harm if we choose bad ones or apply them in an unskillful way, apart from their proper place and in excess of their due number.

3. For this reason, those who in their pieces clearly indicate the embellishments that belong to them have always followed a safer procedure than if they had left their works to the discretion of unskilled performers.

4. Also in this respect we must do justice to the French for being unusually careful in the marking of their pieces. In Germany, the greatest masters of our instrument have done the same, and who knows but what the reasonable choice and number of their embellishments may have given the occasion to the French today of no longer burdening, as formerly, almost every note with such an ornament, thereby concealing the necessary clarity and noble simplicity of the melody.

5. From this we see that we must learn to distinguish good embellishments from bad, to perform the good ones correctly, and to apply them in their proper place and in due number.

6. The embellishments lend themselves readily to a division into two classes. To the first I assign those customarily indicated either by certain accepted signs or by a few small notes; to the second may be assigned the rest, which have no signs and are made up of many small notes.

7. Since this second class of embellishments depends especially on musical taste and is hence all too subject to change, since in works for the clavier it is for the most part found written out, and since we can in any case do without it, in view of the sufficient number of the others, I shall treat it only briefly at the end in connection with fermatas.[1] Otherwise I shall concern myself only with embellishments of the first class, inasmuch as they have for the most part belonged for some time past to the very nature, as it were, of clavier playing, and will no doubt always remain the fashion. To these familiar embellishments I shall add a few new ones; I shall explain them and, as far as possible, determine their position; I shall, for convenience's sake, give at the same time their fingering and, where it is noteworthy, the manner of their delivery; I shall illustrate with examples what cannot always be said with sufficient clarity; I shall say what needs to be said about certain incorrect or at least ambiguous signs, so that one may learn to distinguish them from the correct ones, likewise about embellishments to be rejected; finally I shall refer my readers to the sample pieces,[2] and shall hope, by all these means, to clear away more or less the false notion of the necessity of redundant fancy notes in clavier playing which here and there has taken root.

1. Bach follows this general introduction with sections on the appoggiatura, trill, turn, mordent, compound appoggiatura, slide, and snap, closing the chapter with a section on the elaboration of fermatas.

2. Originally bound with the musical examples of the *Versuch* were *Achtzehn Probestücke in sechs Sonaten* (*Eighteen Sample Pieces in Six Sonatas*). They are available printed separately in modern editions.

8. Regardless of this, anyone who has the skill is at liberty to introduce embellishments more lavish than ours. He need only take care, in so doing, that this occurs seldom, in the right place, and without doing violence to the affect of the piece. Of himself he will understand that, for example, the depiction of innocence or sadness will tolerate less ornamenting than the other passions. He who in this heeds what is needed may be allowed to have his way, for he skillfully combines with the singing style of playing his instrument the elements of surprise and fire in which the instruments have the advantage of the voice and, as a result, knows how to awaken and maintain by means of constant change a high degree of attention in his listeners. This difference between instrument and voice may be preserved unhesitatingly. He who bestows on these embellishments the care they need may be otherwise unconcerned as to whether what he plays can or cannot be sung.

9. At the same time, an overlavish treatment, even of our sort of embellishments, is to be avoided above all things. Let them be regarded as decorations which can overload the finest building, as spices which can spoil the finest food. Many notes, being of no consequence, must be spared them; many notes, sparkling enough in themselves, will likewise not tolerate them, for embellishments should only intensify the weightiness and simplicity of such notes, distinguishing them from others. Failing this, I should commit the same error as the speaker who places an emphatic stress on every word; everything sounds the same and is in consequence unclear.

10. We shall see in what follows that some situations permit more than one sort of embellishment; in such cases, let us take advantage of variation; let us apply, here an ingratiating embellishment, here a sparkling one, and sometimes, for variety's sake, let us use a wholly plain delivery if the notes permit it, without embellishment but in accordance both with the rules of good delivery, to be treated in the next part, and with the true affect.

11. It is difficult to determine the position of each embellishment with absolute precision, for each composer, provided he does no violence to good taste, is at liberty in his inventions to prescribe in most places any embellishment he pleases. In this we are content to instruct our readers by a few well-established rules and examples and by pointing out, in any case, the impossibility of applying a particular embellishment. In those pieces which indicate all embellishments there is no need for concern, while in those which indicate little or nothing the embellishments are customarily supplied in the regular way.

12. Since to this day I can name no one who has anticipated me in this difficult matter and who might have cleared for me this treacherous path, I trust that no one will blame me for believing that, even within certain well-established situations, there may perhaps be still a possibility of exception.

13. And since, to make a reasonable use of this material, he must attend to many small details, the reader should exercise his ear as much as possible by diligent listening to good performances and, the better to understand many things, must have mastered above all the art of thoroughbass. Experience has

shown that he who has no thorough understanding of harmony is, in applying the embellishments, always fumbling in the dark, and that he has to thank mere chance, and never his insight, for a fortunate outcome. To this end, where necessary, I shall always add the bass of the examples.

14. Although the singers and the players of instruments other than ours, if they wish to play their pieces well, can no more do without most of our embellishments than we can ourselves, we players of the clavier have followed the more orderly procedure by giving certain signs to the embellishments, clearly indicating the manner of playing our pieces.

15. Since the others did not observe this praiseworthy precaution, and sought, on the contrary, to indicate everything by a few signs, not only has the teaching of embellishments become more painful to them than to players of the clavier, but we have also seen the rise of many ambiguous, indeed false signs which sometimes, even today, cause many pieces to be performed unsuitably. For example, the mordent is in music a necessary and familiar embellishment, yet there are few, apart from players of the clavier, who know its sign. I know of a piece in which, as a result of this, a particular passage has often been ruined. This passage, if it is not to sound untasteful, must be played with a long mordent, something which no one would hit upon without an indication. The necessity of using as its indication a sign known only to players of the clavier, there being no other, has resulted in its being confused with the sign of a trill. We shall see in what follows how disagreeable an effect has arisen from the great difference between these two embellishments.

16. Since the French are careful in placing the signs of their embellishments, it follows that, in hitherto departing altogether, as we have, unfortunately, from their pieces and from their way of playing the clavier, we have at the same time also deviated from the precise indication of our embellishments to such an extent that today these once so familiar signs are already becoming unfamiliar, even to players of the clavier.

17. The notes comprised in the embellishments take their accidentals from the key signature. Nevertheless, we shall see in what follows that there are frequent exceptions to this rule, readily discovered by a practiced ear, caused sometimes by the preceding notes, sometimes by the following ones, and in general by the modulations of a melody into another key.

18. But in order that the reader may also overcome those difficulties that arise on this account, I have found it necessary to retain that practice according to which the accidentals are indicated along with the embellishments in all cases. One will find them in the sample pieces wherever necessary, now singly, now in pairs.

19. All embellishments must stand in a proportioned relation to the value of their note, to the tempo, and to the content of the piece. Especially in those cases where various sorts of embellishments occur and where the affect is not too restricting, it should be remarked that the more notes an embellishment comprises, the longer the note to which it is applied must be, no matter

whether this length arises from the value of the note or from the tempo of the piece. The player must avoid detracting from the brilliance that an embellishment is intended to produce by allowing too much of the value of its note to remain left over; at the same time, he must also avoid occasioning a lack of clarity by performing certain embellishments too quickly, something which occurs mainly when he applies many embellishments or embellishments of many notes to notes of small value.

20. Although we shall see in what follows that the player may sometimes intentionally apply to a long note an embellishment that does not wholly fill out its value, he may not release the last note of such an embellishment until the following note is due, for the chief aim of all embellishments should be to tie the notes together.

21. We see, then, that embellishments are used more in slow and moderate tempi than in rapid ones, more in connection with long notes than with short ones.

22. Whatever needs to be observed regarding the value of the notes, the signs, and the small notes, I shall always include as a part of my explanations. The reader will also find the small notes with their actual values printed in the sample pieces.

23. All embellishments indicated by small notes belong to the note that follows; the preceding note, in consequence, never diminishes in value, while the following note loses as much as is made up by the small notes taken together. This observation is the more necessary in that it is commonly disregarded and in that I have been unable to avoid sometimes detaching certain small notes from their main note in the sample pieces, the space being so crowded with signs for fingering, embellishments, and delivery.

24. In accordance with this rule, then, these small notes are struck in place of the main note that follows, together with the bass or with the other parts. Through them the player slides into the note following; this too is very often disregarded in that he pounces roughly upon the main note after having, in addition, unskillfully applied or produced the embellishments associated with the small notes.

25. Our present taste being what it is and the good Italian way of singing having made considerable contribution to it, the player cannot manage with the French embellishments alone; for this reason, I have had to compile my embellishments from more than one nation. To these I have added a few new ones. Apart from this, I believe that the best way of playing the clavier or any other instrument is that which succeeds in skillfully combining what is neat and brilliant in the French taste with what is ingratiating in the Italian way of singing. For this union the Germans are particularly well adapted as long as they remain unprejudiced.

26. At the same time, it is possible that a few will not be wholly satisfied with my choice of embellishments, having perhaps embraced one taste alone; I believe, however, that no one can be a thorough judge of anything in music

unless he has heard all kinds and knows how to find what is best in each. What is more, I agree with a certain great man who declared that, while one taste has more good in it than another, there is none the less in every taste some particular thing that is good, no taste being as yet so perfect that it will not still tolerate further additions. By means of such additions and refinements we have reached the point at which we are and shall continue to go on and on. This, however, cannot possibly happen if we work at and, as it were, worship one sort of taste alone; on the contrary, we must know how to profit by whatever is good, wherever it may be found.

27. Therefore, since the embellishments together with the manner of their employment make a considerable contribution to fine taste, the player should be neither so changeable that without further inquiry he accepts at every moment each new embellishment, regardless of its sponsor, nor yet so prejudiced in favor of himself and his own taste that out of vanity he refuses to accept anything new whatsoever. He should of course put the new thing to a rigorous test before he adopts it, and it is possible that in time the introduction of unnatural novelties will make good taste as rare as art. At the same time, to keep pace with the fashion, the player should be, if not the first, then not the last to take up new embellishments. Let him not oppose them if they do not always appeal to him at first. New things, attractive as they are occasionally, sometimes seem to us perverse. And this is often evidence of the worth of a thing which will in the long run last longer than others that are overly pleasing in the beginning. These last are as a rule so run into the ground that they soon become repellent.

28. While most of my examples of embellishments are for the right hand, I by no means deny these graces to the left; on the contrary, I urge every player to exercise each hand alone in all of them, for this brings with it a dexterity and lightness in the production of other notes. We shall see in what follows that certain embellishments also often occur in the bass. Moreover, the player is obliged to reproduce all imitations to the last detail. In short, the left hand must have exercise in this to manage it skillfully; failing this, it will be better to omit the embellishments, which lose their charm if we perform them badly.

9 Leopold Mozart

Leopold Mozart, the father of Wolfgang Amadeus and himself an excellent violinist and a respectable composer, was born at Augsburg in 1719. He entered the service of the Prince-Bishop of Salzburg, served as a composer and assistant *maestro di cappella* to the episcopal court, and died at Salzburg in 1787.

Leopold Mozart was a prolific composer and wrote a large quantity of works

in varied forms of sacred and secular music: masses, motets, symphonies, sere-
nades, concertos, oratorios, operas, etc. His best-known work, however, is
probably his method for the violin, *Versuch einer gründlichen Violinschule*
(*Essay on the Fundamental Principles of Violin Playing*) published in the year of
Wolfgang's birth (1756), one of the oldest and most solid books of its kind. It is,
with Johann Joachim Quantz's method for the flute and C. P. E. Bach's method
for keyboard instruments, an important source for the study of musical practice
in the mid-eighteenth century.

FROM *Essay on the Fundamental Principles of Violin Playing*
(1756)

CHAPTER TWELVE: ON READING MUSIC CORRECTLY AND ON GOOD DELIVERY IN GENERAL

1. Everything turns on good performance: everyday experience confirms this
rule. Many a half-composer is pleased and delighted when he hears his musical
Galimathias performed by good players who know how to apply the passion,
which he has not even thought about, in its proper place, how to make the
greatest possible distinction in the characters, which has never occurred to
him, and consequently how, by means of a good delivery, to render the whole
wretched scribble tolerable to the ears of the listeners. But on the other hand,
who does not know that the best composition is often so miserably performed
that the composer himself has difficulty enough in recognizing his own work?
2. The good delivery of a composition in the present taste is not as simple as
those people believe who think they are doing very well if, following their own
ideas, they ornament and contort a piece in a truly idiotic fashion and who have
no conception whatever of the passion that is supposed to be expressed in it.
But who are these people? In the main they are those who, since they can
scarcely play in time, even tolerably, begin at once with concertos and solos in
order (as they stupidly imagine) to establish themselves as quickly as possible
in the company of the virtuosi. Some actually reach such a point that, in a few
concertos or solos that they have practiced thoroughly, they play off the most
difficult passages with uncommon facility. These they know by heart. But if
they are to perform even a few minuets in the cantabile style directed by the
composer, they are in no position to do so—indeed one sees this already in the
concertos they have studied. For as long as they play an Allegro, things still go
well, but as soon as they come to an Adagio, they betray their gross ignorance
and their poor judgment in every single measure of the piece. They play without order and without expression; they fail to distinguish the loud and the soft;

TEXT: The facsimile reprint of the original edition of 1756 (Vienna, 1922), pp. 252–64. Translation
by Oliver Strunk.

the embellishments are applied in the wrong places, too thickly crowded and for the most part confused; sometimes, just the other way, the notes are too expressionless and one sees that the player does not know what to do. In such players one can seldom hope any longer for improvement, for of all people they are the most prepossessed in their own favor, and he would incur their highest displeasure who sought, out of the goodness of his heart, to persuade them of their mistakes.

3. To read correctly, as directed, the musical compositions of the good masters and to play each piece in accordance with the passion prevailing in it calls for far more art than to study the most difficult concertos and solos. To do the latter does not require much intelligence. And if the player is adroit enough to figure out the fingering he can learn the most difficult passages by himself, provided he practices them diligently. But to do the former is not as easy as this. For the player has not only to attend closely to every annotation and direction and to play the work as it is set down and not otherwise; he has also to enter into the passion that is to be expressed and to apply and to execute all the runs, the legatos and staccatos, the fortes and pianos, in a word, everything that bears in any way on the tasteful delivery of a piece, observing in this a certain good style that can be learned only by sound judgment through long experience.

4. Let the reader now decide for himself whether, among violinists, the good orchestral player ought not to be prized far more highly than the mere soloist. The soloist can play everything as he pleases and adjust its delivery to his own ideas, even to his own hand; the orchestral player must have the ability to grasp at once and to deliver properly the taste, the ideas, and the expression of different composers. The soloist, to bring things out cleanly, has only to practice at home—others must adapt themselves to him; the orchestral player must read everything at sight—often, indeed, passages such as run counter to the natural arrangement of the measure;[1] he must adapt himself to others. The soloist, if only he has a clean delivery, can in general play his concertos acceptably, even with distinction; the orchestral player, on the other hand, must have a considerable grasp of music in general, of the art of composition, and of differences in characters, nay, he must have a peculiarly versatile talent if he is to fill his office creditably, especially if he is ever to act as the leader of an orchestra. Are there some who believe that, among violinists, one finds more good orchestral players than soloists? They are mistaken. Poor accompanists are admittedly numerous enough, but there are very few good ones, for today everyone wants to be the soloist. But as to what an orchestra consisting entirely of soloists is like, I leave

1. *Contra metrum musicum.* Of this I have already given notice in Chapter 1, Section 2, §4, note *d.* And I do not know what I am to think when I see an aria, by one of those Italian composers who are so celebrated just now, which runs so counter to the musical meter that one would suppose it made by a pupil. [Au.] In the note *d* to which Mozart refers, it is pointed out that common time ordinarily has two divisions only and that infractions of this rule are excused only in peasant dances or other unusual melodies.

this to those gentlemen composers who have performed their works under such conditions. Few soloists read well, for it is their habit to be continually introducing details of their own invention and to regard themselves alone, paying little regard to others.[2]

5. Thus, until the player can accompany quite well, he must play no solos. He must first know exactly how to execute all the various strokes of the bow; he must understand how to apply the fortes and pianos in the proper place and to the proper degree; he must learn how to distinguish the characters of pieces and how to deliver each passage according to its required and peculiar taste; in a word, before he begins to play solos and concertos, he must be able to read the works of many gifted persons correctly and elegantly. From a painting, one sees at once whether he who has painted it is a master of drawing; in the same way, many a musician would play his solo more intelligently if he had ever learned to deliver a symphony or trio in accordance with the good taste it required or to accompany an aria with the proper passion and in accordance with the character peculiar to it. I shall endeavor to set down some brief rules which the player can make profitable use of in the performance of a piece of music.

6. The player must of course tune his instrument carefully and exactly to those of his fellows; this he already knows and my mentioning the matter may seem somewhat superfluous. But since even those who wish to pass for first violinists often fail to tune their instruments exactly together, I find it absolutely necessary to mention the matter here, the more so since it is to the first violinist that the rest are supposed to tune. In playing with the organ or harpsichord, these determine the pitch; if neither one is present, the pitch is taken from the wind instruments. Some tune the A-string first, others the D. Both do well, if only they tune carefully and exactly. I would mention only one other point; in a warm room the pitch of the stringed instruments gradually falls, in a cold one it gradually rises.

7. Before beginning to play a piece, the player must thoroughly examine and consider it. He must discover the character, the tempo, and the sort of movement that it requires and must carefully determine whether there is not concealed in it some passage, seemingly unimportant at first sight, which will nonetheless be far from easy to play, demanding a special style of delivery and expression. Then, during the performance itself, he must spare no pains to discover and deliver correctly the passion that the composer has sought to apply and, since the mournful and the merry often alternate, he must be intent on delivering each of these in its own style. In a word, he must play everything in such a way that he will himself be moved by it.[3]

---

2. But what I say does not at all apply to those great virtuosi who, in addition to being extraordinarily gifted as players of concertos, are also good orchestral players. Such people are really deserving of the highest esteem. [Au.]

3. It is bad enough that many a player never gives a thought to what he is doing and simply plays off his music as though in a dream or as though he were actually playing for himself alone. If

8. From this it follows that the player must pay the strictest attention to the prescribed pianos and fortes and not always be scraping away on one level. Nay, without direction and, as a rule, of himself, he must know how to relieve the soft with the loud and how to apply each of these in its proper place, for, following the familiar expression in painting, this is called light and shade. Notes that are raised by a sharp or natural he ought always to attack somewhat more vigorously, reducing his tone again for the continuation of the melody:

In the same way he should differentiate in intensity a note that is momentarily lowered by a flat or natural:

With half notes that occur among shorter values, the invariable custom is to attack them vigorously and then to diminish the tone again:

Indeed, quarters are sometimes also played in just this way:

And this is the expression actually called for by the composer when he marks a note with an *f* or *p*, that is, with a forte or piano. But after the player has vigorously attacked the note, he must not let his bow leave the strings, as some clumsy players do; the stroke must be continued and consequently the tone still heard, though it will gently taper off.[4]

---

such a player, at the beginning of a piece, gets a few beats ahead of the tempo, he does not notice it, and I will wager that he would finish the piece several measures before his fellows if his neighbor or the leader himself did not call his attention to it. [Au.]

4. Let the reader look up what I have said about this on p. 44, note *k*. [Au.] In this note (chap. 1, sec. 3, §18), Mozart complains of those who cannot play a half note or even a quarter without dividing it into two parts.

9. The accent,[5] expression, or intensity of the tone will fall as a rule on the strong or initial note that the Italians call the *nota buona*. But there are distinct varieties of these initial or "good" notes. The particularly strong notes are the following: in every measure, the note beginning the first quarter; in the half measure, the first note, or, in $\frac{4}{4}$ time, the first note of the third quarter; in $\frac{6}{4}$ and $\frac{6}{8}$ time, the first notes of the first and fourth quarters; in $\frac{12}{8}$ time, the first notes of the first, fourth, seventh, and tenth quarters. These, then, are the initial notes on which the maximum intensity of the tone will fall, wherever the composer has indicated no other expression. In the ordinary accompaniments for an aria or concerto, in which as a rule only eighth and sixteenth notes occur, they are usually written nowadays as separate notes or are at least marked for a few measures at the beginning with a little stroke:

f p f p f p f p

The player must accordingly continue in this way to attack the first note vigorously until a change occurs.

10. The other "good" notes are those which are always distinguished from the rest by a slightly increased intensity, but to which this increased intensity must be very moderately applied. They are: in alla breve time, the quarters and eighth notes, and, in the so-called half triple time, the quarters; further, in common time and in $\frac{2}{4}$ and $\frac{3}{4}$ time, the eighth and sixteenth notes; finally, in $\frac{3}{8}$ and $\frac{6}{8}$ time, the sixteenth notes; and so forth. When several notes of this sort follow one after another, slurred two and two, the accent will fall on the first of each two, and this first note will not only be attacked somewhat more vigorously but will also be sustained somewhat longer while the second note will be bound to it quite gently and quietly, and somewhat retarded.[6] It often happens, however, that three, four, and even more such notes are bound together by a slur of this sort. In such a case, the player must attack the first of them somewhat more vigorously and sustain it longer and must bind the rest to it in the same bow, without the slightest stress, by reducing the intensity more and more.[7]

---

5. By the word "accent" I understand here, not the French *port de voix*, which Rousseau tries to explain in his *Méthode pour apprendre à chanter*, p. 56, but a pressure (*expression*) or stress, an emphasis, from the Greek ἐν (*in*) and φάσις (*apparitio, dictio*). [Au.]
6. Let the reader look at the illustration of this in Chapter 7, Section 1, §3, and in particular let him read §5 in Chapter 7, Section 2, and look at the musical examples. [Au.] Chapter 7, "On the many different sorts of bowing," deals in Section 1 with notes of equal value and in Section 2 with figures consisting of notes of unequal value.
7. Let the reader call Chapter 7 to mind from time to time, especially what was said there in Section 1, §20. [Au.] The concluding paragraph (§20) of Section 1 explains that after mastering the various ways of bowing the examples that have been given, the student must learn to play them with taste and so that their variety is immediately perceptible.

11. From Chapters 6[8] and 7 the reader has seen how much the melody may be differentiated by the legatos and staccatos. The player, then, must not only pay the strictest attention to such legatos as are written out and indicated, but since in many a composition nothing is indicated at all, he must know how to apply the legato and staccato himself in a tasteful manner and in the proper place. The chapter on the many varieties of bowing, particularly in its second section, will serve to show the player how to go about making such alteration in this as he thinks proper, provided always that it is in keeping with the character of the piece.

12. Today, in certain passages, one finds the skillful composer applying the expression in a quite special, unusual, and unexpected way which would puzzle many if it were not indicated.

For the expression and the intensity of the tone fall here on the last quarter of the measure, and the first quarter of the measure following is to be bound to it very quietly, without being stressed. The player, then, is by no means to distinguish these two notes by a pressure from the bow, but is to play them as though they formed a single half note.[9]

13. In cheerful pieces, to make the delivery really lively, the accent is usually applied to the highest note. This leads to the stress falling on the last note of the second and fourth quarters in common time and on the end of the second quarter in $\frac{2}{4}$ time, especially when the piece begins with an upbeat.

But in pieces that are slow and sad, this may not be done, for here the upbeat must be not detached but sustained, and delivered in a singing style.

14. In $\frac{3}{4}$ and $\frac{3}{8}$ time the accent may also fall on the second quarter.

8. Chapter 6 is titled "On the so-called triplets."
9. Here too let the reader call to mind §18 and note *k* in Chapter 1, Section 3. [Au.] The paragraph in question deals in greater detail with the correct performance of syncopations like those just described; for Mozart's "Note *k*," see p. 126, n. 4.

15. The player will notice that, in the example last given, the dotted quarter (d) in the first measure is slurred to the eighth note (c) that follows. Accordingly, at the dot he must not bear down with his bow, but, as in all other situations of this kind, he must attack the quarter with a moderate intensity, hold out the time of the dot without stress, and very quietly bind the following eighth note to it.[10]

16. In the same way, such notes as these, which would otherwise be divided off according to the measure, must never be divided, nor may their division be indicated by a stress; on the contrary, the player must simply attack them and sustain them quietly, exactly as though they stood at the beginning of the quarter.[11] This manner of delivery gives rise to a sort of broken tempo which makes a very strange and agreeable impression, since either the inner voice or the bass seems to separate itself from the upper voice; it has the further effect that in certain passages the fifths do not sound together, but are heard alternately, one after the other. Here, for example, are three voices.

17. Not only in the situation just discussed, but wherever a forte is prescribed, the player must moderate the intensity, not foolishly sawing away, above all in accompanying a concerto. Some people either do not do a thing at all or, in doing it, are certain to exaggerate it. The player must be guided by the passion. Sometimes a note requires a rather vigorous attack, at other times a moderate one, at still other times one that is barely perceptible. The first usually occurs in connection with a sudden expression that all the instruments make together; as a rule, this is indicated by the direction *fp*.

The second occurs in connection with those especially prominent notes that were discussed in §9 of this chapter. The third occurs in connection with all the remaining notes first enumerated in §10; to these the player must apply a barely perceptible stress. For even though he sees many fortes written into the accompaniment of a concerto, he must apply the intensity in moderation and

10. I have already drawn attention to this in Chapter 1, Section 3, §9. [Au.]
11. Let the reader just look at §§21, 22, and 23 in Chapter 4, where he will also find examples enough. Here belongs also what was said at the end of Chapter 1, Section 3, §18, by no means forgetting note k. [Au.] The several paragraphs in Chapter 4 deal with various ways of bowing such rhythms as eighth, quarter, eighth, or sixteenth, eighth, sixteenth; for Mozart's references to Chapter 1, see p. 126, n. 4 and p. 128, n. 9

not so exaggerate it that he drowns out the soloist. Quite the other way, such intensity, sparingly and briefly applied, must set off the solo part, give spirit to the melody, help out the soloist, and make easier for him the task of properly characterizing the piece.

18. The player, just as he must pay the strictest attention to the legatos, staccatos, fortes, and pianos required by the expression, must also avoid playing away continually with a dragging heavy bow and must be guided by the passion predominating in each passage. Lively and playful passages must be distinguished by light short strokes and played off joyously and rapidly, just as pieces that are slow and sad must be delivered with long-drawn strokes, richly and tenderly.

19. As a rule, in accompanying a concerto the player must not sustain the notes but must play them off quickly, and in $\frac{6}{8}$ and $\frac{12}{8}$ time, to avoid making the delivery drowsy, must cut off the quarters almost as though they were eighth notes. But let him see to it that the tempo remains steady and that the quarters are more audible than the eighth notes.

It is written thus   and it is played almost like this

20. Many who have no notion of taste are never willing to maintain a steady tempo in accompanying a concerto, but are constantly at pains to yield to the soloist. These are accompanists for bunglers and not for masters. If the player has before him some Italian prima donna who cannot even carry off in the proper tempo what she has learned by heart, or any other fancied virtuoso of this sort, he must admittedly skip over whole half-measures if he is to prevent a public disgrace. But when he accompanies a true virtuoso, one who is worthy of this title, he must not allow himself to be seduced into hesitating or hurrying by the prolongations and anticipations of the notes that the soloist knows how to bring in so skillfully and touchingly, but must at all times continue to play in the same steady tempo. Otherwise what the soloist has sought to build up will be torn down again by his accompanying.[12]

21. Furthermore, if the performance is to be good, the players must pay strict attention to one another and especially to their leader in order that they may not only begin together but may also play throughout in the same tempo and with the same expression. There are certain passages in playing which one

12. The skillful accompanist, then, must be able to judge his soloist. To a respectable virtuoso he must by no means yield, for to do so would ruin the soloist's *tempo rubato*. But what this "stolen time" is may be more easily demonstrated than described. Has he to do, on the contrary, with a fancied virtuoso? Then, in an Adagio cantabile, he may often sustain an eighth note for half a measure until the soloist comes to himself, as it were, after his paroxysm, and nothing goes in time, for the soloist plays in the style of a recitative. [Au.]

easily falls to hurrying.[13] Aside from this, the players must take care to play off the chords quickly and together, the short notes following a dot or a rest of small value somewhat after the beat and rapidly.[14] If several notes are to be played as an upbeat or after a short rest, the usual thing is to take them in a down-bow, including the first note of the following quarter in the same stroke. Here the players must pay special attention to one another and not begin too early. This is an example with chords and rests of small value.

Allegro

22. All that I have set down in this last chapter bears in particular on reading music correctly and in general on the clean and sensible delivery of a well-written piece of music. And all the pains that I have taken in the writing of this book have been directed toward one end: to set the beginner on the right path and to prepare him for the recognition and perception of a good musical taste. So I shall stop here, although I have still many things to say to the musical fraternity. Who knows? I may make bold to enrich the musical world with another book if I see that this my desire to serve the beginner has not been altogether useless.

13. Let the reader just call to mind §38 in Chapter 4. And in Chapters 6 and 7 I have stressed the importance of a steady tempo more than once. [Au.] Paragraph 38 of Chapter 4 deals with the bowing and correct performance of continuous sixteenths; for Chapters 6 and 7, see p. 127, n. 6 and p. 128, n. 8.
14. Let the reader look up what I have written in §§2 and 3 of Chapter 7, Section 2, and also the musical examples given in this connection. [Au.] These two paragraphs deal more explicitly with the correct performance of the short note or notes following a dot.

10 Giambattista Mancini

The first edition of Giambattista Mancini's *Riflessioni pratiche sul canto figurato* (*Practical Reflections on Singing*) was published in Vienna in 1774. Charles Burney, who called the treatise "admirable" and "useful," saw it as a supplement to Pier Francesco Tosi's *Thoughts on Ancient and Modern Singers* (1723); the two works were the preeminent practical treatises on singing written in the eighteenth century. Born in 1714, Mancini studied voice in Naples and Bologna, as well as counterpoint and composition with Padre Giovanni Battista Martini. Mancini, a castrato, had an operatic career in Italy and Germany but gained his primary reputation as a teacher. In 1757 the Empress Maria Theresa invited him to Vienna to teach her daughters singing. He remained there until his death in 1800.

The second Italian edition of Mancini's treatise (entitled as above, a slight variation on the original title) was issued in controversy. Published in 1777, with the encouragement of his friend Padre Martini, it contained long interpolations in several chapters responding to attacks by Vincenzo Manfredini on his teaching techniques. The differences between Mancini and Manfredini were those of practical musician versus theorist, conservative versus progressive, and apostle of agility versus proponent of simple, direct expression (Mancini was particularly stung by Manfredini's attack on his veneration of the trill). In his remarks about declamation and recitative Mancini urged the expressive claims of reform opera, rendering extravagant praise to the genius of Gluck.

FROM *Practical Reflections on Singing*
(1777)

ARTICLE XIII: ABOUT THE ATTAINMENTS NECESSARY TO RECITE WELL IN THE THEATER

As I have already said, it is not the beauty and agility of the voice alone that single out an artist. In addition a fine style of reciting should yield one a proper success, and with it approbation and greater profit.

An actor recites well when, entering thoroughly into the character of the person he represents, he unfolds that character naturally, using action, the voice, and the proper affects, and when he brings that character so clearly to life that the spectator says, for example, that man is *Caesar,* or this man is *Alexander.*

Now, an actor will never be able to express those affects naturally, nor make the spectators recognize their effects clearly, if he does not understand the force of the words; if he does not know the true character of the person he represents; if he does not speak a good Tuscan; and if above all he does not project an exact, clear, and complete pronunciation of the words, although without exaggeration.

I have heard reports of the diligence and serious study that the famous *Pistocchi*[1] put into teaching his students in order to make their pronunciation perfect. As a result the audience would be able to hear all the words, to the

TEXT: The third edition (Milan, 1777), pp. 218–47. Translation by Wye J. Allanbrook.

1. Francesco Antonio Pistocchi (1659–1726) was a castrato who later in his career established a preeminent singing school in Bologna. He taught Mancini's teacher, Antonio Bernacchi, and Mancini praises him highly in Article 2 of this treatise.

point of distinguishing, when they were uttered, certain doubled letters like *tt, rr, ss,* and so on.

In order to acquire these different attainments, an actor needs to undertake three different courses of study—*grammar, history,* and the *Italian* language.

The force and power of a word do not always emerge from its nature alone; very often the manner with which it is uttered diminishes or increases its power. One learns this style of utterance from the study of grammar. In fact one should speak as one writes. For without commas and periods a person reading would not be able to understand the true sense of a text, or at least would easily be deceived in making it out. In the same way a person who is listening to someone speak at length and never hears him pause or change the tone of his voice will never be able to understand him well.

One learns this ordered mode of writing, reading, and speaking from grammar.

Just listen to the speech of a good orator, and hear how many rests, what variety of tones, how many different emphases he uses to express its meanings. Now he raises his voice, now he lowers it; now he hurries a bit, now he grows harsh and now gentle, according to the various passions that he wishes to stir in the listener. But since grammatical rules are only theoretical, you must learn the practice by reading Tuscan books and listening to Italian orators.

When you happen to be alone in your room it would be useful to read aloud some good book, especially of poetry. This is the most useful training, and an easy way of coming to speak with the necessary pauses and tonal inflections. As a consequence you will also speak well in public.

The study of grammar should be followed by the study of *sacred, secular,* and *mythological* history.

You will find professors who certainly do not spend the whole day in leisure, and are not unlearned in any literature. They read about the origin of nations, their vicissitudes, the overthrow of authority, wars, truces, the consequent peace, and the like. This knowledge can certainly serve them as pleasure and ornament, but it cannot be said to be a necessary attainment for an actor. A virtuoso in music must be a traveller, but it is fully sufficient that he know about the predominant merits and passions of one nation. He should know the most common manner of speaking there, habits of dress, and, in short, the kinds of things that usually distinguish one nation from another of the ones in which he may chance to be. But *sacred, secular,* and *mythological* history is an indispensable necessity for an actor.

For example, suppose you want an actor to play *Julius Caesar* in the scene when he was betrayed and assaulted in the Senate by the conspirators. Would it not be ridiculous if he did not know how to vest himself with the powerful spirit of such a hero; if instead of having Caesar suffer an unexpected attack with a firm brow and brave spirit, he represented the man with acts of fear, retreat, and cowardice?

Would it not be ridiculous if in a mythological drama, Mercury appearing on stage from one side, Neptune from the other, the actor performed the part of the young god with the actions, habits, and manners of an old man, and the part of the old god, on the other hand, with agility, vivacity, and spirit?

Would it not be ridiculous if in a sacred drama representing the famous sacrifice of Abraham the actor showed us the knife trembling in the hands of that most obedient patriarch, and resistance and tears in the religious resignation of Isaac? But all this could happen if that actor had not at least tasted the first pages of history.

It remains to say something about those two languages *Latin* and *Italian*. Of the first I will not speak, since every professor sees how necessary it is for vocal music in church, in order at least to know how to distinguish the longs and the shorts. Furthermore, I have limited the scope of these articles of mine strictly to vocal music in the theater.

So let us speak of Italian. All nations are constrained to confess, whether they want to or not, that this language of all others is the most harmonious, the sweetest, and the easiest to adapt to good music. Read the *Lettre sur la musique française* of Monsieur *Rousseau,*[2] and you will see if I speak the truth; yet he is a French writer. By the Italian language he means the language when it is most purified and unblemished—as the saying goes, the *Florentine* tongue on the lips of a *Sienese*, with the grace of a *Pistoian*.

All the other languages, Italian though they may be, have defects for use in the theater. They lack that melody and sweetness that, thanks to a good accent, the purified language possesses. On the contrary, the further their open vowels are from having a complete, precise, and finished sound, the more those vowels are incompatible with good music. For they are a species of diphthong, or compound of two different sounds. And this is precisely the reason why the French language is so little suited to music.

Now not all those who choose the profession of singing can be Tuscan; that choice is not equally free to all the states and provinces that make up fair Italy. But Bolognese, Modenese, Milanese, Venetians, and distinguished Neapolitans learn the true language from their teachers, and learn it almost better sometimes than those very Florentines. For it is difficult for them to rid themselves of a bad habit of the throat that is native to them, commonly called *gorgia*.[3]

A far easier and more effective approach for a young man who is already devoted to this profession is to live for some years in Tuscany. Many have done this—even I myself. For young people converse easily and take in the language unthinkingly, as a baby does milk—without school, without study, and without art. In these circumstances nature and age are the perfect teachers. But since for various reasons this approach is not open to everyone, I suggest another one, namely reading books and conversing with men who speak with a pure pronunciation and good diction.

2. See pp. 161–74.
3. *La gorgia toscana* is the Tuscan habit of adding an 'h' sound to 'c' before 'a,' 'o,' and 'u.'

Here, succinctly set down, are the three most effective methods for correcting a bad pronunciation and a bad accent. How necessary for a singer are a perfect pronunciation, a perfect accent, and a perfect delivery of the words has been demonstrated by the example of all those excellent professors I mentioned in the second chapter.[4]

Even though these men were mostly Neapolitans, Bolognese, Lombards, and who knows what else, no matter in what theater of any nation or country they performed they were taken by all to be true Tuscans.

The divine *Demosthenes* was also aware of this excellence in an actor; he knew how prejudicial defective pronunciation was to anyone who must orate and declaim in public. Therefore this great man, although he was acclaimed as the first orator of Greece and knew in fact that he was such, feared that the shortcomings in his speech could easily cause him to lose both his name and his reputation, and the universal esteem of his and other nations. So with infinite discomfort he declaimed aloud in isolated places, holding little pebbles in his mouth in order to loosen the native constrictions of his tongue. With this useful example he showed us how important it is to remove the defects of our tongue, no matter what the cost.

I hope that the examples I have set down have persuaded my young lovers of vocal music to spare no labor or toil in becoming skilled in this arena. I value it highly, since it seems to me to be the cause of all that is perfect, graceful, and attractive in every melody.

ARTICLE XIV: ABOUT RECITATIVE AND DELIVERY

Once the student has completed the studies necessary for good declamation as I have described them—the study of the *Latin and Italian* languages, and of history—and has acquitted himself in them with profit, he can without hesitation take up the study of the dramatic art.

This notable art, through what fate I know not, in our times counts few good students in its numbers, having declined from that high degree of splendor and excellence it inhabited forty years ago.

Many of our actors believe that they have sufficiently discharged their duty in the theater when they sing the solo arias perfectly, even though their articulation of the recitative has nothing genuine in it, and is not accompanied by a suitable delivery.

Others are certainly aware of the necessity for good declamation and for good delivery, but justify themselves with false excuses. They indict modern writers, saying that it is impossible to declaim the recitatives that are written these days because they interrupt and upset the true sense of the words by constant motions and sudden modulations in the bass, and so on.

So they sigh, affecting to envy the fortunate lot of those actors who could perform the operas written by an Alessandro *Scarlatti, Bononcino, Gasparini,*

4. Article 2 contains an extensive discussion of Italian singers of the previous hundred years.

Francesco *Mancini,* Domenico *Sarro,* Federico *Hendel,* Francesco *Durante,* and other famous men of this sort.[5]

But to convince our actors of their error and affectation, and to make them recognize that most of the time the blame for bad declamation is theirs, one need only remind them of operas written by *Porpora,* Leonardo *Vinci,* Leonardo *Leo,* Francesco *Feo,* or *Pergolese.*[6] Let them take a look, and then say if they find in these recitatives the kind of interruption and confusion they claim is caused by the music.

Let them take into consideration the operas of a Giovanni *Hasse,* Baldassare *Galuppi (Buranello),* Niccolò *Jommelli,* Gaetano *Latilla,* Pasquale *Cafaro,* Davide *Perez,* Gennaro *Manna,* Tommaso *Trajetta,* Niccola *Piccinni,* Antonio *Sacchini, Reichart,* J. C. *Bach,* Antonio *Mazzoni* Bolognese, Pietro *Guglielmi,* Amadeo *Naumann Misliweózek,* Pasquale *Anfossi,* Giovanni *Paisiello,* Carlo *Monza, Tozzi, Borroni, Bertoni,* Giambattista *Borghi,* Tommaso *Giordano,* and Floriano *Gassmann,* most recently deceased.[7] In addition to his commendable service in this Imperial Court, Gassmann has left us notable operas and even more notable students; among them Antonio *Salieri,* the chamber virtuoso of the Imperial Court, clearly stands out.

Let them consider those operas of Giuseppe *Bonno,*[8] successor to *Gassmann* in the imperial service and a name very well known to the republic of music.

Let them consider the other operas of the Cavaliere Christophe *Gluck,* also in the service of the Imperial Court. The vast and penetrating creative genius

5. This list and the two that follow it enumerate well-known composers of vocal music throughout the eighteenth century. This first group flourished around the turn of the century, and includes names that would have been canonical to Mancini's readers. Four of them—Durante, Mancini, Sarro, and Scarlatti—are associated with the Neapolitan school.
6. This second group, all of them Neapolitan in origin and training, were of a slightly later generation, flourishing in the second quarter of the century. Leo was Mancini's teacher in Naples when the author was fourteen.
7. With this group, Mancini moves to the generation of composers who flourished in the second half of the century, most of whom were alive and productive at the time he was writing. The list in the first edition included only Galuppi, Gluck, Jommelli, Cafaro, and Hasse, and was enormously expanded for this edition of 1777.
8. The noble Signora Marianna *Martinez* of Vienna bears witness most genuinely to the praises owed this celebrated master. This incomparable damsel, gifted with a superior talent for music, received both rudiments and refinement from the esteemed Signor *Bonno.* Her progress in these was so rapid that in a short time she became the object of the admiration of all the most famous masters of music. Her compositions have been in great demand, receiving acclaim in Naples, Bologna, and many of the most renowned cities of Italy.
    I myself heard her sing in her earliest years, playing the cembalo with a surprising mastery to accompany her own vocal compositions. She sang and expressed them with such power of musical measure that Signore Abbate *Metastasio* himself experienced in them that emotion he knew so well how to stir in the human heart with his inimitable dramatic poems. Thus among the other unanimous acclamations, the celebrated Padre Martini begged the honor of numbering in our Accademia Filarmonica of Bologna this woman who, although a dilettante, could justly be called a great mistress and rare genius of music. [Au.]
    This note was added in the 1777 edition. For Burney's equally glowing account of Signora Martinez, see *Dr. Burney's Musical Tours in Europe,* P. Scholes, ed. (Oxford: Oxford University Press, 1959), II, 106–7, 109, 117, 119–20, 122.

of this man has not only made him possessor of the most profound secrets and hidden insights of philosophy and other sciences, but has unfolded from the breast of that immense talent all things rare, noble, interesting, and sublime that music was concealing. I speak particularly of French music, of which he was the reformer, or, better, the dictator. What can I say of such merit? What luster can my weak voice add to the glory and fame of a man who is immortalized and venerated as the tutelary deity of music not only in his country, but in all the corners of Europe? What can one say further, having remembered that the French nation, oversolicitous of the glory of its own sons and harsh in scrutinizing that of foreigners, gave high praise to the composer of *Orfeo,* of *Ifigenia,* of *Alceste,* and of *Paride e Elena,* and erected a bust of him halfway through the eighteenth century?[9]

If the theatrical art is in decline, as it surely is, this ought not to be blamed on the *maestri di cappella,* but without a doubt on the actors alone. They are the ones who beat and batter the recitatives because they will not take the trouble to learn the rules of perfect declamation.

•   •   •   •   •

How have the *opere buffe* and dances that at one time served only as intermezzos in *opere serie* both come to stand on their own, and to become principal spectacles instead of accessories, if not by means of the dramatic art? The actors and comics with their gesticulation and the dancers with their pantomime are today effectively the only ones who still use and appreciate good acting, and are consequently also the only ones who receive the good effects of applause and esteem.

I hope by this to have succinctly but sufficiently proved that to be a good actor it is not enough just to sing well: one must also have good declamation and acting skills. It remains for me to speak my mind about how recitative ought to be declaimed, and with what sort of delivery.

It is a given that we have two kinds of recitative: the one has come to be called *simple,* and we term the other *instrumental.* We call *simple* the type that is accompanied by bass alone. This recitative was invented by Giacomo *Peri* about 1600, in order not to allow the dialogue that occurs in plays among the arias, duets, terzets, and choruses to languish completely. When spoken recitative has been written by a learned and knowledgeable master, it is extremely natural. For not only are the simple notes that constitute it placed in the natural range of each voice, but they are articulated and shaped in such a way that they perfectly imitate a natural discourse. Hence all the periods can be distinguished throughout, and question marks, exclamation marks, and full stops can

9. I will not go on to mention many others who would clearly deserve it, both so as not to diverge too far from my path, and because they are well enough known. For who does not know the worth of a *Wagenseil,* lost to the Imperial Court on March 1, 1777? Or of Giuseppe *Steffan,* also in the imperial service, who is, without challenge, the best harpsichord performer in Europe? [Au.] The paragraph in praise of Gluck and this footnote were added in the 1777 edition.

be apprehended. All this is expressed in the vocal line, which varies with the motion and diversity of tones. And the tones vary precisely as the sentiments of the words are diverse, and according to the various emotions that the words are intended to arouse in the souls of the audience.

The other recitative is called *instrumental* because it requires the accompaniment of the orchestra. Its vocal line is not at all different from that of the *simple*. The methods of the two are always the same, except that in the *instrumental* orchestral accompaniment is added so that the orchestra can act when the actor is constrained to a dumb show. Thus the orchestra always follows the actor, even when he is speaking, in order to give greater prominence and embellishment to what he says. Customarily the voice and orchestra are required to perform strictly in tempo in order not to intrude on the feeling and power of the expression. This type of recitative was invented for no other end than to give prominence to the sort of primary and interesting scene that closes with some kind of stirring aria of rage or tenderness, distinguishing it from the others. When such recitatives are written well and well performed they cause universal satisfaction, and are sometimes the mainstay of an entire opera.

Now the vocal line of these various recitatives, although sung, ought always to have a looseness of style that resembles a perfect and simple spoken declamation. Thus it would be a failing if instead of declaiming the recitative loosely an actor wanted to sing it with a constant legato style, without ever thinking to distinguish the periods and the various meanings of the words by restraining and reinforcing, detaching and smoothing his tone, as an educated man does when he speaks or reads. This is the appropriate time to mention that recitative stands or falls entirely on the knowledge of the placement of appoggiaturas, or the musical accent, as it is commonly called. This priceless accent, which constitutes all that is agreeable in a fine vocal line, consists, to be brief, of a note one tone higher than what is written. It is customarily performed only on the occasion when a few syllables making up a word are found on notes of the same pitch. For greater clarity here is an example:

Example 5.111

On - de mai   tu ve - des - ti . . .

I ought to inform you now that we have two accents. The one is called "restrained," as in the exclamation, *O Dio!*, and the second "relaxed."[10] This latter can be languid, or hasty, or serious and sustained, depending on the various affects it expresses. The virtue of teacher and student consists in knowing how to recognize these accents and use them well.

10. *Trattenuto* and *sciolto*.

Since I already discussed in the preceding chapter what kind of study the student needs in order to understand the importance of these vocal inflections, it is not necessary for me to repeat it here. I shall say only that I advise the student to undertake this study while he is still under the direction of a good teacher, who can show him the right way to take advantage of it.

I know that at one time the opinion was current among our professors that the recitatives for the chamber should be delivered differently than those for the theater, and likewise those for the concert hall or the church. As much as I have thought about this, I have not found any convincing reason why this difference should exist. I think that no matter whether they are intended for church, theater, or chamber, recitatives ought always to be delivered in the same fashion. By this I mean with a clear and natural voice, which gives each word the full force due it, and that articulates the commas and periods so that the spectators can understand the meaning of the poetry. So I have concluded that if there exists any difference among these recitatives relative to place, it consists in the quantity of the voice alone, so that the singer, whatever his powers, ought always to adapt to the place in which he sings.

But above all, even if the recitative is uttered with the necessary vocal inflections, pauses, and periods, it will still always be languid and slack if it is not accompanied by a suitable delivery. This is what gives power, expression, and liveliness to the discourse. Gesture is the thing that miraculously expresses the nature of the character one wishes to represent. In the last analysis it is delivery that makes a true actor; so Cicero himself said that all the nobility and excellence of an actor consists in delivery: *actio, actio, actio.*[11]

But do not deceive yourself that this is a pure gift of nature. Learning it requires art and study. Granted, by nature one person more than another has a good disposition for performance, but the disposition for learning something does not in itself cause that thing to be already learned. What comes from nature flawed and crude must be polished and refined with art and study. People say—and it is very true—that one's delivery should be natural rather than studied, and never, above all, too affected, which is a defect that still prevails among many. This does not mean, however, that one should not study the true style of acting, but only that one should not make delivery affected, adapting and conforming it to the words being spoken and the character being represented. This power to adapt and conform is what we call naturalness, which is precisely what is to be learned from study. The good that nature can provide for an actor is restricted to a fine physique and perhaps to some elegance in the movements of the arm.

It is true that the study of delivery does not have sure and precise rules from which a diligent student can learn exactly what posture he ought to assume on any particular occasion. But it does have general rules that will suffice to mold

---

11. Delivery—*actio* (*hypocrisis* in the Greek)—was the all-important fifth and last division of classical rhetoric; see Cicero, *De oratore* 3.56–61.

a good actor. The particular rules that teach one what gestures to make in a given situation are all practical, and should be either spelled out by someone with mature judgment, or learned from attentive observation of the movements of fine actors in those situations. The general rules are also theoretical, and can thus be learned both from teachers and from books.

Principal among these is that of making an entrance gracefully, and of knowing how to walk the boards with a natural decorum. All this can be nowhere learned better than in a dancing school, where one finds out how to move the feet with grace, to control the arms, to turn the head, and to move the whole body with refinement. Schools of fencing and horseback riding are also of some benefit, especially in situations where the actor must perform one of these actions. In addition, all of them make the body robust, agile, and relaxed.

The power to make easy and pliant changes of countenance—or, as they say, knowing how to "work in mask"—is also a necessity for an actor. Knowing how to change expression, to appear first proud, or gentle, or tender and passionate, then angry and scornful, according to the affects and to the impression that is to be aroused or received, is the finest part of delivery that the actor can use. It all depends on these inflections happening naturally and at the right time. Hence an actor is guilty of a great failing when, while listening to his companion on stage tell a story of disgrace or good fortune, he remains indifferent and in his original mood during the whole time of the narrative, and only shows signs of wonder or pleasure or pain at the end of it—and all at once. These signs, to be expressed naturally, should be manifested little by little, starting at the moment when one can understand from the story something of the whole deed, and growing as the grief or agitation to be elicited by the story naturally ought to grow. Hence an actor must always be attentive and collected not only when he himself is speaking but also when he is being spoken to. When he speaks and is distracted, it is very likely not only that he will fail in delivery, but also that he will sing out of tune. In addition to offending the ears of the listeners, this error is likely to disconcert his companion and place him in real danger of failing, for he will have to start again. If an actor does not pay attention to the one who is speaking, he cannot engage in byplay with that person nor display the internal agitations that the other's speech ought to arouse in him. Nevertheless one sees too many actors who, instead of paying attention to what they are saying and to what has just been said to them, amuse themselves by admiring the scenery, looking in the boxes, or greeting friends, all actions that reflect badly not just on the part they are playing, but also on the wisdom of a knowledgeable singer, and on one's sense of duty.

For his delivery to succeed perfectly the actor must also have accurately in his memory both the words and the music of his part. If he goes on stage without knowing them perfectly, founding all his hopes of success on the help of the prompter and the motives in the orchestra, he will not be able to accompany everything he says with a suitable natural delivery. For since in that situation he has to think about the words and the music, he cannot at the same time

living there until his death in 1813. Although early efforts at composition included symphonies and cantatas, he made keyboard music his principal preoccupation, publishing fifteen volumes of keyboard sonatas during his years in Halle. He was a serious scholar, known for his extensive library.

Türk wrote his *Klavierschule (School of Clavier Playing)* after he retired from general teaching to a position as organist and music director of a church in Halle. It is the last of the great eighteenth-century keyboard manuals and has the broadest range of them all. Reaching a larger and less well-educated audience than did earlier manuals, it provided its users with a context for taste and style that they could no longer be assumed to possess of themselves.

FROM *School of Clavier Playing*
(1789)

CHAPTER SIX: CONCERNING EXECUTION

PART ONE: CONCERNING EXECUTION IN GENERAL AND ITS
GENERAL REQUIREMENTS

1. I have already taken the opportunity to touch upon one thing or another required for good execution, but in order that the student can comfortably survey the entire subject, I have arranged the various components of good execution in sequence in the present chapter, and now and then have added some observations which are perhaps not generally known.

2. Whoever performs a composition so that its intrinsic affect (character, etc.), even in every single passage, is most faithfully expressed (made perceptible) and that the tones become, so to speak, a language of feelings, of this person it is said that he is a good executant. Good execution, therefore, is the most important, but at the same time, the most difficult task of making music.

3. One knows from experience that a composition leaves a very different impression depending on whether it is more or less effectively executed. Mediocre works can be uncommonly improved by a good and expressive execution, and on the contrary, the most moving Adagio, poorly executed, loses almost all of its effect, or even provokes unpleasant feelings. In the latter instance it can scarcely be believed that one is hearing the same composition which during a good performance evoked so much delight.

> Composers are to be pitied because they must so often surrender their works to players who have no feeling and sense, for in such cases their aims are either not at all or only half achieved. Other artists are more certain of well-deserved applause for they perform their own works themselves most of the time.

TEXT: Translation by Raymond H. Haggh in *School of Clavier Playing* (Lincoln: University of Nebraska Press, 1982), pp. 321–22, 337–42, 347–53, 358–60, 360–64, 397–400, with minor alterations.

pay attention to and reflect on his delivery; being completely occupied in w
he should say and at what point, he cannot prepare himself for what cor
next.

Finally, so that the delivery be well adapted to the words and to the char
ter, the actor ought thoroughly to understand what he is saying and the partic
lar character he is representing, or else he may make embarrassing mistakes.

I certainly do not consider it useless to repeat my concerns to diligent stu
dents, so that they will not neglect this very necessary study of delivery.

This science is more difficult than can be imagined, but still we have sure
ways and means for learning the true rules, and for acting with power. The
general rules are spelled out by teachers; the particular rules are learned practi-
cally, from observation of the most convincing actors and from the instruction
of expert practitioners, who should be consulted about the precise cases in
which a particular action or gesture takes place.

There are many of these experts; in fact all refined cities abound in them,
especially in Italy, where noblemen, men of letters, and statesmen recite plays
for their own private pleasure. Insofar as they are fine actors themselves, they
will willingly instruct whoever asks them. For example, the Marchese *Teodoli*
in Rome, the Marchese *di Liveri*, the lawyer Giuseppe *Santoro* in Naples,[12]
and many, many others had excellent students, including in our own times our
celebrated *Metastasio* in Vienna. His students Signora Teresa *de Reutter*[13] and
Angelo Maria *Monticelli*,[14] who learned so well following his instructions, demonstrate clearly how capable he was in this art.

If an actor fails in dramatic action, he has only himself to blame; he cannot
excuse himself by saying that he had no means by which to learn the art of the
theater.

12. These particular amateur actors have not been identified.
13. According to Mancini, Reutter was a singer in the Imperial Court at Vienna.
14. Italian castrato soprano (c.1712–1758) who had a considerable career in Italy, London, and
    Dresden. His acting skills were praised by Charles Burney and others.

11 Daniel Gottlob Türk

Daniel Gottlob Türk was a German pedagogue and composer of great intellect,
energy, and education. Born in Saxony in 1750, he studied music from childhood; the teacher of his formative years was Johann Adam Hiller in Leipzig,
where he studied from 1772 to 1774. Under Hiller's guidance, Türk gained
experience in music of all types, including opera and choral music; he also
studied keyboard using C. P. E. Bach's *Versuch*. In 1774, he moved to Halle to
take a teaching position, and he became a mainstay of that city's musical life,

4. It becomes sufficiently clear from these few words that execution must be of the utmost importance for the musician. For even with all his facility in reading notes and in playing,[1] he will never attain his main purpose, which is to move the heart of his listener, without good execution. Whoever possesses both extraordinarily facility and good execution has attributes which are not only praiseworthy but also rare.

5. In my opinion, the following characteristics are particularly typical of good execution: (1) in general, an already achieved facility in playing and note reading, security in rhythm, and knowledge of thoroughbass as well as of the composition to be performed; but in particular (2) clarity of execution, (3) expression of the predominant character, (4) appropriate use of ornaments and other devices of the same sort, and (5) genuine feeling for all the emotions and passions which are expressed in music.

· · · · ·

PART THREE: CONCERNING THE EXPRESSION OF THE PREVAILING CHARACTER

26. If everything that has been taught in the last two parts is followed in the most meticulous way, it is still not possible to have good execution because the most essential part is missing, namely the expression of the prevailing character, without which no listener can be moved to any great degree. This effect, which is the highest goal of music, can only be induced when the artist has the capacity to become infused with the predominant affect and to communicate his feelings to others through the eloquence of music. Expression is therefore that part of a good execution in which the true master, full of genuine feeling for his art, distinguishes himself noticeably from the average musician. Mechanical skill can ultimately be learned by much practice; only expression presupposes—other than mechanical facility—a broad range of knowledge, and above all things, a sensitive soul. It certainly would be a futile endeavor, therefore, if one were to attempt to enumerate in order everything that is required for expression and to specify all of this through rules, because expression depends so much on that which no rule can teach, namely on the individual feelings themselves. Nevertheless, there are some means which can more or less contribute to the strengthening of expression and which to some extent can be put down in the form of written instruction, although it is even in this regard incomparably better to listen to singers and players of great sensitivity. For as has been said, certain subtleties of expression cannot really be described; they must be *heard*.

27. The words "Will he come soon? " can merely through the tone of the speaker receive a quite different meaning. Through them a yearning desire, a vehement impatience, a tender plea, a defiant command, irony, etc., can be

---

1. It is possible to read notes with skill, that is, to be able to perceive several at one glance, and in spite of this not to be able to achieve particular dexterity in playing. [Au.]

expressed. The single word "God!" can denote an exclamation of joy, of pain, of despair, the greatest anxiety, pity, astonishment, etc., in various degrees. In the same way tones by changes in the execution can produce a very different effect. It is therefore extremely necessary to study the expression of feelings and passions in the most careful way, make them one's own, and learn to apply them correctly.

28. Outside of those requirements mentioned in the two previous paragraphs that are indispensable for expression, I also include (1) the suitable degree of loudness and softness of tone, (2) the detaching, sustaining, and slurring of tones, and (3) the correct tempo.

29. Even with the most painstaking marking, it is not possible to specify every degree of loudness and softness of tone. As many words as we have for this purpose, they are by far not sufficient for the indication of all possible gradations. The player must himself feel and learn to judge what degree of loudness and softness of tone is required by the character of the music to be expressed in any given case. The adding of *forte* and *piano* specifies the expression only approximately and in general; to what an excess would these words have to be added if every note which required a special shading would be so indicated.

30. Concerning the intensity of tone required in any given case, I content myself in remarking that generally, compositions of a spirited, happy, lively, sublime, magnificent, proud, daring, courageous, serious, fiery, wild, and furious character[2] all require a certain degree of loudness. This degree must even be increased or decreased according to whether the feeling or passion is represented in a more vehement or more moderate manner. What a number of degrees of loudness are thus required for all this! And now let us consider that in each composition various gradations are again necessary which must all be in a proper relation to the whole. A *forte* in an Allegro furioso must therefore be a great deal louder than in an Allegro in which only a moderate degree of joy prevails, etc.

Compositions of a gentle, innocent, naive, pleading, tender, moving, sad, melancholy, and the like character all require a softer execution. The degree of loudness, however, must exactly correspond to each sentiment being expressed and as a result is different in most of the cases just mentioned. As with compositions which are to be played forcefully, other than the strength already due to them,[3] a still even greater degree for a *fortissimo* must be possible, and in the same manner, a *piano* and *pianissimo* should be possible in compositions that are to be played softly.

---

2. I indicate here and further below a few character types one at a time which border closely on each other and which must almost be treated in the same way, in order that the student generally knows whether by this or that title of a composition, loudness or softness must be applied. I gladly admit that the above-mentioned gradations are not always possible to a perceptible degree of loudness on the clavichord. [Au.]

3. That is, what is marked in the music. [Tr.]

Note 1. The composer often specifies the main degree of loudness or softness by the words *sempre forte* or *sempre piano* which are placed at the beginning of the composition. The *sempre*, however, should not be taken too literally, for the composer is only saying that the execution should be generally loud or soft. Certain musical thoughts, in spite of this, must be suitably modified according to the affect (played stronger or weaker).

Note 2. In the application of *forte* and *fortissimo*[4] I must warn against a very common mistake. Many players strike the keys with such force or press them down so violently in order to maintain the sounding of the tone that (particularly in one-part passages) the pitch becomes too high and consequently impure. It is probably for this reason, among others, that some persons, of whom I myself know a few, do not value the clavichord as much as they should, or even might have an antipathy toward it, because they believe that playing expressively and impurely are inseparable. However, the overemphasis of the tone is for the most part the player's fault or comes from a too weak stringing of the instrument.[5] Even played with the greatest possible degree of strength, the tone must not go higher in pitch; it is simply a matter of the way in which the key is struck or pressed down. That it is possible, however, to play with expression and not to commit this mistake is proved by all really good clavichord players.

31. To specify whether a specific passage must be played somewhat louder or softer than the preceding and following is utterly impossible; nevertheless, one can generally assume that the livelier parts of a composition can be played louder and the tenderly singing, etc., parts can be played softer, even if in the first case no *forte*, and in the second, no *piano* has been indicated. When a musical thought is repeated, then it is customary to play it softly the second time, provided it has been played loudly the first. On the other hand, a repeated passage may also be played louder, especially when the composer has made it livelier through elaborations. In general, one must even play single tones of importance with more emphasis than the others.

32. Good taste has made it a rule that dissonances or dissonant chords must generally be struck with more force than consonant ones, for the reason that the passions should be especially aroused by dissonances.[6] If one considers this rule particularly with relation to the degree of the dissonance, it then follows that the sharper the dissonance or the more dissonances contained in a chord, the louder must the harmony be played. Yet this rule cannot and should not always be strictly followed, because otherwise too much variety is likely to result.

4. Also for tones which are slurred, or when *tenuto* is written over a note. [Au.]
5. A clavichord which is properly strung and yet does not tolerate a full and emphatic stroke is a poor instrument and therefore does not come into consideration. [Au.]
6. Since the passions are not of a single kind and since certain passions can also be aroused without dissonances, etc., then when viewed from this position, this principle, which has become a rule, is probably not so generally valid. At least it would not follow that dissonances be struck in all cases with more force than consonant chords. There are other reasons, however, which appear to be more convincing to me and which illuminate the necessity of the rule given above. A continuing pleasant sensation will gradually become weaker, or if it continues longer, will cease to be pleasant if it is not interrupted at times. If this interruption is of an unpleasant nature, one finds the ensuing pleasure so much the more stimulating. Since through dissonances a kind of unpleasant sensation, or at least a hoping and expectation, a desire for repose and the like, is

Here are some harmonies which are strongly dissonant and must therefore be played with emphasis.

Example 1a

The following chords are less dissonant. Therefore they require a more moderate degree of loudness.

Example 1b

and so on.

That chords which are more or less consonant should be played with varying degrees of loudness is probably too great a subtlety and only a matter for the very skilled player.

33. The harmonies by means of which a modulation into a somewhat distant key is suddenly made or through which the modulation takes an unexpected turn are also played relatively loudly and emphatically in order that they surprise even more in a manner that accords with their purpose. For example:

Example 2

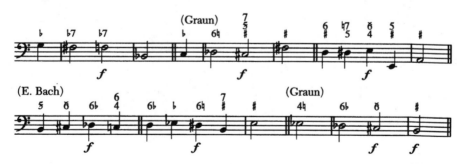

awakened, it follows that dissonant chords among others must for this reason be played with force, so that the consonant chords will then effect an even more pleasant sensation and an even more reassuring resolution, etc. Moreover, dissonances make the particular contribution that the spirit is not so quickly fatigued as it would be from a sequence of nothing but consonances, and that as a result, a composition, if I may say so, becomes appetizing. Therefore dissonances, as it were, are for music just what spices are for food. [Au.]

34. The so-called deceptive cadences (*cadenze d'inganno*) also require a greater or lesser degree of loudness according to whether they are more or less unexpected, and whether they lead to a more distant or more closely related key. For example:

Example 3

After the second d in the bass, g should actually follow; since this does not occur and the expected does not materialize, then the unexpected harmony must be played with force in order that it surprise more. When similar deceptions (deceptive cadences) occur only in the melody, the unexpected tone is played more loudly. For example:

Example 4

•   •   •   •   •

43. The particular ways in which a heavy or light execution can be brought about have been described in §36 to §42. For a *heavy* execution every tone must be played firmly (with emphasis) and held out until the very end of the prescribed duration of the note. *Light* execution is that in which every tone is played with less firmness (emphasis), and the finger lifted from the key somewhat sooner than the actually prescribed duration. In order to avoid a misunderstanding I must also remark that the terms heavy and light in general refer more to the sustaining or detaching of a tone than to the softness or loudness

of the same. For in certain cases, for example in an Allegro vivo, scherzando, Vivace con allegrezza, etc., the execution must be rather light (short) but at the same time more or less loud, whereas pieces of a melancholy character, for example an Adagio mesto, con afflizione, etc., although played slurred and consequently with a certain heaviness, must nevertheless not be executed too loudly. In most cases, however, heavy and loud are indeed to be combined.

Whether the execution is to be heavy or light may be determined (1) from the character and the purpose of a composition (§45); (2) from the designated tempo; (3) from the meter; (4) from the note values used; and (5) from the manner in which the notes progress, etc. In addition, national taste, the style of the composer, and the instrument for which the composition is written must be taken into consideration.

44. Compositions of an exalted, serious, solemn, pathetic, and similar character must be given a heavy execution with fullness and force, strongly accented and the like. To these types of compositions belong those which are headed *grave, pomposo, patetico, maestoso, sostenuto,* and the like. A somewhat lighter and markedly softer execution is required by compositions of a pleasant, gentle, agreeable character, consequently those which are customarily marked *compiacevole, con dolcezza, glissicato, lusingando, pastorale, piacevole,* and the like. Compositions in which lively, humorous, and joyous feelings are predominant, for example, *Allegro scherzando, burlesco, giocoso, con allegrezza, risvegliato,* etc., must be played quite lightly whereas melancholy and similar affects particularly call for the slurring of tones and portato. Compositions of the latter type are designated by the words *con afflizione, con amarezza, doloroso, lagrimoso, languido,* and *mesto* among others.

It is understood that in all of the aforementioned cases various degrees of heavy or light execution must be applied.

45. Compositions which have a more serious purpose, such as fugues, well-composed sonatas, religious odes and songs, etc.,[7] call for a heavier execution than, for example, certain playful divertimentos, humorous songs, lively dances, and the like.

46. Whether a heavy or light execution is to be chosen may also be determined from the tempo. A Presto must be played more lightly than an Allegro; this in turn must be played more lightly than an Andante, etc. In general, the heaviest execution is called for by compositions in slow tempos.

47. That meter has very marked influence on heavy or light execution, or certainly should have, has already been mentioned in passing.[8] The following

7. If I were not writing primarily for the clavichord player, then I would include everything written for the church in this category. [Au.]
8. Türk refers here to a brief discussion of strong and weak beats in Chap. 1, §55, n. 3. The simple duration of a note is called its "external value," its emphasis in the measure its "internal value." Strong beats—usually downbeats—are "internally long," non-thetic beats "internally short." "Long" and "short," however, seem to imply greater emphasis rather than an actual change in duration.

should be noted in this connection. The larger the values of the main beats of a measure, the heavier must be the execution. Therefore, a composition in $\frac{3}{2}$ (Ex. 5a), for example, is played more heavily than it would be if it were in $\frac{3}{4}$ (Ex. 5b)[9] or even in $\frac{3}{8}$ (Ex. 5c). Thus Graun wanted to specify a heavier execution by the meter in Example 5d[10] in combination with a faster tempo.

Example 5

For this reason all tones in Examples 5a and 5d must be played with emphasis and held down for their full value. In 5b and 5e the execution must already be lighter and in 5c and 5f it must be very light. Even if *Adagio* were written over Examples 5c and 5f, a good player would not play these tones with as much emphasis as in the *alla breve* in 5a and 5d. Moreover, it follows from what has been said that the meters $\frac{2}{8}$, $\frac{4}{8}$, $\frac{3}{16}$, $\frac{6}{16}$, and the like require the lightest execution.

Incidentally, I should like to note that compositions in triple meters with short note values can be given a sort of comically hopping motion if the player accents the first note too strongly.

48. Various species of notes require, without regarding the kind of meter, a more or less heavy execution. For example, if in a composition there occur mostly larger note values, namely whole, half, and quarter notes, then the execution must be generally heavier than if many eighth and sixteenth notes, etc., were intermingled. Dotted notes especially—in addition to the attention which

9. For reasons of space I had to omit the bass and the middle voices. [Au.]
10. Carl Heinrich Graun, "Christus hat uns ein Vorbild gelassen [Christ has left us a model]," *Der Tod Jesu*, fourteenth movement. [Tr.]

must be given to the proper arrangement of note values as well as to heavy or light execution—require a very varied treatment according to the context in which they occur. It is customary, for the most part,[11] to dwell on dotted notes longer (and therefore to play the following shorter notes even more quickly) than the notation indicates. For example:

Examples 6a–d

The realization of dotted notes as shown in Example 6b is generally chosen when the character of the composition is serious, solemn, exalted, etc.; so it is not only for an actual Grave but also for overtures or compositions which are marked *sostenuto*, and the like. The dotted notes are executed in this case with emphasis, consequently they are prolonged. For the expression of livelier or more joyous feelings, the playing must be somewhat lighter, approximately as in 6c. The execution shown in Example 6d is particularly chosen for compositions which are to be played in a vehement or defiant manner or those which are marked *staccato*.[12] The keys are to be struck firmly, but the fingers should be raised sooner than they would be for places which are to be played with a certain solemn dignity. For agreeable and lyric thoughts and the like, dotted notes are prolonged a little as shown below in 6e—even though not too perceptibly; in any case they will be played more gently (less accented). Especially in such cases the short notes after the dot are to be played softly and should be slurred. If a second voice occurs with the voice containing the dotted notes, as in 6f, then the prescribed values are to be retained.

11. All possible cases cannot be specified; nevertheless, one can accept as a rule for this that the value of the dot not be prolonged when the note following it has the full value of a metric unit, or in slower tempo, the value of a beat division. However, even this rule is probably not without its exceptions and for the beginner cannot be of too much value. How necessary it would be, therefore, for dotted notes to be notated more exactly. Since at present the meaning of two dots placed after a note is known by almost everyone, then their usage or another more painstaking notation would cause all doubts to be removed in most cases. [Au.]
12. But this kind of execution is extremely poor and quite contrary to the required expression for—as an example—the closing chorus from Graun's *Tod Jesu:* "Hier liegen wir gerührte Sünder" [Here we lie, awe-struck sinners]; nevertheless, it is not seldom that this splendid chorus is heard performed in such a defiant way. [Au.]

Examples 6e–f

Now and then when several voices are involved, the dotted notes are pro-longed in only one voice and the short notes in both voices are played at the same time in order that the whole be more uniform.

Example 7

The short rests which take the place of dots are also often prolonged in compositions of a lively character and the like, as here in Example 8b.

Example 8

Figures in which the first note is short and the second is dotted are slurred without exception and played for the most part in a caressing manner. The first (short) note, of course, is to be accented but the emphasis should be only a very gentle one.

Example 9

The first note should not be rushed, especially in a slow tempo, because the melody can easily degenerate into flippancy, or lose its essential roundness if the first tone is played too short, and, moreover, if the dot is transformed into an incorrect rest, as in Example 9b.

Formerly, for similar figures the first note was given a very short duration. Even Agricola still writes: "When the short note comes first and a dot is placed after the second note, then the first note is played as quickly as possible and the remainder is given to the note which is dotted."[13] Bach, on the other hand, says on page 113: "The first note should not be done away with too quickly if the tempo is moderate or slow."[14]

49. Even with regard to harmony and the progression of some intervals, a heavy or light execution is required. A composition with many dissonances must therefore be executed more heavily than another in which for the most part light, consonant harmonies are employed. Compositions with much passage work in general require a lighter execution than those in which many singable sections are found. In particular, skipping passages are played more lightly than those which move by step, etc.

50. In consideration of national taste, the style of the composer, and the instrument for which a composition has been written, the following should be noted in illustration of §43.

A composition which has been written in the Italian national taste requires in general[15] a medium (between heavy and light) execution. The performance of a French composition must be lighter. On the contrary, the works of German composers for the most part demand a heavier and more robust execution.

In the same way the style of a composer also presumes an individual mode of treatment. A composition of Handel, Sebastian Bach, etc., must be given a more emphatic execution than, for example, a modern concerto of Mozart or Kozeluch, among others.

Sonatas for the harpsichord do not require the heavy execution which is taken for granted for those composed for the clavichord by C. P. E. Bach.

Heavy or light execution, however, must not only correspond to the whole but also to every single part of a composition. In a composition of animated character which is to be executed lightly there can appear passages which notwithstanding the general character of the composition are more dignified and require a heavier execution. If I might express myself in the terminology of painting, then I would say that certain parts must be given light and others shadow. Therefore in fugues, for example, or compositions in strict style, the theme (subject) in particular, as well as the imitative parts must be executed with emphasis, in order that they be more conspicuous. A majestic *all'unisono* also requires a heavy and forceful execution, unless the composer has specified the opposite for certain reasons.

13. Johann Friedrich Agricola's *Anleitung zu Singkunst* (*Introduction to the Art of Singing*, Berlin, 1757) is a translation with running commentary of Pier Francesco Tosi's *Opinioni de' cantori antichi e moderni* ((*Opinions of Ancient and Modern Singers*, Bologna, 1723). See p. 10, n. 8.
14. Carl Philipp Emanuel Bach, *Versuch über die wahre Art das Clavier zu spielen* (Berlin, 1753). Türk owned the second, 1759 edition of Bach's *Versuch*. The quotation he cites is on p. 128, §24, of the 1753 edition. See *Essay on the True Art of Playing Keyboard Instruments, by Carl Philipp Emanuel Bach*, trans. and ed. William J. Mitchell (New York: W. W. Norton 1949), 158.
15. Of course, there are many exceptions to this. [Au.]

51. Besides what has been mentioned in this part, correct tempo contributes to expression to a very large degree. In order to be convinced of this, one ought to play a well-known composition in its proper tempo and then too slowly or too fast immediately afterward. If the tempo is taken too slowly then even the most excellent composition will become feeble or dull; if the tempo is taken too fast, the clarity and at the same time the intended effect are either completely lost or at least partly forfeited. I have especially noted that compositions which are marked *Vivace* are usually played too fast. Presumably this term, which particularly specifies the kind of execution, is incorrectly applied only to the tempo. This must then be the reason that, for example, Graun's aria "So stehet ein Berg Gottes,"[16] etc., is often played much too fast. This is also frequently the case with compositions marked *Grave, maestoso, Marcia*, etc.

·   ·   ·   ·   ·

PART FIVE: CONCERNING THE NEED FOR PERSONAL AND GENUINE FEELING FOR ALL THE EMOTIONS AND PASSIONS WHICH CAN BE EXPRESSED IN MUSIC

63. Even when the composer has indicated the proper manner of expression as well as he can—in general and for specific parts—and the player has appropriately made use of all the means discussed in the preceding sections, there still remain special cases for which the expression can be heightened by *extraordinary* means. Among these I include particularly the following: (1) playing without keeping steady time; (2) quickening and hesitating; (3) the so-called *tempo rubato*. These three resources *when used sparingly and at the right time* can be of great effect.

64. In addition to free fantasies, cadenzas, fermatas, and the like, those passages marked *Recitativo* must be played more according to feeling than to meter. Some passages of this sort are found now and then in sonatas, concertos, and the like, for example in the Andante of the first sonata by C. P. E. Bach dedicated to the King of Prussia. Such passages would have a poor effect if they were played strictly according to the specified values of the notes (measured). The more important notes must therefore be played slower and louder, and the less important notes more quickly and softer, approximately the way a sensitive singer would sing these notes or a good orator would declaim the words thereto.

65. It is difficult to specify all of the places where quickening and hesitating can take place; nevertheless, I will seek to make at least some of them known. I am assuming, however, that the means which I am about to describe will only be used when one is playing alone or with a very attentive accompanist.

---

16. "So stands a mountain of God," *Der Tod Jesu*, thirteenth movement.

That this intentional quickening or hesitating should not be mistaken for the faulty hurrying, etc., mentioned in the Introduction, is obvious.

66. In compositions whose character is vehemence, anger, rage, fury, and the like, the most forceful passages can be played with a somewhat hastened (*accelerando*) motion. Also, certain thoughts which are repeated in a more intensified manner (generally higher) require that the speed be increased to some extent. Sometimes, when gentle feelings are interrupted by a lively passage, the latter can be played somewhat more rapidly.[17] A hastening of the tempo may also take place in a passage where a vehement affect is unexpectedly to be aroused.

67. For extraordinarily tender, longing, or melancholy passages, in which the emotion, as it were, is concentrated in one point, the effect can be very much intensified by an increasing hesitation (*Anhalten, tardando*). The tempo is also taken gradually slower for tones before certain fermatas as if their powers were gradually being exhausted. The passages toward the end of a composition (or part of a composition) which are marked *diminuendo, diluendo, smorzando,* and the like can also be played in a somewhat more lingering manner.

68. A tenderly moving passage between two lively and fiery thoughts (as in the first part of my easy clavichord sonatas, pages 10, 11, 25ff.) can be executed in a somewhat hesitating manner; but in this case, the tempo is not taken gradually slower, but *immediately* a little slower (however, only a *little*). Compositions in which two characters of opposite types are represented especially provide a suitable opportunity for a gradual slowing of the tempo. Thus Bach has written a most excellent sonata "which as it were constitutes a conversation between *Melancholicus* and *Sanguineus.*"[18] In a similar manner, E. W. Wolf, in his six little sonatas from the year 1779, page 10ff., describes an estranged married couple of the common folk. In general, the gradual slowing of tempo can take place most appropriately in slow tempos.

•   •   •   •   •

72. The so-called *tempo rubato* or *robato* (actually *stolen* time) I have specified in §63 as the third resource whose application should be left to the sensitivity and insight of the player. This term appears with more than one meaning. Commonly it is understood as a kind of shortening or lengthening of notes, or the displacement (dislocation) of these. There is something taken away (stolen) from the duration of a note and for this, another note is given that much more, as in the following Examples 10b and c.

17. There are some passages of this type in the first sonata of the second collection of my longer sonatas. [Au.]
18. Sulzer's words in the article *Sonate*. [Au.] The work is a trio sonata by C. P. E. Bach for two violins and bass (W. 161, no. 1) published in 1751. Bach prefaces the sonata, the first of two, with a detailed description of the conversation between the two characters, *Melancholicus* and *Sanguineus*.

Example 10a–c

(a)   (b)   (c)

Example 10a shows the basic notes; in 10b *tempo rubato* is put to use by means of the *anticipation* (*anticipatio*) and in 10c by means of the *retardation* (*retardatio*). From this it can be seen that through this kind of execution, the tempo, or even more, the meter as a whole is not displaced. Consequently, the customary but somewhat ambiguous German term *verrücktes Zeitmaß* ["displaced tempo"] is not very fitting, for the bass voice goes its way according to the meter (without displacement), and only the notes of the melody are moved out of place, as it were. For this reason the expression *Versetzen* (or *Verziehen*) ["changing the place of" or "dragging out"] the *notes* or the *beat divisions* would be more correct. Even when more notes are added to the melody, as in Examples 10e and 10f, both voices must nevertheless correctly coincide each time at the beginning of the measure. In this case then there results no actual displacement of the tempo.

Example 10d–f

(d)   (e)   (f)

This dragging out of notes, as it is otherwise called, must be applied with great care, because errors in the harmony could result. The anticipating in Example 10f would only be bearable in rather slow tempo.

•   •   •   •   •

SUPPLEMENT, PART FIVE: CONCERNING STYLE, MANNER, COUNTERPOINT, AND INVERSION

54. By *style* (manner of writing) is meant a certain individual character of composition, or the way in which each person composes. Diversity of style, therefore, also requires diversity of execution (see pt. 6, §50). Style is particularly varied in consideration of the locality and the nation. With regard to the locality, one namely differentiates between church, theater, and chamber style, and with regard to nations, chiefly between the Italian, French, and German styles (taste).

55. The *church style* requires a serious character united with dignity, solem-

nity, magnificence, sublime greatness, powerful harmonies, and the strict following of the rules, etc. The strict style[19] is particularly put to use.

> Compositions written in the church style are oratorios, passions, sacred cantatas,
> masses, hymns, and such special church compositions as psalms, motets, and the like.

The *theater style* is to a certain degree less reliant upon strict observance of
the rules,[20] and in contrast, the expression must be fiery, brilliant, and characteristic to a high degree. This kind of expression often borders on the pictur-
esque. In short, the theater style seeks to represent the feelings and passions
in their totality and, in order to achieve this purpose, makes use of means that
are not allowed in the church style.

> Serious operas, comic operettas, the pastorale, serenades, and the like are written in
> theater style.

The *chamber style* holds, as it were, a middle ground between church and
theater style and unites things found only occasionally in the aforementioned
styles of writing. Artful harmony, striking turns of expression, boldness, fire,
expression of feelings, magnificence, beautiful sound, in short everything that
does not run contrary to the rules of composition and strict setting is here in
its proper place. Composers in this style of writing take special note of the
facility of the player or singer and seek to use every instrument as much as
possible.

> Pieces in chamber style are some cantatas, vocal pieces, and songs; besides these,
> there are symphonies, sonatas, duos, trios, quartets, and the like, concertos, solos,
> divertimenti, partitas, certain dances, etc.

56. The *Italian style* is pleasing, singing, full (often overladen), brilliant,
diverse, and expressive. At least it was so characterized formerly. At present,
there is to be sure also much that is aimless, often heard, insignificant, shallow,
and the like in the works of various Italian composers; nevertheless, for the
most part it must be conceded to their merit that their melodies have a certain
(captivating) suppleness.

The *French style* is supposed to be, according to Rousseau's judgment, stale,
dull or hard, poorly cadenced, and monotonous,[21] a judgment which is certainly too harsh and testifies to the exclusive preference which the author had
for Italian music.[22] For outside of the fact that French composers do at times
write in a somewhat dry and empty manner, or neglect the harmonic aspect a

---

19. Concerning this there is more to say in §57. [Au.]
20. I would like to say that the theater style needs to be less according to academic precepts;
    nevertheless, mistakes against the rules of harmony and the like are not excused. [Au.]
21. See the *Dictionnaire de musique* under the article *Style*. [Au.]
22. Even Germans give a more favorable judgment of French music. Walther, for example, writing
    before Rousseau, says that the French style is natural, flowing, tender, etc. In Scheibe's *Der
    critische Musicus* on page 146 (2d ed.) it is said: "The manner of writing of the French is
    concise and very natural, far removed from all exotic and bombastic excesses." Even Quantz
    does not degrade the French style to such a degree as Rousseau. [Au.]

little, in spite of this, at present their taste must be more justly acknowledged. Among composers for keyboard instruments they have already long achieved an imposing position and it is beyond all doubt that in this regard they deserve to be much preferred over the Italian composers.

Rousseau also did not view the *German style* of writing from an advantageous position. He says that it is hopping (*sautillant*), mincing (*coupé*), but harmonic for all that. Although this may have been formerly somewhat the case in pieces for the keyboard (with regard to "hopping" and "mincing"), it is certainly no longer true at present. I think that our style manifests itself much more by its effort, solidity, and powerful harmonies. Moreover, we have taken some things from the Italians and the French, and probably not always the most inferior. We are also able to set many really great masters in composition and on instruments, yes, even in singing, over against the foreigners. Be that as it may, we could have left many things to the Italians, for it seems to be that our excellent and powerful style has in recent times begun to degenerate into facile trifling, etc.

> Until now there has still been no individual style attributed to the English. It is remarkable, of course, that a large number of their important composers were Germans, for example, Handel, C. Bach, Fischer, Abel, and Schröter among others.
>
> In earlier writings can be found diverse stylistic divisions which are in part superfluous and in part even ridiculous. Thus, for example, Walther, among others, also mentions a fawning and a base style.

57. Besides the classification of styles which has been given, it is also customary to distinguish between the strict style and the free. A strict (contrapuntal) style is the one in which the composer follows all the rules of harmony and modulation in the strictest manner, mixing in artful imitations and many tied notes, working out the theme carefully, and the like, in short, allowing more art to be heard than euphony. In the free (*galant*) manner of composition, the composer is not so slavishly bound to the rules of harmony, modulation, and the like. He often permits bold changes, which could even be contrary to the generally accepted rules of modulation, assuming that the composer in doing this proceeds with proper insight and judgment, and with it is able to attain a certain goal. In general, the free style of writing has expression and euphony rather than art as its chief purpose.

58. When speaking of the special way in which a composer, without taking into consideration national taste, differs from others with regard to design and execution, one means his manner of composition. Therefore, one speaks of the Bach manner, the Benda manner, the Gluck manner, the Haydn manner, and so on. Since almost every composer has his own manner of composition, the one more or less different from the other, the player must adjust his execution accordingly (pt. 6, §50).

IV

CRITICAL VIEWS OF FRENCH AND ITALIAN OPERA

12 Jean-Jacques Rousseau

Jean-Jacques Rousseau was born at Geneva in 1712 and died in 1778 near Paris. With his battle cry, "Retournons à la nature," Rousseau exerted a deep and lasting influence on the music of his time. He was not technically trained as a musician, but this did not prevent him from taking a passionate interest in things musical. In the "Querelle des Bouffons" Rousseau fought on the side of the partisans of the Italian *opera buffa*. His most important writing in this field is his *Lettre sur la musique française* (*Letter on French Music,* 1753); a reference to its sweeping indictment of French music is almost *de rigueur* in later writings of the period.

Rousseau even tried his hand as composer of a comic opera on a French text in which he attempted to follow the principles of the *opera buffa*. The work— *Le Devin du village* (*The Village Soothsayer,* 1752)—was extremely successful and played an important role in forming the style of French *opéra comique*. Rousseau was also the author of a valuable *Dictionnaire de musique* (1768).

Letter on French Music

(1753)

To The Reader:

Since the quarrel which arose last year at the Opéra[1] produced nothing but abuse, bestowed by the one party with much wit and by the other with much animosity, I was unwilling to take any part in it, for that kind of contest was wholly unsuited to me and I was well aware that it was not a time to speak only reason. Now that the buffoons are dismissed, or the next thing to it, and there is no more question of cabals, I think I may venture my opinion, and shall state it with my customary frankness, without fear of offending anyone by so doing. It even seems to me that in a subject of this kind, any reserve would be an affront to my readers, for I admit that I should have a poor opinion of a people who attached a ridiculous importance to their songs, who made more of their musicians than of their philosophers, and among whom one needed to speak more circumspectly of music than of the gravest questions of morality.

Do you remember, sir, the story, told by M. de Fontenelle,[2] of the Silesian infant who was born with a golden tooth? Immediately all the doctors of Germany exhausted themselves in learned disquisitions on how it was possible to be born with a golden tooth; the last thing that anyone thought of was to verify

TEXT: The original edition (Paris, 1753). Translation by William Strunk, Jr., and Oliver Strunk. Except for notes 1, 12, 19, and 20, the editorial notes in this selection are by Harvey Olnick.

1. See p. 9
2. Bernard Le Bovier de Fontenelle (1657–1757), *littérateur,* perpetual secretary of the Académie des Beaux-Arts, and author of the famous remark, "Sonate, que me veux-tu?"

the fact; and it was found that the tooth was not golden. To avoid a similar embarrassment, it would be well, before speaking of the excellence of our music, to make sure of its existence, and to examine first, not whether it is made of gold, but whether we have one.

The Germans, the Spaniards, and the English have long claimed to possess a music peculiar to their own language; they had, in fact, national operas which they admired in perfect good faith, and they were firmly persuaded that their glory would be at stake if they allowed those masterpieces, insupportable to any ears but their own, to be abolished. Pleasure has at last prevailed over vanity with them, or, at least, they have found a pleasure more easily understood in sacrificing to taste and to reason the prejudices which often make nations ridiculous by the very honor which they attach to them.

We still have in France the same feeling about our music that they had then about theirs, but who will give us the assurance that because we have been more stubborn, our obstinacy has been better grounded? Would it not then be fitting, in order to form a proper judgment of French music, that we should for once try to test it in the crucible of reason and see if it can endure the ordeal?

It is not my intention to delve deeply into this subject; that is not the business of a letter; perhaps it is not mine. I wish only to try to establish certain principles by which, until better have been found, the masters of the art, or rather the philosophers, may direct their researches; for, as a sage once said, it is the office of the poet to write poetry and that of the musician to compose music, but it is the province only of the philosopher to discuss the one and the other well.[3]

· · · · ·

The Italians pretend that our melody is flat and devoid of tune, and all the neutral nations[4] unanimously confirm their judgment on this point. On our side we accuse their music of being bizarre and baroque.[5] I had rather believe that both are mistaken than be reduced to saying that in countries where the sciences and the arts have arrived at so high a degree of perfection, music has still to be born.

The least partial among us[6] content themselves with saying that Italian music

3. Omitted here is an extended section in which Rousseau seeks to prove that the Italian language is best suited for musical setting.
4. There was a time, says Milord Shaftesbury, when the practice of speaking French had made French music fashionable among us. But Italian music, by giving us a nearer view of nature, soon gave us a distaste for the other and made us see it as dull, as flat, and as doleful as it really is. [Au.]
5. It seems to me that people no longer dare make this reproach so frequently since it has been heard in our country. Thus this admirable music has only to show itself as it is in order to clear itself of all the faults of which it is accused. [Au.]
6. Many condemn the total exclusion of French music unhesitatingly pronounced by the amateurs of music; these conciliatory moderates would have no exclusive tastes, as if the love of what is good ought to compel a love of what is bad. [Au.]

and French music are both good, each in its kind, each for its own language; but besides the refusal of other nations to agree to this parity, there still remains the question, which of the two languages is by its nature adapted to the best kind of music. This is a question much agitated in France, but which will never be agitated elsewhere, a question which can be decided only by an ear perfectly impartial, and which consequently becomes every day more difficult to resolve in the only country in which it is a problem. Here are some experiments on this subject which everyone is free to verify, and which, it seems to me, can serve to give the answer, at least so far as regards melody, to which alone almost the whole dispute is reducible.

I took, in the two kinds of music, airs equally esteemed each in its own kind, and divesting them, the one of its *ports-de-voix*[7] and its perpetual *cadences* the other of the implied notes which the composer does not trouble to write, but leaves to the discretion of the singer;[8] I sol-fa'd them exactly by note, without any ornament and without adding anything of my own to the sense or connection of the phrases. I will not tell you what effect this comparison produced upon my mind, because I have the right to offer my reasons but not to impose my authority. I merely report to you the means which I adopted to form my own opinion, in order that you, in turn, may employ them yourself if you find them good. I must warn you only that this experiment requires more precautions than one would think. The first and most difficult of all is that one must maintain good faith and be equally fair in choosing and in judging. The second is that, in order to attempt this examination, one must necessarily be equally acquainted with both styles; otherwise the one which happened to be the more familiar would constantly present itself to the prejudice of the other. And this second condition is hardly easier than the first, for of all those who are well acquainted with both kinds of music, no one hesitates in his choice, and one can tell from the absurdly confused arguments of those who have undertaken to attack Italian music, how much they know of it and of the art in general.

I must add that it is essential to proceed in exact time, but I foresee that this warning, superfluous in any other country, will be quite useless in France, and this sole omission necessarily involves incompetence in judgment.

With all these precautions taken, the character of each kind of music is not slow in declaring itself, and then it is quite hard not to clothe the phrases with

---

7. The *port-de-voix* is a specifically French *agrément*, an upward resolving appoggiatura executed by means of a mordent. *Cadence* is the French word for trill. See musical illustrations in Rousseau's *Dictionnaire de musique* (Paris, 1768), Plate B, Figure 13.

8. This procedure gives all the advantages to the French music, for the implied notes in Italian music are no less of the essence of the melody than those which are written out. It is less a question of what is written than of what should be sung, and this manner of writing notes ought simply to pass as a sort of abbreviation; whereas the cadences and ports-de-voix of French music are indeed, if you will, demanded by the style, but are not essential to the melody; they are a kind of make-up which covers its ugliness without removing it and which only makes it the more ridiculous to sensitive ears. [Au.]

the ideas which are suited to them and not to add to them, at least mentally, the turns and ornaments which one is able to refuse them in singing; nor must one rest the matter on a single trial, for one air may give more pleasure than another without determining which kind of music has the preference, and a rational judgment can be formed only after a great number of trials. Besides, by foregoing a knowledge of the words, one remains ignorant of the most important element in the melody, namely the expression, and all that can be determined in this way is whether the modulation is good and whether the tune is natural and beautiful. All this shows us how hard it is to take enough precautions against prejudice and what great need we have of reasoning to put us in a condition to form a sane judgment in matters of taste.

I made another experiment which requires fewer precautions and which may perhaps seem more decisive. I gave to Italians the most beautiful airs of Lully to sing, and to French musicians some airs of Leo and of Pergolesi,[9] and I observed that while the French singers were very far from apprehending the true taste of these pieces, they were still sensible of their melody and drew from them in their own fashion melodious, agreeable, and well-cadenced musical phrases. But the Italians, while they sol-fa'd our most pathetic airs with the greatest exactness, could never recognize in them either the phrasing or the time; for them it was not a kind of music which made sense, but only a series of notes set down without choice and as it were at random; they sang them precisely as you would read Arabic words written in French characters.[10]

Third experiment. I saw at Venice and an Armenian, a man of intelligence, who had never heard any music, and in whose presence were performed, in the same concert, a French monologue which began with these words:

Temple sacré, séjour tranquille,[11]

and an air of Galuppi, which began with these:

Voi che languite
Senza speranza.[12]

9. Jean-Baptiste Lully (1632–1687) was the creator of the essential form of French opera, the *tragédie lyrique*. Born in Florence as Giovanni Battista Lulli (a form of his name he consistently avoided), he left Italy at the age of eleven to become a servant in a noble French household. Leonardo Leo (1694–1744) was an opera composer of the Neapolitan school and the teacher of Jommelli, who is mentioned below. Giovanni Battista Pergolesi (1710–1736) is best known for his setting of the *Stabat mater* and the comic intermezzo *La serva padrona* (1733), which became the rallying point for the Italian faction in the "Querelle des bouffons" after it was performed in 1752 by an Italian troupe on the stage of the Paris Opéra.
10. Our musicians profess to derive a great advantage from this difference. "We can perform Italian music," they say, with their customary pride, "and the Italians cannot perform ours; therefore our music is better than theirs." They fail to see that they ought to draw a quite contrary conclusion and say, "therefore the Italians have melody and we have none."[Au.]
11. From Jean Philippe Rameau's *Hippolyte et Aricis* (text by Simon Joseph Pelegrin) performed in 1733: Act I, Scene I (*Oeuvres completes*, vol. 6, p. 53).
12. A pasticcio of the opera *Arsace* performed in Venice in 1743 contains an aria set to this text by Baldassare Galuppi.

Both were sung, the French piece indifferently and the Italian badly, by a man familiar only with French music and at that time a great enthusiast for that of M. Rameau. I observed that during the French song the Armenian showed more surprise than pleasure, but everybody observed that from the first bars of the Italian air his face and his eyes grew soft; he was enchanted; he surrendered his soul to the impressions of the music; and though he understood little of the language, the mere sounds visibly enraptured him. From that moment he could not be induced to listen to any French air.

But without seeking examples elsewhere, have we not even among us many persons who, knowing no opera but our own, believe in good faith that they have no taste for singing and are disabused only by the Italian intermezzi? It is precisely because they like only the true music that they think they do not like music.

I allow that the great number of its faults has made me doubt the existence of our melody and has made me suspect that it might well be only a sort of modulated plainsong which has nothing agreeable in itself and which pleases only with the aid of certain arbitrary ornaments, and then only such persons as have agreed to consider them beautiful. Thus our music is hardly endurable to our own ears when it is performed by mediocre voices lacking the art to make it effective. It takes a Fel or a Jélyotte[13] to sing French music, but any voice is good in Italian music, because the beauties of Italian singing are in the music itself, whereas those of French singing, if there are any, are all in the art of the singer.[14]

Three things seem to me to unite in contributing to the perfection of Italian melody. The first is the softness of the language, which makes all the inflections easy and leaves the taste of the musician free to make a more exquisite choice among them, to give a greater variety to his combinations, and to provide each singer with a particular style of singing, so that each man has the character and tone which are proper to him and distinguish him from other men.

The second is the boldness of the modulations, which, although less servilely prepared than our own, are much more pleasing from being made more perceptible, and without imparting any harshness to the song, add a lively energy

13. Marie Fel (1713–1794) and Pierre Jélyotte (1713–1797), the two leading singers of the French lyric stage, are best known for their performances in traditional French opera. Although they sang in Rousseau's *Le Devin du village*, they avoided taking sides in the aesthetic battle of the time.

14. Besides, it is a mistake to believe that the Italian singers generally have less voice than the French. On the contrary they must have a stronger and more harmonious resonance to make themselves heard in the immense theaters of Italy without ceasing to keep the sound under the control which Italian music requires. French singing demands all the power of the lungs, the whole extent of the voice. "Louder," say our singing masters; "more volume; open your mouth; use all your voice." "Softer," say the Italian masters; "don't force it; sing at your ease; make your notes soft, flexible, and flowing; save the outbursts for those rare, brief moments when you must astonish and overwhelm." Now it seems to me that when it is necessary to make oneself heard, the man who can do so without screaming must have the stronger voice. [Au.]

to the expression. It is by this means that the musician, passing abruptly from one key or mode to another, and suppressing, when necessary, the intermediate and pedantic transitions, is able to express the reticences, the interruptions, the falterings, which are the language of impetuous passion so often employed by the ardent Metastasio, which a Porpora, a Galuppi, a Cocchi, a Jommelli, a Perez, a Terradellas have so often successfully reproduced,[15] and of which our lyric poets know as little as do our musicians.

The third advantage, the one which gives to melody its greatest effect, is the extreme exactness of time which is felt in the slowest as well as in the liveliest movements, an exactness which makes the singing animated and interesting, the accompaniments lively and rhythmical; which really multiplies the tunes by making as many different melodies out of a single combination of sounds as there are ways of scanning them; which conveys every sentiment to the heart and every picture to the mind; which enables the musician to express in his air all the imaginable characters of words, many of which we have no idea of;[16] and which renders all the movements proper to express all the characters,[17] or at the will of the composer renders a single movement proper to contrast and change the character.

These, in my opinion, are the sources from which Italian music derives its charms and its energy, to which may be added a new and strong proof of the advantage of its melody, in that it does not require so often as ours those frequent inversions of harmony which give to the thoroughbass a melody worthy of a soprano. Those who find such great beauties in French melody might very well tell us to which of these things it owes them or show us the advantages it has to take their place.

On first acquaintance with Italian melody, one finds in it only graces and believes it suited only to express agreeable sentiments, but with the least study of its pathetic and tragic character, one is soon surprised by the force imparted to it by the art of the composer in their great pieces of music. It is by the aid of these scientific modulations, of this simple and pure harmony, of these lively and brilliant accompaniments that their divine performances harrow or enrap-

15. With the exception of the *buffa* composer Galuppi, this list names the more prominent opera composers associated with the Neapolitan school. Galuppi was performed by the Italian troupe, but few of the works of the others appeared on the Paris stage, their operas gaining standing by performances of isolated arias and by the accounts of those who had heard them elsewhere.
16. Not to depart from the comic style, the only one known to Paris, consider the airs, "Quando sciolto avrò il contratto," "Io ho un vespaio," "O questo o quello t'hai a risolvere," "Ha un gusto da stordire," "Stizzoso mio, stizzoso," "Io sono una donzella," "Quanti maestri, quanti dottori," "I sbirri già lo aspettano," "Ma dunque il testamento," "Senti me, se brami stare, o che risa! che piacere!" all characters of airs of which French music has not the first elements and of which it is incapable of expressing a single word. [Au.]
17. I shall content myself with citing a single example, but a very striking one: the air, "Se pur d'un infelice," in *The Intriguing Chambermaid* [*La Finta cameriera*], a very pathetic air with a very lively movement, which lacks only a voice to sing it, an orchestra to accompany it, ears to hear it, and the second part, which should not be suppressed. [Au.]

ture the soul, carry away the spectator, and force from him, in his transports, the cries with which our placid operas were never honored.

How does the musician succeed in producing these grand effects? Is it by contrasting the movements, by multiplying the harmonies, the notes, the parts? Is it by heaping design upon design, instrument upon instrument? Any such jumble, which is only a bad substitute where genius is lacking, would stifle the music instead of enlivening it and would destroy the interest by dividing the attention. Whatever harmony several parts, each perfectly melodious, may be capable of producing together, the effect of these beautiful melodies disappears as soon as they are heard simultaneously, and there is heard only a chord succession, which one may say is always lifeless when not animated by melody; so that the more one heaps up inappropriate melodies, the less the music is pleasing and melodious, because it is impossible for the ear to follow several melodies at once, and as one effaces the impression of another, the sum total is only noise and confusion. For a piece of music to become interesting, for it to convey to the soul the sentiments which it is intended to arouse, all the parts must concur in reinforcing the impression of the subject: the harmony must serve only to make it more energetic; the accompaniment must embellish it without covering it up or disfiguring it; the bass, by a uniform and simple progression, must somehow guide the singer and the listener without either's perceiving it; in a word, the entire ensemble must at one time convey only one melody to the ear and only one idea to the mind.

This unity of melody seems to me to be an indispensable rule, no less important in music than the unity of action in tragedy, for it is based on the same principle and directed toward the same object. Thus all the good Italian composers conform to it with a care which sometimes degenerates into affectation, and with the least reflection one soon perceives that from it their music derives its principal effect. It is in this great rule that one must seek the cause of the frequent accompaniments in unison which are observed in Italian music and which, reinforcing the idea of the melody, at the same time render its notes more soft and mellow and less tiring for the voice. These unisons are not practicable in our music, unless it be in some types of airs chosen for the purpose and adapted to it. A pathetic French air would never be tolerable if accompanied in this manner, because, as vocal and instrumental music with us have different characters, we cannot employ in the one the same devices which suit the other without offending against the melody and the style; leaving out of account that as the time is always vague and undetermined, especially in slow airs, the instruments and the voice would never be in agreement and would not keep step well enough to produce a pleasing effect together. A further beauty resulting from these unisons is to give a more sensible expression to the vocal melody, now by letting it unexpectedly reinforce the instruments in a passage, now by letting it make them more tender, now by letting it give them some striking, energetic phrase of the melody of which it is itself incapable, but for which the listener, skillfully deceived, never fails to give it credit when the orchestra knows how to bring it to the fore at the right moment. From this arises also that perfect correspondence between the ritornelli and the melody, as the result of which all the strokes which we admire in the one are only the development of the other, so that the source of all the beauties of the accompaniment is always to be sought in the vocal part; this accompaniment is so wholly of a piece with the singing and corresponds so exactly to the words that it often seems to determine the action and to dictate to the actor the gesture which he is to make,[18] and an actor who would be incapable of playing the part with the words alone might play it very correctly with the music, because the music performs so well its function of interpreter.

Besides this, the Italian accompaniments are very far from always being in unison with the voice. There are two very frequent cases in which the music separates them. One is when the voice, lightly singing a passage over a series of harmonies, so holds the attention that the accompaniment cannot share it; yet even then this accompaniment is made so simple that the ear, affected only by agreeable harmonies, does not perceive in them any harmony which could distract it.

The other case demands a little more effort to be comprehended. "When the musician understands his art," says the author of the *Letter on the Deaf and Dumb*,[19] "the parts of the accompaniment concur either in reinforcing the expression of the vocal part, or in adding new ideas demanded by the subject and beyond the capacity of the vocal part to express." This passage seems to me to contain a very useful precept, and this is how I think it should be understood.

If the vocal part is of such a nature as to require some additions, or as our old musicians used to say, some divisions, which add to the expression or to the agreeableness without thereby destroying the unity of the melody, so that the ear, which would perhaps blame them if made by the voice, approves of them in the accompaniment and allows itself to be gently affected without being made less attentive to the vocal part, then the skillful musician, by managing them properly and disposing them with taste, will embellish his subject and give it more expression without impairing its unity; and although the accompaniment will not be exactly like the vocal part, the two will nevertheless constitute only a single air and a single melody. For if the sense of the words connotes some accessory idea, the musician will superimpose this during the pauses of the voice or while it sustains some note, and will thus be able to present it to the hearer without distracting him from the idea expressed by the voice. The

18. Numerous examples may be found in the intermezzi which have been performed for us this year, among others in the air "Ha un gusto di stordire" in The Music Master [*Il Maestro di musica*]; in that of "Son padrone" in *The Vain Woman* [*La Donna superba*]; in that of "Vi stò ben" in [*Livietta e*] *Tracollo*; in that of "Tu non pensi" in *The Bohemian* [*La Zingara*]; and in nearly all of those which require acting. [Au.]
19. Denis Diderot's *Lettre sur les sourds et muets* (Paris, 1751), an essay that takes as a central theme the relation between language and gesture. Its assertion that the French language in its logical clarity is unsuited to poetry gave additional support to Rousseau's position.

advantage will be still greater if this accessory idea can be expressed by a restrained and continuous accompaniment, producing a slight murmur rather than a real melody, like the sound of a river or the twittering of birds, for then the composer can completely separate the vocal part from the accompaniment, and assigning to the latter only the expression of the accessory idea, he will dispose his vocal part in such a way as to give frequent openings to the orchestra, taking care to insure that the instrumental part is always dominated by the vocal, a matter depending more upon the art of the composer than on the execution of the instruments; but this demands a consummate experience, in order to avoid a double melody.

This is all that the rule of unity can concede to the taste of the musician in order to ornament the singing or to make it more expressive, whether by embellishing the principal subject or by adding to this another which remains subordinate. But to make the violins play by themselves on one side, the flutes on another, the bassoons on a third, each with a special motive and almost without any mutual relation, and to call all this chaos music is to insult alike the ear and the judgment of the hearers.[20]

•   •   •   •   •

If I may be allowed to state my frank opinion, I find that the further our music advances toward apparent perfection, the more it is actually deteriorating.

It was perhaps necessary that it should reach its present state, in order that our ears might insensibly become accustomed to reject the prejudices of habit and to enjoy airs other than those with which our nurses sang us to sleep; but I foresee that to bring it to the very mediocre degree of merit of which it is capable, we shall sooner or later have to begin by once more descending (or reascending) to the state to which Lully brought it. Let us agree that the harmony of that famous musician is purer and less inverted; that his basses are more natural and proceed more directly; that his melody is more flowing; that his accompaniments, less burdened, spring more truly from the subject and depart from it less; that his recitative is much less mannered than ours, and consequently much better. This is confirmed by the style of the execution, for the old recitative was sung by the actors of that time in a way wholly different from that of today. It was livelier and less dragging; it was sung less and declaimed more.[21] In our recitative the *cadences* and *ports-de-voix* have been multiplied; it has become still more languid and has hardly anything left to distinguish it from what we call "air."

20. Omitted here is a section in which Rousseau praises Italian accompaniments for the sparseness of their harmonic doublings; in comparison, French accompaniments, as he states at the end of the *Lettre*, suggest the "padding of a pupil."
21. This is proved by the time of the representation of Lully's operas, much longer now than in his day by the unanimous report of those who have seen them long ago. Thus, whenever these operas are revived, they call for considerable cutting. [Au.]

Now that airs and recitatives have been mentioned, you will permit me, sir, to conclude this letter with some observations on the one and the other which will perhaps throw some helpful light on the solution of the problem involved.

One may judge of the idea our musicians have of the nature of an opera by the singularity of their nomenclature. Those grand pieces of Italian music which ravish the soul, those masterpieces of genius which draw tears, which offer the most striking pictures, which paint the liveliest situations and fill the soul with all the passions they express, the French call "ariettes." They give the name of "airs" to those insipid little ditties which they interpolate in the scenes of their operas, and reserve that of "monologues" particularly to those long-drawn-out and tedious lamentations which if only sung in tune and without screams would put everybody to sleep.

In the Italian opera all the airs grow out of the situation and form a part of the scene. Now a despairing father imagines he sees the ghost of a son whom he has unjustly put to death upbraid him with his cruelty; now an easygoing prince, compelled to give an example of severity, entreats the gods to deprive him of his rule or to give him a less susceptible heart. Here a tender mother weeps to recover her son whom she thought dead; there we hear the language of love, not filled with that insipid rigmarole of "flames" and "chains,"[22] but tragic, animated, ardent, and faltering, and befitting impetuous passion. Upon such words it is appropriate to lavish all the wealth of a music full of force and expression and to enhance the energy of the poetry by that of harmony and melody.

The words of our ariettes, on the contrary, always detached from the subject, are only a wretched medley of honeyed phrases which one is only too glad not to understand. They are a random assemblage of the small number of sonorous words that our language can furnish, turned and twisted in every manner except the one that might give them some meaning. It is upon such impertinent nonsense that our musicians exhaust their taste and knowledge and our actors waste their gestures and lungs; it is over these extravagant pieces that our women go into ecstasies of admiration. And the most striking proof that French music is incapable of either description or expression is that it cannot display the few beauties at its command except upon words which have no meaning.

Meanwhile, to hear the French talk of music, one would imagine that in their operas it depicts great scenes and great passions, and that only ariettes are found in Italian operas, to which the very word "ariette" and the ridiculous thing it signifies are equally unknown. We must not be surprised by the grossness of these prejudices: Italian music has no enemies, even among ourselves, but those who know nothing about it, and all Frenchmen who have tried to

22. The special attention given to the musical setting of such words in the *tragédie-lyrique* grew out of classical French declamation. Compare Diderot, who has the same complaint (see pp. 190–93, 196–98).

study it with the sole aim of criticizing it understandingly have soon become its most zealous admirers.[23]

After the "ariettes," which constitute the triumph of modern taste in Paris, come the famous monologues which are admired in our old operas. In this connection it is to be noted that our most beautiful airs are always in the monologues and never in the scenes, for, as our actors have no art of pantomime and the music does not indicate any gesture or depict any situation, the one who remains silent has no notion what to do with himself while the other is singing.

The drawling nature of our language, the little flexibility of our voices, and the doleful tone which perpetually reigns in our opera, give a slow tempo to nearly all our French monologues, and as the time or beat is not made perceptible either in the melody or in the bass or in the accompaniment, nothing drags so much or is so relaxed, so languid, as these beautiful monologues, which everybody admires while he yawns; they aim to be sad and are only tiresome; they aim to touch the heart and only distress the ear.

The Italians are more adroit in their Adagios, for when the time is so slow that there is any danger of weakening the sense of the rhythm, they make their bass proceed by notes of equal value which mark the movement, while the accompaniment also marks it by subdivisions of the beats, which, keeping the voice and the ear in time, make the melody more pleasing and above all more energetic by this exactness. But the nature of French music forbids our composers this resource, for if the actor were compelled to keep time, he would immediately be prevented from displaying his voice and his action, from dwelling on his notes, from swelling and prolonging them, and from screaming at the top of his lungs, and in consequence he would no longer be applauded.

But what still more effectively prevents monotony and boredom in the Italian tragedies is the advantage of being able to express all the passions and depict all the characters in whatever measure and time the composer pleases. Our melody, which in itself expresses nothing, derives all its expression from the tempo one gives to it. It is of necessity sad in a slow tempo, furious or gay in a lively one, serious in a moderate one; the melody itself counts for almost nothing in this; the tempo alone, or, to put it more accurately, the degree of rapidity alone determines the character. But Italian melody finds in every tempo expressions for all characters, pictures for all objects. When the musician so chooses, it is sad in a slow tempo, and, as I have already said, it changes character in the same movement at the pleasure of the composer. Contrasts are thereby made easy, without depending for this on the poet and without the risk of conflicts with the sense.

Here is the source of that prodigious variety which the great masters of Italy were able to display in their operas without ever departing from nature, a

23. A presupposition little favorable to French music appears in this: those who despise it most are precisely those who know it best, for it is as ridiculous when examined as it is intolerable when heard. [Au.]

variety which prevents monotony, languor, and ennui, and which French musicians cannot imitate because their tempi are prescribed by the sense of the words and they are forced to adhere to them unless they are willing to fall into ridiculous inconsistencies.

With regard to the recitative, of which it remains for me to speak, it seems to me that to judge it properly we must begin by knowing exactly what it is, for of all those who have discussed it I am so far unaware of any one who has thought of defining it. I do not know, sir, what idea you may have of that word; as for myself, I call recitative a harmonious declamation, that is, a declamation of which all the inflections are formed by harmonious intervals. It therefore follows that as each language has its own peculiar declamation, each language ought also to have its own peculiar recitative. This does not preclude one from very properly comparing one recitative with another to discover which of the two is the better, that is, the better adapted to its purpose.

Recitative is necessary in lyric drama, first, to connect the action and preserve the unity; second, to set off the airs, of which a continuous succession would be insupportable; third, to express a number of things which cannot be expressed by lyric, cadenced music. Mere declamation cannot be suitable for all that in a lyric work, because the transition from speech to song and especially that from song to speech has an abruptness which the ear does not readily accept, and presents a shocking contrast which destroys all the illusion and in consequence the interest.[24] For there is a kind of probability which must be preserved even at the Opéra, by making the language so homogeneous that the whole may at least be taken for a hypothetical language. Add to this that the aid of the harmonies augments the energy of musical declamation and compensates advantageously for what is less natural in its intonations.

It is evident, according to these notions, that the best recitative, in any language whatever, if this language fulfills the necessary conditions, is that which comes the nearest to speaking; if there were one which came so near to it as to deceive the ear or the mind while still preserving the required harmony, one might boldly pronounce that it had attained to the highest perfection of which any recitative is capable.

Let us now examine by this rule what in France is called "recitative." I pray you, tell me what relation you find between that recitative and our declamation. How can you ever conceive that the French language, of which the accent is so uniform, so simple, so modest, so unlike that of song, can be properly rendered by the shrill and noisy intonations of that recitative, and that there should be any relation whatever between the soft inflection of speech and these prolonged and exaggerated sounds, or rather these perpetual shrieks which form the tissue of that part of our music even more than that of the airs? For instance, let anyone who knows how to read recite the first four lines of the

24. Rousseau refers to the Opéra-Comique, which was then giving performances of mixed song and declamation (comédies mêlées d'ariettes) at the fairs of St. Germain and St. Laurent.

famous recognition scene of Iphigénie; you will barely detect a few slight ine-
qualities, a few feeble inflections of the voice, in a tranquil recital which has
nothing lively or impassioned, nothing which compels the speaker to raise or
lower the voice. Then have one of our actresses deliver the same lines as set to
music by the composer, and try, if you can, to endure that extravagant shrieking
which shifts at each moment from low to high and from high to low, traverses
without a subject the whole vocal register, and interrupts the recital in the
wrong place to string some beautiful notes upon syllables without meaning,
which correspond to no pause in the sense. Add to this the *fredons*,[25] *cadences*,
and *ports-de-voix* which recur at every moment, and tell me what analogy there
can be between speech and this pretended recitative, or at least show me some
ground on which one may find reason to vaunt this wonderful French recitative
whose invention is Lully's title to glory.

It is very amusing to see the partisans of French music take refuge in the
character of the language and attribute to it the faults of which they do not
dare to accuse their idol, whereas it is evident on all grounds that the recitative
most suitable to the French language must be almost the opposite of that which
is in use; that it must range within very small intervals, without much raising
or lowering of the voice; with few prolonged notes, no sudden outbursts, still
fewer shrieks; especially, nothing which resembles melody; little inequality in
the duration or value of the notes or in their intensity either. In a word, the
true French recitative, if one is possible, will be found only by a path directly
opposite to that taken by Lully and his successors, by some new path which
assuredly the French composers, so proud of their false learning and consequently so far from feeling and loving what is true, will not soon be willing to
seek and which they will probably never find.

Here would be the place to show you, by the example of Italian recitative,
that all the conditions which I have postulated in a good recitative can actually
be found there; that it can have at the same time all the vivacity and all the
energy of harmony; that it can proceed as rapidly as speech and be as melodious as veritable song; that it can indicate all the inflections with which the most
vehement passions animate discourse, without straining the voice of the singer
or deafening the ears of the listeners. I could show you how, with the aid of a
particular basic progression, one may multiply the modulations of the recitative
in a way suitable to it and which contributes to distinguishing it from the airs
when, in order to preserve the graces of the melody, the key must be less
frequently changed; how, especially, when one wishes to give passion the time
to display all its movements, it is possible, by means of a skillfully managed
interlude, to make the orchestra express by varied and pathetic phrases what
the actor can only relate—a master stroke of the musician's art, by which, in an
accompanied recitative,[26] he may combine the most affecting melody with all

25. Literally a short roulade, here implying excessive ornamentation.
26. I had hoped that Signor Caffarelli would give us, in the concert of sacred music, some example
   of grand recitative and of pathetic melody, in order to let the pretended connoisseurs hear for

the vehemence of declamation without ever confusing the one with the other. I could unfold to you all the numberless beauties of that admirable recitative of which in France so many absurd tales are told, as absurd as the judgments which people presume to pass on them, as if one could judge of a recitative without a thorough knowledge of the language to which it belongs. But to enter into these details it would be necessary, so to speak, to create a new dictionary, to coin terms every moment in order to present to French readers ideas unknown among them, and to address them in language which would seem meaningless to them. In a word, one would be obliged, in order to make oneself clear, to speak a language they understood, and consequently to speak of any science or art whatever except music alone. Therefore I shall not go into this subject with an affected detail which would do nothing to instruct my readers and concerning which they might presume that I owed the apparent force of my arguments only to their ignorance in this matter.

•   •   •   •   •

I think that I have shown that there is neither measure nor melody in French music, because the language is not capable of them; that French singing is a continual squalling, insupportable to an unprejudiced ear; that its harmony is crude and devoid of expression and suggests only the padding of a pupil; that French "airs" are not airs; that French recitative is not recitative. From this I conclude that the French have no music and cannot have any;[27] or that if they ever have, it will be so much the worse for them.

I am, etc.

---

once what they have so long been passing judgment on, but I found, from his reasons for doing nothing of the kind, that he knew better than I the capacity of his hearers. [Au.]

Gaetano Majorano, called Caffarelli after his earliest protector (1703–1783), one of the leading Italian castrati. Louis XV engaged him to entertain the Dauphine, according to the *Mémoires du duc de Luynes* (vol. 12, p. 471 and vol. 13, p. 10), and while in Paris he was also heard at the Concert Spirituel on November 5, 1753—an event Rousseau presumably attended.

27. I do not call it having a music to import that of another language and try to apply it to one's own, and I had rather we kept our wretched and absurd singing than that we should still more absurdly unite Italian melody with the French language. This distasteful combination, which will perhaps from now on constitute the study of our musicians, is too monstrous to be accepted, and the character of our language will never lend itself to it. At most, some comic pieces will succeed in passing by reason of their orchestral part, but I boldly predict that the tragic style will never be attempted. At the Opéra-Comique this winter the public applauded the work of a man of talent who seems to have listened with good ears, and who has translated the style into French as closely as is possible; his accompaniments are well imitated without being copied; and if he has written no melody, it is because it is impossible to write any. Young musicians who feel that you have talent, continue in public to despise Italian music; I am well aware that your present interest requires it; but in private make haste to study that language and that music if you wish to be able some day to turn against your comrades the disdain which today you affect for your masters. [Au.]

13 Francesco Algarotti

Born at Venice in 1712 and educated in Rome and Bologna, Francesco Algarotti was a cosmopolitan savant who was welcomed into educated circles in London and Paris, where he lived for a time with Voltaire. In 1740 he went to Berlin at the invitation of Frederick the Great, and remained there for nine years in close touch with the King, assisting him in the translation of opera librettos. He returned to Italy in 1753 because of ill health, and died in Pisa in 1764.

Algarotti's *Saggio sopra l'opera in musica* (*An Essay on the Opera*, 1755) became the principal text of reform opera. Comparing the singer-driven opera of Italy to the better integrated operatic productions he had seen in the north, he advocated subsuming all elements of the spectacle under a unifying poetic idea, calling for a return to the austerities of Greek tragedy. In the service of this neoclassical program, he argued the appropriateness of subjects like the story of Iphigenia or of Virgil's Dido. His influence can be seen clearly in later reform documents such as Gluck's Preface to *Alceste*.

FROM *An Essay on the Opera*
(1755)

CHAPTER I. OF THE POEM, ARGUMENT, OR BUSINESS OF AN OPERA

As soon as the desired regulation shall have been introduced on the theatre it will then be incumbent to proceed to the various constituent parts of an opera in order that those amendments should be made in each whereof they severally now appear the most deficient. The leading object to be maturely considered is the nature of the subject to be chosen, an article of much more consequence than is commonly imagined; for the success or failure of the drama depends, in a great measure, on a good or bad choice of the subject. It is here of no less consequence than, in architecture, the plan is to an edifice, or the canvas, in painting, is to a picture; because thereon the poet draws the outlines of his intended representation, and its coloring is the task of the musical composer. It is therefore the poet's duty, as chief engineer of the undertaking, to give directions to the dancers, the machinists, the painters; nay, down even to those who are entrusted with the care of the wardrobe and dressing the performers. The poet is to carry in his mind a comprehensive view of the *whole* of the drama; because those parts which are not the productions of his pen ought to flow from the dictates of his actuating judgment, which is to give being and movement to the whole.

TEXT: The original edition of the anonymous English translation of 1767, pp. 10–49.

At the first institution of operas, the poets imagined the heathen mythology to be the best source from which they could derive subjects for their dramas. Hence Daphne, Eurydice, Ariadne, were made choice of by Ottavio Rinuccini and are looked upon as the eldest musical dramas, having been exhibited about the beginning of the last century. There was, besides, Poliziano's *Orpheus*,[1] which also had been represented with instrumental accompaniments, as well as another performance that was no more than a medley of dancing and music, contrived by Bergonzo Botta for the entertainment of a Duke of Milan in the city of Tortona.[2] A particular species of drama was exhibited at Venice for the amusement of Henry the Third; it had been set to music by the famous Zarlino.[3] Add to these some other performances, which ought only to be considered as so many rough sketches and preludes to a complete opera.

The intent of our poets was to revive the Greek tragedy in all its lustre and to introduce Melpomene on our stage, attended by music, dancing, and all that imperial pomp with which, at the brilliant period of a Sophocles and Euripides, she was wont to be escorted. And that such splendid pageantry might appear to be the genuine right of tragedy, the poets had recourse for their subjects to the heroic ages and heathen mythology. From that fountain, the bard, according to his inventive pleasure, introduced on the theatre all the deities of paganism; now shifting his scene to Olympus, now fixing it in the Elysian shades, now plunging it down to Tartarus, with as much ease as if to Argos or to Thebes. And thus, by the intervention of superior beings, he gave an air of probability to most surprising and wonderful events. Every circumstance being thus elevated above the sphere of mortal existence, it necessarily followed that the singing of actors in an opera appeared a true imitation of the language made use of by the deities they represented.

This then was the original cause why, in the first dramas that had been exhibited in the courts of sovereigns or the palaces of princes in order to celebrate their nuptials, such expensive machinery was employed; not an article was omitted that could excite an idea of what is most wonderful to be seen either on earth or in the heavens. To superadd a greater diversity and thereby give a new animation to the whole, crowded choruses of singers were admitted, as well as dances of various contrivance, with a special attention that the execution of the ballet should coincide and be combined with the choral song; all which pleasing effects were made to spring naturally from the subject of the drama.

No doubt then can remain of the exquisite delight that such magic representations must have given to an enraptured assembly; for although it consisted but of a single subject, it nevertheless displayed an almost infinite variety of entertainment. There is even now frequent opportunity of seeing, on the

1. Performed at Mantua, probably in the Carnival season of 1480.
2. The medley referred to was a festal play with music to celebrate the wedding of Gian Galeazzo Sforza and Isabella of Aragon. The performance of this unnamed work took place in 1488.
3. A reference to Cornelio Frangipane's *Tragedia* of 1574, the music not by Zarlino but by Claudio Merulo.

French musical theatre, a spirited likeness to what is here advanced; because the opera was first introduced in Paris by Cardinal Mazarin, whither it carried the same magnificent apparatus with which it had made its appearance at his time in Italy.

These representations must, however, have afterwards suffered not a little by the intermixture of buffoon characters, which are such ill-suited companions of the dignity of heroes and of gods; for by making the spectators laugh out of season, they disconcert the solemnity of the piece. Some traces of this theatric impropriety are even now observable in the eldest of the French musical dramas.[4]

The opera did not long remain confined in the courts of sovereigns and palaces of princes, but, emancipating itself from such thralldom, displayed its charms on public theatres, to which the curious of all ranks were admitted for pay. But in this situation, as must obviously occur to whoever reflects, it was impossible that the pomp and splendor which was attendant on this entertainment from its origin could be continued. The falling off, in that article, was occasioned principally by the exorbitant salaries the singers insisted on, which had been but inconsiderable at the first outset of the musical drama; as for instance, a certain female singer was called *La Centoventi*, "The Hundred-and-Twenty,"[5] for having received so many crowns for her performance during a single carnival, a sum which hath been amazingly exceeded since, almost beyond all bounds.

Hence arose the necessity for opera directors to change their measures and to be as frugally economical on the one hand as they found themselves unavoidably profuse on the other. Through such saving, the opera may be said to have fallen from heaven upon the earth and, being divorced from an intercourse with gods, to have humbly resigned itself to that of mortals.

Thenceforward prevailed a general renunciation of all subjects to be found in the fabulous accounts of the heathen deities, and none were made choice of but those derived from the histories of humble mankind, because less magnificent in their nature, and therefore less liable to large disbursements for their exhibition.

The directors, obliged to circumspection for their own safety, were induced to imagine they might supply the place of all that costly pomp and splendid variety of decoration, to which the dazzled spectators had been accustomed so long, by introducing a chaster regularity into their drama, seconded by the auxiliary charms of a more poetical diction as well as by the concurring powers of a more exquisite musical composition. This project gained ground the faster from the public's observing that one of these arts was entirely employed in modeling itself on our ancient authors, and the other solely intent on enriching itself with new ornaments; which made operas to be looked upon by many as

4. Comic characters appear in the first three operas of Lully (*Cadmus*, 1673; *Alceste*, 1674; *Thésée*, 1675) but not in the later works.
5. This singer has not been further identified.

having nearly reached the pinnacle of perfection. However, that these representations might not appear too naked and uniform, interludes and ballets, to amuse the audience, were introduced between the acts; and thus, by degrees, the opera took that form which is now practised on our theatres.

It is an incontrovertible fact that subjects for an operatical drama, whether taken from pagan mythology or historians, have inevitable inconveniences annexed to them. The fabulous subjects, on account of the great number of machines and magnificent apparatus which they require, often distress the poet into limits too narrow for him to carry on and unravel his plot with propriety; because he is not allowed either sufficient time or space to display the passions of each character, so absolutely necessary to the completing of an opera, which, in the main, is nothing more than a tragic poem recited to musical sounds. And from the inconvenience alluded to here, it has happened that a great number of the French operas, as well as the first of the Italian, are nothing better than entertainments for the eyes, having more the appearance of a masquerade than of a regular dramatic performance; because therein the principal action is whelmed, as it were, under a heap of accessories, and, the poetical part being so flimsy and wretched, it was with just reason called a string of madrigals.

On the other hand, the subjects taken from history are liable to the objection of their not being so well adapted to music, which seems to exclude them from all plea of probability. This impleaded error may be observed every day upon the Italian stage. For who can be brought to think that the trillings of an air flow so justifiably from the mouth of a Julius Caesar or a Cato as from the lips of Venus or Apollo? Moreover, historical subjects do not furnish so striking a variety as those that are fabulous; they are apt to be too austere and monotonous. The stage, in such representations, would forever exhibit an almost solitary scene unless we are willing to number, among the ranks of actors, the mob of attendants that crowd after sovereigns, even into their closets. Besides, it is no easy matter to contrive ballets or interludes suitable to subjects taken from history; because all such entertainments ought to form a kind of social union and become, as it were, constituent parts of the whole. Such, for example, on the French stage, is the "Ballet of the Shepherds," that celebrates the marriage of Medoro with Angelica and makes Orlando acquainted with his accumulated wretchedness.[6] But this is far from being the effect of entertainments obtruded into the Italian operas, in which, although the subject be Roman and the ballet consist of dancers dressed like Roman soldiers, yet so unconnected is it with the business of the drama that the scozzese or furlana might as well be danced. And this is the reason why subjects chosen from history are for the most part necessitated to appear naked or to make use of such alien accoutrements as neither belong, nor are by any means suitable to them.

In order to obviate such inconveniences, the only means left to the poet is to exert all his judgement and taste in choosing the subject of his drama, that thereby he may attain his end, which is to delight the eyes and the ears, to

6. In Jean Baptiste Lully's *Roland* (1685), act 2, scene 5.

rouse up and to affect the hearts of an audience, without the risk of sinning against reason or common sense. Wherefore the most prudent method he can adopt will be to make choice of an event that has happened either in very remote times, or in countries very distant from us and quite estranged from our usages, which may afford various incidents of the marvellous, notwithstanding that the subject, at the same time, be extremely simple and not unknown, two desirable requisites.

The great distance of place where the action is fixed will prevent the recital of it to musical sounds from appearing quite so improbable to us. The marvellousness of the theme will furnish the author with an opportunity of interweaving therewith dances, choruses, and a variety of scenical decorations. The simplicity and notoriety of it will exempt his muse from the perplexing trouble and tedious preparations necessary to make the personages of a drama known, that, suitable to his notification, may be displayed their passions, the main spring and actuating spirit of the stage.

The two operas of *Didone* and *Achille in Sciro*, written by the celebrated Metastasio, come very near to the mark proposed here.[7] The subjects of these dramatic poems are simple and taken from very remote antiquity, but without being too far-fetched. In the midst of their most impassioned scenes, there is an opportunity of introducing splendid banquets, magnificent embassies, embarkations, choruses, battles, conflagrations, &c, so as to give a farther extension to the sovereignty of the musical drama, and make its rightfulness be more ascertained than has been hitherto allowed.

The same doctrine may be advanced in regard to an opera on the subject of Montezuma, as much on account of the greatness, as of the novelty of such an action as that emperor's catastrophe must afford. A display of the Mexican and Spanish customs, seen for the first time together, must form a most beautiful contrast; and the barbaric magnificence of America would receive various heightenings by being opposed in different views to that of Europe.[8]

Several subjects may likewise be taken from Ariosto and Tasso, equally fitting as Montezuma for the opera theatre; for besides these being so universally known, they would furnish not only a fine field for exercising the passions, but also for introducing all the surprising illusions of the magic art.

An opera of Aeneas in Troy, or of Iphigenia in Aulis, would answer the same purpose;[9] and to the great variety for scenes and machinery, still greater height-

---

7. Metastasio's *Didone abbandonata* was first set to music by Domenico Sarro in 1724; the first setting of his *Achille in Sciro* (1736) was by Antonio Caldara.
8. Montezuma has been chosen for the subject of an opera, performed with the greatest magnificence at the Theatre Royal of Berlin. [Au.] Carl Heinrich Graun's *Montezuma*, a setting of G. P. Tagliazucchi's Italian version of a French libretto by Frederick the Great, was first performed on January 6, 1755, in Berlin. Algarotti signed the dedication of his *Saggio* on October 6, 1754. Yet this reference to the subject of Montezuma was surely written with the forthcoming performance in mind; Frederick had written to Algarotti about his plans for the opera as early as October 1753.
9. Algarotti outlines an opera on the first of these subjects at the end of his *Saggio* and after this prints his own libretto on the second.

enings might be derived from the enchanting *poetry* of Virgil and Euripides.

There are many other subjects to the full as applicable to the stage and that may be found equally fraught with marvellous incidents. Let then a poet who is judicious enough make a prudent collection of the subjects truly dramatic that are to be found in tracing the fabulous accounts of the heathen gods, and do the same also in regard to more modern times. Such a proceeding relative to the opera would not be unlike to what is oft-times found necessary in states, which it is impossible to preserve from decay and in the unimpaired enjoyment of their constitutional vigor without making them revert from time to time to their original principles.

CHAPTER II. ON THE MUSICAL COMPOSITION FOR OPERAS

No art now appears to stand so much in need of having the conclusive maxim of the preceding chapter put in practice as that of music; so greatly has it degenerated from its former dignity. For by laying aside every regard to decorum, and by scorning to keep within the bounds prescribed, it has suffered itself to be led far, very far astray in a bewildering pursuit of new-fangled whimsies and capricious conceits. Wherefore it would now be very seasonable to revive the decree made by the Lacedaemonians against that man who, through a distempered passion for novelty, had so sophisticated their music with his crotchety innovations that, from noble and manly, he rendered it effeminate and disgusting.

Mankind in general, it must be owned, are actuated by a love of novelty; and it is as true that, without it, music, like every other art, could not have received the great improvements it has. What we here implead is not a chaste passion for novelty, but a too great fondness for it; because it was that which reduced music to the declining state so much lamented by all true connoisseurs. While arts are in their infancy the love of novelty is no doubt essential, as it is to that they owe their being, and after, by its kindly influence, are improved, matured, and brought to perfection; but that point being once attained, the indulging this passion too far will, from benign and vivifying, become noxious and fatal. The arts have experienced this vicissitude in almost every nation where they have appeared, as, among the Italians, hath music at this time in a more remarkable manner.

On its revival in Italy, though in very barbarous times, this elegant art soon made its power be known throughout Europe; nay more, it was cultivated to such a degree by the tramontane nations that it may without exaggeration be asserted, the Italians themselves were, for a certain period of time, glad to receive instructions from them.

On the return of music to Venice, Rome, Bologna, and Naples, as to its native place, such considerable improvements were made there in the musical art, during the two last centuries, that foreigners, in their turn, repaired thither for instruction; and such would be now the case were they not deterred from so doing by the raging frenzy after novelty that prevails in all the Italian schools. For, as if music were yet unrudimented and in its infancy, the mistaken professors spare no pains to trick out their art with every species of grotesque imagination and fantastical combination which they think can be executed by sounds. The public too, as if they were likewise in a state of childhood, change almost every moment their notions of, and fondness for things, rejecting today with scorn what yesterday was so passionately admired. The taste in singing, which, some years ago, enraptured audiences hung upon with wonder and delight, is now received with a supercilious disapprobation; not because it is sunk in real merit, but for the very groundless reason of its being old and not in frequent use. And thus we see that in compositions instituted for the representation of nature, whose mode is ever one, there is the same desire of changing as in the fluctuating fashions of the dresses we wear.

Another principal reason that can be assigned for the present degeneracy of music is the authority, power, and supreme command usurped in its name; because the composer, in consequence, acts like a despotic sovereign, contracting all the views of pleasing to his department alone. It is almost impossible to persuade him that he ought to be in a subordinate station, that music derives its greatest merit from being no more than an auxiliary, the handmaid to poetry. His chief business then is to predispose the minds of the audience for receiving the impression to be excited by the poet's verse, to infuse such a general tendency in their affections as to make them analogous with those particular ideas which the poet means to inspire. In fine, its genuine office is to communicate a more animating energy to the language of the muses.

That old and just charge, enforced by critics against operatical performances, of making their heroes and heroines die *singing,* can be ascribed to no other cause but the defect of a proper harmony between the words and the music. Were all ridiculous quavering omitted when the serious passions are to speak, and were the musical composition judiciously adapted to them, then it would not appear more improbable that a person should die singing, than reciting, verses.

It is an undeniable fact that, in the earliest ages, the poets were all musical proficients; the vocal part, then, ranked as it should, which was to render the thoughts of the mind and affections of the heart with more forcible, more lively, and more kindling expression. But now that the twin sisters, poetry and music, go no longer hand in hand, it is not at all surprising, if the business of the one is to add coloring to what the other has designated, that the coloring, separately considered, appear beautiful; yet, upon a nice examination of the whole, the contours offend by not being properly rounded and by the absence of a social blending of the parts throughout. Nor can a remedy be applied to so great an evil otherwise but by the modest discretion of a composer who will not think it beneath him to receive from the poet's mouth the purport of his meaning and intention; who will also make himself a competent master of the author's sense before he writes a note of music and will ever afterwards confer with him concerning the music he shall have composed; and, by thus proceeding, keep up such a dependence and friendly intercourse as subsisted between Lully and Quinault, Vinci and Metastasio, which indeed the true regulation of an operatical theatre requires.

Among the errors observable in the present system of music, the most obvious, and that which first strikes the ears at the very opening of an opera, is the hackneyed manner of composing overtures, which are always made to consist of two allegros with one grave and to be as noisy as possible. Thus are they void of variation, and so jog on much alike. Yet what a wide difference ought to be perceived between that, for example, which precedes the death of Dido and that which is prefixed to the nuptials of Demetrius and Cleonice. The main drift of an overture should be to announce, in a certain manner, the business of the drama, and consequently prepare the audience to receive those affecting impressions that are to result from the whole of the performance, so that from hence a leading view and presaging notions of it may be conceived, as is of an oration from the exordium. But our present composers look upon an overture as an article quite detached and absolutely different from the poet's drama. They use it as an opportunity of playing off a tempestuous music to stun the ears of an audience. If some, however, employ it as an exordium, it is of a kindred complection to those of certain writers, who with big and pompous words repeatedly display before us the loftiness of the subject and the lowness of their genius; which preluding would suit any other subject as well and might as judiciously be prefixed for an exordium to one oration as another.[10]

After the overture, the next article that presents itself to our consideration is the recitative; and as it is wont to be the most noisy part of an opera, so is it the least attended to and the most neglected. It seems as if our musical composers were of opinion that the recitative is not of consequence enough to deserve their attention, they deeming it incapable of exciting any great delight. But the ancient masters thought in a quite different manner. There needs no stronger proof than to read what Jacopo Peri, who may be justly called the inventor of the recitative, wrote in his preface to *Euridice*.[11] When he had applied himself to an investigation of that species of musical imitation which would the readiest lend itself to theatric exhibitions, he directed his tasteful researches to discover the manner which had been employed by the ancient Greeks on similar occasions. He carefully observed the Italian words which are capable of intonation or consonance and those which are not. He was very exact in minuting down our several modes of pronunciation, as well as the different accents of grief, of joy, and of all the other affections incident to the human frame, and that in order to make the bass move a timing attendance to them, now with more energy, now with less, according to the nature of each. So

10. Compare the criticism of Johann Joachim Quantz (pp. 70–71 above).
11. See *SR* 4.

nicely scrupulous was he in his course of vocal experiments that he scrutinized intimately the very nature of the Italian language; on which account, in order to be more accurate, he frequently consulted with several gentlemen not less remarkable for the delicacy of their ears, than for their being uncommonly skilled both in the arts of music and poetry.

The final conclusion of his ingenious inquiry was that the groundwork of all such imitation should be an harmony chastely following nature step by step; a something between common speaking and melody; a well-combined system between that kind of performance which the ancients called the *diastematica*,[12] as if held in and suspended, and the other, called the *continuata*.[13] Such were the studies of the musical composers in former times. They proceeded in the improvement of their art with the utmost care and attention; and the effect proved that they did not lose their time in the pursuit of unprofitable subtleties.

The recitative in their time was made to vary with the subject and assume a complection suitable to the spirit of the words. It sometimes moved with a rapidity equal to that of the text and at others with an attendant slowness; but never failed to mark, in a conspicuous manner, those inflections and sallies which the violence of our passions can transfuse into the expression of them. All musical compositions finished in so masterly a manner were heard with delight. Numbers now living must remember how certain passages of simple recitative have affected the minds of an audience to a degree that no modern air is able to produce.

However, the recitative, all disregarded as it may be, has been known to excite emotions in an audience when it was of the *obbligato* kind, as the artists term it, that is, when strictly accompanied with instruments.[14] Perhaps it would not be improper to employ it oftener than is now the custom. What a kindling warmth might be communicated to the recitative if, where a passion exerts itself, it were to be enforced by the united orchestra! By so doing, the heart and mind at once would be stormed, as it were, by all the powers of music. A more evincing instance of such an effect cannot be quoted than the greater part of the last act of *Didone*, set to music by Vinci,[15] which is executed in the taste recommended here; and no doubt but Virgil's self would be pleased to hear a composition so animating and so terrible.

Another good purpose which must be derived from such a practice is that then would not appear to us so enormous the great variety and disproportion

12. Diastematic implies, according to the sense of the ancients, a simple interval, in opposition to a compound one, by them called a system. [Note from translator's glossary.]
13. Continuata, in vocal music, means to continue or hold on a sound with an equal strength or manner, or to continue a movement in an equal degree of time all the way. [Note from translator's glossary.]
14. For Metastasio's views on the subject, see his letter to Johann Adolph Hasse, published by Charles Burney in his *Memoirs of the Life and Writings of the Abate Metastasio* (London, 1796), vol. 1, pp. 315–330.
15. The *Didone abbandonata* of the Neapolitan composer Leonardo Vinci, set to Metastasio's libretto, was first performed in Rome in January, 1726.

now observable in the *andamento* of the recitative and that of the airs; but, on the contrary, a more friendly agreement among the several parts of an opera would be the result. The connoisseurs have often been displeased with those sudden transitions where, from a recitative in the *andantissimo* and gentlest movement, the performers are made to skip off and bound away into *ariettas* of the briskest execution, which is to the full as absurd as if a person, when soberly walking, should all on the sudden set to leaping and capering.

The surest method to bring about a better understanding among the several constituent parts of an opera would be not to crowd so much art into the airs and to curb the instrumental part more than is now the custom. In every period of the opera these two formed the most brilliant parts of it; and, in proportion as the musical composition has been more and more refined, so have they received still greater heightenings. They were naked formerly in comparison of what we see them now and were in as absolute a state of simplicity as they had been at their origin, insomuch that, either in point of melody or accompaniments, they did not rise above recitative.

Old Scarlatti was the first who infused life, movement, and spirit in them. It was he who clothed their nakedness with the splendid attire of noble accompaniments, but they were dealt out by him in a sober and judicious manner. They were by no means intricate or obscure, but open and obvious; highly finished, yet free from all the minuteness of affectation; and that not so much on account of the vastness of the theatres, by means of which many of the minor excellencies in musical performances may be lost, as in regard to the voices, to which alone they should be made subservient.

But unwarrantable changes have happened, since that great master's time down to ours, in which all the bounds of discretion are wantonly overleapt. The airs now are whelmed under and disfigured by crowded ornaments with which unnatural method the rage of novelty labors to embellish them. How tediously prolix are those *ritornelli* that precede them; nay, and are often superfluous! For can anything be more improbable than that, in an air expressive of wrath, an actor should calmly wait with his hand stuck in his sword-belt until the *ritornello* be over to give vent to a passion that is supposed to be boiling in his breast? And after the *ritornello* then comes on the part to be sung, but the multitude of fiddles, etc., that accompany it in general produce no better an effect than to astonish the faculty of hearing and to drown the voice of a singer? Why is there not more use made of the basses, and why not increase the number of bass viols, which are the shades of music? Where is the necessity for so many fiddles, with which our orchestras are now thronged? Fewer would do, for they prove in this case like too many hands on board of a ship which, instead of being assistant, are a great impediment to its navigation. Why are not lutes and harps allowed a place? With their light and piercing notes they would give a sprightliness to the *ripienos*. Why is the *violetta* excluded from our orchestras, since from its institution it was intended to act a middle part between the fiddles and the basses in order that harmony might thence ensue?

But one of the most favorite practices now, and which indeed makes our theatres to resound with peals of applause, is, in an *air*, to form a contest between the voice and a hautboy or between the voice and a trumpet so as to exhibit, as it were, a kind of musical tilting-match with the utmost exertion on either side. But such a skirmishing of voices and instruments is very displeasing to the judicious part of the audience, who, on the contrary, would receive the greatest delight from the airs being accompanied by instruments differently qualified from the present in use, and perhaps even by the organ, as hath been formerly practiced.[16] The consequence then would be that the respective qualities of instruments would be properly adapted to the nature of the words which they are intended to accompany, and that they would aptly glide into those parts where a due expression of the passion should stand most in need of them. Then the accompaniment would be of service to the singer's voice by enforcing the pathetic affections of the song, and would prove not unlike to the numbers of elegant and harmonious prose, which, according to the maxim of a learned sage, ought to be like the beating on an anvil by smiths, at once both musical and skilfully labored.

These faults, however considerable, are not the greatest that have been introduced in the composition of airs; we must go farther back to investigate the first source of this evil, which, in the judgment of the most able professors, is to be found in the misconduct of choosing the subject of an air, because rarely any attention is paid to the *andamento* of the melody being natural and corresponding to the sense of the words it is to convey; besides, the extravagant varieties which it is now made to shift and turn about after cannot be managed to tend to one common center or point of unity. For the chief view of our present musical composers is to court, flatter, and surprise the ears, but not at all either to affect the heart or kindle the imagination of those who hear them; wherefore, to accomplish their favorite end, they frequently bound over all rules. To be prodigal of shining passages, to repeat words without end, and musically to interweave or entangle them as they please are the three principal methods by which they carry on their operations.

The first of these expedients is indeed big with danger when we attend to the good effect that is to be expected from melody, because through its middle situation it possesses more of the *virtù*. Moreover, music delights to make an use of acute notes in her compositions similar to that which painting does with striking lights in her performances.

In regard to brilliant passages, common sense forbids the introduction of them excepting where the words are expressive of passion or movement; otherwise they deserve no milder an appellation than being so many impertinent interruptions of the musical sense.

The repeating of words and these chiming rencounters that are made for the

---

16. In the orchestra of the theatre in the famous villa of Cataio an organ is now to be seen. [Au.] The villa Cataio, near Padua, was erected in 1570 by Pio Enea degli Obizzi, a Paduan nobleman with a strong interest in the theater.

sake of sound merely and are devoid of meaning prove intolerable to a judicious ear. Words are to be treated in no other manner but according as the passion dictates; and, when the sense of an air is finished, the first part of it ought never to be sung over again; which is one of our modern innovations and quite repugnant to the natural process of our speech and passions, that are not accustomed to thus turn about and recoil upon themselves.

Most people who frequent our Italian theatres must have observed that, even when the sense of an air breathes a roused and furious tendency, yet, if the words "father" or "son" be in the text, the composer never fails to slacken his notes, to give them all the softness he can, and to stop in a moment the impetuosity of the tune. Moreover he flatters himself, on such an occasion, that, besides having clothed the words with sentimental sounds suitable to them, he hath also given to them an additional seasoning of variety.

But in our sense he hath entirely spoiled all with such a dissonance of expression that will ever be objected to by all who have the least pretensions to judgment and taste. The duty of a composer is to express the sense, not of this or that particular word, but the comprehensive meaning of all the words in the air. It is also his duty to make variety flow from the several modifications the subject in itself is capable of, and not from adjuncts that adventitiously fasten themselves thereon and are foreign from, preposterous, or repugnant to the poet's intention.

It seems that our composers take the same mistaken pains which some writers do, who, regardless of connection and order in a discourse, bend all their thoughts to collect and string together a number of finely sounding words. But, notwithstanding such words are ever so harmonious, a discourse so written would prove an useless, vain, and contemptible performance. The same may be said of every musical composition which is not calculated either to express some sentiment or awaken the idea of some imagery of the mind.[17] Like what we have compared it to, it must turn out but an useless and a vain production, which, should it be received with a temporary and slight applause, must soon be consigned to perpetual silence and oblivion, notwithstanding all the art that might have been employed in choosing the musical combinations. On the contrary, those airs alone remain forever engraven on the memory of the public that paint images to the mind or express the passions, and are for that reason called the speaking airs because more congenial to nature; which can never be justly imitated but by a beautiful simplicity, which will always bear away the palm from the most labored refinements of art.

Although poetry and music be so near akin to each other, yet they have pursued different views here in Italy. The muse presiding over harmony was

17. "All music that paints nothing is only noise, and, were it not for custom that unnatures everything, it would excite no more pleasure than a sequel of harmonious and finely sounding words without any order or connection."—Preface of the *Encyclopédie*. [Au.] Algarotti's quotation is from the "Discours preliminaire" of Jean le Rond d'Alembert.

too chaste in the last century to give in to those affectations and languishing airs which she is at present so fond of indulging. She then knew the way to the human heart and how to stamp permanent impressions thereon; she possessed the secret of incorporating herself, as it were, with the meaning of the words, and, that the probability might seem the greater, she was to the last degree simple, yet affecting, though at the same time the poetic muse had run away from all semblance of truth to make a parade of hyperbolical, far-fetched, fantastical whimsies. Since that time, by a strange vicissitude, as soon as poetry was made to return into the right path, music ran astray.

Such excellent masters as a Cesti and a Carissimi had the hard fate of composing music for words in the style of the Achillino,[18] men who were equal to the noble task of conveying in musical numbers the sighs and love-breathings of a Petrarch. But now, alas, the elegant, the terse, the graceful poems of Metastasio are degraded into music by wretched composers. It must not, however, be hence concluded that no vestige of true music is to be perceived among us, because, as a proof against such an opinion, and that no small one, may be produced our intermezzi and comic operas, wherein the first of all musical requisites, that of expression, takes the lead more than in any other of our compositions; which is owing perhaps to the impossibility the masters found of indulging their own fancy in a wanton display of all the secrets of their art and the manifold treasures of musical knowledge, from which ostentatious prodigality they were luckily prevented by the very limited abilities of their singers. Wherefore, in their own despite, they found themselves obliged to cultivate simplicity and follow nature. Whatever may have been the cause, this style soon obtained the vogue and triumphed over every other although called plebeian. Why did it succeed? Because it was fraught with truth, that in all arts and sciences must ultimately prevail.

To this kind of performance we owe the extending of our musical fame on the other side of the Alps among the French, who had been at all times our rivals in every polite art. The emulous contention which had so long subsisted between them and us for a pre-eminence in music is universally known. No means could be hit on by our artists to make their execution agreeable to Gallic ears, and the Italian melody was abhorred by them as much as had been, in former times, an Italian regency.

But no sooner was heard upon the theatre of Paris the natural yet elegant style of the *Serva padrona*, rich with airs so expressive and duets so pleasing, than the far greater part of the French became not only proselytes to, but even zealous advocates in behalf of the Italian music. A revolution so sudden was caused by an intermezzo and two comic actors.[19] The like had been attempted in vain in the most elaborate pieces of eminent composers through a long series

18. G. F. Achillini (1466–1538), prolific author of pedantic verse.
19. For the "Querelle des bouffons," see pp. 9–11, 161–74, and 188–98.

of years, although bedizened over with so many brilliant passages, surprising shakes, etc. Nor did the repeated efforts of our most celebrated performers, vocal or instrumental, fare better.

Nevertheless, all the good musical composition modern Italy can boast of is not absolutely confined to the intermezzi and comic operas; for it must be confessed that in some of our late serious pieces there are parts not unworthy of the best masters and the most applauded era of music. Several instances are to be found in the works of Pergolesi and Vinci, whom death too soon snatched from us, as well as in those of Galuppi, Jommelli, "Il Sassone,"[20] that are deserving to be for ever in esteem.

Through the energy of the composition of these masters, music makes an audience feel sometimes from the stage the very same effects that were formerly felt in the chapels under the direction of Palestrina and Rodio.[21] We have likewise proofs of the like powerful influence in the skilful productions of Benedetto Marcello, a man second in merit to none among the ancients and certainly the first among the moderns. Who ever was more animated with a divine flame in conceiving and more judicious in conducting his works than Marcello? In the cantatas of Timotheus and Cassandra and in the celebrated collection of psalms[22] he hath expressed in a wonderful manner not only all the different passions of the heart, but even the most delicate sentiments of the mind. He has, moreover, the art of representing to our fancy things even inanimate. He found out the secret of associating with all the gracefulness and charms of the modern the chaste correctness of ancient music, which in him appears like the attractive graces of a beloved and respected matron.

20. Johann Adolph Hasse.
21. Rocco Rodio, a Neapolitan composer of the sixteenth century and the author of a treatise, *Regole di musica*, published in 1609.
22. Benedetto Marcello's *Timoteo* (1726) has the subtitle *Gli effetti della musica;* the four volumes of his *Estro poetico-armonico*, collected settings of fifty paraphrases from the Psalms, were first published in Venice from 1724 to 1727.

14 Denis Diderot

Denis Diderot, *philosophe* and principal editor of the *Encyclopédie,* playwright and art critic, scattered discussions of musical issues throughout his writings, often in an important thematic way. Such is the case with this extraordinary dialogue, *Le neveu de Rameau (Rameau's Nephew),* a work written in the 1760s or 1770s that remained unpublished in Diderot's lifetime (it first appeared in 1805, in a German translation by Goethe). The dialogue takes place between a Diderot-like figure and a certain nephew of Jean-Philippe Rameau who was a music teacher and professional parasite. Apparently in life as in fiction, the

Nephew was extravagantly changeable—a strange mixture of utter baseness and nobility. Their encounter occurs in a Parisian café frequented by chess players. Although Diderot at first pretends mere amusement at his old friend's antics, he is clearly transfixed by the man's strange blend of nihilism and innocent candor. The Nephew turns up in Hegel's *Phenomenology of Spirit* as the exemplar of "alienated consciousness."

Near the end of the dialogue, a conversation about music arises after the Nephew, having related with cheerful detachment the tale of a despicable extortion by a fabled renegade, asks for a chorus of praise in honor of his own degradation. He proceeds to render it himself in mime, and the conversation turns on this peculiar pivot to a critique of French opera in the vein of Rousseau. Although it could stand alone as a straightforward entry in the "Querelle des bouffons," embedded in this dialogue the musical discussion raises serious questions about the relation of seeming to being and art to morality. In the words of the Nephew, "Can the style of an evil man have any unity?"

FROM *Rameau's Nephew*

(?1760s–70s)

I: I don't know which strikes me as more horrible, the villainy of your renegade or the tone in which you talk about it.

He: That's just what I was saying to you. The enormity of the deed carries you beyond mere contempt, and that is the explanation of my candor. I wanted you to know how I excelled in my art, I wanted to force you to admit that at least I was unique in my degradation, and classify me in your mind with the great blackguards, and then exclaim: *Vivat Mascarillus, fourbum imperator!*[1] Come on, join in, Mr. Philosopher, chorus: *Vivat Mascarillus, fourbum imperator!*

(Thereupon he began to execute a quite extraordinary fugue. At one moment the theme was solemn and full of majesty and at the next light and frolicsome, at one moment he was imitating the bass and at the next one of the upper parts. With outstretched arms and neck he indicated the held notes, and both performed and composed a song of triumph in which you could see he was better versed in good music than in good conduct.

As for me, I didn't know whether to stay or run away, laugh or be furious. I stayed, with the object of turning the conversation on to some other subject which would dispel the horror that filled my soul. I was beginning to find irksome the presence of a man who discussed a horrible act, an execrable

TEXT: As translated by Leonard Tancock, *Diderot: Rameau's Nephew, D'Alembert's Dream* (New York: Penguin Books, 1966), pp. 96–108, with minor alterations. Reproduced by permission of Penguin Books Ltd.

1. "Long live Mascarille, king of the rogues!" In Molière's *L'Étourdi* (act 2, scene 8) the conniving valet Mascarille, at a moment when his projects are going particularly well, fantasizes a portrait of himself painted as a hero, with this legend in gold letters at the base.

crime, like a connoisseur of painting or poetry examining the beauties of a work of art, or a moralist or historian picking out and illuminating the circumstances of a heroic deed. I became preoccupied in spite of myself. He noticed it and said:)

He: What's the matter? Do you feel ill?

I: A bit, but it will pass off.

He: You have that worried look of a man hag-ridden by some disturbing thought.

I: That's so.

(After a moment of silence on his part and mine, during which he walked up and down whistling and singing, I tried to get him back to his own talent by saying:) What are you doing just now?

He: Nothing.

I: Very tiring.

He: I was silly enough as it was; I have been to hear this music by Duni[2] and our other youngsters, and that has finished me off.

I: So you approve of this style of music?

He: Of course.

I: And you find beauty in these modern tunes?

He: Do I find beauty? Good Lord, you bet I do! How well it is suited to the words! What realism! What expressiveness!

I: Every imitative art has its model in nature. What is the musician's model when he writes a tune?

He: Why not go back to the beginning? What is a tune?

I: I confess the question is beyond me. That's what we are all like: in our memories we have nothing but words, and we think we understand them through the frequent use and even correct application we make of them, but in our minds we have only vague notions. When I pronounce the word "tune" I have no clearer idea than you and most of your kind when you say "reputation, blame, honor, vice, virtue, modesty, decency, shame, ridicule."

He: A tune is an imitation, by means of the sounds of a scale (invented by art or inspired by nature, as you please), either by the voice or by an instrument, of the physical sounds or accents of passion. And you see that by changing the variables the same definition would apply exactly to painting, rhetoric, sculpture, or poetry. Now to come to your question: what is the model for a musician or a tune? Declamation, if the model is alive and thinking; noise, if the model is inanimate. Declamation should be thought of as a line, and the tune as another line that snakes its way over the first. The more vigorous and true the declamation, which is the basis of the tune, and the more closely the tune fits it and the more points of contact it has with it, the truer that tune will be and

2. Egidio Romoaldo Duni (1709–1775; Diderot gives his name the French spelling *Douni*), Italian composer who successfully adapted French declamation to the musical style of *opera buffa*. With Pierre Alexandre Monsigny and François-André Danican Philidor, Duni is regarded as having defined the shape and style of the *opéra comique*.

the more beautiful. And that is what our younger musicians have seen so clearly. When you hear *Je suis un pauvre diable* you think you can tell it is a miser's plaint, for even if he didn't sing he would address the earth in the same tone when hiding his gold therein: *O terre, reçois mon trésor.*[3] And that young girl, for example, who feels her heart beating, who blushes and in confusion begs his lordship to let her go—how else could she express herself?[4] There are all kinds of characters in these works, and an infinite variety of modes of declamation. Sublime, I tell you! Go and listen to the piece when the young man, feeling himself on the point of death, cries: *Mon coeur s'en va.*[5] Listen to the air, listen to the instrumental setting, and then try and tell me the difference there is between the real behavior of a dying man and the turn of this air. You will see whether the line of the melody doesn't coincide exactly with that of the declamation. I am not going into time, which is another condition of song; I am sticking to expression, and nothing is more obvious than the following passage which I have read somewhere: *Musices seminarium accentus.*[6] Accent is the nursery-bed of melody. Hence you can tell how difficult the technique of recitative is, and how important. There is no good tune from which you cannot make a fine recitative, and no recitative from which a skilled person cannot make a fine tune. I would not like to guarantee that a good speaker will sing well, but I should be surprised if a good singer could not speak well. Believe all I say on this score, for it is the truth.

I: I should be only too willing to believe you if I were not prevented by one little difficulty.

He: What difficulty?

I: Just this: if this kind of music is sublime, then that of the divine Lully, Campra, Destouches, and Mouret, and even, between ourselves, of your dear uncle,[7] must be a bit dull.

He (whispering into my ear): I don't want to be overheard, and there are lots of people here who know me, but it *is* dull. It's not that I care twopence about dear uncle, if "dear" he be. He is made of stone. He would see my

3. "I am a poor devil"; "Oh earth, receive my treasure"—words from airs sung by the crazy miser Sordide in Duni's *L'Isle des fous* (*The Isle of Madmen*, 1760).
4. The young girl is Nicette, another character in Duni's *L'Isle des fous.*
5. "My heart is failing"—from *Le Maréchal-ferrant* (*The Blacksmith*, 1761), by François-André Danican Philidor (1726–1795), the most famous member of a family prominent in French musical life for over a century. He was also a master chess player, who frequented the café where this dialogue takes place. "The French are much indebted to M. Philidor, for being among the first to betray them into a toleration of Italian music, by adopting French words to it, and afterwards by imitating the Italian style in several comic operas, which have had great success, particularly, *Le Marechal Ferrant*" (Charles Burney, *The Present State of Music in France and Italy* [London, 1771], pp. 26–27).
6. A phrase Diderot quotes several times in his writings, always without attribution. It is found in the works of Martianus Capella, a fifth-century writer on the liberal arts. Rousseau also quotes it, in the article "Accent" in his *Dictionnaire*, but attributes it to Dionysius of Halicarnassus.
7. Composers favored by the partisans of French opera in the "Querelle des bouffons." For the "Querelle des bouffons," see pp 9–11, 161–74, and 187–88.

tongue hanging out a foot and never so much as give me a glass of water, but for all his making the hell of a hullabaloo at the octave or the seventh—la-la-la, dee-dee-dee, tum-te-tum—people who are beginning to get the hang of things and no longer take a din for music will never be content with that. There should be a police order forbidding all and sundry to have the *Stabat* of Pergolesi[8] sung. That *Stabat* ought to have been burned by the public hangman. Lord! these confounded Bouffons, with their *Serva Padrone*, their *Tracollo*,[9] have given us a real kick in the backside. In the old days a thing like *Tancrède, Issé, L'Europe galante, Les Indes* and *Castor, Les Talents lyriques* ran for four, five, or six months.[10] The performances of *Armide*[11] went on for ever. But nowadays they all fall down one after the other, like houses of cards. And Rebel and Francoeur breathe fire and slaughter and declare that all is lost and they are ruined, and that, if these circus performers are going to be put up with much longer, national music will go to the devil and the royal academy in the cul-de-sac will have to shut up shop.[12] And there is some truth in it, too. The old wigs who have been going there every Friday for the past thirty or forty years are getting bored and beginning to yawn, for some reason or other, instead of having a good time as they used to. And they wonder why, and can't find the answer. Why don't they ask me? Duni's prophecy will come true, and the way things are going I'll be damned if, four or five years after *Le Peintre amoureux de son modèle*,[13] there will be as much as a cat left to skin in the celebrated Impasse.[14] The good people have given up their own symphonies to play Italian ones, thinking they would accustom their ears to these without detriment to their vocal music, just as though orchestral music did not bear the same relationship to singing (allowances being made for the greater freedom

8. Giovanni Battista Pergolesi's setting of the *Stabat mater* (1736), for two solo voices and strings, was first published in London in 1749. Almost universally admired, it was the most frequently printed work in the eighteenth century. It entered the regular repertoire of the Concert Spirituel in Paris after its first performance there in 1753. See pp. 9, 194, n. 22, and 245.
9. Operas by Pergolesi: *La serva padrona* (Naples, 1733; first performed in Paris in 1746), the comic intermezzo that touched off the "Querelle des bouffons," and *Livietta e Tracollo* (Naples, 1734; see n. 9, p. 164, and n. 18, p. 168).
10. *Tancrède* (1702) and *L'Europe galante* (1697) are by André Campra, *Issé* (1697) by André Cardinal Destouches, *Les Indes galantes* (1735), *Castor et Pollux* (1737), and *Les Talents lyriques* (1739) by Rameau.
11. *Armide* (1686), an opera by Jean-Baptiste Lully to a libretto by Philippe Quinault, was revived at the Opéra as late as 1766.
12. The composers François Rebel (1701–1775) and François Francoeur (1698–1787) were co-directors of the Paris Opéra (the Académie Royale de Musique) from 1741 to 1767, with a brief intermission from 1753 to 1757. Because at that time the Académie was located at the end of a cul-de-sac or *impasse*, it was nicknamed the "Royal Academy of the cul-de-sac"—the Dead-End Academy. The Nephew surely had this in mind a few lines earlier when he rather rudely referred to the triumph of the *bouffons* as "a real kick in the *cul*" (politely, "backside").
13. *The Painter Who Fell in Love with his Model* (1757), *opéra comique* by the Italian composer Egidio Duni. See n. 2, p. 190. By "Duni's prophecy" the Nephew probably meant this opera, which was enormously popular and was considered by some to have been the work that set the French taste for Italian music.
14. See n. 12.

due to range of instrument and nimbleness of finger) as singing to normal declamation. As though the violin were not the ape of the singer, who in his turn will become the ape of the violin one of these days, when technical difficulty replaces beauty. The first person to play Locatelli was the apostle of modern music.[15] What nonsense! We shall become inured to the imitation of the accents of passion and of the phenomena of nature by melody or voice or instrument, for that is the whole extent and object of music; and shall we keep our taste for rapine, lances, glories, triumphs, and victories?[16] *Va-t-en voir s'ils viennent, Jean.*[17] They supposed they could weep or laugh at scenes from tragedy or comedy set to music, that the tones of madness, hatred, jealousy, the genuine pathos of love, the ironies and jokes of the Italian or French stage could be presented to their ears and that nevertheless they could still admire *Ragonde* and *Platée.*[18] You can bet your boots that even if they saw over and over again with what ease, flexibility, and gentleness the harmony, prosody, ellipses, and inversions of the Italian language suited the art, movement, expressiveness and turns of music, and relative length of sounds, they would still fail to realize how stiff, dead, heavy, clumsy, pedantic, and monotonous their own language is. Well, there it is. They have persuaded themselves that after having mingled their tears with those of a mother mourning the death of her son, or trembled at the decree of a tyrant ordering a murder, they won't get bored with their fairy-tales, their insipid mythology, their sugary little madrigals which show up the bad taste of the poet as clearly as they do the poverty of the art which uses them. Simple souls! It is not so, and cannot be. Truth, goodness, and beauty have their claims. You may contest them, but in the end you will admire. Anything not bearing their stamp is admired for a time, but in the end you yawn. Yawn, then gentlemen, yawn your fill, don't you worry! The reign of nature is quietly coming in, and that of my trinity, against which the gates of hell shall not prevail: truth, which is the father, begets goodness, which is the son, whence proceeds the beautiful, which is the holy ghost. The foreign god takes his place unobtrusively beside the idol of the country, but little by little he strengthens his position, and one fine day he gives his comrade a shove with his elbow and wallop! down goes the idol. That, they say, is how the Jesuits planted Christianity in China and the Indies. And the Jansenists can say what they like, this kind of politics which moves noiselessly, bloodlessly, towards its goal, with no martyrs and not a single tuft of hair pulled out, seems the best to me.

15. When the French began to play the music of Pietro Antonio Locatelli (1695–1764), considered an innovator in Italian instrumental music, they were unknowingly accustoming themselves to Italian vocal music as well, or to the "modern" style.
16. This list is a paraphrase of one that Diderot the interlocutor uses at the beginning of the dialogue, when introducing the Nephew, to characterize the subject matter of the operas of Rameau.
17. "Go see if they're coming, John"—the refrain of a popular song that came to be a proverbial expression of disbelief.
18. *Le mariage di Ragonde* (1714), opera by Jean-Joseph Mouret, and *Platée* (1745), *comédie lyrique* by Rameau.

I: There is a certain amount of sense in everything you have been saying.

He: Sense! It's as well, for devil take me if I have been trying. It just comes, easy as wink. I am like those musicians in the Impasse, when my uncle arrived; if I hit the mark, well and good. A coal-heaver will always talk better about his own job than a whole Academy and all the Duhamels[19] in the world . . .

(And off he went, walking up and down and humming some of the tunes from *L'Isle des fous*, *Le Peintre amoureux de son modèle*, *Le Maréchal-ferrant*, and *La Plaideuse*,[20]) and now and again he raised his hands and eyes to heaven and exclaimed: "Isn't that beautiful! God, isn't it beautiful! How can anyone wear a pair of ears on his head and question it?" He began to warm up and sang, at first softly; then as he grew more impassioned, he raised his voice and there followed gestures, grimaces, and bodily contortions, and I said: "Here we go, he's getting carried away and some new scene is working up." And indeed off he went with a shout: *Je suis un pauvre misérable. . . . Monseigneur, Monseigneur, laissez-moi partir. . . . O terre, reçois mon or, conserve bien mon trésor. . . . Mon âme, mon âme, ma vie! O terre!. . . . Le violà le petit ami, le voilà le petit ami!. . . Aspettare e non venire. . . . A Zerbina penserete. . . . Sempre in contrasti con te si sta. . . .*[21] He sang thirty tunes on top of each other and all mixed up: Italian, French, tragic, comic, of all sorts and descriptions, sometimes in a bass voice going down to the infernal regions, and sometimes bursting himself in a falsetto voice he would split the heavens asunder, taking off the walk, deportment, and gestures of the different singing parts: in turn raging, pacified, imperious, scornful. Here we have a young girl weeping, and he mimes all her simpering ways; there a priest, king, tyrant, threatening, commanding, flying into a rage, or a slave obeying. He relents, wails, complains, laughs, never losing sight of tone, rhythm, the meaning of the words, and the character of the music. All the chess players had left their boards and gathered round him. Outside, the café windows were thronged with passers-by who had stopped because of the noise. There were bursts of laughter fit to split the ceiling open. He noticed nothing, but went on, possessed by such a frenzy, an enthusiasm so near to madness that it was uncertain whether he would ever get over it, whether he should not be packed off in a cab straight to Bedlam. Singing a part of the Jommelli *Lamentations*[22] he rendered the finest bits of

19. Henri-Louis Duhamel du Monceaux (1700–82), a French savant, engineer, and agriculturalist, who wrote a vast number of treatises on botanical subjects. Diderot used several of them in writing technical articles for the *Encyclopédie*.

20. For the first three works, see nn. 3, 13, and 5. *Le procès, ou La plaideuse* (*The Lawsuit, or The Maid-Litigant*), *opéra comique* by Duni (1762).

21. Ariettes from *l'Isle des fous*: "I am a poor wretch . . . O Milord, Milord, let me leave. . . . O earth, receive my gold, preserve my treasure. . . . My soul, my soul, my life! O earth! . . . There's my little friend, my little friend!" Arias from *La serva padrona*: "To wait and have no one come. . . . Think about Zerbina. . . . With you it's always strife. . . ."

22. Like Pergolesi's *Stabat mater*, Niccolò Jommelli's *Lamentations of Jeremiah* (1751) had been performed at the Concert Spirituel.

each piece with incredible accuracy, truth, and emotion, and the fine accompanied recitative in which the prophet depicts the desolation of Jerusalem was mingled with a flood of tears which forced all eyes to weep. Everything was there: the delicacy of the air and expressive power as well as grief. He laid stress upon the places where the composer had specially shown his great mastery, sometimes leaving the vocal line to take up the instrumental parts, which he would suddenly abandon to return to the voice part, intertwining them so as to preserve the connecting links and the unity of the whole, captivating our souls and holding them in the most singular state of suspense I have ever experienced. Did I admire? Yes, I did. Was I touched with pity? Yes, I was. But a tinge of ridicule ran through these sentiments and discolored them.

But you would have gone off into roars of laughter at the way he mimicked the various instruments. With cheeks puffed out and a hoarse, dark tone he did the horns and bassoons, a bright, nasal tone for the oboes, quickening his voice with incredible agility for the stringed instruments to which he tried to get the closest approximation; he whistled the recorders and cooed the flutes, shouting, singing, and throwing himself about like a mad thing: a one-man show featuring dancers male and female, singers of both sexes, a whole orchestra, a complete opera house, dividing himself into twenty different stage parts, tearing up and down, stopping, like one possessed, with flashing eyes and foaming mouth. The weather was terribly hot, and the sweat running down the furrows of his brow and cheeks mingled with the powder from his hair and ran in streaks down the top of his coat. What didn't he do? He wept, laughed, sighed, his gaze was tender, soft, or furious: a woman swooning with grief, a poor wretch abandoned in the depth of his despair, a temple rising into view, birds falling silent at eventide, waters murmuring in a cool, solitary place or tumbling in torrents down the mountainside, a thunderstorm, a hurricane, the shrieks of the dying mingled with the howling of the tempest and the crash of thunder; night with its shadows, darkness, and silence, for even silence itself can be depicted in sound. By now he was quite beside himself. Knocked out with fatigue, like a man coming out of a deep sleep or long trance, he stood there motionless, dazed, astonished, looking about him and trying to recognize his surroundings. Waiting for his strength and memory to come back, he mechanically wiped his face. Like a person waking up to see a large number of people gathered round his bed and totally oblivious or profoundly ignorant of what he had been doing, his first impulse was to cry out "Well, gentlemen, what's up? What are you laughing at? Why are you so surprised? What's up?" Then he went on: "Now that's what you call music and a musician. And yet, gentlemen, you mustn't look down on some of the things in Lully. I defy anyone to better the scene *Ah, j'attendrai,*[23] without altering the words. You mustn't look down on some parts of Campra, or my uncle's violin airs and

23. "Ah! I shall await . . ." The first words of the monologue of Roland in Lully's *Roland* (1685).

his gavottes, his entries for soldiers, priests, sacrificers ... *Pâles flambeaux, nuit plus affreuse que les ténèbres ... Dieu du Tartare, Dieu de l'oubli....*"[24] At this point he raised his voice, held on to the notes, and neighbors came to their windows while we stuck our fingers in our ears. "This," he went on, "is where you need lung-power, a powerful organ, plenty of wind. But soon it will be good-bye to Assumption; Lent and Epiphany have already come and gone. They don't yet know what to set to music, nor, therefore, what a musician wants. Lyric poetry has yet to be born. But they will come to it through hearing Pergolesi, the Saxon,[25] Terradellas, Traetta, and the rest; through reading Metastasio they will have to come to it.")

I: You mean to say that Quinault, La Motte, Fontenelle[26] didn't know anything about it?

He: Not for the modern style. There aren't six lines together in all their charming poems that you can set to music. Ingenious aphorisms, light, tender, delicate madrigals, but if you want to see how lacking all this is in material for our art, which is the most forceful of all, not even excepting that of Demosthenes, get someone to recite these pieces, and how cold, tired, and monotonous they will sound! There is nothing in them that can serve as a basis for song. I would just as soon have to set the *Maximes* of La Rochefoucauld or the *Pensées* of Pascal to music. It is the animal cry of passion that should dictate the melodic line, and these moments should tumble out quickly one after the other, phrases must be short and the meaning self-contained, so that the musician can utilize the whole and each part, omitting one word or repeating it, adding a missing word, turning it inside out like a polyp,[27] without destroying it. All this makes lyric poetry in French a much more difficult problem than in languages with inversions, which have these natural advantages.[28] ... *Barbare, cruel, plonge ton poignard dans mon sein. Me voilà prête à recevoir le coup fatal. Frappe. Ose.... Ah! je languis, je meurs.... Un feu secret s'allume dans mes sens.... Cruel amour, que veux-tu de moi?... Laisse-moi la douce paix*

24. "Pale torches, night more frightful than the shadows ... God of Tartarus, God of the forgotten man." The first is an air of Telaire in Rameau's *Castor et Pollux* (1737), the second the air of Envie in Rameau's *Le Temple de la gloire* (1745).

25. Johann Adolf Hasse.

26. All three wrote opera libretti for French tragic opera and *opéra ballet*, Philippe Quinault (1635–88) for Lully, Antoine Houdar La Motte (1672–1731) for Campra and Destouches among others, and Bernard le Bovier de Fontenelle (1687–1757) for Lully.

27. In 1740 the naturalist Abraham Trembley observed that the tiny creature known as the freshwater polyp was capable of regeneration: when it was cut into any number of parts, each part would become a complete animal. He also performed experiments showing that the polyp could live and function when turned inside out. The discovery became a subject of intense controversy not only among naturalists, but also among philosophers.

28. A reference to a contemporaneous debate about the relation of word order to expression in French and Classical languages. Against a popular claim that French word order was the most natural order for a language, Charles Batteux had recently argued that in fact its rigid rules of word succession prevented inversion, which more heavily inflected languages like Greek and Latin allow, and which Batteux saw as more "natural" (*Letters on the French Phrase as Compared to the Latin Phrase* [1747–48]).

dont j'ai joui. . . . Rends-moi la raison. . . .[29] The passions must be strong and the sensibility of composer and poet must be very great. The aria is almost always the peroration of a scene. What we want is exclamations, interjections, suspensions, interruptions, affirmations, negations; we call out, invoke, shout, groan, weep, or have a good laugh. No witticisms, epigrams, none of your well-turned thoughts—all that is far too removed from unvarnished nature. And don't imagine that the technique of stage actors and their declamation can serve as a model. Pooh! we want something more energetic, less stilted, truer to life. The simple language and normal expression of emotion are all the more essential because our language is more monotonous and less highly stressed. The cry of animal instinct or that of a man under stress of emotion will supply them.

(While he was saying all this the crowds round us had melted away, either because they understood nothing he was saying or found it uninteresting, for generally speaking a child like a man and a man like a child would rather be amused than instructed; everybody was back at his game and we were left alone in our corner. Slumped on a seat with his head against the wall, arms hanging limp and eyes half shut, he said: 'I don't know what's the matter with me; when I came here I was fresh and full of life and now I am knocked out and exhausted, as though I had walked thirty miles. It has come over me all of a sudden."

I: Would you like a drink?

He: I don't mind if I do. I feel hoarse. I've no go left in me and I've a bit of a pain in my chest. I get it like this nearly every day, I don't know why.

I: What will you have?

He: Whatever you like. I'm not fussy. Poverty has taught me to make do with anything.

(Beer and lemonade are brought. He fills and empties a big glass two or three times straight off. Then, like a man restored, he coughs hard, has a good stretch, and goes on:)

But don't you think, my lord Philosopher, that it is a very odd thing that a foreigner, an Italian, a Duni should come and teach us how to put the stress into our own music, and adapt our vocal music to every tempo, measure, interval, and kind of declamation without upsetting prosody? And yet it wouldn't have taken all that doing. Anyone who had ever heard a beggar asking for alms in the street, a man in a towering rage, a woman mad with jealousy, a despairing lover, a flatterer—yes, a flatterer lowering his voice and dwelling on each syllable in honeyed tones—in short a passion, any passion, so long as it was strong enough to act as a model for a musician, should have noticed two things: one, that syllables, whether long or short, have no fixed duration nor even a settled

---

29. "Barbarous one, cruel one, plunge your dagger into my breast. I am here, ready to receive the fatal blow. Strike. Dare. . . . Ah! I languish, I die. . . . A secret fire is kindled in my senses. . . . Cruel love, what do you want of me? . . . Leave me the sweet peace that I have enjoyed. . . . Give me back my reason."

connection between their durations, and the other, that passion does almost what it likes with prosody; it jumps over the widest intervals, so that a man crying out from the depths of his grief: *"Ah, malheureux que je suis!"*[30] goes up in pitch on the exclamatory syllable to his highest and shrillest tone, and down on the others to his deepest and most solemn, spreading over an octave or even greater interval and giving each sound the quantity required by the turn of the melody without offending the ear, although the long and short syllables are not kept to the length or brevity of normal speech. What a way we have come since we used to cite the parenthesis in *Armide: Le vainqueur de Renaud (si quel-qu'un le peut être)*, or: *Obéissons sans balancer* from *Les Indes galantes*[31] as miracles of musical declamation! Now these miracles make me shrug my shoulders with pity. The way the art is advancing I don't know where it will end! Meanwhile let's have a drink.

(And he had two or three without realizing what he was doing. He would have drowned himself, just as he had exhausted himself, without noticing, had I not moved away the bottle he was absentmindedly feeling for. Then I said:)

I: How is it that with a discrimination as delicate as yours and your remarkable sensitiveness for the beauties of the musical art, you are so blind to the fine things of morality, so insensitive to the charms of virtue?

He: Apparently because some things need a sense I don't possess, a fiber that hasn't been vouchsafed me, or a slack one that you can tweak as much as you like but it won't vibrate; or again it may be that I have always lived with good musicians and bad people. Hence it has come about that my ear has become very sharp and my heart very deaf.

30. "Ah, how unhappy I am!"
31. See nn. 11 and 10.

15 Christoph Willibald Gluck

Born in 1714 near the German-Bohemian border, Christoph Willibald Gluck is the master who liberated the opera from the conventions of contemporary Italian *opera seria* and created a new operatic style based on truly dramatic expression. After studying for four years with Sammartini in Milan and visiting London and various cities on the Continent, Gluck settled in Vienna in 1750.

The opera *Orfeo ed Euridice,* written in 1762, marks a turning point in Gluck's career. Here he applied for the first time his new ideas, supported by his able and original librettist, Ranieri de' Calzabigi. Gluck gives an explanation of his aims in the prefaces to the printed scores of his operas *Alceste* (1768) and *Paride ed Elena* (1770). In 1772, Gluck found a new and congenial collaborator in F. L. G. le Bland Du Roullet, who had adapted Racine's *Iphigénie* as an opera libretto. The new score—*Iphigénie en Aulide*—was accepted by the Paris Opéra, and Gluck himself went to Paris to direct the rehearsals. After reinforcing his position with *Armide* (1777) and *Iphigénie en Tauride* (1779), Gluck returned, crowned with fresh laurels, to Vienna, where he died in 1787.

Dedication for *Alceste*
(1769)

YOUR ROYAL HIGHNESS:

When I undertook to write the music for *Alceste*, I resolved to divest it entirely of all those abuses, introduced into it either by the mistaken vanity of singers or by the too great complaisance of composers, which have so long disfigured Italian opera and made of the most splendid and most beautiful of spectacles the most ridiculous and wearisome. I have striven to restrict music to its true office of serving poetry by means of expression and by following the situations of the story, without interrupting the action or stifling it with a useless superfluity of ornaments; and I believed that it should do this in the same way as telling colors affect a correct and well-ordered drawing, by a well-assorted contrast of light and shade, which serves to animate the figures without altering their contours. Thus I did not wish to arrest an actor in the greatest heat of dialogue in order to wait for a tiresome *ritornello*, nor to hold him up in the middle of a word on a vowel favorable to his voice, nor to make display of the agility of his fine voice in some long-drawn passage, nor to wait while the orchestra gives him time to recover his breath for a cadenza. I did not think it my duty to pass quickly over the second section[1] of an aria of which the words are perhaps the most impassioned and important, in order to repeat regularly four times over those of the first part, and to finish the aria where its sense may perhaps not end for the convenience of the singer who wishes to show that he can capriciously vary a passage in a number of guises; in short, I have sought to abolish all the abuses against which good sense and reason have long cried out in vain.

I have felt that the overture ought to apprise the spectators of the nature of the action that is to be represented and to form, so to speak, its argument; that the concerted instruments should be introduced in proportion to the interest and the intensity of the words, and not leave that sharp contrast between the

TEXT: As translated by Eric Blom in Alfred Einstein, *Gluck* (London: J. M. Dent & Sons, 1936), pp. 98–100.

1. By "second section" Gluck means the central or contrasting section of the da capo aria. The first section of such an aria regularly presented its full text twice and had then to be repeated after the central or contrasting section, hence Gluck's reference to repeating the words of the first part "four times over." Frederick the Great says much the same thing in a letter of May 4, 1754, quoted in *Denkmäler der Tonkunst in Österreich*, vol. 15 (1904), p. ix.

aria and the recitative in the dialogue, so as not to break a period unreasonably nor wantonly disturb the force and heat of the action.

Furthermore, I believed that my greatest labor should be devoted to seeking a beautiful simplicity, and I have avoided making displays of difficulty at the expense of clearness; nor did I judge it desirable to discover novelties if it was not naturally suggested by the situation and the expression; and there is no rule which I have not thought it right to set aside willingly for the sake of an intended effect.

Such are my principles. By good fortune my designs were wonderfully furthered by the libretto, in which the celebrated author, devising a new dramatic scheme, for florid descriptions, unnatural paragons, and sententious, cold morality, had substituted heartfelt language, strong passions, interesting situations and an endlessly varied spectacle. The success of the work justified my maxims, and the universal approbation of so enlightened a city has made it clearly evident that simplicity, truth, and naturalness are the great principles of beauty in all artistic manifestations. For all that, in spite of repeated urgings on the part of some most eminent persons to decide upon the publication of this opera of mine in print, I was well aware of all the risk run in combating such firmly and profoundly rooted prejudices, and I thus felt the necessity of fortifying myself with the most powerful patronage of YOUR ROYAL HIGHNESS, whose August Name I beg you may have the grace to prefix to this my opera, a name which with so much justice enjoys the suffrages of an enlightened Europe. The great protector of the fine arts, who reigns over a nation that had the glory of making them arise again from universal oppression and which itself has produced the greatest models, in a city that was always the first to shake off the yoke of vulgar prejudices in order to clear a path for perfection, may alone undertake the reform of that noble spectacle in which all the fine arts take so great a share. If this should succeed, the glory of having moved the first stone will remain for me, and in this public testimonial of Your Highness's furtherance of the same, I have the honor to subscribe myself, with the most humble respect,

Your Royal Highness's

Most humble, most devoted, and most obliged servant,

CHRISTOFORO GLUCK

16 Vincenzo Manfredini

Born in Pistoia in 1737, Vincenzo Manfredini spent the middle years of his life in Bologna writing and teaching. In his twenties, however, he had served as *maestro di cappella* in the court at St. Petersburg until he was replaced by Baldessare Galuppi in 1769, and he returned to that city just before his death in 1799.

Whether nature or circumstance made Manfredini a polemicist is not entirely clear, but both his major publications involved him in public disputes. His quarrel with Giambattista Mancini he seems to have initiated, at least in print, in his *Rules of Harmony* (1775), to which Mancini responded in a new edition of his treatise on singing. After Manfredini reviewed the first volume of Stefano Arteaga's history of opera in a Bologna journal in 1785, Arteaga, a Spanish musician who had been a student of Padre Giovanni Battista Martini in Bologna, printed extracts from the review in the third volume of his history, accompanying them with acid commentary. Manfredini retaliated in kind in his *Difesa della musica moderna, e de' suoi celebri esecutori (A Defense of Modern Music and its Distinguished Practitioners)*, yet another entry in the continuing dialogue between *musica antica* and *musica moderna*. As one of the few music pedagogues to go on record against the "Hellenicizing," antiquarian tendencies of reform opera, Manfredini defended the expressive directness of the new aria styles against those who put ancient music forward as a model for simplicity and expressiveness. His style, however, is flatfooted and bombastic, achieving none of the virtues of the music he praises.

FROM *A Defense of Modern Music and Its Distinguished Practitioners*
(1788)

CONCLUSION

Now I have finished my *responses,*[1] and consequently the occasion to extend any further my defense of modern music and its excellent practitioners, whether professors or dilettantes. But the cause is so good and just that it in no way required a wordy discourse to sustain it. Nevertheless, anyone who thinks that Signor Arteaga was the only person to believe that modern music was not the equal of ancient would be very much mistaken. On the contrary,

TEXT: The original edition (Bologna, 1788), pp. 189–207. Translation by Wye J. Allanbrook.

1. The "responses" referred to are Manfredini's section-by-section critique of Arteaga's commentary on Manfredini's review of Arteaga's history of opera; see the introduction.

he has only been following in the footsteps of certain scholars and learned composers, who have gone so far as to suppose that something is a defect when it is actually a virtue.[2] Unfortunately prejudices, fierce enemies of the truth, are adopted sometimes even by preeminent men. This comes about, in my opinion, from a principle common to all the arts, but one that ought not to be a consideration in music and all other creative arts. Without innovation, as I said earlier, all the arts would still be in their infancy. Yet innovation has always been a theme that artists have raised their voices to denounce, especially those artists who are already developed and with reputations. This may be because they have too much veneration for tradition, or because they are not capable of doing otherwise. But certainly if there is any art in which one ought to strive for innovation, for a means of making the art more pleasing and expressive, that art ought properly to be music. For as was said, it has been the last to be revived, and only in these recent times has it been carried, if not to the summit, at least to the nearest degree of perfection. Thanks for this are due precisely to certain sublime geniuses and creators who knew how to conquer and overthrow the barriers of prejudice by means of innovation. These individuals have brought about a more pleasing, more expressive, and truer music, a music that is not at all that of the ancients, which had too many *voices, fugues, points of imitation, ligatures, countersubjects,* and in sum was more harmonic than melodic. There is general agreement about instrumental music, therefore, that it is in a lofty position now, and that ancient music did not achieve so much.

But what else does this kind of music contain, if not vocal lines or melodies that are more spirited, more pleasing, and more meaningful than the ancient ones? They are melodies almost all of which derive from vocal music, whose follower and companion instrumental music has been and always will be. It is simply true that instrumental music is for the most part a copy and imitation of the vocal. When it doesn't sing, it doesn't express—that is, it says nothing and it is worth nothing at all. So while instrumental music has greatly improved, it first had to be made into vocal music, and whoever denies this can deny anything. But to convince oneself that modern music, whether instrumental or vocal, is absolutely better than ancient music, it is enough to compare good

2. In the music of our day (says the aforesaid Padre Martini) they look only for variety in ideas; a choice of intervals most apt to stimulate the senses; the most delicate and tender affects; a combination of those movements, those figures, and those instruments that produce the most surprise, and stir up the most racket; and in the singers and instrumentalists they seek only something that is on the lips of every professor, which they call *good taste.* (See *History of Music,* vol. 2, p. 281). All this that Padre Martini said with an air of contempt is in my opinion the finest praise that can be given to modern music. God willing, the assertions of Padre Martini would turn out to be true, that is, composers would always seek out tender and delicate affects when circumstances require it, and singers and instrumentalists would always look for *good taste,* without which no music will ever be able to be perfect. [Au.]

Padre Martini was the mentor of both Giambattista Mancini and Stefano Arteaga; he himself wrote a comic intermezzo, *Il maestro di musica* (1746), in which he contrasted the old and the new—expressive and virtuoso—styles of singing.

modern compositions with ancient ones. It is enough to observe the change
that occurs between musical works written at various periods by the same fine
modern masters, who managed by means of repeated experience to alleviate
some improbabilities, inconsistencies, and prejudices. For since the art of
music was new, the time had to be right for it to be brought to a degree of
excellence it had not yet attained. This happy transaction was reserved for our
century, which was destined if not to perfect completely certain arts and sciences, at least to clarify and improve them in great part, and among these arts
one should certainly number music. In fact does there not exist a great difference between music written seventy, forty, twenty years ago, and that of the
present? Then to believe that such a difference arises because music does not
have a fixed style, and because now it is generally in decline—both of these
opinions seem to me to be false. They have been advanced too easily by a
person who, since he is not acquainted with this art nor has he practiced it, as
is required, cannot form of it a reasonable judgment.

It is natural that all the arts and sciences that have not yet reached their total
perfection must undergo alteration. Since music (as I have said many times,
and it is indisputable) has recently been reborn, cultivated, and improved, the
changes it has had to undergo are not few. Some writers have believed these
changes to be imperfections, when it is completely the contrary.

One must remember that since music is a very rich art, like poetry, painting
and so on, it has many manners and styles, and even more fashions. Hence one
must be acquainted with them all and have a solid knowledge of what music is
in order to make a sound decision about whether a certain manner or style is
good or bad; or whether a particular fashion that differs from another is good
or bad, or if they are both good. I think further that among the fine works in
every class, by the same fine authors and different ones, comparisons to the
benefit or disadvantage of one or the other should not be so easily proposed.
For any one of those works can be excellent, one because of one merit, another
because of another. Anyone who would assert, for example, that the St. Cecilia
of Raphael is a better and more beautiful work than the St. Peter of Guido,[3]
or Orlando furioso better than Gerusalemme liberata,[4] or the Pergolesi Stabat
better than the Jommelli Miserere, etc., or would assert the contrary, would be
making a bad argument. For each of these very beautiful works has its particular merit, as do their respective creators, who themselves ought to be admired
and not compared. The same can be said of many other things, provided they
are good, for each has its own worth, and can be most perfect in its class. But
let us look separately at the stronger reasons that cause some of the proponents
of ancient music to think that the music of our opera seria is in decline (for no

3. Guido Reni, Italian painter who flourished in the first half of the seventeenth century.
4. The two great Italian epics were published in the sixteenth century. Orlando furioso by Lodovico
   Ariosto in 1516 (with subsequent editions in 1521 and 1532) and Gerusalemme liberata by
   Torquato Tasso in 1581.

one would be so untutored as to try to maintain of the music of *opera buffa* that it has not made incredible progress from the time when Buranello[5] flourished up until now.) People say, "You no longer hear a truly cantabile aria. Now they only compose *rondòs*, noisy arias, bravura arias . . . and all this because musicians no longer know how to sing . . . it is the orchestra that sings," and so on. These finicky gentlemen know that the term *rondò*, taken from the French, is often badly applied, since not all those arias that partly resemble *rondòs* are true *rondòs*. On the contrary, they are grand and sublime arias that contain two *themes* or subjects, one slow and the other spirited, repeated only two times. These arias are certainly better than the so-called *arie cantabili* of old, because they are more natural, more genuine, and more expressive.[6]

In the first place, many *arie cantabili* of thirty or forty years ago contained so much passagework or brilliant figuration (almost always quite remote from the sentiment of the words and the character of the aria), put there expressly in order that the singer should demonstrate his learning in varying them. These passages did great harm to the expression, to the authenticity, to the power of the action, and so on.

Second, many things about these arias were badly conceived and consequently harmful to reason and verisimilitude, for example: the habit of repeating the words of the first part of an aria four times and the words of the second only once; having two and sometimes four cadenzas; being condemned to death and going off calmly, without fury; saying good-bye but never leaving; vocalizing on words before their end, and so on. These things even occur sometimes in the arias of well-known composers, who have written them either to indulge the singer or through habit. Are our arias not much more natural and more pleasing, especially those with two themes and two perceptibly different tempos? If they contain one such bit of passagework that is nothing compared to the many that would have been used in times past. Moreover, arias like these lack the aforesaid inconveniences of the *da capo*, the cadenza, and so on. They finish convincingly, with the expression that the situation requires and in the tempo in which they are being executed. Now not all arias written some years ago that have a cadenza or a *da capo*, and so on, are defective; there are some excellent ones, written by fine composers. That came about precisely because, as I said, music is rich in fashions and styles. Hence the most important study for a composer consists in knowing how to discover those styles that will always be attractive, especially when they have been adapted to the situation and the circumstances. Besides, it is simply true that the aforementioned arias in two tempos are not true *rondòs*, although they bear some resemblance to them. Instead they are magnificent and truly heroic arias, which the masters who

5. Baldassare Galuppi (1706–1785), often known as Buranello, after his birthplace.
6. Manfredini is referring here to the fashionable new two-tempo rondò, with a slow first section and a faster, more showy second section, frequent in operas of the 1760s and after, such as those of Galuppi, Niccolò Piccinni, Giovanni Paisiello, and Mozart. Fiordiligi's rondò "Per pietà, ben mio," in Mozart's *Così fan tutte,* is a good example of a rondò.

composed them very rarely—perhaps never—had distinguished with the term *rondò*. They did not even distinguish true *rondòs* with this term, but called them instead cavatinas, or "little arias," such as "Che farò senza Euridice" by Gluck, "Idol mio, che fiero istante" by Buranello, "Idol mio se più non vivi" by Sacchini, and many others of this type.[7]

As for the arias written in past years called *arie di bravura*, without taking merit from those that possess it, many of them contain so much passagework or brilliant figuration that they come off rather badly. Ours also contain some of these passages, but they have more relation to the sentiment of the words, and they are more tasteful, because more varied. In short, because they are adapted more to the themes and characters of the arias, they are not tiresome, boring, and out of place, but highly interesting, pleasing, and agreeable. So I conclude by saying that if for the aforesaid reasons modern arias are more perfect than ancient ones, it is certain too that our musicians know how to sing with more expression and more naturalness than did ancient musicians. And if the orchestra also sings, so much the better, because music is only singing. It is enough that the orchestra sings well, that is, that the instruments moderate their unisons with the voice part in order not to cover it, so that the words can be heard clearly; that when the vocal line is proceeding, the instruments wait on it, so to speak, by playing few notes, and *piano*. But when the poetry and the situation require more significant instrumental accompaniments, consisting of a kind of melody that is more eloquent and richer, it ought to be composed in such a way that the principal melody, which should always be that of the vocal line, stands out clearly, and is not destroyed. Now in all this our fine composers certainly do not fail, nor do our good orchestras fail nor our fine instrumentalists, nor are we lacking in the finest singers.[8] So let Signor Arteaga repeat that most composers do not write music as one ought, that most singers do not sing from the heart, that most players do not perform with clarity and expression. These objections (as I hope I have already demonstrated to him)

7. For example, unlike the new-fangled two-tempoed Italian *rondò* that Manfredini had previously praised, Gluck's well-known "Che farò senza Euridice" from *Orfeo ed Euridice* (Vienna, 1762) displays the features usually characteristic of rondo construction. The aria consists of a closed musical couplet on a single text performed three times, and framing two "episodes" of freer, more declamatory material.
8. Take note that I speak here, as always throughout this defense, of skilled professionals only. For I too willingly agree with Signor Arteaga, and with anyone who has asserted it before him, that there are many mediocre and unfortunate practitioners who were probably intended for something else than the pursuit of music. I also agree that many masters very often destroy the melody, covering and mixing the voice part with a hodge-podge of unsuitable and poorly conceived accompaniments. They make use of certain extravagant innovations, jeopardizing the most reasonable laws of modulation, of spontaneity, and of verisimilitude. They may do this to support the talent of a person who lacks training when they ought to do just the contrary, for praise from the unskilled is not genuine praise. Again I candidly confess that in churches they introduce inappropriately, and against the spirit of devotion, a theater style of the most brazen sort. But I will never agree that all masters fall into such errors, and through them have caused music to decline. For on the contrary, music owes a great debt to the fine modern composers who are bringing it to a degree of perfection unattained in the past. [Au.]

are frivolous, and an insufficient basis for deducing the decline of music. For the general run of practitioners in all the arts and sciences will always be less skilled and less perfectly accomplished.

I cannot better close this defense of modern music than by reproducing for the public the genuine and impartial eulogy for one of its better creators, Maestro Sacchini, who died in Paris last year.[9] Because this eulogy was composed in the capital of France, in a language different from ours, it will perhaps not be known to all Italians. So I set it forth here with great pleasure, because while it is written with great musical learning that can instruct young composers, it also serves as a eulogy, so to speak, for the celebrated Maestro Piccinni himself, the author, one of the solid supporters and creators of modern music—that is to say, of the best music. Yes, of the best without doubt; since it is obvious that good modern music surpasses not only the most ancient music, but in general also that of fifty and sixty years ago. It does this in many regards, but especially in that of melody, which is the most essential part of all music. Rousseau wrote, in the letter on French music already cited,[10] that Corelli, Bononcini, Vinci, and Pergolesi are the first men who made music. He meant by this that the music of masters previous to those men cannot be called music, since it was too little melodic, too artificial, and full of counterpoint. To these four masters, however, one ought to add the two Scarlattis (Alessandro and Domenico), Porpora, Marcello, Handel, Clari, and so on. Yet our good music assuredly surpasses that of these great masters mentioned above (except for Pergolesi, some of whose compositions were invented and perfected in an instant, as it were, by that sublime genius). It surpasses their music, as I have already said, in its most essential part, which is without a doubt good melody, and this consists in a pleasing and varied singing line. If you examine the music of those composers—Pergolesi always excepted—you will find much counterpoint there, and great exertion, but melody is rare, and hence there is little spontaneity and variety. The style of their pieces is for the most part a fugato or point of imitation that is drawn out too long. That is to say that since they lacked invention, they thought that a few thoughts or scraps of melody would suffice to constitute an entire and lengthy composition. How monotonous and boring such music must turn out to be, I leave to the consideration of anyone who has just a simple idea of good taste. How much more to be preferred is the music of the fine modern masters (into whose number, however, I do admit, besides Pergolesi, also Leo, Durante, Hasse, Galuppi, Jommelli, Traetta, and various others, who contributed greatly to its improvement and left monuments that will always be sound and lovely, even though written many years ago). Because these masters adapt and unite harmony to melody, the *imitative* style to the ideal and varied style, art to nature, etc., their music does not appear so uni-

9. The eulogy is omitted here.
10. Manfredini cites the *Lettre sur la musique française* in his last "response," p. 185, note, where he praises Rousseau as a man "who could speak of music because he understood it deeply." The excerpt from Rousseau's *Letter* on pp. 161–74 of this volume omits this passage.

form and tedious; it pleases connoisseurs and amateurs alike.

Is it not the same with modern *fugues?* Since they are divided up and interwoven with new thoughts that are not derived from those of the same *fugues,* are they not very much more pleasing and more perfect than the ancient ones? We agree, and openly avow that ancient music was never so animated, ordered, and expressive as is the modern. Well I know that Algarotti, Sulzer, Brown, Padre Martini, and so many others whom Signor Arteaga has supported in many matters did not think this way. But not all the music he thought to be imperfect was truly so, and so much the less is ours. I wonder if those well-known men had heard and carefully considered all this fine music, truly expressive and eloquent, and composed by so many fine modern masters who are still alive, would they have dared to denounce it? Or again, after having heard so much of Hasse, Buranello, Jommelli, Perez, Gluck, and so on, how could they ever ignore its superiority over ancient music, and the progress that it has always been making? Did they perhaps contend that music was all fine and irreproachable, and, like the goddess Minerva, born in an instant, completely formed and perfect? And why attribute to the music the great abuses to which operas are often subjected? For they derive from worse abuses, like those of bad direction at the hand of almost any impresario, without subordination to the poet or the composer, and so on. But in spite of such excesses fine composers have always made every effort to sustain and improve music. They have been encouraged in that effort not by the enormity of the rewards nor by the justice rendered to them (for these things happen rarely), but by the particular character of their art, which like all the arts depends on talent and inspiration. One does not attain excellence in it simply by means of wealth, rank, and study but by an wholly natural inclination, and after the means of success have been rendered easier by the repeated labors of our predecessors.

V

EXPRESSION AND SENSIBILITY

17 Jean-Jacques Rousseau

FROM *Essay on the Origin of Languages, Which Treats of Melody and Musical Imitation*

(c. 1760)

CHAPTER TWELVE: THE ORIGIN OF MUSIC
AND ITS RELATIONS

With the first voices came the first articulations or sounds formed according to the respective passions that dictated them. Anger produces menacing cries articulated by the tongue and the palate. But the voice of tenderness is softer: its medium is the glottis. And such an utterance becomes a sound. It may occur with ordinary or unusual tones, it may be more or less sharply accented, according to the feeling to which it is joined. Thus rhythm and sounds are born with syllables: all voices speak under the influence of passion, which adorns them with all their éclat. Thus verse, singing, and speech have a common origin. Around the fountains of which I spoke,[1] the first discourses were the first songs. The periodic recurrences and measures of rhythm, the melodious modulations of accent, gave birth to poetry and music along with language. Or, rather that was the only language in those happy climes and happy times, when the only pressing needs that required the agreement of others were those to which the heart gave birth.

The first tales, the first speeches, the first laws, were in verse. Poetry was devised before prose. That was bound to be, since feelings speak before reason. And so it was bound to be the same with music. At first, there was no music but melody and no other melody than the varied sounds of speech. Accents constituted singing, quantity constituted measure, and one spoke as much by natural sounds and rhythm as by articulations and words. To speak and to sing were formerly one, says Strabo,[2] which shows that in his opinion poetry is the source of eloquence.[3] It should be said that both had the same source, not that they were initially the same thing. Considering the way in which the earliest

---

TEXT: *Essay on the Origin of Languages, Which Treats of Melody and Musical Imitation*. Translation by John H. Moran (Chicago: University of Chicago Press, 1966), pp. 50–65. Original title: *Essai sur l'origine des langues où il est parlé de la mélodie et de l'imitation musicale*.

1. "There at last was the true cradle of nations: From the pure crystal of the fountains flow the first fires of love." (Chapter 9, "Formation of the Southern Languages.")
2. Greek geographer and historian (63 B.C.E.–24 C.E.) known for his seventeen-volume geography, which provides information about the Mediterranean countries in the early common era.
3. *Geography*, Bk. I. [Au.]

societies were bound together, is it surprising that the first stories were in verse and the first laws were sung? Is it surprising that the first grammarians subordinated their art to music and were professors of both?[4]

A tongue which has only articulations and words has only half its riches. True, it expresses ideas; but for the expression of feelings and images it still needs rhythm and sounds, which is to say melody, something the Greek tongue has and ours lacks.

We are always astonished by the prodigious effects of eloquence, poetry, and music among the Greeks. These effects are incomprehensible to our minds because we do not try to do such things any more. All that we can manage is to appear to believe them out of kindness toward our scholars.[5] Burette,[6] having translated certain Greek musical pieces as well as could be, into our musical notation, was simple enough to have them played at the Academy of Belles-Lettres; and the academicians were patient enough to listen to them. Such an experiment is admirable, in a country whose music all other nations find indescribable. Ask any foreign musician to perform a French operatic monologue and I defy you to recognize any part of it. Yet these are the same Frenchmen who purport to determine the melody of an ode of Pindar set to music two thousand years ago!

I have read that the Indians in America, having seen the amazing results of firearms, would gather musket balls from the ground; they would throw them by hand, making a loud noise with the mouth. They were quite surprised that

---

4. "*Archytas atque Aristoxenes etiam subjectam grammaticen musicae putaverunt, et eosdem utriusque rei praeceptores fuisse. . . . Tum Eupolis, apud quem Prodamus et musicen et litteras docet. Et Maricas, qui est Hyperbolus, nihil se ex musicis scire nisi litteras confitetur.*" Quintillian, Bk. I, ch. 10. [Au.] "Archytas and Aristoxenes also considered grammar to be included under music, and the same masters taught both. . . . Then too, Eupolis has Prodamus teaching both music and letters. And Maricas, who is Hyperbolus, admits that he knows nothing of music except letters." [Tr.]

5. No doubt allowance must be made for Greek exaggeration in all such matters; but one concedes too much to modern prejudice if one pushes such discounting to the point where all differences vanish. "When Greek music in the time of Amphion and Orpheus had reached the level it has attained today in the remotest provincial cities," says Abbé Terrasson, "it would interrupt the course of rivers, attract oak trees, and move cliffs. Today, having reached a very high degree of perfection, it is very much loved, it is just as pervasively beautiful, but it leaves everything in place. Thus, for example, it includes the verses of Homer, a poet born in the infancy of the human spirit, compared to those who followed. We are enraptured by these verses, but today we are content simply to enjoy and esteem those good poets." Undoubtedly the Abbé Terrasson has had some acquaintance with philosophy, but he does not show it in this passage. [Au.]

   The Abbé Jean Terrasson (1670–1750), professor of Greek and Latin at the Collège de France, is best known for his romance *Sethos*, the tale of an Egyptian prince's initiation into the mysteries, which is considered a source for the libretto of Mozart's *Die Zauberflöte*. In the ongoing discussions about the competing virtues of the ancients and the moderns, Terrasson took the part of the moderns. In his *Critical Dissertation on Homer's "Iliad"* he enumerated the faults in Homer and called for a poetics "founded on reason."

6. Pierre-Jean Burette (1665–1747), Parisian musician and scholar of great erudition who gave himself to the study of ancient music. His essays on the subject are cited frequently by his contemporaries.

they did not kill anyone. Our orators, our musicians, and our scholars are like these Indians. It is not remarkable that we do not do as much with our music as the Greeks did with theirs. On the contrary, it would be remarkable if one produced the same results with such different instruments.

CHAPTER THIRTEEN: ON MELODY

No one doubts that man is changed by his feelings. But instead of distinguishing the changes, we confuse them with their causes. We attach far too little importance to sensations. We do not see that frequently they have no effect on us merely as sensations, but as signs or images, and also that their moral effects have moral causes. Just as the feelings that a painting excites in us are not at all due to colors, the power of music over our souls is not at all the work of sounds. Beautiful, subtly shaded colors are a pleasing sight; but this is purely a pleasure of the sense. It is the drawing, the representation, which gives life and spirit to these colors. The passions they express are what stir ours; the objects they represent are what affect us. Colors entail no interest or feeling at all. The strokes of a touching picture affect us even in a print. Without these strokes in the picture, the colors would do nothing more.

The role of melody in music is precisely that of drawing in a painting. This is what constitutes the strokes and figures, of which the harmony and the sounds are merely the colors. But, it is said, melody is merely a succession of sounds. No doubt. And drawing is only an arrangement of colors. An orator uses ink to write out his compositions: does that mean ink is a very eloquent liquid?

Imagine a country in which no one has any idea of drawing, but where many people who spend their lives combining and mixing various shades of color are considered to excel at painting. Those people would regard our painting precisely as we consider Greek music. If they heard of the emotions aroused in us by beautiful paintings, the spell of a pathetic scene, their scholars would rush into a ponderous investigation of the material, comparing their colors to ours, determining whether our green is more delicate or our red more brilliant. They would try to find out which color combinations drew tears, which could arouse anger. The Burettes of that country would examine just a few tattered scraps of our paintings. Then they would ask with surprise what is so remarkable about such coloring.

And if a start were made in a neighboring country toward the development of line and stroke, an incipient drawing, some still imperfect figure, it would all be treated as merely capricious, baroque daubing. And, for the sake of taste, one would cling to this simple style, which really expresses nothing, but brilliantly produces beautiful nuances, big slabs of color, long series of gradually shaded hues, without a hint of drawing.

Finally, the power of progress would lead to experiments with the prism. And immediately some famous artist would base a beautiful system on it. Gentlemen, he will tell you, true philosophy requires that things be traced to physical causes. Behold the analysis of light; behold the primary colors; observe their relations, their proportions. These are the true principles of the pleasure that painting gives you. All this mysterious talk of drawing, representation, figure, is just the charlatanry of French painters who think that by their imitations they can produce I know not what stirrings of the spirit, while it is known that nothing is involved but sensation. You hear of the marvels of their pictures; but look at my colors.

French painters, he would continue, may have seen a rainbow. Nature may have given them some taste for nuance, some sense of color. But I have revealed to you the great and true principles of art. I say of art! of all the arts, gentlemen, and of all the sciences. The analysis of colors, the calculation of prismatic refractions, give you the only exact relations in nature, the rule of all relations. And everything in the universe is nothing but relations. Thus one knows everything when one knows how to paint; one knows everything when one knows how to match colors.

What are we to say of a painter sufficiently devoid of feeling and taste to think like that, stupidly restricting the pleasurable character of his art to its mere mechanics? What shall we say of a musician, similarly quite prejudiced, who considers harmony the sole source of the great effects of music. Let us consign the first to housepainting and condemn the other to doing French opera.[7]

Music is no more the art of combining sounds to please the ear than painting is the art of combining colors to please the eye. If there were no more to it than that, they would both be natural sciences rather than fine arts. Imitation alone raises them to this level. But what makes painting an imitative art? Drawing. What makes music another? Melody.

CHAPTER FOURTEEN: ON HARMONY

The beauty of sounds is natural. Their effect is purely physical. It is due to the coincidence of various particles of air set in motion by the sonorous body and all their aliquots, perhaps to infinity: the total effect is pleasing. Everyone in the world takes pleasure in hearing beautiful sounds. But if the pleasure is not enlivened by melodious inflections that are familiar to them, it will not be at all delightful, will not become at all voluptuous. The songs most beautiful to us will only moderately move those to whom they are quite unfamiliar. It is a tongue for which one needs a dictionary.

Harmony, properly speaking, is a still more difficult matter. Being only conventionally beautiful, it does not in any way please the completely unpracticed ear. Development of sensitivity and taste for it requires long exposure. To the

7. In this paragraph and in Chapter 14 Rousseau is attacking Jean-Philippe Rameau, who considered music a science of which the universal principle was harmony. Rousseau also attacks Rameau in his *Lettre sur la musique française* (see pp. 161–74.

uncultured ear, our consonances are merely noise. It is not surprising that when natural proportions are impaired, the corresponding natural pleasure is destroyed.

A sound is accompanied by all its concomitant harmonic sounds so related in terms of power and interval as to harmonize most perfectly with that sound. Join to it the third or fifth or some other consonance; you do not join anything to it, you redouble it. You retain the relation of interval while changing that of force. By intensifying one consonance and not the others, you break up the proportion. In trying to do better than nature, you do worse. Your ear and your taste are impaired by a poor understanding of the art. Naturally, the only harmony is unison.

M. Rameau proposes that, by a certain unity, each treble naturally suggests its bass and that an untrained person with a true ear will naturally begin to sing that bass. That is the prejudice of a musician, against all experience. Not only will those who have no idea of either bass or harmony fail to find it, but even if they could be made to understand it, they would be displeased by it, preferring simple unison.

Even if one spent a thousand years calculating the relations of sounds and the laws of harmony, how would one ever make of that art an imitative art? Where is the principle of this supposed imitation? Of what harmony is it the sign? And what do chords have in common with our passions?

When the same question is applied to melody, the reply is the same: it is in the mind of the reader beforehand. By imitating the inflections of the voice, melody expresses pity, cries of sorrow and joy, threats and groans. All the vocal signs of passion are within its domain. It imitates the tones of languages, and the twists produced in every idiom by certain psychic acts.[8] Not only does it imitate, it bespeaks. And its language, though inarticulate, is lively, ardent, passionate; and it has a hundred times the vigor of speech itself. This is what gives music its power of representation and song its power over sensitive hearts. In certain systems, harmony can bring about unification through binding the succession of sounds according to laws of modulation; rendering intonation more appropriate and offering some definite aural evidence of this aptness; fixing and reconciling consonant intervals, and coordinating imperceptible inflections. But in the process it also shackles melody, draining it of energy and expressiveness. It wipes out passionate accent, replacing it with the harmonic interval. It is restricted to only two types of songs, within which its possibilities are determined by the number of oral tones. It eliminates many sounds or intervals which do not fit into its system. Thus in brief, it separates singing from speech, setting these two languages against each other to their mutual deprivation of all authenticity, so that it is absurd for them to occur together in a pathetic subject. That is why the expression of strong and serious passion in song always seems ridiculous, for it is known that in our languages the passions

8. *Mouvemens de l'âme.* [Tr.]

have no musical inflection at all, and that northern peoples do not die singing any more than swans do.[9]

By itself, harmony is insufficient even for those expressions that seem to depend uniquely on it. Thunder, murmuring waters, winds, tempests, are but poorly rendered by simple harmonies. Whatever one does, noise alone does not speak to the spirit at all. The objects of which one speaks must be understood. In all imitation, some form of discourse must substitute for the voice of nature. The musician who would represent noise by noise deceives himself. He knows nothing of either the weakness or the strength of his art, concerning which his judgment is tasteless and unenlightened.

Let him realize that he will have to render noise in song; that to produce the croaking of frogs, he will have to have them sing. For it is not enough to imitate them; he must do so touchingly and pleasantly. Otherwise, his tedious imitation is nothing, and will neither interest nor impress anyone.

CHAPTER FIFTEEN: THAT OUR MOST LIVELY SENSATIONS FREQUENTLY ARE PRODUCED BY MORAL IMPRESSIONS

As much as one might want to consider sounds only in terms of the shock that they excite in our nerves, this would not touch the true principle of music, nor its power over men's hearts. The sounds of a melody do not affect us merely as sounds, but as signs of our affections, of our feelings. It is thus that they excite in us the emotions which they express, whose image we recognize in them. Something of this moral effect is perceivable even in animals. The barking of one dog will attract another. When my cat hears me imitate a mewing, I see it become immediately attentive, alert, agitated. When it discovers that I am just counterfeiting the voice of its species, it relaxes and resumes its rest. Since there is nothing at all different in the stimulation of the sense organ, and the cat had initially been deceived, what accounts for the difference?

Unless the influence of sensations upon us is due mainly to moral causes, why are we so sensitive to impressions that mean nothing to the uncivilized? Why is our most touching music only a pointless noise to the ear of a West Indian? Are his nerves of a different nature from ours? Why are they not excited in the same way? Or, why should the same stimulus excite some people very much and others so little?

The healing of tarantula bites is cited in proof of the physical power of sounds. But in fact this evidence proves quite the opposite. What is needed for curing those bitten by this insect are neither isolated sounds, nor even simply tunes. Rather, each needs tunes with familiar melodies and understandable lyrics. Italian tunes are needed for Italians; for Turks, Turkish tunes. Each is

9. "In southern climes, where nature is bountiful, needs are born of passion. In cold countries, where she is miserly, passions are born of need, and the languages, sad daughters of necessity, reflect their austere origin" (Chapter 10, "Formation of the Languages of the North").

affected only by accents familiar to him. His nerves yield only to what his spirit predisposes them. One must speak to him in a language he understands, if he is to be moved by what he is told. The cantatas of Bernier[10] are said to have cured the fever of a French musician. They would have given one to a musician of any other nation.

The same differences can be observed relative to the other senses, even the crudest. Suppose a man has his hand placed and his eyes fixed upon the same object, while he alternately believes it to be alive and not alive: the effect on his senses would be the same, but what a different impression! Roundness, whiteness, firmness, pleasant warmth, springy resistance, and successive rising would give him only a pleasant but insipid feeling if he did not believe he felt a heart full of life beating under it all.

I know of only one affective sense in which there is no moral element: that is taste. And, accordingly, gluttony is the main vice only of those who have no sense of taste.

If those who philosophize about the power of sensations would begin by distinguishing pure sense impressions from the intellectual and moral impressions received through the senses, but of which the senses are only the occasional causes, they would avoid the error of attributing to sense objects a power they do not have, or that they have only in relation to affections of the soul which they represent to us. Colors and sounds can do much, as representatives and signs, very little simply as objects of sense. Series of sounds or of chords will perhaps amuse me for a moment; but to charm me and soften me, these series must offer something that is neither sound nor chord, and moves me in spite of myself. Even songs that are merely pleasant but say nothing, are tiresome. For the ear does not so much convey pleasure to the heart as the heart conveys it to the ear. I believe that through developing these ideas, we shall be spared stupid arguments about ancient music. But in this century when all the operations of the soul have to be materialized, and deprived of all morality and human feeling, I am deluded if the new philosophy does not become as destructive of good taste as of virtue.

CHAPTER SIXTEEN: FALSE ANALOGY BETWEEN COLORS AND SOUNDS

There is no kind of absurdity that has not been given a place in the treatment of fine arts by physical observation. The same relations have been discovered in the analysis of sound as in the analysis of light. This analogy has been seized upon immediately and eagerly, with no concern for reason or experience. The systematizing spirit has confused everything, and presumes, out of ignorance, to paint for the ears and sing for the eyes. I have seen the famous clavichord

---

10. Nicolas Bernier (1665–1734), French composer and teacher, *sous-maître* of the king's chapel from 1723 to his death, who in addition to sacred vocal motets composed a number of secular cantatas.

on which music is supposedly made with colors. It would be a complete misunderstanding of the workings of nature not to see that the effect of colors is in their stability and that that of sounds is in their succession.

All the riches of color display themselves at a given moment. Everything is taken in at first glance. But the more one looks, the more one is enchanted; one need only admire and contemplate, endlessly.

This is not true of sound. Nature does not analyze sounds or isolate harmonics. On the contrary, it hides such distinctions under the appearance of unison. Or, if it does sometimes separate them, as in the modulated singing of man and the warbling of some birds, it is in succession, one after the other. Nature inspires songs, not accords; she speaks of melody, not harmony. Colors are the clothing of inanimate objects. All matter is colored. But sounds manifest movement. A voice bespeaks a sensitive being. Only living bodies sing. It is not an automatic flute player that plays the flute; it is the engineer who measured the wind and made the fingers move.

Thus each sense has its proper domain. The domain of music is time; that of painting is space. To multiply the sounds heard at a given time, or to present colors in sequence, is to alter their economy, putting the eye in the place of the ear, and the ear in the place of the eye.

You say: Just as color is determined by the angle of refraction of the ray it emits, each sound is determined by the number of vibrations of a sounding object in a given time period. But the relations of these angles and of these numbers will be the same. The analogy is evident. Agreed. Yet this analogy is rational, not experiential. So this is not an issue. The angle of refraction is primarily experiential and measurable, while the number of vibrations is not. Sounding bodies, subject to air currents, incessantly change in volume and tone. Colors are durable, sounds vanish. And one is never sure that later sounds will be the same as those that preceded. Further, each color is absolute and independent while each sound is, for us, only relative, distinguished only by comparison. A sound, considered in itself, has no absolute character by which it is recognizable. It is hard or soft, has an acute or grave accent in relation to another. In itself, none of this applies to it. Even in the harmonic system, no sound is anything by nature. It is neither tonic, nor dominant, nor harmonic nor fundamental, because all these properties are only relational; and because the whole system could vary from grave to acute, each sound changing its rank and position in the system according to the extent to which the system itself changes. But the properties of colors are not at all relational. Yellow is yellow, independently of red and of blue. Everywhere it is sensate and recognizable. As soon as its angle of refraction is determined, one can be certain that one has the same yellow at all times.

The locus of colors is not in colored bodies, but in light. For an object to be visible, it must be illuminated. Sounds also need a mover, and in order for them to exist, a sonorous body must be struck. This is another advantage of sight, for the perpetual emanation of the stars is its natural stimulus, while nature alone engenders little sound. And, unless one believes in the harmony of the celestial spheres, it must be produced by living beings.

From this it is evident that painting is closer to nature and that music is more dependent on human art. It is evident also that the one is more interesting than the other precisely because it does more to relate man to man, and always gives us some idea of our kind. Painting is often dead and inanimate. It can carry you to the depths of the desert; but as soon as vocal signs strike your ear, they announce to you a being like yourself. They are, so to speak, the voice of the soul. If you hear them in the wilderness, they tell you you are not there alone. Birds whistle; man alone sings. And one cannot hear either singing or a symphony without immediately acknowledging the presence of another intelligent being.

It is one of the great advantages of the musician that he can represent things that cannot be heard, while it is impossible to represent in painting things which cannot be seen. And the greatest marvel, for an art whose only medium is motion, is to represent repose. Sleep, the calm of night, even silence, enter into musical pictures. It is known that noise can produce the effect of silence, and silence the effect of noise, as when one falls asleep at a dull monotonous lecture and wakes up as soon as it ends. But music affects us more deeply, arousing through one sense feelings similar to those aroused through another. But, since its result must be perceptible, and its impression weak, painting lacks this power: it cannot imitate music as music can imitate it. Even if the whole of nature were asleep, those who contemplate it would not be. And the musician's art consists of substituting for an imperceptible image of the object the movements which its presence excites in the heart of the contemplator. Not only will it agitate the sea, fan flames, and engorge a stream, but it will depict the horrors of a frightening wilderness, darken the walls of a dungeon, calm a tempest, subdue the winds, and the orchestra will lavish new freshness upon the forest. It does not represent these things directly, but excites in the soul the same feelings one experiences in seeing them.

CHAPTER SEVENTEEN: AN ERROR OF MUSICIANS HARMFUL TO THEIR ART

See how everything continually takes us back to the moral effects of which I spoke, and how far from understanding the power of their art are those many musicians who think of the potency of sounds only in terms of air pressure and string vibrations. The more they assimilate it to purely physical impressions, the farther they get from its source and the more they deprive it of its primitive energy. In dropping its oral tone and sticking exclusively to the establishment of harmonics, music becomes noisier to the ear and less pleasing to the heart. As soon as its stops singing, it stops speaking. And then, with all its accord and all its harmony it will have no more effect upon us.

18 Johann Jakob Engel

As a student of philosophy and theology in Leipzig, Johann Jakob Engel (1741–1802) grew interested in musical theater, and wrote a libretto based on Carlo Goldoni's *Lo speziale* that was later set to music by Christian Gottlob Neefe (*Der Apotheker,* 1771). Appointed professor of philosophy and liberal arts in Berlin in 1775, he continued writing for the theater, publishing a collection of comedies in 1785. He became an important figure in Berlin intellectual life and in 1788 was appointed director of the newly established National Theater of Berlin. His writings went through several editions and were translated into French and Italian.

Über die musikalische Malerey (*On Painting in Music*) is primarily concerned with representation in music. Music must "paint," Engel writes, but it is least effective when it tries to paint external objects: it should depict instead the impression an object makes on the soul. Thus representation becomes internalized, its proper subject the expression of the passions. Expression does not, however, translate into *self*-expression; the passions are affects common to all, and music's means to depict them can to some extent be codified. Engel's concept of mediated representation has been connected by modern writers such as Adolf Sandberger with Beethoven's famous characterization of the "Pastorale" Symphony as "mehr Ausdruck der Empfindung als Mahlerey" ("more an expression of feeling than painting").

FROM *On Painting in Music*

(1780)

To the Royal Capellmeister Herr Reichardt[1]

Dearest Friend!

As I see it, the investigation you have assigned me amounts to the following four questions:

First: What does "painting" mean?

Second: What means does music have for painting?

Third: What is it in a position to paint by these means?

Fourth: What should it paint, and what should it refrain from painting?

If one wanted to give an exhaustive answer to these questions, it would lead hither and yon, in a very rarefied, almost hairsplitting investigation. I will avoid

---

Text: *Schriften* (Berlin, 1844), vol. 4, pp. 136–56. Translation by Wye J. Allanbrook.

1. Johann Friedrich Reichardt became Capellmeister at the court of Frederick the Great in the same year that Engel took up residence in Berlin; see pp. 295–307.

these subtleties, introducing only the premises that seem to me absolutely necessary and hurrying on to practical matters.

Painting does not mean bringing an object to the understanding by means of signs that have been agreed upon in a merely arbitrary fashion, but bringing that object before the perception of the senses by means of natural signs. The word "lion" merely stimulates a representation in my understanding; the picture of a lion actually places the visible phenomenon before my eyes. The word "roar" already has a sort of pictorial content; Benda's expression of it in *Ariadne* is an even more complete painting of a roar.

Certainly in poetry the word is used in a somewhat different fashion. A poet is considered all the more a painter:

First: the more he goes into the particular and individual in his representations; the more he gives them sensuousness and animation through more precise specification. Language usually furnishes him only with general notions for the understanding, which the listener or reader must first change into images for the imagination. Through a more precise specification of these notions the poet comes to the aid of the imagination, and stimulates it to think of images from a specific viewpoint, with a superior power and clarity.

Second: the more he brings the mechanical—the sound of the words and the cadence of the meter—into agreement with the inner meaning of the discourse. In other words, the more he introduces a resemblance with the represented object itself into the perception of the signs that signify these objects. Or in other words still, the more he makes his merely arbitrary signs approximate the natural ones.

In music this first understanding of the word "painting" does not apply, leaving only the second. Musical tones are not arbitrary signs, since there is no agreement about what they are supposed to make one think. They make their effect not by something signified through them, but by themselves alone, as particular kinds of impressions on our hearing. The composer has nothing general to individualize; he has no notions of the understanding to beautify by making them specific. But by means of his tones as by means of natural signs, he can stimulate representations of other related objects. He can suggest these objects to us by means of tones just as the painter tries to suggest his through colors. And then he must do what the poet does as painter in the second sense: he must make his tones as imitative as possible, and lend them as much similarity to the objects as possible.

Now this painting is either *complete* or *incomplete.* The one type brings the entire phenomenon before our perception, while the other presents only its separate parts or *properties.*

Complete painting obviously takes place only when the object itself is audible, and compatible with regular tones and measured rhythm.

As regards incomplete painting:

First: the object can be a phenomenon compounded of the impressions of different senses, where the audible is mixed with the visible and so forth. By imitating the audible the composer arouses in the imagination the representation of the whole. This is the way to paint a battle, a storm, or a hurricane, for example.

Second: the object may contain absolutely nothing audible, but still share with audible tones certain general properties, which provide the imagination with an easy passage from one to the other.

That is, there are similarities not merely between objects of a single sense, but also between those of different senses. Slowness and quickness, for example, occur just as much in a sequence of tones as they do in a sequence of visual impressions. I will call all such similarities *transcendental* similarities.

Now the composer ferrets out such transcendental similarities, and manages at least an incomplete painting of the quick dash of an *Atalanta*—which of course only mime can imitate completely—by means of the quick sequence of his tones. If he can put it together with the imitation of painting, then he has depicted at the same time the audible part of the phenomenon: his painting is twofold.

This possibility multiplies the objects that the composer can paint. Many objects of the other senses, especially of sight—the external sense most fertile in concepts—are susceptible to musical imitation by means of their transcendental similarities with tones.

At the same time, however, it becomes clear, at least in part, why musical imitation remains generally so indefinite—why it is so difficult, without the help of words, to understand the painting composer. Imitation is almost always only incomplete, only partial, only with respect to general properties, whether an externally sensed object or an inner feeling is imitated. For the feeling is also imitated only in a general way; it can be individualized only through a particular representation of the object arousing it. More about this is soon to follow.

To list all the transcendental similarities that serve this imitation would be as superfluous as it would be impossible. Nature goes into such fine detail on this that the most detailed investigation could hardly follow her. But those who have investigated the origins of language, among others a well-known sect of ancient philosophers,[2] have already provided some ideas that are also useful for this theory.

These ancient philosophers remind me that for our incomplete painting there is still another powerful means at hand. That is, the composer still paints:

Third: when he imitates not a part or a property of the object itself, but the impression that this object tends to make on the soul. Imitation in music obtains its broadest range by this means. For now we no longer require in the object itself those qualities I called transcendental similarities. Even color is paintable. For the impression of a delicate color bears some resemblance to the impression of a gentle tone on the soul.

---

2. The Stoics. See Tiedemann's *System of Stoic Philosophy*, vol. 1, p. 147ff. [Au.] Dietrich Tiedemann was a German philosopher whose *Geist der spekulativen Philosophie* (6 vols., Marburg, 1791–97) was the first modern history of philosophy.

In order to understand how these impressions, or indeed all inner feelings of the soul, can be painted, and why such painting succeeds best in music, and further, why even such painting must still always remain incomplete, we must answer the second question we posed above: What means has music for painting?

I put down here what I know, and as well as I know it. It is the task of a master in the art to amend any incorrect ideas I may have, and to supplement any deficient ones.

The means for musical painting are, to my knowledge:

First: The choice of *mode*—major and minor.

Second: The choice of the *tone* from which the piece should proceed. Each of the twelve major and minor scales differs from the others through its own different intervals, and receives from that its own character. *C major* and *A major* diverge in character most of all because the progressions of their scales are the least similar; and a characteristic instrumental piece transposed out of *C major* into *A major* will be almost unrecognizable. The same holds for the minor modes.

Third: Melody. It is of great importance whether the tones progress in either small or large intervals, in light or heavy ones, whether in uniformly long or short notes, or in mixed ones. Also whether this mixing comes about according to a manifest order or with apparent irregularity, whether the embellishments are simple, or manifold and rich, etc. I doubt that everything that comes under consideration here can be listed.

Fourth: Movement. Under this head are included measures that are duple or triple, long or short; quick or slow, simple or varied and manifold movement in different voices; parallel, non-parallel, or even contrary motion, and so on.

Fifth: Rhythm. The periods and their sections are either long or short, equal or unequal.

Sixth: Harmony, the combining of simultaneously sounding tones in direct or indirect consonances. In consideration here are: the way to combine simpler or more complex, lighter or heavier proportions; the way these compounded proportions progress, which can occur in an endless number of shifts; the slowness or rapidity of the shifts; the fullness or emptiness, clarity or obscurity, purity or impurity, of the harmony (an impurity that is often only apparent), and so on.

Seventh: The choice of *voices.* Deep, high, medium voices, a particular mixture of the voices—each has a different effect.

Eighth: The choice of *instruments,* according to their own very different characters, and the way in which they are mixed.

Ninth: Loudness and softness, their shading in its different degrees, and the manner of the shading.

How by using these devices to their fullest extent the composer can paint the inner feelings and movements of the soul will become clear in the following observations.

First: All representations of the passions in the soul are inseparably bound up with certain corresponding movements in the nervous system, and are maintained and strengthened by the perception of these movements. But it is not just that these corresponding natural vibrations arise in the body when the representations of the passions have already been stimulated in the soul; these representations also arise in the soul if the related vibrations are already produced in the body. The action is reciprocal: the same path that runs from the soul into the body runs back from the body into the soul. By nothing else, however, are these vibrations so certainly, so powerfully, so variously produced, as by tones. Thus nature herself makes use chiefly of tones in order to stir up the instinctive sympathy that exists among beasts of the same species. The howls of a beast in pain set the nerves of a beast that is not in pain into a similar vibration, and that similar vibration arouses a similar feeling in the latter beast's soul. Hence this feeling takes the name of com-passion, or shared pain. The same goes for con-celebration, or shared joy.[3]

Second: The various kinds of representations of the passions differ in the fullness and wealth of the several representations united in each; in the greater variety of the multiplicity that is united in each; in the greater or lesser accord within this variety, which poses a greater or lesser obstacle to comprehending the whole representation and thinking it through; in the slower or quicker succession of representations; in the smaller or larger steps according as more or fewer intermediate representations are skipped over; in the greater or lesser uniformity of the progression, since some are slow and others quick in their progression while others, extremely irregular, are sometimes halting in their course and sometimes move more quickly, and so on.

I will give just a few examples. Representations of the exalted have a very weighty content, so their movement is slow. Representations of joy have a content that is easily grasped, so their movement is sprightly, the leaps not large. Fear works more quickly, but in a broken style, with a handful of discordant ideas. Melancholy steals off in slow and lingering steps, using closely related ideas.

Have I made it clear in these remarks:

First: how music can paint or imitate the inner feelings of the soul? It chooses tones that have a certain effect on the nerves, which is similar to the impression of a given feeling. To this end it also chooses particular instruments and higher or lower tones. If the tones of a Franklin harmonica[4] fling a man of only somewhat sensitive nerves irresistibly into melancholy, then on the other hand the blare of the trumpet and the roll of the drums move him just as

3. There is no precise English equivalent for the German word pair *Mitleiden* and *Mitfreude*— feelings of sympathy for another's pain and for another's joy.
4. The "armonica," Benjamin Franklin's mechanized version of the musical glasses, proved very popular in Europe; Mozart wrote his Quintet K. 617 for armonica, flute, oboe, viola, and cello for the blind virtuoso Marianne Kirchgessner. The instrument was reputed to have an unsettling effect on the nerves of the player.

irresistibly to transports of joy and exaltation. And while the higher tones are more appropriate to all the sprightly, happy feelings and the middle tones to all the soft, gentle ones, so are the lower tones most suited for all the sad, gruesome, mournful ones. Thus in the first three words of the line

Sacri orrori, ombre felici![5]

Hasse sank ever further into the depths; but the last word he suddenly set on high.

But music paints the feelings infinitely better still when in the representation of these corresponding nerve vibrations, and especially in their succession, it brings out all the analogies with the feelings noted above by means of a wise choice of pitch, of key, of harmony, melody, meter, and tempo. It accomplishes this by giving the harmony more or less richness or poverty, lightness or heaviness, by letting the melody proceed in closer or more distant intervals, by making the tempo faster or slower, more or less uniform, and so on.

Second: Have I made it clear why music succeeds best when painting the feelings? For it takes effect here with all its powers assembled; here it applies all its devices as one; here it concentrates all its effects. This will very rarely be the case if it only paints the objects that give rise to feelings. These objects it can usually signify only by single, weak, and distant similarities, while the feelings it can signify by a multitude of very particular similarities.

Third: Have I made it clear why nevertheless even this kind of painting still remains incomplete? As has already been remarked above, a feeling cannot be individualized except by a particular representation of the object arousing it. In this respect music must always be far behind. All it can do, with the concentrated power of all its devices, is indicate classes or types of feelings, even if they consist of low-level, more specific types of feelings. The more special and individual aspects—whatever must be first apprehended from the particular nature and context of the object—remains consistently unspecified, precisely because music cannot also indicate that special nature and context.

From these two last remarks, which I believe to be clear and evident, two rules follow directly:

The *first* rule is that the composer should always paint feelings rather than objects of feelings; always the state into which the soul and with it the body are conveyed through contemplation of a certain matter and event, rather than this matter and event itself. For one should prefer to execute with every art whatever it allows one to execute best—most perfectly. So in the kind of storm symphony that appears in various operas, it is always better to paint the inner movements of the soul in a storm than the storm that occasions these movements. Even though there is much in that phenomenon that would be audible, the former method is always more successful than the latter. On this basis alone

---

5. "Sacred terrors, fortunate shades!" Engel drew this and two other examples in this essay from arias in Johann Adolf Hasse's oratorio *Sant'Elena al Calvario* (Dresden, 1746; rev. Vienna, 1753, 1772).

Hiller's storm symphony in *Der Jagd* is undoubtedly superior to *Philidor's*.[6]

But there is still another and, as it seems to me, more powerful ground for this rule. For since music is essentially created for the feelings, since everything in it works toward this goal, the composer cannot fail, even if he is merely painting an object, to express certain feelings that the soul enters into and wants to pursue. But it almost always turns out that, despite the effort of the composer to imitate a particular thing or event, the soul is driven unpleasantly from feeling to feeling, and is led astray in the entire sequence of its representations.

The *second* rule is that the composer must not try to paint a sequence of feelings that, because it is dependent on some other sequence of occasions or considerations, will have an incomprehensible or nonsensical effect if one does not have in mind simultaneously that other sequence on which this one depends. Let me explain further.

Suppose that the most beautiful accompanied recitative of a *Hasse* were performed without the voices, or, even better perhaps, that a duodrama of *Benda's* were performed by the orchestra alone, without the characters.[7] What would you think you heard in the best work, one composed with the finest taste and the most correct judgment? Nothing other than the wild fantasy of a person delirious with fever. But why? Clearly because the sequence of ideas or events, which is what makes the sequence of feelings comprehensible, has been removed from the whole. And will it not be the same thing when a composer makes up his mind, as has actually happened, to put in the overture to an opera the whole sequence of feelings that is to be aroused in the spectators during the course of the action? In my opinion at least, the overture with which *Monsigny* opens his *Deserteur*—it has many admirers—as well as the one with which he opens his *Bel Arsène*, have always just seemed very tasteless.[8]

If a symphony or a sonata—any musical work not supported by speech or the art of gesture—is intended to be more than just an agreeable noise, a pleasing buzz of tones, it must contain the realization of a single passion, although certainly that realization can take the form of a variety of feelings. It must contain the sort of sequence of feelings that would evolve by itself in a soul completely immersed in a passion, unhindered by externals, and uninterrupted in the free flow of its ideas. If I may be permitted to assume a theory

6. The comparison is apt, since Johann Adam Hiller (1728–1804) turned to French models for *The Hunt* (Weimar, 1770) and other of his operas written in the 1760s and '70s.

7. Georg Benda wrote three stage works consisting of a spoken text with musical accompaniment— *Ariadne auf Naxos* and *Medea* in 1775 and *Pygmalion*, to Rousseau's text, in 1780 (see p. 247, n. 2). Called generically "melodramas," they were also often termed "duodramas" or "monodramas" after the number of participating characters; they were generally short pieces involving only a soloist or a duo.

8. *The Deserter* (1769) and *The Fair Arsene* (1775), by Pierre Alexandre Monsigny (1729–1817), a native French composer of meager musical training but who, with François-André Danican Philidor and Pierre Alexandre Duni, is ranked among the founders of the *opéra comique*. He was known for the richness of his writing for instruments.

of the various sequences of ideas and their principles that has not yet become well-known, I would say that this sequence of ideas must not be other than the *lyric*.

I am coming to what you most expect from me—the specification of rules for vocal composition. Before all else I must distinguish between the voices and the accompaniment. I will take up the former first.

Everything I have to say here is based on the distinction between *painting* and *expression*. This distinction has existed for a long time, but nevertheless, I fear, has not been given proper attention.

A pure idea of the understanding that has no reference to our desire, the pure, passionless representation of a thing as it is, without associated representations concerning whether it is good or bad, whether it compliments or counters our natural inclinations—this is not an aesthetic notion suited to the fine arts. It is not the sort of thing that the true poet will write, and least of all that he will write to be set to music. In every true poetic notion, and still more in every musico-poetic notion, we must be able to distinguish two things—the representation of the object, and the representation of the relation this object has to our desires. For we will esteem or despise it, love or hate it, be angry at it, frightened by it, or delight in it, stand in awe of it or pine for it, and so on.

In short, in any such notion two things must be distinguishable—the *objective* and the *subjective*.

In order to anticipate any confusion or misinterpretation, let me remind you that something that originally was subjective can become objective. That is, the representation of a feeling, whether someone else's or our own, can become the source of a new feeling, and sometimes even of a different, a contrary feeling. Someone else's joy can stir me to anger; I can be saddened to see myself take pleasure in something that my reason does not accept. In these examples the joy and pleasure are objective, the anger and sadness subjective.

In vocal music now, *painting* means the depiction of the *objective*, while the depiction of the *subjective* is no longer considered painting, but *expression*.

Fundamentally, of course, both are contained in our previous understanding of painting. Expression one could explain as the painting of the subjective— the painting of feeling. But I would prefer not to use the word feeling because a feeling is not always subjective, that is, the feeling prevailing in the soul right now. The subjective, as I said before, can become the objective; in the same way, I now say, can expression become painting. For example, if feeling is the object of a feeling, and the musician expresses the former feeling that is the object and not the latter, then he is painting. Or perhaps an object usually causes a certain feeling, but in the present case causes a different feeling, possibly one that is completely the opposite. If the composer takes the former for the latter, he has not expressed, but painted.

I hope by the above to have thoroughly specified and clarified the rule we so often repeat to the composer of vocal music, that it should express, and not paint.

This rule hardly needs proof. For:

First: If the objective is not in itself subjective, if it is an external matter or event, then according to one of the previous remarks, the vocal composer who would rather paint than express would be working for the very effect he can least obtain. And even if the objective is originally subjective, then it would still be quite absurd to prefer to paint the feeling that is not at the moment the ruling one rather than the one that now should engage the singer's entire soul.

Second: What else should song be but the most lively, sensuous, passionate speech? And what above all does a man in a passion want to use his speech for? What to him is the most important thing? Certainly not to describe the nature of the object that puts him in the passion, but to pour out and communicate the passion itself. Everything in him works toward this end—the tone of the voice, the facial muscles, the hands and feet.

Thus only expression attains the goal of song; painting destroys it.

But what if painting and expression sometimes coincide? That is, what if the painting of the objective sometimes serves as the expression of the subjective? Indeed if the expression of the subjective sometimes cannot occur without the painting of the objective?

This is in fact so often the case that I would like people to understand the previous rule differently. Instead of saying "The vocal composer should not paint, but express," we should rather say, "The vocal composer should take care not to paint against the expression." That he has painted is not in itself an error, for he can and should paint. It is only an error when he has painted the wrong thing or in the wrong place.

This insight is based on a distinction in our feelings to which we still probably pay too little attention. On the spur of the moment the following is the best way I know to state it. In the one kind of feeling the subjective fuses with— loses itself in—the objective. The passion can only satisfy itself by embracing the object as much as possible, the entire soul by imitating the object as much as possible. In the other kind of feeling the subjective and objective are in clear contrast with one another, and the passion satisfies itself by putting the soul in a setting that is completely opposed to the nature of the object. Since this distinction subdivides the feelings differently than do any of the well-known classifications, I suggest a new designation, in order to be able to express myself more succinctly. The former kind of feeling I will call *homogeneous,* the latter *heterogeneous.*

Examples will make everything clearer. Admiration of a great or noble object is a homogeneous feeling. The contemplating subject assumes as much as possible the nature and quality of the contemplated object. When one thinks on great objects, says *Home,*[9] the voice becomes full, and the breast expands. People who are thinking exalted thoughts raise their heads and lift their voices

9. Henry Home, Lord Kames (1696–1782), a Scottish judge whose *Elements of Criticism* (1762), praised by Samuel Johnson, was a systematic attempt to look beyond the conventional rules of literary composition to investigate the metaphysical principles of the fine arts.

and hands. The subject seeks in every way to imitate the object.

The case is already different with respect and adoration. Here the subject is in contrast with the object. He feels his own weakness, baseness, insignificance, and imperfection in relation to this object: the head is bowed; voice and hands sink down.

This is even more the case with fear. The greatness and strength that are perceived in the object are directed against the subject. The grander and stronger the one, the baser and weaker is the other. The fuller, more exalted, and more splendid the painting, the weaker, more diminished, and subdued is the expression.

From this the following rule directly emerges: in homogeneous feelings painting is expression; with heterogeneous ones painting destroys expression.

Nonetheless even when painting is actually justifiable, the composer should not paint recklessly. I will record here the cautions that are to be noted with this rule. But I will not bring proof, because I think that they are demonstrated by the previous remarks.

First: In the object to be painted there may be several attributes that music is capable of painting. The composer must take care to include only the ones in the prevailing sequence of ideas to which the soul attends. In the concept *sea,* for example, one should probably take into consideration in the actual association of ideas only its dangers, its depths, its broad expanse. It would be the most obvious sin against expression in this case to paint the gentle washing of the waves. If I remember correctly after so many years, *Hasse* did not avoid this error in the aria mentioned above, from the *Sant'Elena.* In the lines:

> Questo è il suol, per cui passai
> Tanti regni e tanto mar,[10]

he gave the last word an extension in the Italian manner expressing a gentle undulation, which must have been far from the mind of St. Helen as she sang. Generally this idea is certainly not suitable to be painted. But it is astonishing to what extent the Italian singsong has destroyed expression, even in the work of our most talented composers.

Second: If in the whole concept there is no precise, musically paintable attribute in the actual sequence of ideas that particularly attracts the attention, then the composer must refrain from descriptive painting altogether, and use simple declamation.

Third: He must judge the importance of each member of the whole sequence of representations—how long, with what degree of attention, the soul would linger on it. And then, if painting should turn out to become expression, he must decide how deeply he should venture to engage in painting. If instead of the main concept on which the soul is concentrating its full attention and around which all the others build and unite, he seizes on one of the secondary

10. "This is the hallowed ground [the tomb of Christ] for the sake of which I have travelled so far on land and sea."

concepts as the focus of his painting, he has committed the very same blunder as if he had set a misplaced stress. It is actually one that is even more unpleasant, because a passage of painting does not slip by as quickly as a tone.

Fourth: The severest offences against expression would be for the composer to paint not the idea but the word, to develop a representation that the words deny and negate, or to hold to the mere picture—to the metaphor—rather than to the things themselves. But we need not give warnings against errors of this sort; all warning is wasted on a person who could actually commit them.

I will still add a couple of remarks, however, in order to anticipate possible objections you might make.

First: Sometimes even in heterogeneous feelings painting accidentally becomes expression. For example, the object of veneration may be the humility, gentleness, and submissiveness of a holy man, or the object of fear may be the uncertainty of the surrounding darkness and a deep, distant, intermittent roar heard in this darkness. In this case the composer can choose almost no other expression than the one with which he would also paint the object.

Second: Occasionally the painting of a secondary detail, which, strictly speaking, should not be considered in the sequence of ideas, turns out either to aid the expression, or at least not to hinder it. *Hasse* in the aria:

> Del Calvario già sorger le cime
> Veggo altere di tempio sublime,
> E i gran Duci del Rè delle sfere
> Pellegrini la tomba adorar![11]

from the oratorio mentioned several times earlier, has introduced the sort of painting of a secondary detail that does not offend my sensibilities at any rate. He paints the arrival of the great commanders-in-chief with a magnificent phrase in march style, which seems remarkably well suited to the joyously exalted feeling that should dominate the whole of the aria. Genius commits those apparent transgressions of the rules in all the arts, and the critic is wrong to find fault with them. But it is equally wrong to allow genius to set itself above all the rules on this account. As long as genius is really genius it remains within the rules, and seems to be violating them only because the rules are still not sufficiently defined and modified. In fact the relation that prevails between theory and practice in most of the arts is still the following: theory is far less useful for perfecting works than are works useful for correcting theory.

As to the instrumental accompaniment, this is primarily what I have to say: far more painting is allowed there than in the voice. Hence in the accompaniments of their arias, and especially in their recitatives, even the best, most expressive composers have not limited themselves to carrying on the expression of the feeling, but have often tried as well to support and enhance that feeling by depicting the object that gave rise to it. *Graun* in the well-known aria:

11. "Already from Calvary I see the proud spires of the lofty temple rising, and the grand Dukes of the King of the heavens coming as pilgrims to worship at the tomb!"

Wenn ich am Rande dieses Lebens
Abgründe sehe . . . [12]

introduced a splendid painting of the dreadful judge into the accompaniment, and this was no error. In the voice, on the other hand, it would be an obvious error.

Nevertheless even in the accompaniment the painting must depict only essential attributes of the object that have a connection with the feeling, and the painting must not be so heterogeneous to the expression that it destroys the feeling instead of maintaining it. This would be the case, for example, if a serious sequence of thoughts were interrupted by a bit of comic painting. This error has been made often by one recent composer—or rather, a composer only lately become well-known, who is otherwise excellent. It makes the most adverse impression in the world when in a thoroughly serious and uplifting piece the beating of the heart is accompanied with *pizzicato*, or the hissing of the serpent is imitated by the violins.

If it were not unsuitable in a letter to you, I would also apply the rules I have established to declamation and mime. For in truth these rules hold for all the kinetic arts. But you can apply them automatically as soon as you have just the slightest notion of those arts and the means by which they operate.

I am with the greatest esteem, etc.

12. "When I see the abysses at the brink of this life . . . " This text is the second section of a da capo aria from Carl Heinrich Graun's Passion cantata *Der Tod Jesu* (1755). It continues: "When I hear the Judge approach with his scales and thunderbolts, and the globe quakes at his step, who then will be my protector?" Engel must be referring to the disjunct dotted figures in the accompaniment that alternate with its pulsing bass line.

19 Wolfgang Amadeus Mozart

We have few substantive statements from Mozart about the nature of the musical art and the process of composition. Fortunately, however, he was in lively correspondence with his father from Vienna while he was composing *Idomeneo*, in 1780–81, and *Die Entführung aus dem Serail*, in the fall of 1781. In the case of *Idomeneo*, Leopold Mozart was the intermediary between his son and the librettist, the Jesuit-trained Giovanni Battista Varesco, a chaplain to the Archbishop of Salzburg. Hence son and father had long exchanges about issues of dramatic effectiveness—where best to place an aria, for example, how to make the action seem natural, or how long a section should last. Mozart was anxious to keep the speech of the subterranean voice tellingly brief, remarking that the Ghost's speech in *Hamlet* (which he had most probably seen in a Salzburg adaptation) would be far more effective if it were not so long. In composing *Die Entführung*, Mozart again worked closely with a compliant librettist,

Gottlieb Stephanie, the director of the National-Singspiel in Vienna. In the following two letters to his father about this collaboration, Mozart touched on a wide range of subjects—characterization in music and the nature of musical expression, the relation of words to music, the success of the Italian comic style, and the problems attendant on meeting the demands of performers and audience.

Letters to His Father

Vienna, September 26, 1781

Mon Trés Cher Pére!

Forgive me for having made you pay an extra heavy postage fee the other day. But I happened to have no necessary business to report and thought that it would afford you pleasure if I gave you some idea of my opera. As the original text began with a monologue,[1] I asked Herr Stephanie to make a little arietta out of it—and then to put in a duet instead of making the two chatter together after Osmin's short song.[2] As we have given the part of Osmin to Herr Fischer,[3] who certainly has an excellent bass voice (in spite of the fact that the Archbishop[4] told me that he sang too low for a bass and that I assured him that he would sing higher next time), we must take advantage of it, particularly as he has the whole Viennese public on his side. But in the original libretto Osmin has only this short song and nothing else to sing, except in the trio and the finale; so he has been given an aria in Act 1, and he is to have another in Act 2. I have explained to Stephanie the words I require for this aria—indeed I had finished composing most of the music for it before Stephanie knew anything whatever about it. I am enclosing only the beginning and the end, which is bound to have a good effect. Osmin's rage is turned into the comic mode by bringing in Turkish music. In working out the aria I have (in spite of our Salzburg Midas)[5] allowed Fischer's beautiful deep notes to glow. The passage "Drum beim Barte des Propheten"[6] is indeed in the same tempo, but with rapid notes; and as Osmin's rage gradually increases—just as one thinks the aria is at an end—the Allegro assai, in a totally different tempo and in a different key, is bound to make the very best effect. For a person who finds himself

TEXT: Translation by Emily Anderson, *The Letters of Mozart and His Family* (2 vols.; London: St. Martin's Press, 1966), vol. 2, pp. 768–70, 772–73, with minor alterations. Used by permission of The Macmillan Press Ltd.

1. The original text, *Belmonte und Konstanze* (1780), was the work of Christoph Friedrich Bretzner (1748–1807), a Leipzig merchant who had written several popular light-opera libretti.
2. It is worthy of note that the part of Osmin, which in Bretzner's libretto is negligible, was transformed by Mozart in collaboration with Stephanie into a towering figure in *Die Entführung*. Possibly Mozart was encouraged to do this as he was composing for a magnificent singer. [Tr.]
3. Ludwig Fischer (1745–1825), a preeminent German bass, worked in Vienna from 1780 to 1783.
4. Hieronymus, Count Colloredo, Archbishop of Salzburg since 1772, was Mozart's patron.
5. That is, the Archbishop. [Tr.]
6. "Thus by the beard of the prophets . . . " (Act 1, no. 3).

in such a towering rage oversteps all bounds of order, proportion, and purpose—he does not recognize himself; so the music, too, must no longer recognize itself. But since the passions, whether violent or not, must never be expressed to the point of exciting disgust, and music, even in the most terrible situations, must still give pleasure and never offend the ear, that is, must always remain *music*, so I have not chosen a key remote from F (in which the aria is written) but one related to it—not the nearest, D minor, but the more remote A minor. Let me now turn to Belmonte's aria in A major, "O wie ängstlich, o wie feurig."[7] Would you like to know how I have expressed it—and even indicated his throbbing heart? By the two violins playing octaves. This is the favorite aria of all those who have heard it, and it is mine also. I wrote it expressly to suit Adamberger's voice.[8] You feel the trembling—the faltering—you see how his throbbing breast begins to swell; this I have expressed by a crescendo. You hear the whispering and the sighing—which I have indicated by the first violins with mutes and a flute playing in unison.

The Janissary chorus is, as such, all that can be desired, that is, short, lively, and written to please the Viennese. I have sacrificed Constanze's aria a little to the flexible throat of Mlle Cavalieri,[9] "Trennung war mein banges Los and nun schwimmt mein Aug' in Tränen."[10] I have tried to express her feelings, as far as an Italian bravura aria will allow it. I have changed the "Hui" to "schnell," so it now runs thus—"Doch wie schnell schwand meine Freude."[11] I really don't know what our German poets are thinking of. Even if they do not understand the theater, or at all events operas, yet they should not make their characters talk as if they were addressing a herd of swine. Hui, sow!

Now for the trio at the close of Act I. Pedrillo has passed off his master as an architect—to give him an opportunity of meeting his Constanze in the garden. Bassa Selim has taken him into his service. Osmin, the steward, knows nothing of this, and being a rude churl and a sworn foe to all strangers, is impertinent and refuses to let them into the garden. It opens quite abruptly— and because the words lend themselves to it, I have made it a fairly respectable piece of three-part writing. Then the major key begins at once *pianissimo*—it must go very quickly—and wind up with a great deal of noise, which is always appropriate at the end of an act. The more noise the better, and the shorter the better, so that the audience may not have time to cool down with their applause.

I have sent you only fourteen bars of the overture, which is very short with

7. "O how fearfully, O how passionately [beats my loving heart]" (Act 1, no. 4).
8. Josef Valentin Adamberger (1743–1804) was a German tenor based in Vienna during the 1780s who was particularly known for his performance of expressive arias in moderate tempos.
9. Caterina Cavalieri, an Austrian soprano, was known for her imposing upper range and impressive flexibility. She also appeared as Donna Elvira in the first Vienna production of Mozart's *Don Giovanni*.
10. "Parting was my dreadful fate, and now my eyes swim with tears" ("Ah ich liebte," Act 1, no. 6).
11 "But how quickly my joy vanished."

alternate *fortes* and *pianos,* the Turkish music always coming in at the *fortes.*
The overture modulates through different keys; and I doubt whether anyone,
even if his previous night has been a sleepless one, could go to sleep over it.
Now comes the rub! The first act was finished more than three weeks ago, as
was also one aria in Act II and the drunken duet[12] (*per i signori viennesi*) which
consists entirely of *my Turkish tattoo.* But I cannot compose any more, because
the whole story is being altered—and, to tell the truth, at my own request. At
the beginning of Act 3 there is a charming quintet or rather finale, but I should
prefer to have it at the end of Act 2.[13] In order to make this practicable, great
changes must be made, in fact an entirely new plot must be introduced—and
Stephanie is up to the eyes in other work. So we must have a little patience.
Everyone abuses Stephanie. It may be that in my case he is only very friendly
to my face. But after all he is arranging the libretto for me—and, what is more,
as I want it—exactly—and, by Heaven, I do not ask anything more of him.
Well, how I have been chattering to you about my opera! But I cannot help it.
Please send me the march[14] that I mentioned the other day.[15] Gilowsky says
that Daubrawaick[16] will soon be here. Fräulein Auernhammer[17] and I are longing to have the two double concertos.[18] I hope we shall not wait as vainly as
the Jews for their Messiah. Well, adieu. Farewell. I kiss your hands a thousand
times and embrace with all my heart my dear sister, whose health, I hope, is
improving, and am ever your most obedient son

W: A: MOZART

Vienna, October 13, 1781

Mon Trés Cher Pére!

·   ·   ·   ·   ·

Now as to the libretto of the opera. You are quite right so far as Stephanie's
work is concerned. Still, the poetry is perfectly in keeping with the character
of stupid, surly, malicious Osmin. I am well aware that the verse is not of the
best, but it fitted in and it agreed so well with the musical ideas which already
were buzzing in my head, that it could not fail to please me; and I would like

---

12. The duet between Pedrillo and Osmin, "Vivat Bacchus, Bacchus lebe." [Tr.]
13. This is the quartet at the end of Act 2. [Tr.]
14. Probably K. 249, written in 1776 for the wedding of Elizabeth Haffner to F. X. Späth, for
    which Mozart also composed K. 250 [248b], the Haffner serenade. [Tr.]
15. The letter in which Mozart made this request has unfortunately been lost. [Tr.]
16. Franz Wenzel Gilowsky von Urazowa (1757–1816) was a young surgeon in Vienna and had
    been best man at Mozart's wedding. Daubrawaick was possibly a son of Johann Anton Dau-
    brawa von Daubrawaick, Court Councillor in Salzburg, who was to bring Mozart music from
    Salzburg. [Tr.]
17. Fräulein Josepha Auernhammer (1758–1820) became Mozart's pupil on the clavier, and he
    wrote for her his sonata for two pianos, K. 448 [375a]. [Tr.]
18. K. 365 [316a], composed in 1779, and K. 242, a concerto for three claviers, composed in 1776,
    which Mozart himself had arranged for two. [Tr.]

to wager that when it is performed, no deficiencies will be found. As for the poetry which was there originally, I really have nothing to say against it. Belmonte's aria "O wie ängstlich" could hardly be better written for music. Except for "Hui" and "Kummer ruht in meinem Schoss"[19] (for sorrow—cannot rest), the aria too is not bad, particularly the first part. Besides, I should say that in an opera the poetry must be altogether the obedient daughter of the music. Why do Italian comic operas please everywhere—in spite of their miserable libretti—even in Paris, where I myself witnessed their success? Just because there the music reigns supreme and when one listens to it all else is forgotten. Why, an opera is sure of success when the plot is well worked out, the words written solely for the music and not shoved in here and there to suit some miserable rhyme (which, God knows, never enhances the value of any theatrical performance, be it what it may, but rather detracts from it)—I mean, words or even entire verses which ruin the composer's whole idea. Verses are indeed the most indispensable element for music—but rhymes—solely for the sake of rhyming—the most detrimental. Those high and mighty people who set to work in this pedantic fashion will always come to grief, both they and their music. The best thing of all is when a good composer, who understands the stage and is talented enough to make sound suggestions, meets an able poet, that true phoenix; in that case no fears need be entertained as to the applause even of the ignorant. Poets almost remind me of trumpeters with their professional tricks! If we composers were always to stick so faithfully to our rules (which were very good at a time when no one knew better), we should be concocting music as unpalatable as their libretti.

Well, I think I have chattered enough nonsense to you; so I must now enquire about what interests me most of all, and that is, your health, my most beloved father! In my last letter I suggested two remedies for giddiness, which, if you do not know them, you will probably not think any good. But I have been assured that they would certainly have a splendid effect; and the pleasure of thinking that you might recover made me believe this assurance so entirely that I could not refrain from suggesting them with my heart's wishes and with the sincere desire that you may not need them—but that if you do use them, you will recover completely. I trust that my sister is improving daily. I kiss her with all my heart and, my dearest, most beloved father, I kiss your hands a thousand times and am ever your most obedient son.

W. A. Mozart

[P. S.:] As soon as I receive the watch, I shall return yours. Adieu.

19. "Sorrow rests in my bosom."

20 Michel-Paul-Guy de Chabanon

Michel-Paul-Guy de Chabanon was a well-educated man of broad interests: in addition to musical pursuits, he wrote translations and commentaries of ancient Greek texts. Born in the West Indies in 1729 or 1730, he was educated in Paris, where he lived until his death in 1792. He was a violinist of considerable reputation and a composer of instrumental works as well as a youthful opera and several librettos. Although Jean-Philippe Rameau was his mentor and friend (he published a eulogy for the composer after his death in 1764), and he remained faithful to the conviction that the French did indeed have a music, nonetheless his notions about the primacy of melody in music were closer to those of Rousseau. With this independence of mind, and perhaps also because of his involvement with instrumental music, he was able to stand outside the wrangles of the "Querelle des bouffons" and its successors.

In his essay *De la musique considérée en elle-même et dans ses rapports avec la parole, les langues, la poésie, et le théâtre* (*On Music Considered in Itself and in Its Relations with Speech, Languages, Poetry, and the Theater*) he became one of the first writers to argue for the autonomy of music, for its independence from the strictures of imitation. Music to him was most appropriately nonrepresentational, and imitation an unnatural conjuring trick. He did not, however, take the position to the conclusions that would be reached by some nineteenth-century aestheticians. His proposal—that music can offer to the ear only voluptuous sensation—showed a willingness to accept disappointing limits for the art in return for the gift of autonomy.

FROM *On Music Considered in Itself and in Its Relations with Speech, Languages, Poetry, and the Theater*

(1785)

CHAPTER III. CONTINUATION OF THE SAME INVESTIGATION

Let us extend the principle I have just established[1] as far as it can go; let us carry it to the point of exaggeration. None of the steps we take beyond the truth will be wasted in our investigations; to go beyond our limits in this way is to explore the approaches to the place in which we are trying to make ourselves unassailable.

To take the words in their strict sense, song can only imitate that which sings. What am I saying? Its power does not always extend as far as that. The warbling of birds could never be well rendered by our music. For music is subject to laws, to harmonic relationships, while the birds, inaccurate melodists that they are, connect their tones according to an order that harmony does not approve. Also since the time when the lyric poets called the birds to the aid of the art that they favored, this art, ineffectual in its means of imitation, has not gained one step toward the object that people have so often prescribed that it imitate. A strange art of imitation, that renders the things most analogous to it in such a way that the copy never resembles the model!

I should not suppress the response that M. l'Abbé Morellet makes to this difficulty, which he himself proposed; the more ingenious it is, the more it is our duty to cite it.[2]

> All the arts make a kind of contract with the soul and the senses they affect: this contract consists in demanding liberties, and promising pleasures that they would not give without these happy liberties .... Music takes such liberties: it demands that its movement be rhythmic and its periods rounded off, that the voice be supported and strengthened by the accompaniment, *which is certainly not in nature.*

TEXT: The original edition (Paris, 1785; Slatkin Reprints: Geneva, 1969), pp. 46–63, 104–113. Translation by Wye J. Allanbrook.

1. In Chapter 2 Chabanon states that the essence of music is song, or melody, and that only through singing can music please. Music in its primitive state is only song, and we should look to this primitive state to know its essence.
2. The brief essay in which M. l'Abbé Morellet discusses musical expression is full of shrewd and accurate opinions: I doubt that anything better has been written on music. [Au.] In his short essay *On Expression in Music and Imitation in the Arts* (1771), André Morellet argued that music, like the other arts, is imitative, and that proper imitation is a selective activity—the embellishment of nature rather than its slavish simulation.

Without a doubt this alters the truth of the imitation, but increases its beauty at the same time, and gives the copy a charm that nature refused to the original.

Nothing resembles the song of the nightingale so much as the sounds of that little pipe that children fill with water, and set to chirping with their breath. What pleasure does this imitation give us? None. But if we hear a flexible voice and a pleasing symphony expressing (less clearly, to be sure) the song of the same nightingale, the ear and the soul are in rapture. For the arts are something more than a precise imitation of nature.

I understand everything that is ingenious and true in this response. But may I be permitted to ask M. l'Abbé Morellet why poetry, painting, and sculpture are obliged to give us faithful, precise images that resemble the objects they imitate, and why music is exempt? Isn't it because this art is less than the others an art of imitation? The children's pipe that we take for the nightingale itself gives us no pleasure, and the light symphony, which resembles the bird song almost not at all, pleases and charms us. Do not these two facts demonstrate that imitation has very little place in the pleasure that music gives us, and that that pleasure depends almost entirely on the charm of melody?

Man's instinct is prodigiously imitative; he demonstrates this from infancy. But if I am not deceived, imitation only amuses him in so far as he understands its difficulty and its success astonishes him: if a child with his mouth alone were to mimic the nightingale as perfectly as he did with the pipe, we would hear him with more pleasure and interest than we did the pipe. Thus it is certainly wrong that, in the theory of the arts, we pretend to count as nothing a difficulty conquered; it ought to be of great account in the pleasure that the arts provide. The noble impression of the sublime arises partly from the surprise that a conception that is very remote from us causes in us. What we discover easily we enjoy only slightly.

But, you may say, if music is not the imitation of nature, then what is it? What a strange need of the human mind to torment itself with difficulties that it conjures up gratuitously, and that it cannot resolve because they are meaningless! Music is for the hearing what the objects that affect them agreeably are for each of our senses. Why then do you not want the ear to have its immediate pleasures, its voluptuous sensations, just as do sight and smell? And in music are they other than those pleasures that result from tones harmoniously combined? Is it because it pleased you to call music an art that you mean to subject it to all things characteristic of the arts? Come now! Do you know to what extent this term *art* is suited to music? We will examine that eventually; first let us finish demonstrating that music pleases independently of all imitation.

CHAPTER IV. MUSIC PLEASES INDEPENDENTLY OF ALL IMITATION

Animals are susceptible to music. Thus music need not imitate in order to please, for the most perfect imitation is nothing to an animal. If you show one its image drawn on canvas, it will be neither moved nor surprised by the sight. We only enjoy imitation to the extent that we understand its difficulty, but this understanding exceeds the intelligence of animals.

The baby who delights in the songs of his nurse does not seek in them anything that is imitative; he enjoys them like the milk that nourishes him.

The savage, the black, the sailor, the common man—they repeat the songs that amuse them without at the same time requiring the character of the songs to accord with the actual disposition of their souls.

A skilled hand preluding on the harp or harpsichord engages the most knowledgeable listeners. Imitation counts for nothing in the formation of a prelude.

Music has soothed, even cured, sick people: this fact is attested by the Academy of Sciences, and I have seen proof of it. A young person bled six times for an acute pain in the eye forgot his sufferings for two hours while hearing someone play the harpsichord. Is it by virtue of the imitation that such a spell is brought about? Is a mind seized by suffering in a state to enjoy a pleasure that requires reflection?

Thus music acts immediately on our senses. But the human mind, that quick, active, curious, reflective intelligence, interferes with the pleasure of the senses; it cannot be an idle and indifferent spectator. What part can it take in sounds, which because they have in themselves no determinate meaning never offer clear and distinct ideas? It searches for relationships there, for analogies with various objects and with various natural effects. And what happens? Among the nations where intelligence has been brought to perfection, music, anxious to obtain in some way the approval of the intellect, strives to present to it the kinds of relationships or analogies that will please it. Music imitates to the extent that it can, and at the express command of the intellect, which, enticing the art further than its end directs, proposes imitation to it as a secondary goal. But the intellect, which for its own part appreciates the weakness of the means that music uses in order to succeed in imitation, makes few difficulties on this point. The slightest analogies, the most flimsy relationships suffice for it. It calls this art *imitative*, when it scarcely imitates. It bears in mind the efforts that music makes to please it, and is content with the part that has been assigned it in pleasures that would seem to have been designed uniquely for the ear.

No one who has not been completely blinded by the systematic spirit, which one should not want to impose either on oneself or on others, should silence objections that are contrary to the opinion one holds. Here is an objection that at first intimidated me in my opinion: If the pleasure of music is for the ear what a handsome face is for our eyes, why is it more necessary to make one of these sensations imitative than it is the other? Aristotle, in his *Problems*,[3] pro-

---

3. The *Problemata*, attributed to Aristotle and assembled around 100 C.E., were collections of materials compiled by his successors.

poses to himself almost the same difficulty, in different terms. This is how he answers it:

> No sensation produced by an object without movement can be imitative; it cannot have any conformity with our actions, our customs, or our characters. If you have the ear hear only one tone, and you continue its duration, this lifeless and inactive sensation will not represent anything to the intellect. On the other hand, if several tones succeed one another, as in music, their progression, be it slow or rapid, uniform or varied, will give them a character, and make them capable of being likened to other objects.

Thus a handsome face, presenting just the same sight and same object, is at the most capable of being compared only to another handsome object itself. But for want of variation and difference, it does not lead the intellect to make it the symbol of disparate actions and effects.

I want to note that it is only proper for music to link to one another the successive sensations it causes in us, so that they relate to and modify one another. Let us try to make that clearer. If you affect the senses of sight, smell, or touch successively by the presence of various objects that replace one another, these sensations will not be bound to one another, and the one that is ceasing will have no effect on the one that supplants it.[4] But in music the tone you no longer hear is bound by memory to those that follow it. Together they are a body; they are parts of the same whole. To distort the phrase you are hearing, sometimes all that is needed is to detach it from the one that came before.

CHAPTER V. IN WHAT MANNER MUSIC PRODUCES ITS IMITATIONS.[5]

See how quickly we have moved away from the paradox that we seemed at first to want to maintain, that music lacks the proper means for imitation. In the process of pruning from that assertion what was exaggerated in it, we are brought to the examination of the means by which music imitates. Music likens (as much as it can) its sounds to other sounds, its movements to other movements, and the sensations that it produces to affections that are analogous to them. This last means of imitating will be the subject of another chapter.

Musical imitation is perceptibly genuine only when it has songs for its object. In music one truthfully imitates military fanfares, hunting airs, rustic songs, etc. It is only a question of giving one melody the character of another melody. In that case, art suffers no violence. When it moves beyond that, however, imitation grows weak, because of the insufficiency of means that music may employ.

4. In *Observations on Music* (1779), an earlier version of this essay, Chabanon adds by way of example that if you smell a rose after having smelled another flower, the rose's perfume will not be modified.
5. This chapter is one of those where our ideas happen to be in agreement with those of M. l'Abbé Morellet. [Au.]

Is it a question of representing a brook? The continual slight fluctuation of two notes that are neighbors to each other makes the music ripple rather like the water that flows along. This relationship, which presents itself first to the intellect, is the only one of which the art has availed itself up to now, and I doubt we will ever discover another one more striking. The desire to depict a brook thus necessarily unites all the musicians who have it and who will have it with a melodic configuration that is common knowledge and almost worn out. The disposition of the notes is as it were foreseen and given in advance. Melody, the slave of this constraint, will have less grace and novelty. According to this calculation, the ear loses by that representation almost everything that the intellect gains from it.

Now add to the depiction of the brooks the twittering of the birds. In this case the imitative musician makes the voice and instruments sustain long cadences; he mixes in roulades, although there has never been a bird that used roulades in its song. This imitation has the double inconvenience of being quite imperfect on the one hand, and on the other, of constraining musician to forms that have been often used. M. l'Abbé Morellet is lavish in his praise of the Italian air whose words are *If the nightingale loses [its mate]*. Although I do not recall that air precisely, I would venture to guarantee that the part of it that is the most agreeable is not that part that strives to imitate the song of the nightingale.

Given a skillful composer forced by the text to depict the brook that murmurs and the bird that twitters, would we dare to blame him if he reasoned as follows? "My art cannot render with truth the effects that my poet expects of it: in striving to achieve them, I run the risk of resembling all those who have attempted the same picture. The depiction of the water, of the flowers, of the zephyrs, of the greenery, is considered so lyrical only because the view of a cheerful and pastoral site produces a gentle impression on our senses, and disposes our souls to a blissful calm. If then, refraining from imitating what I cannot render, I were to imagine only a suave and tranquil melody, the sort one would like to hear when resting in the cool shade, in sight of the most beautiful countryside, would I be failing my poet and my art?" As long as this reasoning artist was a man of talent, so that he could execute such a plan, I know no way in which the partisans of imitation could reproach him.

The sky is overcast, the winds whistle, the thunder prolongs its long reverberations from one end of the horizon to the other. . . . How ineffective music is in depicting such effects, especially if the musician strives to detail them, and introduces the expectation of a painted likeness! Here a volley of ascending or descending notes will express either the lightning, or the force of the wind, or the thunderclap. For he has a choice among all these effects; the same vivid trait belongs to them all, and suits them equally. Instead, do away with all these busy pictures that depict nothing, and paint in broad strokes! Let the fracas, the tumult, the disorder of the symphony depict the disorder and the noise of the storm, and above all let the melody be such that no one can say: *All this is mere noise, without expression or character.*

One day I was present at an evening concert on the boulevard; the orchestra was numerous and quite loud. They were performing the overture from *Pygmalion.*[6] It looked as though it was going to storm. At the *fortissimo* of the reprise we heard a thunder clap. We all felt an extraordinary relation between the symphony and the meteor that rumbled in the sky. Rameau turned out in that moment to have made a picture with an intention and a resemblance that neither he nor anyone else would have suspected. Musical artists, you who reflect on your art, does this example teach you anything?

There is one effect in nature that music renders rather truthfully—the moaning of the angry waves. Many basses playing in unison, and making the melody roll like waves that rise and fall, create a tumult similar to that of an agitated sea. We all once heard a symphony in which the author had used this unison, without pictorial intent. The imitative effect of it was so generally felt that this symphony was called *The Tempest,* although there was nothing else there that could justify this designation. Given such facts, would one not be right to call music *the art of painting without suspecting it?*

Let us speak of another imitation, the kind that depicts to one of our senses what is subject to another, as when sound imitates light.

Everyone knows the story of the blind man who was given a picture in which one could see men, trees, and herds. The incredulous blind man carefully ran his hand over all the parts of the canvas, and finding there only a plane surface, could not imagine that so many different objects were represented on it. This example proves that one sense is not the judge of something that another sense experiences. Also, it is not properly for the ear that we depict in music what strikes the eyes: it is for the intellect, which, situated between the two senses, combines and compares their sensations.

If you tell a musician to depict the light taken abstractly, he will confess the impotence of his art. But tell him to paint the dawn, and he will feel that the contrast of clear and piercing sounds, put into opposition with mute and veiled sounds, can resemble the contrast between light and darkness. From this point of comparison he knows how to imitate. But what is he actually depicting? Not day and night, but only a contrast, and a contrast of any kind. The first one that comes into your mind will be expressed just as well by the same music as that of light and darkness.

Let us not fear to repeat this for the instruction of artists: the musician who produces such pictures does nothing if he does not produce them with felicitous melodies. To paint is only the second of his duties; to sing is the first. If he does not satisfy that, what is he worth? Because of the weakness in his art he paints imperfectly; because of the weakness in his own talent, he fails in the principal functions of his art.

---

6. An *acte de ballet* composed by Jean-Philippe Rameau and first performed in 1748.

How can music paint what strikes the eyes, while painting makes no attempt to render what is in the province of hearing? Painting is bound by its essence to imitate, and that faithfully; if painting does not imitate, it is no longer anything. Speaking only to the eyes, it can only imitate what strikes the sight. Music, on the contrary, pleases without imitation, by the sensations that it brings about. Since its pictures are always imperfect, consisting often of a simple and slender analogy with the object it wishes to paint, such relationships multiply easily. In short, painting imitates only what is proper to it, because it must imitate rigorously. Music can paint everything, because it paints it all imperfectly.

• • • • •

CHAPTER X. OF THE MUSICAL SENSATIONS APPLICABLE TO OUR VARIOUS AFFECTIONS, AND OF THE NATURAL MEANS OF EXPRESSION PROPER TO MUSIC

A particular song pleases you—you love to hear it. That can only be because it produces in you an impression of some kind. Study this impression; examine its nature and character. It is impossible that you would not recognize whether it is bitter or sweet, lively or tranquil; the movement alone should indicate this to you. Is it sweet or tender? Adapt to it words of the same sort, and you will render expressive a piece of music that earlier you wouldn't have suspected of being so. From a sensation that is all but vague and indeterminate, you shape a sentiment of which you can give an account.

I beg the reader to master his imagination, and not to let it go faster than this discussion allows. A little further on he will find the developments and clarifications that he has a right to expect from us.

The air that we would call *tender* does not perhaps dispose us precisely in the same circumstance of body and mind as we would experience if we were actually moved to pity by a wife, a father, or a friend. But between these two situations, the one actual, the other musical (if I may be allowed this manner of speaking), the analogy is such that the mind agrees to accept the one for the other.

Why, it will be said, do you want the effect of such music to be only a sensation, and not a distinct sentiment? — Reader, I wish it for this reason: because in questioning you about an air without words that may have given you pleasure, if I ask you what distinct sentiment it arouses in you, you would not know how to tell me. I suggest a tender air, and I ask you if it is the tenderness of a happy or an unhappy lover that the air inspires in you; if it is that of a lover for his mistress, or of a son for his father, etc., etc., etc. If all these different feelings equally suit the air of which we are speaking, am I wrong if I would sooner call its effect a rather vague sensation than a determinate sentiment? Moreover—I repeat this once more—let us not go any faster than necessary. What we are advancing here in a general and superficial manner will be determined elsewhere with more precision.

What are the natural means that give melody a character of sadness or of gaiety, of gentleness or of resolution? In undertaking to resolve such questions, I advance, so to speak, into the shadows with which nature cloaks and surrounds all first causes. I will go wherever the torch of experience leads me. And the more obscure the subject is, the more I will make it my duty only to lay down incontestable assertions.

It is the nature of sustained tones to impart a character of sadness. Don't think that this is a fact of convention. No; men have not made a contract among themselves to find the cry of the turtle-dove plaintive and the song of the blackbird joyful. If the nightingale mingles several tones with one another and sounds them together, you will associate with this musical language a notion less sad than if the solitary bird had made a sound in the night that he drew out for several beats. Is it not recognized that a uniform sound, like that of a voice that reads on the same tone, induces us to sleep? If the sound has this direct an effect on us, why should we deny other effects that are no more astonishing?

In general the minor mode produces an impression that is gentler, softer, and more sensitive than that of the major mode. Don't ask the reason for it; no one is in a position to tell you. But a move from one of these modes to the other makes this different impression perceptible to every musical ear. The sixth note of the scale in the minor mode is more sensitive than all the others; each time it appears, even in the most joyful Allegro, it requires from the performer a softer and more expressive inflection. The fourth note of the scale has this quality in the major mode. It is the note that by means of its intrinsic quality summons the performer to a pathetic expression even when the rest of the melody is directing him to a different sensation. High-pitched tones have a certain clarity and brilliance that seem to invite the soul to joy. Compare the high strings of the harp to the low strings of the same instrument, and you will feel how the latter dispose the soul more easily to tenderness. Who knows if these broad undulations of strings that are long and less taut do not communicate similar vibrations to our nerves, and if this disposition of our body is not what gives us affective sentiments? Believe me, man is only an instrument; his fibers respond to the strings of the lyrical instruments, which assail these fibers and interrogate them. Each tone, each instrument has its own qualities, from which melody profits handily, but which she also controls at her pleasure; for the most sensitive instrument can successfully articulate joyful songs.

Tender music uses movements without rapidity. It binds the sounds, rather than contrasting them or making them collide with one another. In music of this character the staccato breve does not imperiously control the dotted long that is joined to it, and the performer tempers his tones with broad vibrato. Those whom taste inclines to sadness draw out the sounds (following the observation that we have already made), and their bow fears to leave the string; their voice gives the song a certain indolent idleness. Joyful music dots the notes and makes the tones leap; the bow is always in the air, and the voice imitates it.

These are pretty much the natural means that music has at its disposal, and with the aid of which it produces sensations in us. The composer, man of genius that he is, who has experienced all these effects and applies them appropriately to words and situations, is an expressive musician. It will be obvious to the reader that all the means of expression are in the province of melody, not of harmony.

An essential observation, and one that stands at the very foundation of our doctrine, is that in the most expressive air, almost always—I would even say necessarily—there are ideas and passages contradictory to the character of the expression that ought to dominate it. Let us cite an example. In the first verset of the *Stabat*,[7] I see no verse or word that does not require the same nuance of sadness.

> Stabat mater dolorosa,
> Juxta crucem lacrimosa,
> Dum pendebat Filius.[8]

At the beginning of the work music makes use of all its expressive means. The tempo is slow, the sounds weak and veiled; they progress slowly, and legato. The expression is well established here. In the tenth measure, however, everything changes: a *fortissimo* succeeds a *piano,* and the sounds that cringed darkling in the bass of the *octave* suddenly rise up, reinforced to excess, and combat with and contradict those that preceded them with their proud *détaché.* Where does this incongruity come from? From the fact that music, in its essence, is not an imitative art. It lends itself to imitation as much as it can, but this act of complaisance cannot distract it from the functions that its actual nature imposes on it. One of these necessary functions is to vary its modifications from moment to moment, combining in the same piece the *gentle* and the *strong,* the *legato* and the *détaché,* the proud articulation and the tender one. This art, so considered, is of an ungovernable inconstancy; all its charm depends on its rapid transformations. I know that it often comes back to the same things in each piece, but without lingering on them. Now across all these fleeting and fugitive forms how do you expect the imitation to be unified, and to progress with an even step? On limping foot it follows this playful and changeable thing that is music, overtaking it sometimes, and sometimes letting it go its way alone. If the proof I advance for this is found in the first couplet of the *Stabat*—so beautiful, so expressive, so short, and composed of only two ideas—in what Italian air will this proof not manifest itself with even more clarity?

Reader, no matter how little of a musician you may be, you are now in a position to judge the dramatic system of M. Gluck. Now you understand how, being devoted to expression, which he rightly regards as the foundation of all theatrical illusion, he only permits himself an entire air when the situation itself

7. Most probably the setting of the *Stabat mater* by Pergolesi; see pp. 9 and 192, n. 8.
8. "There stood the grieving mother / Weeping beside the cross, / While her son was crucified."

permits music those digressions, those indeterminate wanderings in which melody delights. Whenever a periodic and coherent song would make the action languish, and would transform the actor into a singer at his music stand, M. Gluck quickly cuts off this melody that has just begun, and by another movement, or a simple recitative, he restores the singing to the continuity of the action, and makes them flow together. It is inconceivable that a system so true could have been disapproved of in a country where the art of the theater is so well known. It is even more inconceivable that among its critics there could have been men who in their position and their wisdom ought to have defended the rights of the stage against the rights of music. In Italy men of letters have said that theater music was no longer for the enjoyment of intellectuals. Here the intellectuals, not being real musicians, have maintained that the operas of M. Gluck were made more for the intellect than for the ear. But while they were entertaining this judgment, the most delicate and trained ears were nourishing themselves with delights from M. Gluck's music. I do not think that there have ever been judgments more calculated to astonish.

21 Germaine de Staël

Germaine de Staël (1766–1817) was a fresh young intelligence shaped in the salons of pre-Revolutionary Paris. She was the daughter of a middle-class Swiss banker, Jacques Necker, who as the finance minister for Louis XVI managed to keep the loyalty both of the monarch and the people, at least in the Revolution's early days. She became a literary critic and novelist as well as a passionate student of politics who spoke out against the monarchy in a manner uncharacteristic of any private citizen, much less a woman.

De Staël's first published work was her *Lettres sur Rosseau (Letters on Rousseau)* of 1788. Rousseau was clearly a formative influence in her early years, and in fact she understood him well, in both his innocence and his monstrousness, as she makes clear in an essay on his character included in that collection. She also understood and shared his feeling about the relation of sensibility to the intellect; in her preface she remarks that she has found pleasure in recalling to memory—retracing—the sensation of her enthusiasm for him. Her interest in music here, like her interest in botany, is an interest in its objects as profound mnemonic devices, capable of summoning one to reflections about the best and the deepest in the natural state of humankind. Rousseau, composer and theorist, evinced the same Romantic sensibility.

FROM *Letters on Rousseau*
(1788)

ON ROUSSEAU'S TASTE FOR MUSIC AND BOTANY

Rousseau wrote several works on music; he loved this art with passion all his life. *The Village Soothsayer*[1] even shows some talent for composition. He tried to make melodramas adopted in France, using *Pygmalion* as an example, and perhaps this genre should not have been rejected.[2] When words and music follow each other, both effects are increased; sometimes they are improved by not being harnessed together. Music expresses situations; words develop them. Music can take on the portrayal of impulses beyond words; words can portray feelings that are too nuanced for music. Pygmalion's monologue is so eloquent that it seems perfectly likely for the statue to come to life at the sound of his voice, and we are tempted to believe that the gods played no part in this miracle.

Rousseau composed simple, touching airs for a number of romances, the kind of melody that blends in with the situation of one's soul, the kind one can still sing when one is unhappy. A few of them seem national to me; as I heard them I felt myself transported to our mountain peaks, when the sound of the shepherd's flute is slowly prolonged in the distance by a succession of repeated echoes. These airs remind me of the kind of music, calm rather than somber, that lends itself to the listener's sentiments and becomes for him the expression of his own feelings. Where is the sensitive man who has never been touched by music? An unfortunate person who can listen to it is given the sweet satisfaction of shedding tears, and his despair is replaced by melancholy; while one listens, one's sensations are enough for both mind and heart, leaving no emptiness in either. Some melodies put one in ecstasy for a moment; a choir of angels always heralds rapture into heaven. How powerfully memories are retraced by music! how inseparable it becomes from them! What man in the midst of life's passions could be unmoved by hearing the tune that enlivened the dances and games of his peaceful childhood! What woman whose beauty has been withered by time could keep from tears at the sound of the romance her lover once sang for her! The tune of this romance, even more than its words, renews in

---

TEXT: *Major Writings of Germaine de Staël*, trans. Vivian Folkenflik (New York: Columbia University Press, 1987), pp. 50–52.

1. *Le Devin du village*, words and music by Rousseau.
2. Rousseau's *Pygmalion* was composed in 1762 and first performed in Lyons in 1770, with music by Horace Coignet (except for an overture and Andante that Rousseau himself may have composed). This work is generally considered to be the first in which a spoken text alternated with music that reflects the changing affects of the words. Although the genre did not take root in France, it spread to Austria and Germany, where it was taken up enthusiastically. See p. 226 and n. 7.

her heart the emotions of youth. No accessory circumstance such as the sight of places or things that once surrounded us is connected to the events of our lives the way music is. The memories which come to us through music are not accompanied by any regrets; for a moment music gives us back the pleasures it retraces, and we feel them again rather than recollect them. Rousseau loved only melancholy airs; that is the kind of music one wants in the country. All nature seems to accompany the plaintive sounds of a touching voice. To feel such pleasures, one needs a pure and gentle soul. A man disturbed by the remembrance of his errors would not be able to bear the reverie into which we are thrown by touching music. A man tormented by heartrending remorse would be afraid to get that close to himself, to make all his feelings alive again, to feel them all slowly, one at a time. I am inclined to trust anyone who is enraptured by music, flowers, and the country. Ah! a penchant for vice must surely be born within man's heart, because all the sensations he receives from the objects surrounding him draw him away from it. I don't know—but often at the end of a lovely day, in a country retreat, at the sight of a starry sky, it has seemed to me that the spectacle of nature was speaking to the soul of virtue, hope, and goodness.

For a while Rousseau turned his attention to botany; this is one way of taking a detailed interest in the countryside. He had adopted a system which may show the extent of his belief that man's own memory is what spoils the pleasure aroused by his contemplation of nature. Rousseau distinguished plants by their forms, rather than by their properties; he thought it degrading to relate them to the use man could make of them. I must admit I am not in favor of adopting this opinion; to consider the works of the Creator destined to a final cause is no desecration, and the world looks more imposing and majestic to someone who sees in it only a single thought. But Rousseau's poetic, savage imagination could not bear to link the image of a shrub or flower, ornaments of nature, to the memory of men's sicknesses and infirmities. In his *Confessions* he paints an enchanting picture of his rapture at seeing periwinkle again.[3] The sight of it had the same effect on him as that tune it is forbidden to play to the Swiss army when they are out of their country, for fear they will desert.[4] This peri-

3. In the *Confessions*, Book 6, Rousseau gives an account of sighting, while botanizing in 1764, some periwinkle, a creeping plant with a modest blue flower. Madeleine-like, the discovery of the plant instantaneously evokes in him vividly precise memories of the happiest days of his life, nearly fifty years earlier, with his patroness in Les Charmettes, their isolated country retreat.
4. Of the *ranz des vaches*, the Swiss mountain melody that herdsmen play on an alphorn to summon the cows, Rousseau writes the following in his *Dictionnaire* ([Paris, 1768], "Musique"): "This air [is] so dear to the Swiss that playing it among their troops was banned on pain of death, since it made those who heard it melt with tears, desert, or die, so much did it stir in them the passionate desire to see their country again. It would be vain to search in this tune for the powerful accents capable of producing such astonishing effects. These effects . . . only come from habit, from memories, from the thousand circumstances which, retraced by this tune for those who hear it, and recalling for them their country, their early pleasures, their youth, their way of life, stir in them a bitter grief at having lost all that. Thus the *music* does not act precisely like *music*, but like a commemorative sign."

winkle could inspire in Rousseau a passion to return to the Vaud country; this single circumstance made all his memories present to him. His mistress, his country, his youth, his loves—he found and felt every one of them again, and all at one time.

22 Hester Lynch Piozzi

Hester Lynch Piozzi (1741–1821) is best known as the confidante of Dr. Samuel Johnson. Johnson was drawn to her for her intelligence and wit, and for her lively open manner in company; their friendship seems to have been a deep one. Her marriage to Henry Thrale, a wealthy brewer, while supported by little beyond an affection born of habit, persisted through twelve pregnancies (four daughters surviving into adulthood) until Thrale's death in 1781. Fortunately, Thrale was a cultivated man who enjoyed intelligent company. Dr. Johnson attached himself to the pair, often living at their country house and depending on "his dear Master and Mistress" for conversation and consolation. Charles Burney and his daughter Fanny, the actor David Garrick, Sir Joshua Reynolds, and Edmund Burke were also regular visitors. After Thrale's death, Hester Lynch fell passionately in love with Gabriel Piozzi, an Italian singer and teacher. Their marriage brought rejection by her daughters and many of her friends—Johnson and Fanny Burney foremost among them—who were shocked at this unsuitable attachment to a foreigner. Stubbornly enjoying her newfound happiness, she spent several years on the continent with Piozzi, and then returned to London and a thriving social life with a new circle of friends.

Hester Piozzi was a tireless diarist, who committed most of her writing before her second marriage to this form. After Johnson's death, however, she published collections of his letters and of Johnsonian anecdotes. On her return to England Piozzi brought out this book of synonyms, aimed at helping foreigners sort out the subtleties of English usage while offering her opportunities for expansive flights of associative fancy.

FROM *British Synonymy; or, An Attempt at Regulating the Choice of Words in Familiar Conversation*

(1794)

MELODY, HARMONY, MUSICK

These terms are used as synonymes only by people who revert not to their derivation; when the last is soon discovered to contain the other two, while the first means merely the air—or, as Italians better express it, *la cantilena*—because our very word MELODY implies *honey-sweet singing, mellifluous* succession of simple sounds, so as to produce agreeable and sometimes almost enchanting effect. Meanwhile both co-operation and combination are understood to meet in the term HARMONY; which, like every other science, is the result of knowledge operating on genius, and adds in the audience a degree of astonishment to approbation, enriching all our sensations of delight, and clustering them into a maturity of perfection.

MELODY is to HARMONY what innocence is to virtue; the last could not exist without the former, on which they are founded; but we esteem him who enlarges simplicity into excellence, and prize the opening chorus of *Acis and Galatea*[1] beyond the "Voi Amanti" of Giardini,[2] although this last-named composition is elegant, and the other vulgar. Where the original thought, however, like Corregio's Magdalen in the Dresden Gallery set round with jewels, is lost in the blaze of accompaniment, our loss is the less if *that* thought should be somewhat coarse or indelicate; but MUSICK of this kind pleases an Italian ear far less than do Sacchini's sweetly soothing MELODIES, never overlaid by that fulness of HARMONY with which German composers sometimes perplex instead of informing their hearers. *His* choruses in *Erifile*,[3] though nothing deficient either in richness or radiance, are ever transparent; while the charming subject (not an instant lost to view) reminds one of some fine shell coloured by Nature's hand, but seen to most advantage through the clear waves that wash the coast of Coromandel when mild monsoons are blowing. With regard to MUSICK, Plato said long ago, that if any considerable alteration took place in the MUSICK of a country, he should, from that single circumstance, predict innovation in the laws, a change of customs, and subversion of the govern-

TEXT: The original edition (London: G. G. and J. Robinson, 1794), vol. 2, pp. 21–29.

1. Oratorio by Handel, first performed in England in 1718, and in 1732 with added airs.
2. Felice Giardini was an Italian violinist who spent most of his career in London, as director of the King's Theatre opera orchestra and sometime impresario. He wrote several operas, most of which are lost, and arias for pasticcios. He was an intimate of Charles Burney, who called him "the greatest performer in Europe." Later, they parted in bitterness. See also pp. 256 and 268.
3. Antonio Sacchini was an Italian opera composer who lived in London for nearly ten years, from 1772 to 1781. His *Erifile* was performed in London in 1778.

ment.[4] Rousseau, in imitation of this sentiment, which he had probably read *translated* as well as myself, actually foretold it of the French, without acknowledging whence his idea sprung; and truly did he foretell it. "The French," says he, "have no MUSICK now—nor can have, because their language is not capable of musical expression; but if ever they *do* get into a better style—(which they certainly soon did, changing Lulli and Rameau for Gluck, and for Piccinni)—*tant pis pour eux.*"[5]

Rousseau had indeed the fate of Cassandra, little less mad than himself; and Burney justly observed, that it was strange a nation so frequently accused of volatility and caprice, should have invariably manifested a steady perseverance and constancy to one particular taste in this art, which the strongest ridicule and contempt of other countries could never vanquish or turn out of its course. He has however lived to see them change their mode of receiving pleasure from this very science; has seen them accomplish the predictions of Rousseau, and confirm the opinions of Plato; seen them murder their own monarch, set fire to their own cities, and blaze themselves away—a wonder to fools, a beacon to wise men. This example has at least served to shew the use of those three words which occasioned so long a speculation. MELODY is chiefly used speaking of vocal MUSICK, and HARMONY means many parts combining to form composition. Shall I digress in saying that this latter seems the genuine taste of the English, who love plenty and opulence in all things? Our MELODIES are commonly vulgar, but we like to see them richly drest; and the late silly humour of listening to tunes made upon three notes only, is a mere whim of the moment, as it was to dote upon old ballads about twenty or thirty years ago; it will die away in a twelvemonth—for simplicity cannot please without elegance: nor does it really please a British ear, even when exquisitely sweet and delicate. We buy Blair's Works,[6] but would rather study Warburton's;[7] we talk of tender Venetian airs, but our hearts acknowledge Handel. Meantime 'tis unjust to say that German MUSICK is not expressive; when the Italians say so they mean it is not *amorous:* but other affections inhabit other souls; and surely the last-named immortal composer has no rival in the power of expressing and exciting sublime devotion and rapturous sentiment. See his grand chorus, *Unto us a Son is born,* &c. Pleyel's Quartettos[8] too, which have all somewhat of a drum and fife in them, express what Germans ever have excelled in—regularity, order, discipline, arms, in a word, war. When such MUSICK is playing, it reminds one of Rowe's verses which say so very truly, that

4. See, for example, Plato, *Laws* 3. 700a–701d.
5. "So much the worse for them." See p. 174.
6. Hugh Blair (1718–1800), a native of Edinburgh, and author of an essay on rhetoric, *Lectures on Rhetoric and Belles Lettres* (1783), whom the Piozzis had met when traveling in Scotland in 1789.
7. William Warburton (1698–1779), Anglican bishop and literary critic who was a friend of Alexander Pope. Piozzi met Warburton once in her youth.
8. The Parisian music publisher Ignace Pleyel (1757–1831), who was born in Austria and studied with Haydn in the early 1770s, was a prolific composer whose works were enormously popular in the late eighteenth century.

> The sound of arms shall wake our martial ardour,
> And cure the amorous sickness of a soul
> Begun by sloth and nursed with too much ease.
> The idle god of love supinely dreams
> Amidst inglorious shades and purling streams;
> In rosy fetters and fantastic chains
> He binds deluded maids and simple swains;
> With soft enjoyment wooes them to forget
> The hardy toils and labours of the great:
> But if the warlike trumpet's loud alarms
> To virtuous acts excite, and manly arms,
> The coward boy avows his abject fear,
> Sublime on silken wings he cuts the air,
> Scar'd at the noble noise and thunder of the war.[9]

What then do those critics look for, who lament that German MUSICK is not *expressive?* They look for plaintive sounds meant to raise tender emotions in the breast; and this is the peculiar province of MELODY—which, like Anacreon's lyre, vibrates to amorous touches only, and resounds with nothing but love. Of this sovereign power,

> To take the 'prison'd soul, and lap it in Elysium,[10]

Italy has long remained in full possession: the Syren's coast is still the residence of melting softness and of sweet seduction. The MUSICK of a nation naturally represents that nation's favourite energies, pervading every thought and every action; while even the devotion of that warm soil is tenderness, not sublimity;— and either the natives impress their gentle souls with the contemplation of a Saviour newly laid, in innocence and infant sweetness, upon the spotless bosom of more than female beauty—or else rack their soft hearts with the afflicting passions; and with eyes fixed upon a bleeding crucifix, weep their Redeemer's human sufferings, as though he were never to re-assume divinity. Meantime the piety of Lutherans soars a sublimer flight; and when they set before the eyes of their glowing imagination Messiah ever blessed, they kindle into rapture, and break out with pious transport.

> Hallelujah! for the Lord God Omnipotent reigneth, &c.

They think of him that sitteth high above the heavens, begotten before all worlds!

> *Effulgence of the Father! Son beloved!*[11]

With such impressions, such energies, such inspiration—Milton wrote poetry, and Handel composed MUSICK.

---

9. Nicholas Rowe (1674–1718), a dramatist in the sentimental style who succeeded Nahum Tate as poet laureate of England. He also compiled the first critical edition of Shakespeare.
10. John Milton, *Comus* ll. 253–57: "The Sirens three, . . . Who as they sung, would take the prison'd soul, / And lap it in *Elysium.*"
11. John Milton, *Paradise Lost*, bk. 6, l. 680. God speaks: "Effulgence of my Glorie, Son beloved."

VI

DIARISTS AND HISTORIANS

23 Charles Burney

In 1744 Charles Burney, son of a Shrewsbury dancing master, left the country for London to become apprenticed to the composer Thomas Arne. After a period of varied employment as a practical musician both in London and out, he took up permanent residence in London in 1760 as a society music teacher. His real ambition, however, was to make a comprehensive study of the history of music. By 1769 he had taken his doctorate at Oxford and begun to amass a sizable music library. He rapidly gathered distinction as a scholar, in correspondence with Diderot and Rousseau in France, and joined a distinguished London circle that included Dr. Johnson, Joshua Reynolds, and the actor David Garrick. Burney died in 1814.

Burney made extensive journeys to the Continent to assemble the materials for his story—to France and Italy in 1770 and to the Low Countries, Germany, and Austria in 1772. The impressions gathered in the course of these tours he set down in two travel diaries: *The Present State of Music in France and Italy* (1771), and *The Present State of Music in Germany, the Netherlands and United Provinces* (1773). The first volume of his *General History of Music* appeared in 1776, and the fourth and final volume in 1789. Other writings include a biography of Pietro Metastasio and fragments for a set of memoirs (heavily expurgated, unfortunately, by his daughter, the novelist Fanny Burney). Burney's works are of inestimable importance to scholars for their voluminous information and lively opinions about late eighteenth-century musical life.

FROM *The Present State of Music in France and Italy*
(1771)

NAPLES

I entered this city, impressed with the highest ideas of the perfect state in which I should find practical music. It was at Naples only that I expected to have my ears gratified with every musical luxury and refinement which Italy could afford. My visits to other places were in the way of *business,* for the performance of a *task* I had assigned myself;[1] but I came hither animated by the hope of pleasure. And what lover of music could be in the place which had produced the two Scarlattis, Vinci, Leo, Pergolesi, Porpora, Farinelli, Jommelli, Piccinni, and innumerable others of the first eminence among composers and performers, both vocal and instrumental, without the most sanguine expecta-

TEXT: The original edition (London, 1771), pp. 291–93, 298–04, 305–07, 316–19, 324–30, 335–40, 352–58.

1. The collection of materials for his *General History of Music.*

tions. How far these expectations were gratified, the reader will find in the course of my narrative, which is constantly a faithful transcript of my feelings at the time I entered them in my journal, immediately after hearing and seeing, with a mind not conscious of any prejudice or partiality.

I arrived here about five o'clock in the evening, on Tuesday, October 16,[2] and at night went to the Teatro de' Fiorentini to hear the comic opera of *Gelosia per gelosia,* set to music by Signor Piccinni. This theatre is as small as Mr. Foote's in London,[3] but higher, as there are five rows of boxes in it. Notwithstanding the court was at Portici, and a great number of families at their *villeggiature,* or country houses, so great is the reputation of Signor Piccinni, that every part of the house was crowded. Indeed this opera had nothing else but the merit and reputation of the composer to support it, as both the drama and singing were bad. There was, however, a comic character performed by Signor Casaccia, a man of infinite humor; the whole house was in a roar the instant he appeared; and the pleasantry of this actor did not consist in buffoonery, nor was it local, which in Italy, and, indeed, elsewhere, is often the case; but was of that original and general sort as would excite laughter at all times and in all places.

The airs of this burletta are full of pretty passages, and, in general, most ingeniously accompanied: there was no dancing, so that the acts, of which there were three, seemed rather long.

•   •   •   •   •

Thursday 18. I was very happy to find, upon my arrival at Naples, that though many persons to whom I had letters were in the country, yet Signor Jommelli and Signor Piccinni were in town. Jommelli was preparing a serious opera for the great theatre of San Carlo, and Piccinni had just brought the burletta on the stage which I have mentioned before.

This morning I visited Signor Piccinni, and had the pleasure of a long conversation with him. He seems to live in a reputable way, has a good house, and many servants and attendants about him. He is not more than four or five and forty; looks well, has a very animated countenance, and is a polite and agreeable little man, though rather grave in his manner for a Neapolitan possessed of so much fire and genius. His family is rather numerous; one of his sons is a student in the University of Padua. After reading a letter which Mr. Giardini[4] was so obliging as to give me to him, he told me he should be extremely glad if he could be of any use either to me or my work. My first enquiries were concerning the Neapolitan Conservatorios; for he having been brought up in one of them himself, his information was likely to be authentic and satisfactory. In my first visit I confined my questions chiefly to the four following subjects:

2. Burney had left Rome for Naples on Sunday, October 14, 1770.
3. The "New" Theatre in the Haymarket, opened in 1767.
4. Felice de Giardini (1716–96), an Italian composer and violinist resident in London. See pp. 250, n. 2, and 268.

♦

1. The antiquity of these establishments.
2. Their names.
3. The number of masters and scholars.
4. The time for admission, and for quitting these schools.

To my first demand he answered that the Conservatorios were of ancient standing, as might be seen by the ruinous condition of one of the buildings, which was ready to tumble down.[5]

To my second, that their names were *San Onofrio, La Pietà,* and *Santa Maria di Loreto.*

To my third question he answered that the number of scholars in the first Conservatorio is about ninety, in the second a hundred and twenty, and in the other, two hundred.

That each of them has two principal *maestri di cappella,* the first of whom superintends and corrects the compositions of the students; the second the singing and gives lessons. That there are assistant masters, who are called *maestri secolari;* one for the violin, one for the violoncello, one for the harpsichord, one for the hautbois, one for the French horn, and so for other instruments.

To my fourth inquiry he answered that boys are admitted from eight or ten to twenty years of age; that when they are taken in young they are bound for eight years; but, when more advanced, their admission is difficult, except they have made a considerable progress in the study and practice of music. That after boys have been in a Conservatorio for some years, if no genius is discovered, they are dismissed to make way for others. That some are taken in as pensioners, who pay for their teaching; and others, after having served their time out, are retained to teach the rest; but that in both these cases they are allowed to go out of the Conservatorio at pleasure.

I inquired throughout Italy at what place boys were chiefly qualified for singing by castration, but could get no certain intelligence. I was told at Milan that it was at Venice; at Venice that it was at Bologna; but at Bologna the fact was denied, and I was referred to Florence; from Florence to Rome, and from Rome I was sent to Naples. The operation most certainly is against law in all these places, as well as against nature; and all the Italians are so much ashamed of it that in every province they transfer it to some other.

> Ask where's the North? at York, 'tis on the Tweed;
> In Scotland, at the Orcades; and there,
> At Greenland, Zembla, or the Lord knows where.
> —Pope, *Essay on Man*

However, with respect to the Conservatorios at Naples, Mr. Gemineau, the British consul, who has so long resided there and who has made very particular inquiries, assured me, and his account was confirmed by Dr. Cirillo, an eminent

---

5. I afterwards obtained, from good authority, the exact date of each of these foundations; their fixed and stated rules, amounting to thirty-one; and the orders given to the rectors for regulating the conduct and studies of the boys, every month in the year. [Au.]

and learned Neapolitan physician, that this practice is absolutely forbidden in the Conservatorios, and that the young *castrati* come from Leccia in Apuglia; but, before the operation is performed, they are brought to a Conservatorio to be tried as to the probability of voice, and then are taken home by their parents for this barbarous purpose. It is, however, death by the laws to all those who perform the operation, and excommunication to everyone concerned in it, unless it be done, as is often pretended, upon account of some disorders which may be supposed to require it, and with the consent of the boy. And there are instances of its being done even at the request of the boy himself, as was the case of the Grassetto at Rome.[6] But as to these previous trials of the voice, it is my opinion that the cruel operation is but too frequently performed without trial, or at least without sufficient proofs of an improvable voice; otherwise such numbers could never be found in every great town throughout Italy, without any voice at all, or at least without one sufficient to compensate such a loss. Indeed all the *musici*[7] in the churches at present are made up of the refuse of the opera houses, and it is very rare to meet with a tolerable voice upon the establishment in any church throughout Italy. The virtuosi who sing there occasionally, upon great festivals only, are usually strangers, and paid by the time.

•   •   •   •   •

From hence I went directly to the comic opera, which, tonight,[8] was at the *Teatro Nuovo.* This house is not only less than the *Fiorentini,* but is older and more dirty. The way to it, for carriages, is through streets very narrow, and extremely inconvenient. This burletta was called the *Trame per Amore,* and set by Signor Giovanni Paesiello, *Maestro di Cappella Napolitano.* The singing was but indifferent; there were nine characters in the piece, and yet not one good voice among them; however, the music pleased me very much; it was full of fire and fancy, the ritornels abounding in new passages, and the vocal parts in elegant and simple melodies, such as might be remembered and carried away after the first hearing, or be performed in private by a small band, or even without any other instrument than a harpsichord.[9] The overture, of one movement only, was quite comic, and contained a perpetual succession of pleasant passages. There was no dancing, which made it necessary to spin the acts out

6. "*Il Grassetto,* a boy who submitted to mutilation by his own choice and against the advice of his friends for the preservation of his voice, which is indeed a very good one." (Burney, *France and Italy,* p. 259 [Rome, Sept 22].)

7. The word *musico,* in Italy, seems now wholly appropriated to a singer with a soprano or contralto voice, which has been preserved by art. [Au.]

8. The date is still October 18.

9. This is seldom the case in modern opera songs, so crowded is the score and the orchestra. Indeed Piccinni is accused of employing instruments to such excess, that in Italy no copyist will transcribe one of his operas without being paid a zechin more than for one by any other composer. But in burlettas he has generally bad voices to write for, and is obliged to produce all his effects with instruments; and, indeed, this kind of drama usually abounds with brawls and *squabbles,* which it is necessary to enforce with the orchestra. [Au.]

to rather a tiresome length. The airs were much applauded, though it was the fourteenth representation of the opera. The author was engaged to compose for Turin, at the next carnival, for which place he set out while I was at Naples. The performance began about a quarter before eight, and continued till past eleven o'clock.

•   •   •   •   •

Friday 26. This morning I first had the pleasure of seeing and conversing with Signor Jommelli, who arrived at Naples from the country but the night before. He is extremely corpulent, and, in the face, not unlike what I remember Handel to have been, yet far more polite and soft in his manner. I found him in his night-gown, at an instrument, writing. He received me very politely, and made many apologies for not having called on me, in consequence of a card I had left at his house; but apologies were indeed unnecessary, as he was but just come to town, and at the point of bringing out a new opera that must have occupied both his time and thoughts sufficiently. He had heard of me from Mr. Hamilton.[10] I gave him Padre Martini's letter, and after he had read it we went to business directly. I told him my errand to Italy, and showed him my plan, for I knew his time was precious. He read it with great attention, and conversed very openly and rationally; said the part I had undertaken was much neglected at present in Italy; that the Conservatorios, of which, I told him, I wished for information, were now at a low ebb, though formerly so fruitful in great men. He mentioned to me a person of great learning who had been translating David's Psalms into excellent Italian verse; in the course of which work he had found it necessary to write a dissertation on the music of the ancients, which he had communicated to him. He said this writer was a fine and subtle critic; had differed in several points from Padre Martini; had been in correspondence with Metastasio, and had received a long letter from him on the subject of lyric poetry and music; all of which he thought necessary for me to see. He promised to procure me the book, and to make me acquainted with the author.[11] He spoke very much in praise of Alessandro Scarlatti, as to his church music, such as motets, masses, and oratorios; promised to procure me information concerning the Conservatorios, and whatever else was to my purpose, and in his power. He took down my direction, and assured me that the instant he had got his opera[12] on the stage he should be entirely at my service. Upon my telling him that my time for remaining at Naples was very short, that I should even then have been on the road on my way home but for his opera, which I so much wished to hear; that besides urgent business in

10. The British Minister to the Court of Naples.
11. Saverio Mattei, whose biography of Metastasio was published in 1785. For Metastasio's letters to him see Burney's *Memoirs of the Life and Writings of the Abate Metastasio* (London, 1796), vol. 2, pp. 378–420 and vol. 3, pp. 115–53.
12. His *Demofoonte*. Actually, this was an old work; first performed in Padua on June 16, 1743, it had already been heard in London, Milan, and Stuttgart.

England, there was great probability of a war, which would keep me a prisoner on the continent: he, in answer to that, and with great appearance of sincerity, said, if after I returned to England anything of importance to my plan occurred, he would not fail of sending it to me. In short, I went away in high good humor with this truly great composer, who is indisputably one of the first of his profession now alive in the universe; for were I to name the living composers of Italy for the stage, according to my idea of their merit, it would be in the following order: Jommelli, Galuppi, Piccinni, and Sacchini. It is, however, difficult to decide which of the two composers first mentioned has merited most from the public; Jommelli's works are full of great and noble ideas, treated with taste and learning; Galuppi's abound in fancy, fire, and feeling; Piccinni has far surpassed all his contemporaries in the comic style; and Sacchini seems the most promising composer in the serious.

•   •   •   •   •

Wednesday, October 31. This morning I went with young Oliver[13] to his conservatorio of S. Onofrio, and visited all the rooms where the boys practise, sleep, and eat. On the first flight of stairs was a trumpeter, screaming upon his instrument till he was ready to burst; on the second was a French horn, bellowing in the same manner. In the common practising room there was a *Dutch concert,* consisting of seven or eight harpsichords, more than as many violins, and several voices, all performing different things, and in different keys: other boys were writing in the same room; but it being holiday time, many were absent who usually study and practise in this room. The jumbling them all together in this manner may be convenient for the house, and may teach the boys to attend to their own parts with firmness, whatever else may be going forward at the same time; it may likewise give them force, by obliging them to play loud in order to hear themselves; but in the midst of such jargon, and continued dissonance, it is wholly impossible to give any kind of polish or finishing to their performance; hence the slovenly coarseness so remarkable in their public exhibitions; and the total want of taste, neatness, and expression in all these young musicians, till they have acquired them elsewhere.

The beds, which are in the same room, serve for seats to the harpsichords and other instruments. Out of thirty or forty boys who were practising, I could discover but two that were playing the same piece; some of those who were practising on the violin seemed to have a great deal of hand. The violoncellos practise in another room; and the flutes, oboes, and other wind instruments in a third, except the trumpets and horns, which are obliged to fag, either on the stairs, or on the top of the house.

There are in this college sixteen young *castrati,* and these lie upstairs, by themselves, in warmer apartments than the other boys, for fear of colds, which

13. "A young Englishman who has been four years in the Conservatorio of S. Onofrio." (Burney, *France and Italy,* p. 324 [Naples, Oct. 27].)

might not only render their delicate voices unfit for exercise at present, but hazard the entire loss of them forever.

The only vacation in these schools in the whole year is in autumn, and that for a few days only: during the winter, the boys rise two hours before it is light, from which time they continue their exercise, an hour and a half at dinner excepted, till eight o'clock at night; and this constant perseverance, for a number of years, with genius and good teaching, must produce great musicians.

After dinner I went to the theatre of San Carlo, to hear Jommelli's new opera rehearsed. There were only two acts finished, but these pleased me much, except the overture, which was short, and rather disappointed me, as I expected more would have been made of the first movement; but as to the songs and accompanied recitatives, there was merit of some kind or other in them all, as I hardly remember one that was so indifferent as not to seize the attention. The subject of the opera was Demophontes; the names of the singers I knew not then, except Aprile, the first man, and Bianchi, the first woman. Aprile has rather a weak and uneven voice, but is constantly steady as to intonation. He has a good person, a good shake, and much taste and expression. La Bianchi has a sweet and elegant toned voice, always perfectly in tune, with an admirable portamento; I never heard anyone sing with more ease; or in a manner so totally free from affectation. The rest of the vocal performers were all above mediocrity: a tenor with both voice and judgment sufficient to engage attention; a very fine contralto; a young man with a soprano voice, whose singing was full of feeling and expression; and a second woman, whose performance was far from despicable. Such performers as these were necessary for the music, which is in a difficult style, more full of instrumental effects than vocal. Sometimes it may be thought rather labored, but it is admirable in the *tout ensemble,* masterly in modulation, and in melody full of new passages.[14] This was the first rehearsal, and the instruments were rough and unsteady, not being as yet certain of the exact time or expression of the movements; but, as far as I was then able to judge, the composition was perfectly suited to the talents of the performers, who, though all good, yet not being of the very first and most exquisite class, were more in want of the assistance of instruments to mark the images, and enforce the passion, which the poetry points out.

The public expectation from this production of Jommelli, if a judgement may be formed from the number of persons who attended this first rehearsal, was very great; for the pit was crowded, and many of the boxes were filled with the families of persons of condition.

The theatre of San Carlo is a noble and elegant structure: the form is oval, or rather the section of an egg, the end next the stage being cut. There are seven ranges of boxes, sufficient in size to contain ten or twelve persons in each, who sit in chairs, in the same manner as in a private house. In every

14. Jommelli is now said to write more for the *learned few,* than for the *feeling many.* [Au.]

range there are thirty boxes, except the three lowest ranges, which, by the King's box being taken out of them, are reduced to twenty-nine. In the pit there are fourteen or fifteen rows of seats, which are very roomy and commodious, with leather cushions and stuffed backs, each separated from the other by a broad rest for the elbow: in the middle of the pit there are thirty of these seats in a row.

•   •   •   •   •

Sunday 4. At night I went to the first public representation of Signor Jommelli's opera of *Demofoonte,* in the grand theatre of San Carlo, where I was honored with a place in Mr. Hamilton's box. It is not easy to imagine or describe the grandeur and magnificence of this spectacle. It being the great festival of St. Charles and the King of Spain's name-day, the court was in grand gala, and the house was not only doubly illuminated, but amazingly crowded with well-dressed company.[15] In the front of each box there is a mirror, three or four feet long by two or three wide, before which are two large wax tapers; these, by reflection, being multiplied, and added to the lights of the stage and to those within the boxes, make the splendor too much for the aching sight. The King and Queen were present. Their majesties have a large box in the front of the house, which contains in height and breadth the space of four other boxes. The stage is of an immense size, and the scenes, dresses, and decorations were extremely magnificent; and I think this theatre superior, in these particulars, as well as in the music, to that of the great French opera at Paris.

But M. de la Lande, after allowing that "the opera in Italy is very well as to music and words," concludes with saying "that it is not, in his opinion, quite so in other respects, and for the following reasons:

1. There is scarce any machinery in the operas of Italy.[16]
2. There is not such a multitude of rich and superb dresses as at Paris.
3. The number and variety of the actors are less.[17]
4. The choruses are fewer and less labored. And
5. The union of song and dance is neglected."[18]

To all which objections, a real lover of music would perhaps say, *so much the better.*

M. de la Lande, however, allows that the hands employed in the orchestra are more numerous and various, but complains that the fine voices in an Italian opera are not only too few, but are too much occupied by the music and its embellishments to attend to declamation and gesture.

15. The fourth of November is likewise celebrated as the name-day of the Queen of Naples and the Prince of Asturias. [Au.]
16. The Italians have long given up those puerile representations of flying gods and goddesses, of which the French are still so fond and so vain. [Au.]
17. If the characters are fewer, the dresses must be so, of course. [Au.]
18. [Joseph Jerome Lelande], *Voyage d'un François* [*en Italie* (1765–66)], vol. 6. [Au.]

With regard to this last charge, it is by no means a just one; for whoever remembers Pertici and Laschi, in the burlettas of London, about twenty years ago, or has seen the *Buona figliuola*[19] there lately, when Signora Guadagni, Signor Lovatini, and Signor Morigi were in it; or in the serious operas of past times remembers Monticelli, Elisi, Mingotti, Colomba Mattei, Mansoli, or, above all, in the present operas has seen Signor Guadagni, must allow that many of the Italians not only recite well, but are *excellent actors*.

Give to a lover of music an opera in a noble theatre, at least twice as large as that of the French capital, in which the poetry and music are good and the vocal and instrumental parts well performed, and he will deny himself the rest without murmuring, though his ear should be less stunned with choruses, and his eye less dazzled with machinery, dresses, and dances than at Paris.

But to return to the theatre of San Carlo, which, as a spectacle, surpasses all that poetry or romance have painted: yet with all this, it must be owned that the magnitude of the building and noise of the audience are such, that neither the voices or instruments can be heard distinctly. I was told, however, that on account of the King and Queen being present, the people were much less noisy than on common nights. There was not a hand moved by way of applause during the whole representation, though the audience in general seemed pleased with the music: but, to say the truth, it did not afford me the same delight as at the rehearsal; nor did the singers, though they exerted themselves more, appear to equal advantage: not one of the present voices is sufficiently powerful for such a theatre, when so crowded and so noisy. Signora Bianchi, the first woman, whose sweet voice and simple manner of singing gave me and others so much pleasure at the rehearsal, did not satisfy the Neapolitans, who have been accustomed to the force and brilliancy of a Gabrieli, a Taiber, and a De Amici. There is too much simplicity in her manner for the depraved appetites of these *enfants gâtés*, who are never pleased but when astonished. As to the music, much of the *claire obscure* was lost, and nothing could be heard distinctly but those noisy and furious parts which were meant merely to give *relief* to the rest; the mezzotints and background were generally lost, and indeed little was left but the bold and coarse strokes of the composer's pencil.[20]

• • • • •

Wednesday 7. Today I was favored at dinner with the company of Signor Fabio, the first violin of the opera of San Carlo; he was so obliging and so humble as to bring with him his violin. It is very common in the great cities of Italy to see performers of the first eminence carry their own instruments through the streets. This seems a trivial circumstance to mention, yet it strongly marks the difference of manners and characters in two countries not very

19. By Niccolò Piccinni.
20. Leopold Mozart, in a letter written in Milan on December 22, 1770, says that the opera "failed so miserably that people are even wanting to substitute another" (*The Letters of Mozart & His Family*, trans. Emily Anderson [London, 1938], vol. 1, p. 258).

remote from each other. In Italy, the leader of the first opera in the world carries the instrument of his fame and fortune about him, with as much pride as a soldier does his sword or musket; while, in England, the indignities he would receive from the populace would soon impress his mind with shame for himself and fear for his instrument.

I obtained from Signor Fabio an exact account of the number of hands employed in the great opera orchestra: there are 18 first and 18 second violins, 5 double basses, and but 2 violoncellos; which I think has a bad effect, the double bass being played so coarsely throughout Italy that it produces a sound no more musical than the stroke of a hammer. This performer, who is a fat, good-natured man, by being long accustomed to lead so great a number of hands, has acquired a style of playing which is somewhat rough and inelegant, and consequently more fit for an orchestra than a chamber. He sang, however, several buffo songs very well and accompanied himself on the violin in so masterly a manner as to produce most of the effects of a numerous band. After dinner, he had a second to accompany him in one of Giardini's solos, and in several other things.

I spent this whole evening with Barbella,[21] who now delivered to me all the materials which he had been able to recollect, relative to a history of the Neapolitan conservatorios, as well as anecdotes of the old composers and performers of that school: besides these, I wrote down all the verbal information I could extract from his memory, concerning musical persons and things. During my visit, I heard one of his best scholars play a solo of Giardini's composition very well; he was the most brilliant performer on the violin that I met with at Naples.

And now, having given the reader an account of the musical entertainment I received at Naples, I hope I shall be indulged with the liberty of making a few reflections before I quit this city; which has so long been regarded as the center of harmony, and the fountain from which genius, taste, and learning have flowed to every other part of Europe that even those who have an opportunity of judging for themselves take upon trust the truth of the fact, and give the Neapolitans credit for more than they deserve at present, however they may have been entitled to this celebrity in times past.

M. de la Lande's account of music at Naples is so far from exact, that it would incline his reader to suppose one of two things, either that he did not attend to it, or that he had not a very distinguishing ear.

> Music [says this author] is in a particular manner the triumph of the Neapolitans; it seems as if the tympanum in this country was more braced, more harmonical, and more sonorous, than in the rest of Europe; the whole nation is vocal, every gesture and inflection of voice of the inhabitants, and even their prosody of syllables in conversation, breathe harmony and music. Hence Naples is the principal source of Italian music, of great composers, and of excellent operas.[22]

21. Emanuele Barbella, an Italian composer and violinist, at one time resident in London.
22. *Voyage d'un François*, vol. 6. The inaccuracy with which M. de la L. speaks about music and musicians runs through his work. He places Corelli and Galuppi among the Neapolitan com-

I am ready to grant that the Neapolitans have a natural disposition to music; but can by no means allow that they have voices more flexible and a language more harmonious than the inhabitants of the other parts of Italy, as the direct contrary seems true. The singing in the streets is far less pleasing, though more original than elsewhere; and the Neapolitan language is generally said to be the most barbarous jargon among all the different dialects of Italy.[23]

But though the rising generation of Neapolitan musicians cannot be said to possess either taste, delicacy, or expression, yet their compositions, it must be allowed, are excellent with respect to counterpoint and invention, and in their manner of executing them, there is an energy and fire not to be met with perhaps in the whole universe: it is so ardent as to border upon fury; and from this impetuosity of genius, it is common for a Neapolitan composer, in a movement which begins in a mild and sober manner, to set the orchestra in flames before it is finished. Dr. Johnson says that Shakespeare, in tragedy, is always struggling after some occasion to be comic; and the Neapolitans, like high bred horses, are impatient of the rein, and eagerly accelerate their motion to the utmost of their speed. The pathetic and the graceful are seldom attempted in the Conservatorios; and those refined and studied graces, which not only change, but improve passages, and which so few are able to find, are less sought after by the generality of performers at Naples, than in any other part of Italy.

---

posers; whereas it is well known that Corelli was of the Roman school, and he himself says in another place (vol. 5) that Galuppi was of the Venetian. [Au.]

23. A sufficient proof of the Neapolitan language being only a *patois* or provincial dialect, is that it remains merely oral, the natives themselves, who are well educated, never daring to write in it. [Au.]

24 Susannah Burney

Susannah Elizabeth Burney (1755–1800) was the daughter of the music historian Dr. Charles Burney. Although overshadowed by her sister Fanny, the celebrated novelist, Susan (as she was known to her family) was also a gifted writer, especially about music. From 1779 to 1780 she wrote a series of long letters from London to her sister, who was in the country working on a novel. The letters give a vivid account of the famous musicians Susan met and the Italian operas she attended. She was much more concerned than her father about dramatic aspects of opera, and she was more knowledgeable about musical style and technique than Fanny. In the following excerpts from the letter-diary, Susan describes a rehearsal of the pasticcio *Alessandro nell'Indie* in November 1779 and the bumpy reception accorded to Antonio Sacchini's *Rinaldo* later in the same season.

FROM Letter-Journal
(1779–80)

20 November 1779. Yesterday Morning Mr. Burney[1] and my sister came. I went to the Opera House a little *entremblant;* however, upon naming my father, we were very civilly allowed to pass. The opera was begun. We had lost the overture and a song or two I believe; Manzoletto[2] was then singing. We went into the pit, where there were two or three people. But two boxes were occupied—one by Lady Mary Duncan, the other by two ladies I did not know. I believe the rehearsal was intended to be quite private.... The opera is a pasticcio, and has been got together in such a hurry that though advertised to be under the *direction of Bertoni*[3] I fancy he can have composed nothing purposely for it, and indeed that there are but few songs of his introduced. This I supposed by observing that he did not stand forwards as *direttore* to above three or four throughout the opera; all the singers acted as *maestro* during their own songs. As I had read the opera [libretto] previous to the rehearsal I found that the scene which contains Porus's first song, "Vedrai con tuo periglio," was over, which I regretted infinitely. However I afterwards found it was omitted. But Pacchierotti[4] in a beautiful cavatina "Se mai più sarò geloso" which is placed about the middle of the first act charmed me indeed more than anything that followed in his part, or in course in that of any body else, throughout the whole opera. It is elegant, charming music, and admits of all those refinements and graces in which Pacchierotti so peculiarly excells. And he *did* sing it like a very angel. To *you* [her sister Fanny] it will give little trouble to conceive the pleasure I felt at hearing his most sweet voice, and that in such sweet music; but I would not answer for the *conception.* ... As an opera, I confess I have heard few that seemed to me possessed of a smaller number of fine, or even of *pleasing* airs than the present *Alessandro;* and I am sorry to say that, except the cavatina I have already mentioned, I am far from being charmed with anything even in Pacchierotti's part. Madame Le Brun[5] sings a

TEXT: British Library Egerton MS 3691, edited by Curtis Price, Judith Milhous, and Robert D. Hume. The notes are by these editors and Wye J. Allanbrook.

1. Susan's cousin and brother-in-law, Charles Rousseau, a well-known pianist.
2. The stage name of Angiolo Monanni (fl. 1779–82), a well-respected castrato of the second rank.
3. Ferdinando Bertoni (1725–1813), a celebrated composer of *opera seria* who was a friend of the castrato Pacchierotti (see n. 4), and accompanied him to England. He later (1785) was appointed maestro di capella of San Marco in Venice.
4. Gasparo Pacchierotti (1740–1821), generally regarded as one of the greatest castratos of the eighteenth century.
5. The soprano Franziska Lebrun, née Danzi (1756–1791), a singer of great skill and clarity, but of whom Charles Burney complains that having lived so long with an oboist her voice had taken on a "cold and instrumental" quality. She also turned her hand to composition, writing some ballet music and sonatas for keyboard and violin.

great deal in it, in *her* style very well—her voice being generally clear and her intonation extremely good, but her singing seems to me in almost every particular exactly the reverse of Pacchierotti's. Hers seems a bad imitation of an instrument; his what no instrumental performer on earth can equal: all softness, feeling, expression, while she is ever *trilling*, and diminishing instead of adding to the merit of her songs by the graces she introduces.

Madame Le Brun's songs, except two, I cannot I confess recollect anything of, but I believe their style was unmasked, for she cannot sing a cantabile, which prevents there being much variety in her airs; but one of the two I remember was a *chicherichi*[6] song in the second act—a bravura composed purposely for her which goes *up to the high*, and a very unpleasing one I think. Her husband,[7] who looks a conceited fop, gave the time etc. when she sung, and the *composition* for ought I know might be his. I should suspect her rondeau in the last act at least to be his, as it is very French. Tessier[8] in his advertisement of this opera, says that in it *many songs of Handel* will be introduced; the *many* however consist in *two*, one of which, being sung by Manzoletto, may be fairly said to be *too many*. Such an impertinent imitation it is of Pacchieriotti as makes one sick. His other songs I don't remember nor anything of Trebbi's[9] part, except that it was very heavy, and that he sang very much out of tune. Micheli[10] has a song, the instrumental parts of which are interesting. Pozzi[11] has a minuet in the first act, the music of which is vile; in the second a bravura by Bertoni which is *pretty enuff!* But in the third she has, perhaps, the best song in the opera, at least that which, excepting "Se mai più sarò geloso," seemed to *me* much the best. It is a bravura, and a very difficult one, yet full of elegant and pleasing passages, very much in Sacchini's[12] style. They led it so fast, that before she came to the end of it, she *non poteva più*,[13] and was obliged to stop for breath lery for merry.[14] Cramer[15] then with his accustomed good humour began it again slower, which I was very glad of, as we had an opportunity of hearing this charming song again, and to more advantage, as Pozzi being then more at her ease, executed it infinitely better.

Pacchierotti sings in the first act only "Se mai più sarò geloso" and the duet

6. Italian for "cock-a-doodle-do."
7. The oboist Ludwig August Lebrun (1752–1790).
8. Antoine Le Texier (c. 1737–1814), the manager of the opera company.
9. Giuseppi Trebbi (fl. 1775–82), a buffo singer, whom Charles Burney also criticizes.
10. Leopoldo De Michele (fl. 1761–91), a regular singer of the second rank, mentioned several times by Charles Burney.
11. Anna Pozzi (fl. 1776–88), a young Italian soprano who had greater success later in Italy than in her three London seasons.
12. See p. 266, n. 3. For Charles Burney's opinion of Sacchini, see p. 260.
13. "She could do no more," that is, she ran out of steam.
14. Helter-skelter.
15. Wilhelm Cramer (1745–1799), a German violinist, born in Mannheim, who after a stint in the famous Mannheim orchestra came to London, where he took up permanent residence. One of England's foremost violinists, he was concertmaster not only of the opera house orchestra, but also of several concert orchestras.

which I cannot like, though it is Piccinni's;[16] but great men are not always equal, and human genius has a period at which it seldom fails to decline. This it seems is Piccinni's last[17] work. It is in the beginning old fashioned and in the end incoherent, difficult, and unpleasing—*selon moi*,[18] and indeed *selon* every body but one I have heard mention it. But he[19] is a legion! In the second act Pacchierotti sings a song of Handel's, "Return oh God of Hosts," from *Samson*. It is, in its solemn and antique style a fine song. Pacchierotti expressed it like an angel, but, keeping himself I trust in reserve for the time of public performance, was *too* chaste and too *retenue*,[20] a fault of which he is indeed not often guilty. It is adapted to Italian words. After this he sings a bravura by Piccinni which is *extremely* difficult, but which did not seem to me either pleasing or calculated to shew his talents to any advantage. However, he sung so much *a sotto voce* that it was not very easy to form a judgement concerning him in it. He has a pretty rondeau in the last act, which he likewise whispered, owing I believe to the presence of that oaf the Duke of C[umberlan]d, for after he appeared, which was during the second act, Pacchierotti seemed displeased, out of spirits, and exerted himself in nothing. I believe you were at home when Giardini[21] gave us an account of his behavior to poor Pacchierotti when Lady Mary Duncan introduced him to his Royal Highness at Windsor. *Wretched doings! Nothing could be more shabby!* At first we had seated ourselves in a very obscure part of the pit, but when Pacchierotti began his cavatina, he sung, though divinely, so *piano*, that we moved nearer the orchestra. By this means Mr. Burney was soon espied by many who know him in the band. Cramer bowed in the most respectful polite manner that could be to us all. He is a *charming Creachur*, so mild, so gentlemanlike in his manner of speaking to the band, at the same time that it is evident he quite suffers when anything goes wrong. The wind instruments were all out of tune, and though I pitied poor Cramer 'twas impossible not to laugh. After repeatedly desiring the French horn players to make their instruments sharper, at last he called out in a voice which proved that he with difficulty could repress a degree of indignation and with his foreign accent, "Gentlemen [sic] . . . You are not in tune at all?" "It's a very sharp morning, sir," said one of them. "We shall do better another time." Another said that the crook he used was right, but Cramer desired he would try the other. He did so. "Why that is *better*," said Cramer, as indeed it clearly was. "Very well sir," said the stupid, earless wretch, "I'll be sure to use it." Presently after, in another passage the bassoon player was dreadfully and ridiculously out of tune. Cramer stopped again, and Clementi,[22] to point out in the

16. For Charles Burney's opinion of Piccinni, see pp. 256–57 and 260.
17. Most recent.
18. "According to me."
19. Pacchierotti.
20. "Restrained."
21. See pp. 250, n. 2 and 256.
22. Muzio Clementi (1752–1832), composer and piano virtuoso, at the beginning of his distinguished career.

most forcible manner possible why he did so, played over the passage with natural notes in the treble and flat in the bass. I don't know whether you can understand what I mean, but it had the most dissonant and comical effect and produced the best imitation of their accompaniment that can be conceived. Pacchierotti, whose song was playing, then went and whispered something to Cramer, who in consequence of it, called to the bassoon player by his name, and desired he would omit playing that passage. "Yes, sir, to be sure I will," cried the dolt whose stupid, shameless insensibility made everybody laugh, and spite of his evident vexation Cramer [too] at last, till he seemed almost choked by it. Tessier did not appear till the rehearsal was nearly over, and did not know us as we sat in a dark place. Indeed, I believe, had we been in any other, I was the only one he would have known. I was not very miserable at this, especially as the only person I saw by whom I at all wished myself noticed was not long without observing me: this was, need I say, Pacchierotti. We had approached the orchestra very gently during his cavatina; presently after it the weather was so cold that he gave two or three jumps to warm himself. During this performance, he caught our eyes, and almost while he was yet *en l'air* took off his hat, laughing and bowing. "Il fait bien froid," said he, to excuse his exhibition I suppose; "très froid en verité."[23] As soon as the duet which ends the act was over, which is, by the way, preceded by some delightful recitative, I missed Pacchierotti on the stage, and presently heard his voice behind me. "How does Miss Burney do?" said he, "and Mr. Burney and Mrs. Burney? . . . All well I hope?" "Very happy to see and hear him again," I told him. He expressed much good natured concern at hearing my mother was yet confined and said, "I wished much to wait upon you this morning, but there was the rehearsal— tomorrow again . . . but Sunday, in the evening . . . I will try." I told him we should be most happy to see him. "And when," said he, "do you expect your sister?" "I hope next week." "Oh yes . . . when the Parliament makes its meeting." Mr. Burney then began cutting up[24] the duet, in doing which I found, as indeed he might have foreseen, he was in the wrong box. Had Pacchierotti disliked it, certainly in a pasticcio where there could be no obligation to do it, he would not have sung it. He said it was Piccinni's last composition. "Une musique qui n'a pas été entendu encore, et *belle en verité*,"[25] and attributed Mr. Burney's not liking it to its having been ill executed, but hoped Tuesday night it would go better. Because Mr. Burney talks such good French and Italian he would not speak English to poor Pacchierotti as *I* did and, I believe, bothered him to death. He asked me if I had heard the cavatina. I said it was beautiful, and begged to know the composer, but the noise of the instruments was so great I could not hear his answer. However, he said of the music, "Elle est charmante, il est vrai."[26] I then asked if he had not another song before it.

23. "It's very cold, truly very cold."
24. Criticizing.
25. "Music that has not been heard yet, and truly beautiful."
26. "It is charming, it is true."

"No, dans le premier acte rien que ce morceau et le duo," but seeing me look *malcontente,* "Mai j'ai bien assez," added he, "vous verrez, dans le second acte j'ai deux airs, et puis un rondeau dans le troisième. J'ai un beaucoup à fatiguer en verité."[27] The *Sultano Generoso*[28] was in his head I dare say. Micheli was singing: "à present il faut écouter les Instrumens," said I. "Il est vrai,"[29] said he, laughing. The next air was Pozzi's which he *brava'*d away like anything. He told me 'twas Bertoni's song. In this pretty manner did he set with us till recalled on the stage to sing, and indeed the time he spent with us was more agreeably passed by me than any other during which he was *not* singing.

I came home extremely well pleased with my entertainment, though not totally so with the opera in general. There will be another rehearsal Monday, but though we may go to it free gratis, for nothing at all, our dear fastidious sister thinks it not worth while to come to it.

•   •   •   •   •

I had a nice conclusion of my confab with Pacchierotti. I asked him whose was the cavatina he sung in the first act of *Alessandro.* "Piccinni's," he told me, as was the duet. He had particularly wished Madame Le Brun likewise to sing an air of Piccinni's to these words: "Se mai turbo il tuo riposo," and indeed for a very good reason. I don't know whether you are acquainted with the opera, but Porus, whose jealousy occasions the great distress of the piece, having received the strongest proofs of his mistress's attachments sings "Se mai più sarò geloso, mi punirca i sacre nume che dell'India e domator" [*sic*].[30] She in her turn sings "Se mai turbo il tuo riposo, se m'accende pace mai non abbia il cor."[31] Soon after Porus's jealousy being again awakened, they insult each other with their former protestations. This is the subject of the duet. Porus begins it with the words of Cleofida, "Se mai turbo" etc., and she then repeats his "Se mai più sarò geloso" etc. Now, you will readily conceive that the two airs and the duet ought to be the composition of the same master. Piccinni made the subject of the latter the same with that of the two airs, which added much to its effect. "Et quand je l'ai chanté avec la De Amicis,"[32] said Pacchierotti, "dans ces Paroles *Se mai più sarò geloso,* elle a imité ma manière de chanter la cavatina, et moi aussi à mon tour j'a che [*sic*] d'exprimer *Se mai turbo il tuo riposo* de la façon qu'elle l'avait faite. Ce qui a fait un effet je vous assure que je ne puis vous dire. J'avais expliqué à Madame Le Brun comme j'ai l'honneur de vous de faire à vous, et comme j'ai beaucoup d'estime et pour son caractère et

---

27. "No, in the first act there is nothing but this piece and the duo. But I have plenty; you will see, in the second act I have two arias, and then a rondeau in the third. I have enough to tire me, truly."
28. Actually *Il soldano generoso,* a pasticcio arranged by Bertoni and given later in the season, on December 14, 1779.
29. "Now it's necessary to listen to the instruments." "It is true."
30. "If I am ever jealous again, may the gods who conquered India punish me."
31. "If I ever trouble your repose, may my heart have no peace."
32. Anna Lucia De Amicis (c. 1733–1816), Italian soprano who had a distinguished career, primarily in Italy.

pour son mérite je desirais et véritablement que nous nous entendions bien sur ce sujet aussi bien pour son interêt que pour la mienne. Et bien nous nous etions convenus de tout ici et en avions même parlé de nouveau je passé au soir. Eh bien, le matin arrive et, à la répétition, sans me dire un seul mot, je suis tout surpris de l'entendre chanter un autre air, au quel vous avez peut être remarquée que M. Le Brun a donné le ton."[33] How injudiciously and wantonly ill bred and impertinent! Pacchierotti repeated several times that he knew he had no title to expect her to sing an air disagreeable to her, had she objected to it when they were together. But to accept and then change it without deigning to give a reason or make an apology was a want of politeness and consideration which he did not expect. He attributed it however to her husband, I found, who is I believe an insolent, disagreeable man. I mentioned with admiration the sweet recitative before the duet. "Eh le duo aussi est beau je vous assure mademoiselle," said Pacchierotti, "s'il est chanté comme il faut. J'espère une autre fois qu'il vous plaira."[34]

Speaking of the *désagrément* attending his situation, owing to the jealousy, caprice, or caballing spirits of those he had to deal with he said, "Si dieu me fait la grace jamais de me tirer du théâtre je m'estimerai bien heureux je vous assure!"[35] My father promised to send him any English books he could wish for when he should be gone. "Mais sans la conversation," said he, "j'ai peur que j'oublierai tout." "Il faut donc rester," said I. "Ah mademoiselle! Vous voyez, apres cette année je n'aurai plus rien à faire. Et de rester me sera impossible!"[36]

• • • • •

Wednesday morning, 19 April 1780. Etty[37] came and accompanied me to the Opera House. When we went in a dance was rehearsing by Mademoiselle Bacelli and Signor Guiardele.[38] I was however in a relief at hearing from Cramer who was behind the scenes that it would soon be over, and the

33. "And when I sang with De Amicis, at those words *Se mai più sarò geloso* she imitated the way in which I sang the cavatina, and I also in my turn conveyed *Se mai turbo il tuo riposo* in the way that she had done it. I assure you, this had an effect that I cannot describe. I had explained to Madame Le Brun as I have had the honor of explaining to you, and as I had much admiration both for her character and for her talent I would truly desire that we understand one another well on this subject, as well for her interest as for mine. And we certainly were agreed about it all here, and we had even spoken of it again before I left for the evening. Well, the morning came and, at the rehearsal, without saying a single word to me, I was completely surprised to hear her sing another air, to which you perhaps would have observed that M. Le Brun gave the tone."

34. "Ah, I assure you, Mademoiselle, the duo is also fine, if it is sung as it ought to be. I hope that it will please you some other time."

35. "If God did me the favor of taking me away from the theater, I would think myself very happy, I assure you!"

36. But without conversation I'm afraid that I will forget everything." "Then you must stay here." "Ah mademoiselle! You see, after this year I won't have anything more to do. And it will be impossible for me to stay."

37. Susan's elder sister, Hester (1749–1832).

38. Favre Guiardele (fl. 1775–1802), a protégé of the choreographer Jean-George Noverre.

opera[39] was then to be rehearsed. I saw Lady Clarges and Miss Bulls in an opposite box, which made me not ambitious of figuring in the pit. However, as the woman to whom we applied for a box was not kind, we even made the best of our way to the above mentioned place. Here in a minute we were followed and joined by Cramer, to whom my sister and I both paid our compliments concerning his great benefit.[40] "But," said he, "had you not better be in a box Ma'am to day?" We said we could not get one. "Oh dear," said he, "I will get one for you in a minute if you will give me leave. It's very cold here indeed." We made proper speeches, but Cramer with the utmost good humour and readiness opened a side box for us where we sat very comfortably, though at too great a distance from the stage to see well, or be at all discoverable to those upon it, which I was sorry for as by this means Pacchierotti could not see that we had made use of his intelligence concerning the rehearsal. Lady Clarges and Miss Bulls had some other engagement and went away before the end of the second act. Lady Mary Duncan, Lady [Mount] Edgcumbe, the Harris's, and Brudenells, Duke of Dorset, Jack Parsons, Mr. Southwell, Rauzzini, Vachon, and a few others we distinguished in the boxes and on the stage.

There was no *maestro*! Poor Sacchini confined wholly to his bed with the gout, and Mattei says fretting himself to death, that this opera like *Enea e Lavinea*[41] must come out without his being able to act as director, or know whether things go well or ill. Indeed, though Cramer took great pains this morning, nothing seemed to go so well as at the rehearsal in the room[42] of last week, owing to carelessness in some of the performers and forgetfulness in others. Scarce anything was repeated; all hurried over, and Madame Le Brun's great song in the second act and a great deal of recitative not even rehearsed, nor was the rondeau tried, though I heard by Mattei it was quite finished some days before, and though there will be but one more rehearsal of this opera. 'Tis indeed very hard on Sacchini, and may well fret him.

As I gave you so full an account of *Rinaldo* before, I shall have the less to mention concerning it this time. Zampieri, or Lampieri, as some call him,[43] rehearsed a song in the first act, a mezzo bravura not so pretty as his two other songs, and as a singer I like him even less than before. He was insufferably out of tune. Pozzi's bravura in the second act I like far less than that she had in the first act of *Enea e Lavinia*. It does not hang together so well as Sacchini's songs generally do, but her other two airs are indeed beautiful. Madame Le Brun's first song too is full of delightful passages, and must be listened to with pleasure notwithstanding she sings it. This and Trebbi's second song, which is a bravura

---

39. Sacchini's *Rinaldo* (London, King's Theatre, April 1780) was a revival of his *Armida*, first performed in Milan in 1772.
40. A concert for which all the receipts, less the rental of the room and payment of the other artists, went to the star performer, in this case Cramer.
41. Sacchini's *Enea e Lavina* was first performed at King's Theatre, London, in March 1779.
42. The coffee room at the King's Theatre, which doubled as a rehearsal hall.
43. Nicola(?) Sampieri (fl. 1780–1800?).

abounding in new and charming accompaniments, pleased me yet more than at the first rehearsal. Pacchierotti's part I could not be more enchanted with than I was on the first hearing. He sung divinely, and made *sans y pense*[44] a delightful cadence to his first song.

When all was over my sister and I in coming away saw Bertoni with whom we stopped to speak a little while Pacchierotti in the midst of a very animated conversation bowed to me at a distance, but seemed to me to be engaged in a dispute with an Italian who held a letter open in his hand. . . .

Dr. Johnson has just called—but for a minute. He had a coach waiting for him and would not even set down, though he was very smiling and good humoured. He came to tell us he accepted an invitation which was sent him this morning to dine with us next Sunday. Mrs. Williams will likewise come. *I wiss to my art* you were at home!

Friday evening, 21 April 1780. Ah, ma chère Fanni! I have been to another and the last rehearsal of *Rinaldo* this morning; I am returned more distractedly in love with it than ever yet had many little things to abate my pleasure too. My mother, Charlotte,[45] and I went, and were immediately shown to a box, which was rather a wonder, as I never before saw so crowded a rehearsal. Not only the pit and stage were full, and the stage boxes, but much the greater number of the second range of side boxes were occupied. Lady Clarges and Miss Bulls were in a stage box opposite us but could not distinguish us; nor could anybody else indeed, as we were so far back as to be totally in the dark. However, my mother made herself known to Mr. Harris[46] who sat in the box next us, and was very polite and charming, as was Miss Louisa, who came in afterwards, and compared notes with me during all the opera. Lady Mary Duncan, Lady [Mount] Edgcumbe, his honour and Mrs. Brudenell, Jack Parsons, Lady Caermarthen, Lady Lucan, Mr. Southwell, Mr. Price, the Duke of Queensbury, Lady Hales and Miss Coussmaker etc. were there. Cramer found us out in passing from the stage into the pit, and came between every act to speak to us and lament with me that the dances were rehearsed, which were so long and so very tiresome they fatigued us all abominably. I could dwell on the merits of every part of the opera for ages, but think it would be making too free with your time and patience, so shall hold back. However, I must say that even in the most inferior pieces of *Rinaldo* charming passages and infinite entertainment must be met with but all Trebbi's part. Madame Le Brun's, the recitatives throughout, overture, duet, trio, quintetto, Pozzi's first and last song, and Paccheriotti's part are divine indeed. And from what I can remember of the latter, even were *he* not to sing it I am sure it would still yet be charming. Yet most certain it is that he adds infinite grace and beauty to everything he

44. "Without thinking about it."
45. A younger sister of Susan and Fanny.
46. Perhaps James Harris (1709–1780), author of the influential essay *Three Treatises: The First Concerning Art: The Second Concerning Music, Painting and Poetry: The Third Concerning Happiness* (1744), who was a friend of the Burney family.

performs, and can give merit even when it is wholly wanting. His rondo was rehearsed to day, and I have it by heart. It is different from every other I remember, and full of grace and elegance. It ends allegro. 'Tis a most sweet thing!

In the beginning of the last act the Harris's finding one of the stage boxes had been evacuated, and wishing as I did to be nearer the performers, left their box and went into the other. We then moved into their box, but presently Mr. Harris returned to us and stayed during the last act with us, and my dear father joined us at the end.

Soon after this removal we were spied out by Pacchierotti who had before not known us. He bowed smiling to me, and presently, passed by some ladies in the stage boxes to speak to me. "I wished Ma'am," said he, "to have waited upon you this week, but I have been *so* busy I could not. I have been very sorry indeed." I told him we knew how much he must be hurried and scarce had hoped to see him. And then, fearing to inconvenience the ladies in the next box, whom he stood before[,] he retired again, but I just told him I had been charmed with his rondo. He looked very pale indeed, and told my father who spoke to him in coming in he was far from well, and this rehearsal (owing to *three dances* besides those interwoven in the piece being rehearsed) was enough to kill him.

● ● ● ● ●

Monday Morning, 24 April 1780. Mr. Barry[47] was here Saturday evening but left us as did Miss Young who was much fatigued by her journey, before my father returned from the opera. There was a great house, and the opera went off he says with uncommon éclat, though poor Pacchierotti was ill and frightened and sung more flat than he has done before this season. The torches too of some of the furies in the last act went out, which set many fools laughing and so disturbed Pacchierotti that he could scarce sing a note, and this vexatious circumstance ruined the effect of the recitative and air with which I was so struck at the rehearsals. However, I hope this will not happen again, for had I been there I should have been ready to say with disappointment and vexation, as nothing in the opera at the rehearsals affected me so greatly as the composition and performance of this scene. My father could not get behind the scenes to speak to Pacchierotti. His cantabile was encored.

● ● ● ● ●

This morning I was upstairs preparing to go out when a carriage stopped at our door, which on looking out of the window I discovered to be Pacchierotti's. I made all possible haste downstairs and saw Pacchierotti dressed for the day, and looking much better than on Friday, notwithstanding that his face appeared to me not to be quite clean, which was afterwards accounted for. "I intended ma'am," said he, "to come here last night, but I was prevented, and as I have

47. The painter James Barry.

engagements for every night this week, I was determined to wait upon you in the morning." I told him he was very good, and my mother said we had the more obligation to him because he had already seen my father that morning. "Yes ma'am, and I hope," said he laughing, "he will bring you my respects, as I did desire him to do." I enquired after Bertoni. He had just met him he said in Oxford Road and that he was *si enjoué*[48] and looked so gay he was delighted at it! "Were you at the opera ma'am," said he, "Saturday?" I was obliged to answer in the negative. "But you heard that there was some mischief happened?" "Yes. My father told me the furies disturbed you . . ." "Oh! I was so angry, ma'am. My best scene in the last act it was quite spoiled." "And how was it," asked my mother? "Oh! I assure you I never was so *wexed* . . . Indeed! Four *Disgraziate furie!*—ungraceful furies, they came out, and by their bad actions and ridiculous manner they made all the people laugh, and indeed I could not tell how to go on; and all the time they kept beating me like a martyr. You see ma'am my face how it is bruised." I then found that a large discolored spot on his chin which I had taken for dirt, was the effect of a blow given him by these careless and awkward beasts! You'll exclaim as I did, especially when he went on and told us that he had had another blow on his head, which yet pained him extremely, and *several* on his shoulders and back. "Yet," said he, "I spoke to them in every language I knew and bid them stop: 'it is enough'; 'basta'; 'c'est assez.' Indeed, when I found they would not desist, I had a great will to strike them myself, I felt such . . . *rabbia*—rage. Indeed, and then in the newspaper the next day they put it in that I was embarrassed, and sung too much at the private concerts. Now on a first night I never exert myself so much. I never felt more *impegno . . . premura*[49] . . . more desire to succeed, but these *dirty scrubs* . . . indeed they quite made me mad." After compassionating him and railing with all my heart at the *dirty scrubs,* I told him I hoped there would be another rehearsal before Saturday, that these wretches might be better instructed. "Oh," said he, "if this had been properly rehearsed before the time of performance, nothing of this sort could have happened. But the dancing master,[50] he is so *fool* and so *pride*"—"so foolish and so proud," said I. "Yes, ma'am, that he will not do anything he is requested, but all his own way. But we must rehearse the dances on Friday and tomorrow too then will be a rehearsal of the *Olimpiade,* for the sake of Madame Le Brun."

●   ●   ●   ●   ●

Saturday, 29 April 1780. Sacchini appeared at the harpsichord tonight, which he could not do last Saturday. He was much applauded the moment he appeared but looked indeed *à faire compassion!*[51] Very, *very* ill. I hope however he was satisfied with the manner in which his charming opera was per-

48. "So playful."
49. "Zeal . . . eagerness."
50. Gutardele.
51. "Pitiful."

formed and received. I do not now regret I did not go the first night, because though it was greatly applauded, many things failed, and nothing was so correct as at this second performance. 'Tis a very dramatic opera, and I find not Badini's[52] but merely sewn together by him. The scenery is very good and machinery not bad. I like all but some monsters who in the first scene are supposed to terrify Ubaldo from pursuing his way to Armida's enchanted palace, but who appear so very *tame*, that one longs to pat their heads and caress them like a good natured Pomeranian dog. The scene of the furies went off extremely well. There were twelve of them, and they kept a respectful distance from Pacchierotti, and seemed only inclined to guard the myrtle, not to beat him again like a martyr. The music is so fine, and the opera went off so well that though I was in pain from my head to my foot before it began, I felt no complaints during the whole opera. I was in Elysium and will insist upon it that there are medicinal powers in music.

The overture, Trebbi's recitative and first air charmed me as much as ever, and Pozzi's sweet song. Even Sampiere I could bear as there are such pretty passages in his songs, though they are of a second or perhaps third rate. Madame Le Brun's first song is full of charming *pensieri*, and indeed I never liked her better. She acts in Armida really extraordinarily well. But how was I delighted when Rinaldo appeared, surrounded by dancing nymphs, with the sweetest accompanied recitative imaginable, that he *so sings!* 'Tis really worth while to get his part by heart that one may not lose a word. Indeed, every passion, every line of the opera is beautifully set, and with infinite expression and feeling by Sacchini, and Pacchierotti not only in his airs, but in every word of the recitative delights me: so much *sense;* so much *sensibility;* such judicious, such energetic, such affecting expression does he give to everything! His first sweet song "Resta ingrata, io parto, addio," he sung most charmingly. And the duet. But I must not dwell again upon *every thing*. In the second act he sung his fine cantabile very finely, and very *chastely*, but it was not encored. He made the finest cadences I almost ever heard, very recherché, yet simple and in the style of the song. There were some beasts in the house (Tenducci[53] I saw and firmly believe to have been one of them) who blew their noses, coughed, spit, and did everything possible but *hiss* during every one of his songs, in a shameful manner. They meant to disturb him and make him sing ill and out of tune, to prevent people from hearing him, and to persuade him and everyone that the public wished not to listen to him. I am *certain* it was the effect of malice not accident, because the house was stiller during Zampieri's and even Micheli's songs than during Pacchierotti's. Is it not enough to make one sick that there should be such envy and such worthlessness in the world?

52. Carlo Francesco Badini (fl. 1770–1793), house poet at the King's Theatre.
53. Giusto Ferdinando Tenducci (c. 1735–1790), a rival castrato.

These wretches produced in part the effect they desired in his first song, when he was two or three times disturbed I am certain by the noise. The cantabile however could not be better sung, but the rumor of these creatures I am certain prevented it from being *felt* as it ought to be, and consequently from being encored. Pozzi's furious song, which I like less than most in the opera, though it describes a storm and expresses it indeed vastly well, was vehemently applauded by all whose hands had not moved to Pacchierotti, not from admiration of her but to mortify *him!* After this follows a most divine scene of accompanied recitative by Pacchierotti, and one of the sweetest rondeau's in the world; and this was encored, but opposed by the snakes who were *semés ça et la*[54] in the galleries. However, the encore was so strong and so well kept up that he returned, and repeated it better than ever.

A fine scene of accompanied recitative followed by Madame Le Brun, a pretty cavatina, more accompanied recitative and the scene ends with a furious song, of the *chicherichi* sort, but very animated and clever; and then some snakes immediately encored this, though there is not an Italian that can bear Madame Le Brun's singing. During the encore and opposition to the rondo, I observed that Piozzi[55] was totally neutral, and indeed he never stirred his hands to Pacchierotti throughout the opera, but how, though he condemns and hates Madame Le Brun's singing, he encored her with violence. "Mais est-ce-que vous dites encore pour vous moquer d'elle," said I, laughing. "Eh pourquoi voulez vous pas que je dise encore mademoiselle," said he, *fiercement.* "C'est trop juste, pourquoi ne faut il pas qu'elle repète son air *aussi?*"[56] Don't you admire this sort of reasoning? So, because Pacchierotti sung like a divinity and enchanted all that had ears and were not devoured by envy and malice it was *trop juste* that Madame Le Brun should likewise be encored. The trio was strongly encored but two songs having been repeated in the same act the encore was not carried. In the last act I was delighted by Trebbi's sweet song, by the finest recitative in the world of Pacchierotti, by Pozzi's syrenish song, who appears at the head of a number of fair nymphs in defence of the myrtle; by Madame Le Brun's slow song which she sung uncommonly well and acted better, and finally and most strongly was I affected by the recitative of Pacchierotti and air which he sings surrounded by the furies. Yet to say the truth these same furies, the thunder, lightning, scenery etc. add nothing to the effect of the music, but rather I think serve to disturb and interrupt one's attention, in so much that I dare say every one who *heard with ears* at the rehearsals of *Rinaldo* were more touched by this scene than at the public representation. It reminded me of the witches in *Macbeth*, whose speeches when they are *read*

---

54. "Sown here and there."
55. Gabriele Mario Piozzi, tenor and singing teacher, later married to Hester Lynch Piozzi (see p. 249).
56. "But are you saying encore to make fun of her?" "Eh, why do you not want me to say encore, mademoiselle? It's too just, why isn't it necessary for her to repeat her air *also?*"

freeze one with horror, but when repeated on the stage lose all their effect and become even ludicrous by the absurd appearance of gestures of the actors. However, the scene in question yet holds its ground with me, and seems to me the *plus beau morceau de l'opéra*.[57] It ends delightful by the sweet quintetto. Sacchini continued after the curtain was let down to be applauded till he had left the orchestra. Indeed he merited every mark of approbation the opera could receive. There was such a house as only Cramer's [benefit] could exceed. Indeed except on the stage it could not well be fuller. We came away before the last dance.

57. "The finest piece of the opera."

25 Johann Nikolaus Forkel

In his twentieth year Johann Nikolaus Forkel (1749–1818) matriculated at the University of Göttingen, and he remained there until his death, having been appointed music director in 1779. Although he was a practicing musician, his real talents lay in music history and bibliography. He surrounded himself with an extensive library and he conceived of and brought nearly to completion a universal history of music: beginning with the Egyptians, it breaks off in the sixteenth century. What distinguishes Forkel's history from its predecessors is not the breadth of its coverage, however, but its systematizing "introduction," an essay of sixty-eight pages divided into 135 titled sections. The principles outlined in the essay, a taxonomy of music into five essential branches and three evolutionary stages, provide a theoretical framework for the history that follows. The *Allgemeine Geschichte der Musik* (*A General History of Music*) is further supported by a massive annotated bibliography, *Allgemeine Litteratur der Musik* (*General Bibliography of Writings on Music,* 1792), consisting of some three thousand citations from antiquity to the late eighteenth century. This systematizing bent and diligent scholarship earned Forkel his reputation as the founder of modern musicology.

The notion of musical progress outlined in the *Geschichte* was critical to Forkel's thought; music for him had reached its zenith in the works of J. S. Bach and in his own time had fallen into a period of decadence, from which it might be rescued by an accurate extraction of compositional rules from all of music history. In this spirit Forkel wrote the first biography of Bach—a work that, true to his love of system, was to take its place as the culmination of the history he never completed.

FROM *A General History of Music*
(1788–1801)

INTRODUCTION

§ 1. [THE BENEFITS OF AN ACCURATE PRESENTATION OF THE RANGE
OF MUSIC, AND HOW IT HAS GRADUALLY ATTAINED SUCH A GREAT
RANGE.][1]

The different configurations in which music appears in the narrative of its
fortunes over the millennia, among both ancient and modern peoples, cannot
be correctly surveyed and evaluated without a precise conception of its gradual
development, from the first elements to the highest and most perfect union of
all individual parts in the whole. In the first epochs, among the first of earth's
peoples, music appears in its infancy, as it were; only the first and simplest
parts of the whole can be observed. In the periods immediately following,
nations that are somewhat more cultivated augment those few parts and first
elements with some new ones, but without coming noticeably closer to the
perfection of the whole. Finally, while among still later and more developed
peoples this increase in the number of the individual parts can be more or less
apparent, still perhaps no single people may gather all the individual parts of
the whole into one and thereby offer a model of the art in its highest perfection.
How is it possible today to make a correct evaluation of all these variations,
which arise not only from the lesser and greater quantities of individual parts,
but also from the influence of different climates, social conditions, the way of
life, moral values, and other cultural habits of the nations? Only if one knows
how the art has necessarily been constituted as regards its inner nature, in its
infancy as well as step by step in each epoch of its development; only if there
exists a standard by which, at least to some extent, the condition in which it
endured among various peoples can be determined. Such a standard must be
the correct conception of music in its entire extent.

Like all products of nature, the arts and sciences grow to perfection only
gradually. The interval between their first beginning and their highest perfection is filled with such a variety of intermediate creations that not only is the
stepwise progression from the simple to the complex, the small to the large,
everywhere apparent, but also each individual degree in this gradation can be
examined itself as a whole. Thus the sciences and arts resemble polyps, whose

TEXT: The original edition, vol. 1 (Leipzig, 1788), pp. 1–6, 31–35, 91–93. Translation by Wye J.
Allanbrook.

1. The headings following the numbered sections are not included in the text but are supplied
from Forkel's table of contents.

hundred limbs, if cut up, each live on their own—seemingly perfect polyps, but in miniature.[2]

Thus a picture that represents the stepwise development of music from its first beginnings to its highest perfection—one that genuinely manifests the course taken by the human intellect in the development of its capabilities generally, but in particular in our art—seems to be the best means to enable the reader to evaluate more certainly all the possible variations in which this art appears in all the nations that have become known to us, and at least not to be without a basis for determining where and when it had or could have had true inner worth. The drawing of such a picture entails many difficulties, for several reasons. First of all, its individual features are scattered about in the whole of nature, and can be gathered together only with great effort. Second, these features, even if they have been successfully gathered together, can be united in a whole only with great difficulty. And finally, in the third place, it is not sufficient to ascertain from ancient and modern historians what these individual features were and are: one must in addition be a theorist, critic, and even a moralist, in order to be able to demonstrate what they would have had to be. This last requirement compels the painter of such a picture to proceed like Apelles, who in order to paint a perfect Venus united the most beautiful features of several beautiful women into a whole. In music, as in all her works, nature has only scattered about individual things of beauty; it is the task of human beings to search them out, and to produce by means of their appropriate arrangement new creations—creations more perfect than those of nature herself.

§2. [THIS ACCURATE PRESENTATION CAN BE MOST EASILY ACHIEVED BY THE COMPARISON OF MUSIC WITH LANGUAGE.]

The similarity that obtains between the language of human beings and their music—a similarity that extends not only to their origin but also to their full development, from its first beginning to its highest perfection—can furnish the surest guide in these matters. In its genesis music, like language, is nothing other than the expression of a feeling through the passions of the tones. The two of them arise from a common source—sensation. When subsequently they separated, each on its own path became what it was capable of becoming—the one, the language of the intellect, and the other, the language of the heart. Yet there remained to them both so many signs of their common origin that even at their furthest remove they still speak to the understanding and the heart in similar ways. The derivation and multiplication of their expressions from the first utterances of the feelings, the construction and composition of those expressions with a view not only to awakening feelings or concepts, but also to awakening and communicating them precisely and without ambiguity: in brief,

2. For the important biological discovery of the 1740s that suggested this comparison to Forkel, see p. 196, n. 27.

all the qualities that make the one into the consummate language of the understanding make the other similarly into the consummate language of the heart.
Thus whoever knows the nature of the one can be easily brought to a correct
and full understanding of the other by observation of the similarity prevailing
between them. What can be said here only provisionally about the similarity of
the construction of the language of our feelings and the language of our ideas[3]
will best be confirmed if in the course of this introduction that similarity is kept
in mind at all times, and the ground and cause of the relation always pointed
out at appropriate moments.

THE FIRST PERIOD OF THE ART

§ 3. [IT CONSISTS MERELY OF DISCONNECTED TONES AND NOISE.]

Although tone—or rather, as it must be called at this juncture, sound—is
only the means by which music is made perceptible, in primitive, uncultivated
nations it is generally taken for the thing itself. Indeed they consider every
individual sound to be music. Consider pure sound in its various modifications:
loud, soft, sharp and rough, gentle, dark, muffled, thick, thin, and so on. Furthermore, consider how in these various modifications sound is capable of
affecting the hearing, and therefore the feelings, of human beings.[4] Then there
is little reason to be surprised that the pleasure sound can already stimulate in
itself may come to be considered a pleasure that arises from actual music. In

3. In *Dell'origine e delle regole della musica* [*On the Origin and Principles of Music*, 1774], Antonio
   Eximeno has undertaken a similar comparison, but in a wholly different fashion from that undertaken here, as the following will make clear. He does agree that music is a true language, but he
   looks for this similarity not in the like derivation and construction of its means of expression—
   in a word, not in the inner qualities of the art—but only in its externals, namely in prosody. Thus
   in his comparison he does not go beyond the first exclamatory utterances, believing that music
   originated and was developed out of these utterances alone, in gradual combination with prosody. Now this is certainly very superficial; but a man like Eximeno, who at the time of the
   publication of his works had previously studied music for only four years, could scarcely pene-
   trate more deeply into the true nature of the art.
      The Spaniard Francisco Salinas understood this relationship far better. In the preface to his
   treatise *De musica* [in seven books; 1577] he includes the following passage: "They (grammar
   and music), however, are from their very beginnings so similar that they were thought to be not
   merely sisters, but almost twins. For grammar takes its beginning from letters, from which it
   receives its name; then using syllables, which arise from a combination of letters, and words,
   which are constituted from a union of syllables, it strives to arrive at the completion of a complete utterance. Similarly music, named for the Muses, to whom antiquity attributed every
   manner of skill in performing, completes and composes a melody or song from tones, from
   intervals made by a combination of tones, and from consonances, which arise from a union of
   intervals." Salinas was professor of music at Salamanca; his treatise appeared in 1577. [Au.]
4. The natural cause of the pleasure and displeasure arising from the tones of both animate and
   inanimate beings in nature lies in the relationship of these tones to the auditory nerves. The
   tones or voices of living beings are expressions of their various emotional states, and consequently generate another cause of pleasure and displeasure through sympathy. See Dietrich
   Tiedemann's "Aphorisms on the Feelings," in *Das deutsche Museum* (December 1777). [Au.]
   For Tiedemann, see also p. 222, n. 2.

his primal condition man is a passive creature; his soul has not yet been put into action. Sense impressions are thus still the only impressions that he can receive; he is not yet capable of other impressions, in which his intellect first must make a comparison, and derive from the observation of a proportion or a symmetry a feeling of pleasure. These sense impressions must be all the more intense and stirring the less the intellect is cultivated, and capable itself of being engaged.

This explains why we find in all wild and uncivilized nations such great pleasure taken in the clamor of noisy instruments—in drums, for example, and rattles, in blaring trumpets, and extremely loud, ferocious shrieks. Nature has established a wholly unmediated union between the heart and the hearing of human beings; all passions are communicated through their own proper tones, which stir in the heart of the hearer the very passional sensation from which they resulted.[5] This relation of unmediated perception between tone, hearing, and the heart is the same in all peoples, the most savage as well as the most civilized, with this one difference: the more savage a people, the more it remains merely sensuous and poor in mental representations, the more powerful are its sensations and its organs of sense. Thus in this primal state the pure tone, taken for itself alone as an expression of the passions, must be crude and vigorous, and entirely in keeping with the power of these sense organs.

§4. [MAN IN HIS EARLIEST STATE STILL CANNOT CONNECT REPRESENTATIONS AND CONCEPTS WITH FEELINGS.]

It is a generally understood premise that all our knowledge originally proceeds from perception. But it was necessary, in addition, that representations and concepts be gradually united with this perceptual knowledge. A perception in itself is nothing more than the consciousness of an impression on the external or internal senses. In order for it to become a representation, the soul must try to observe in that impression something by which to distinguish it, and must generally strive to bring this consciousness, which previously was only obscure, to full clarity. Only then does the perception turn into a representation, and a person now is able not only to perceive a loud and strong tone, but also to determine whether this loud and strong tone is harsh or tender. If the soul's observational power increases further, so that it can distinguish the entire multiplicity that can be observed in a tone, then the representation attains an even higher degree of clarity, and if the perception's mode of being is grasped along with its cause, it can become a concept in the true sense. Now the person no longer only discerns whether a strong tone is harsh or tender, but also why it is so.

5. See Johann Georg Sulzer's *Allgemeine Theorie der schönen Künste* [Leipzig, 1771–74], article "Musik," and Cicero, *De oratore*, 3.216: "Every motion of the soul has by nature its own look and sound and gesture; one's whole frame and countenance and all the sounds one utters resound like strings in a lyre as they are struck by a motion of the soul." [Au.] See p, 7 and n. 5.

§5. [MAN LEARNS TO DO THIS VERY LATE, AND THUS CANNOT OBSERVE ANY DISTINCTION AMONG THE TONES.]

But before a people reaches this point—before, in other words, it learns to connect representations and concepts with its perceptions of tones—it must first have spent centuries only perceiving. And even when it does begin to connect representations and concepts with perceptions, these representations are long so imperfect and limited that their influence on development of any kind remains unnoticed for just that long a time. Extensive experience and practice are required in order to make the connection between perception and representation as it occurs among cultivated peoples. This can best be observed in all those unfamiliar phemenona that appear to us for the first time. It is thus undeniable—and history attests it—that entire peoples can have loved and practiced music for hundreds of years without coming to an awareness of the primary distinctions discernable in tones. If a man first advances in representations and concepts under civil government, if his body first loses its coarseness and raw force as his intellect gains in ideas, then we must not only be able to conceive of this person in civil circumstances, but we must have conceived of him there for a considerable time before we can presume that the gently fluting tone of a nightingale might please him more—might leave a more pleasant impression on his hearing—than the loud bellowing or screeching sounds from his own throat, or from those of his equally crude brethren. Thus the very first music of rough and uncultivated nations was nothing more than a noisy clamoring without regard to any of the endless modifications that music allows.

§6. [RHYTHM WAS THE SINGLE EXPEDIENT MAN HAD TO MAKE HIS SIMPLE TONES ENTERTAINING.]

One may well ask, however, how this sort of racket could please entire peoples for hundreds of years. If nothing were added to this racket by which it could be more entertaining, and even pleasing for its duration, then it would surely be incomprehensible, and an unbearable monotony even for the roughest and most uncivilized men. In his first stage of development, however, a man soon notices that a certain regular kind of repetition makes all simple things more entertaining. This regular repetition of simple things that in themselves are not susceptible of any diversity we term in music *beat,* or, using the original word, *rhythm.* Tone is in itself the expression of a sensation. Sensation follows the laws of motion, because it is itself a motion. Consequently, the sensation aroused by a simple tone, if it is to be entertaining, must be renewed from time to time by the motion or repetition of the simple tone according to a certain order. The extent of the diversion that can be provided by such a rhythmic repetition of simple tones, whose monotony would otherwise grow wearisome, can be ascertained from the use that in modern times we still make of our drums. These mere variations of rhythmic beats not only facilitate the motion of walking and determine the pace of the step, but also may awaken some feeling of bravery and courage in the hearts of those men for whom this warlike, purely rhythmic music is chiefly intended. There is an excellent discussion of the causes of these rhythmic effects in the article "Rhythm" in Sulzer's *Encyclopedia,* to which I refer the reader in order to avoid prolixity here.[6] Hence not only can we accept this effect of rhythm as certain and undeniable, but we can also be satisfied that all half-wild, half-civilized peoples made their first music—that is, their simple sounds and noises—varied and entertaining by this means alone, and not by modifications in the tones themselves. Abundant proof of this is provided by their instruments—their drums, rattles, clappers, and so on: without additional rhythmic motion and variety these instruments would be capable of generating even for the crudest of peoples only a wearisome and hence intolerable monotony.

§7. [WHAT IS COMPREHENDED UNDER A MUSIC CONSISTING OF SINGLE TONES.]

In order not to cause misunderstanding, however, and to make this first stage of music as clear as possible for the reader, let me suggest that the monotony or simplicity of sound in question here must not be conceived as though it had arisen from a single tone in the most literal sense. It is called monotonous only insofar as the few tones of such a music had no coherence with one another. I will explain further. Music can be called "many-toned" only when a succession of tones, however brief, is arranged in such a way as to bring into being a certain kind of melody—namely, a complete melodic statement, whose various members have various significations. In language this is a sentence, which not only signifies a thing in itself, but also a quality of that thing, joining the two together. For example, I may not only say *tree,* but *tall tree,* or *the tree is tall,* and so on. Now in its language an uncultivated people only very slowly achieves this kind of signifying, through which not only are things signified, but also their difference from other similar things. Likewise it was undoubtedly only very late, probably later still than in the case of speech,[7] that a succession of tones came to be arranged so as to generate for the senses a melody similar to a sentence in speech. And as long as a music lacks this coherence in its tones, as long as a minimum of two or three tones are not so combined that in their connection they achieve a different significance, as long as each tone must be considered for itself alone without any further relationships, connections, and

6. See p. 74, n. 1.
7. The laws that the soul observes in thinking were certainly discovered earlier than those for the feelings. The soul is more conscious of its operations in thinking than it is in feeling. Thus in the latter case the soul must first reassemble by means of recollection the scattered fragments of its state of feeling, examine them in others, and out of these collected observations gradually construct a theory. See Johann August Eberhard's *Allgemeine Theorie des Denkens und Empfindens* [*General Theory of Thinking and Feeling,* 1786], p. 98. [Au.]. Johann August Eberhard (1739–1809) was a philosopher and lexicographer who wrote extensively on esthetics and ethics.

associations, then no matter how many distinct and single, deep or high sounds this music consists of, it cannot be called anything but "single-toned." That no savage and uncultivated nation has had—and still has—such a tone series is proven for us by the musical compositions of such peoples that are known to us; they are merely rhythmic, and have so little coherence in the truly musical sense that they can be compared with sentences in speech that consist only of nouns. Indeed, with their lack of melodic coherence the tones of these pieces are so peculiar that travellers among those peoples who actually heard them could scarcely comprehend them and render them in European notation.

§8. [THIS FIRST STAGE OF MUSIC LASTED FOR A VERY LONG TIME, AND STILL ENDURES AMONG MANY PEOPLES. FOR DESPITE ITS INFERIOR NATURE, UNCULTIVATED PEOPLES STILL FIND IT VERY ENTERTAINING.]

How long a people can tolerate this first crude state of music cannot be precisely determined. We do still find it today, however, among many Asiatic, African, and American peoples, whom we also know to have made no progress for millennia in other branches of culture.

Moreover, as inferior as this crude, barbaric music is in itself, it still serves uncultivated peoples as pleasure and amusement in several ways. They combine it with dance, and use it not only for domestic and social diversion, but also in religious ceremonies and in their wars. But in all these different usages it is always the same deafening and concussive noise, which they love all the more the less their intellect is engaged or capable of engagement.

THE SECOND PERIOD OF THE ART

§9. [THE SIMILARITY BETWEEN THE UTTERANCES OF FEELINGS AND THOUGHTS.]

The similarity that can be observed in more than one respect between feelings and thoughts must necessarily have prompted man, with the growth of his intellect, partly just to increase the expressions not only of thoughts but also of feelings, but partly also gradually to adapt these expressions more precisely to the characteristic and manifold manner in which feelings and thoughts are customarily uttered. Hitherto his speech-sounds had been nothing but interjections and simple words, with which he designated the external objects most closely surrounding him. With increasing observation of these objects, however, he gradually discovered ever new aspects—new characteristics—of the objects, by which to distinguish them from other objects of a similar kind, for the designation of which simple words were no longer sufficient. The speech sounds of his feelings were just as simple—mere sounds without connection. The more often the same feeling was reawakened, the more intimately did the feeling man grow acquainted with it. He had necessarily to notice that there were differentiations among feelings as well as among physical objects and thoughts—that there were primary and secondary feelings, more or less pleasant and unpleasant feelings, happy and sad ones, and so forth—and that for the expression, representation, or imitation of these feelings the individual high or low sounds hitherto in use were just as insufficient as were the single tones of speech for the designation of external objects with their variations and special characteristics.

§10. [THE SIMILARITY BETWEEN SCALES AND PARTS OF SPEECH ARISING FROM THIS SIMILARITY BETWEEN THOUGHTS AND FEELINGS.]

In language this observation of the different qualities and relations of external objects and thoughts gradually gave rise to the discovery of the parts of speech, as we call them, as well as to inflections and diverse alterations of the original sounds of speech. In music, or the language of the feelings, it led to a combination of tones that in their mutual relations consisted of primary and secondary tones, or (to borrow grammatical terminology) of noun-, adjective-, and conjunction-tones. Through these first efforts—these first steps in the development of a true language of tones or feelings—the groundwork was laid for the regular and coherent successions of tones we now call scales. The final development of these scales, however, cost the human intellect so much strain and effort that it could be fully accomplished only after several millennia.

•   •   •   •   •

REFLECTIONS ON MUSICAL NOTATION

§58. III.

The third place among the auxiliary sciences belonging to musical grammar[8] is taken by the art of writing down music, which is also called the art of notation, or is designated by its technical name *semiography* (the doctrine of signs).

Writing presupposes thought, because it is the visible sign of a thought, used when someone wants either to share that thought with another person or to recall it privately. The case is the same with musical notation, which comprises the visible signs of audible interconnected tones, which by its means can either be shared with others or recalled to one's own mind.

§59. [NOTATION CAN HAVE BEEN INVENTED ONLY AFTER MUSIC WAS RATHER MORE DEVELOPED.]

It is not my intention here to investigate the many ways in which such visible signs of tones could have been or actually have been devised. Not only do we not have enough information about the subject, but also this kind of investiga-

---

8. Forkel assigns the first two places to physical and mathematical acoustics (§52–§57).

tion belongs to the history of the doctrine of signs, which will appear in the sequel to this work. I shall only say as a preliminary that the musical art had already to have attained a considerable scope and degree of development before any appropriate signs at all could have been discovered for the tones—signs, that is, that not only could be adapted perfectly to the music of the time, but could also follow it through all the steps of its development and refinement. We know that the first language writing was nothing but a crude picturing of visible objects. In this period what was not visually perceived could also not be visibly expressed. Like air, a tone is a body, but an invisible one; man must thus have devised signs for it at least as late as he devised signs for invisible thoughts. If we now know that in language writing thoughts were initially given signs only according to certain relations and similarities that they had with external visible objects—namely, pictorially, then we ought not to be surprised that as long as tones are still left unconnected, no similarity with external visible objects can be observed, and hence not even this type of inferior pictographic writing can occur. Therefore history also, insofar as it has left us accounts about this matter, confirms that no people could arrive at any method at all for translating its melodies into signs before the invention of alphabetical writing.

§60. [HOW IT HAPPENS THAT NO PEOPLE COULD WRITE DOWN A MELODY BEFORE THE INVENTION OF ALPHABETICAL WRITING.]

This was in all likelihood because a people that was about to devise an alphabetical script already had to be extremely enlightened. It already had to be capable of transferring every external visible or audible perception into the soul as a picture, and of turning it into thoughts or abstract ideas. In other words, perceptions would already have had to be changed into representations and concepts. With this capacity to abstract, a relationship could also gradually be observed among tones, and be put into signs at least to some extent by the very means used to designate the sounds of speech. It is most regrettable that the path by which the human intellect gradually arrived at the discovery of its written characters of all kinds lies so obscure before us—so obscure that we can scarcely make out its least trace. In language writing there are still at least some traces visible, although very slight, by which we can conjecture to some extent how human beings passed step by step from pictographs to syllabic and alphabetical script. In music notation, however, we are completely cast adrift, and apparently must give up even the slightest hope of making discoveries in a matter at once so interesting and so important to human understanding.

§61. [THE INCONVENIENCE AND IMPERFECTION OF THE FIRST MUSIC NOTATION.]

It is well known that letters of the alphabet were used for the designation of tones by all ancient peoples, and still for a good while through the Middle Ages; for the most part, with the exception of a few small alterations, our modern names for tones are written as they were then. But this system of signs, when it was not meant to serve as mere nomenclature as it does with us, had the inconvenience that it must signify with different signs not only each tone but also all the different relations of a tone, necessitating an astonishing multiplicity of signs even if the melody that was to be designated was only of limited range. This condition of the notational art is proof that people had not thoroughly investigated the countless ways in which tones are differentiated, in order to observe how many of these features are essential to the tone and how many are merely accidental. In short, they were still not capable of dividing the whole gamut of tones into classes according to their similarities and differences, or of resolving them into their principal varieties, and consequently could not even designate the tones that were similar to each other with similar signs, or the genuinely different ones with dissimilar signs. A similar situation obtains in syllabic writing, which also had need of an astonishing quantity of signs as long as the words and syllables were not resolved into their simplest sounds. Hence syllabic writing was so inconvenient that with the multiplication of concepts and the ever-increasing need for writing, people necessarily had to abolish it and seek out bettᴖr means. Language and writing always proceeded at an equal pace in their development; therefore music and notation can be presumed to have done the same. Thus we can safely conclude that a people who used this kind of notation must have had an extremely imperfect, extremely unordered music.

§62. [INITIALLY NO ONE CAME UP WITH A PICTORIAL
REPRESENTATION OF SCALES.]

Since at first man arrived at all knowledge through pictorial representations, it is surprising that in music he missed this path, which could have led him most securely and swiftly to his goal. Certainly a single tone cannot be conceived of by way of an image. But once a succession of interconnected tones is present, when one hears it or sees it struck on an instrument there arises an image of an ascent and descent, or a ladder, and what would be easier and more natural in this case than to have a single arbitrary sign of a tone ascending and descending stepwise? We have no evidence whether the Greeks named their tones series merely "systems" (a term found in most Greek writers), or also named them after this image, as happened in the Middle Ages. For what the Romans long after them called *scala* was to the Greeks a rhetorical figure named *climax*, and it had no actual relationship to their music.[9] But no matter whether they had such a nomenclature, it is still certain that, like other ancient peoples whose notation we know something about, they wrote their notes or musical

9. *Climax* (Greek, "ladder") is the term for a rhetorical figure in which there is a gradual ascent in intensity in parallel word forms ("I came, I saw, I conquered"). The word does, however, become a musical term when the Latin *climacus* is used in neumatic notation to denote a neume of three notes descending. Forkel seems to have some awareness here of the medieval neumes as iconic representations of ascending and descending figures.

letters horizontally, completely contrary to the image of a tone series.[10] Thus what man hit on first in language writing—that is, a sign imitating the picture of an object—he hit upon last in musical notation.

§63. [EVEN AFTER ACHIEVING A PICTORIAL REPRESENTATION, FOR A LONG TIME THEY STILL CONFUSED THE TONES AND WORDS OF A SONG WITH ONE ANOTHER.]

Our modern notation is really a sequence of such pictorial representations, but only very slowly has it become what it now is. The habit the ancients had of writing their tone signs horizontally over the text of a melody had been widely propagated in the Middle Ages, but with the already considerable difference that in place of the great variety of Greek letters they used a small

10. The Arabs call their music *ilm el edwar,* or "the science of the circle," and even write their melodies in circles, in which as many lines are drawn on top of one another as the melody contains intervals. These lines, which are drawn inside a circle, all have different colors in addition. Thus if, for example, they are to designate seven tones—which the Arabs call *alif, be, gim, dal, hé, waw, zal'n,* corresponding to our A, B, C, D, E, F, G—they must be of seven different colors. The line that signifies the lowest tones, namely the *Alif* or our A, is green, the second rose-colored, the third a kind of blue, the fourth violet, the fifth brown, the sixth black, and the seventh light blue. The following is an illustration of this kind of Arab notation:

number of Latin ones. Although they now began to sense the ascending and descending motion of the melody, this feeling still appears to have been so obscure that in pictorial representations they confused melody and text with one another, and let words rise and fall between the drawn lines in the place of tones. It was still thus in the time of Hucbald, who lived in the tenth century, as can be seen from the *Musica enchiriadis,* printed in Martin Gerbert, *Scriptores ecclesiastici di musica sacra* [1784] vol. 1, pp. 152ff.[11]

•   •   •   •   •

CHAPTER II. THE HISTORY OF MUSIC IN EGYPT

§30. [REFLECTIONS ON BRUCE'S LETTER[12] AND A DEDUCTION ABOUT THE INTRINSIC CHARACTER OF ANCIENT EGYPTIAN MUSIC.]

From these reports, which are in part very valuable, as well as from the number of musical instruments previously described that according to the testi-

---

To interpret this kind of notation, in German it would mean something like the following:

1) Take the tone D.
2) From here drop down to C.
3) Move from there to F.
4) And drop again to B, through all the tones lying in between.
5) Make a pause here.
6) Climb up again to C and
7) end on B.

Arab notation also has its abbreviations, which, however, are altogether proof of its deficiency. These abbreviations always have the same color as the line on which they stand. *Makhadz* signifies the first note, *sooud,* the rise of the voice, *tertib,* the continuation by one degree, *sooud lilefra,* the quick rise of the voice, *houbouth,* a fall, *houbouth bil tertib,* a gradual fall, *serian,* quickly, *houbouth bil efrâ,* a quick fall, *thafr,* a leap, *afk,* a quick motion, *rikz,* the last note of the piece. Thus the Arabs have no actual notational signs, but only such signs as can suggest the course of a melody only to a certain extent, by very difficult means. Thus Arab musicians know all their melodies by heart, and the one who knows them best is the most honored person among them. Since the Arabs were after all a learned people, and were always great friends of music, as the surviving manuscripts of Avicenna [Ibn Sina], Alpharabius [Al-Farabi], Abdulcadir ['Abd al-Qadir], Alschalahi, and others can testify, and still their notation could not attain even a mediocre degree of perfection, this is fresh proof that finding the true path to the true notation has cost uncommonly great toil and struggle. One finds traces of a notation among the Persians, the Chinese, and several other non-European peoples, ancient as well as modern, but they have all come no further—and not even as far as—the Arabs. [Au.]

This lengthy note on Arab music consists of kernels of truth distorted by a good deal of misinformation. What Forkel's source or sources for the note were is not known. The notational elements he mentions did exist in Arab music: musical modes were thought of as cyclical, as in Forkel's circle (one of the most famous books on Arab music is the *Kitab al-adwar,* or *Book on the Cyclic Forms of Musical Modes*), and colors were used as representations of chords. But Forkel's combination of these elements makes little sense; his source may well have been a person who knew some Arabic but little about Arab music.

11. The treatise *Musica enchiriadis* (c. 900) was incorrectly attributed to Hucbald by Gerbert. Hucbald's treatise *De harmonica institutione* (c. 880) is printed in the same volume. See the excerpt from *Musica enchiriadis, SR* 2.

12. The previous section (§29) consists of Forkel's translation of a letter to Charles Burney from James Bruce, the famous explorer of the sources of the Nile (*Travels to Discover the Source of the Nile* [London, 1790]) concerning Egyptian musical instruments. Burney published the let-

mony of earlier historians were in use among the Egyptians, we can now conclude with certainty that music was practiced and beloved in Egypt from the
earliest times. But how this Egyptian music was constituted cannot easily be
determined: did it attain a considerable degree of development or, as is probably to be concluded from most of their instruments, the Theban harp described
by Bruce included, did it remain a crude beginning for the art, a matter unworthy of the consideration of posterity? The determination of this question would
require accounts of a completely different sort than those that remain to us.
Beyond instruments there are still so many requirements even for a moderate
degree of perfection in this art, which were altogether overlooked by the historians of Egyptian arts and sciences; without them a truly considerable development can be imagined as little in music as in the other arts and sciences. Thus
we are obliged either to give up the determination of this question entirely or
to risk conjectures and inferences that indeed, if they are deduced from things
whose true character is more precisely known, can be brought to a higher
degree of plausibility, but never to full certainty. Nevertheless I will dare a few
such deductions.

§31. [WHETHER THE EGYPTIANS HAD A MUSIC NOTATION.]

The art of notation—or the science of writing down musical thoughts—is as
important to music as the art of writing is to scholarship. If we had not invented
signs for the various utterances of a language by means of which these utterances could be made visible and permanent, so to speak, they might have
developed much later, or more probably might never have attained the perfection in which we now see them. The situation is the same with the language of
music: its utterances vanish just as quickly as do the utterances of the spoken
language, and it is an undeniable truth that all peoples who do not know how
to write down their melodies continue to have an extremely insignificant music.
The entire music of such peoples consists of songs of such a small range that
everyone is able to remember them easily by heart; there is no use thinking of
anything that even begins to resemble a coherent musical discourse. Language
and writing, music and notation—the elements of both these pairs stand in
such a natural and necessary relation with each other that they can only attain
perfection at an equal pace, and neither can thrive without the other.

§32. [GENERAL REFLECTIONS ON THE WRITING OF EARLY PEOPLES.]

At present most writers unanimously consider the Phoenicians[13] to
have been the first people in the ancient world to possess writing and the

---

ter in his *General History of Music* (vol. 1, pp. 177–83), along with Bruce's sketch of a "Theban
harp" (plate 1, vol. 1, p. 391).

13. "If rumor is to be believed, it was the Phoenicians who first dared to capture an utterance by
marking it down with crude figures." Lucan. [Au.] This remark—actually two dactyllic-hexame-
ter verses from the Roman poet Lucan's *Bellum civile* (*Pharsalia*), an epic account of the civil

Egyptians the second; but it is recognized just as unanimously that this early writing was still extremely deficient. Naturally the first attempts were simply intended to preserve the memory of events and discoveries that these people believed would be of consequence to posterity. There is sufficient proof that in the first millennia the means to attain these ends were not only columns, altars, and other devices of a similar sort, but also— indeed primarily—songs and regular festivals. The most common of these devices were songs, which were introduced by all peoples in the most remote past, and in more modern times as well as in the ancient world. The Egyptians,[14] Phoenicians,[15] Arabs,[16] Chinese,[17] Gauls,[18] Greeks,[19] Mexicans,[20] Peruvians,[21] and even the ancient inhabitants of the North, of Brazil,[22]

---

wars between Caesar and Pompey—seems to have served eighteenth-century writers as a *locus classicus* for the account of the Phoenicians' invention of writing. See Charles Burney, *A General History of Music*, vol. 1, 220.

14. Clemens of Alexandria, *Stromata libri VIII* [*Tapestries, Eight Volumes*], I.6. p. 757. [Au.]

15. Sanchoniathon in Eusebius, [*De evangelica praeparatione (Preparation for the Gospel)*], Bk. 1, p. 38. [Au.] Sanchoniathon was a Phoenician writer of great antiquity (conjectures range from the thirteenth to the sixth century B.C.E.) whose writings about Phoenician mythology and religion were translated by Philo of Biblos around 100 C.E. The fourth-century Christian bishop and church historian Eusebius of Caesarea included extracts from this translation in his essay on the Gospels.

16. The Book of Job, chap. 36, v. 24. [Au.]

17. *Lettres edifiantes [et curieuses, écrites des missions étrangères, par quelques missionaires de la Compagnie de Jesus]* (*Curious and Edifying Letters Written from Foreign Missions, by some Jesuit Missionaries*), (Paris, 1729), vol. 19, p. 477, [Au.] A letter from a Jesuit in China describes the ancient ethical books of the Chinese, one type of which contains songs describing paradigmatic deeds of Chinese heroes.

18. Tacitus, *De moribus Germanorum*, chap. 2, cited in *Bibliothéque universelle*, vol. 6, p. 299. [Au.] In this passage Tacitus states that ancient songs were the only source of historical tradition among the German tribes.

19. *Mémoires [de Littérature tirés des Registers] de l'Académie des Inscriptions [et belles lettres* (43 vols.; Paris, 1728–86)], vol. 6, p. 165. Tacitus, *Annales*, lib. 4. chap. 43. [Au.] In this passage from the *Annals* Tacitus tells of a dispute between the Spartans and their neighbors the Messenians over the possession of a temple, in which both sides cited the songs of ancient poets as evidence for their case. The Tacitus passage is cited in the *Mémoires* by a certain M. Freret in an essay on the validity of the evidence in the works of ancient historians.

20. Theodore de Bry, *Historia Americae* [1590–1634], vol. 2, p. 4.; p. 123. [Au.] The fourteen lavish volumes about travels in the Americas published by de Bry and his family were the first such series to contain accurate illustrations of life in the New World.

21. *Histoire des Incas, rois du Perou*, [trans. Thomas François Dalibard from the Spanish of Garcileso de la Vega; 2 vols. (Paris, 1744)], vol. 1, p. 321; vol. 2, p. 56, 57, 145. It is said that the Peruvians still sing an ode from their earliest times that contains the history of the world according to their ancient theology. [Au.] Vega, the illegitimate son of a Spanish knight and an Inca princess who was raised in Peru, wrote histories of the Indians of South America and of the expeditions of the Spanish conquistadors.

22. *Voyages de [François] Coreal [aux Indes Occidentales*, 1666–97, trans. from the Spanish; 2 vols. (Paris, Noel Pissot, 1722)], vol. 1, pp. 199, 203. J[ean] de Léry, *Histoire d'un voyage faict en la terre du Brésil* [1578], p. 248. [Au.] Coreal in these passages mentions songs of Brazilian savages containing a flood narrative much like the story of Noah, a description of a paradise resembling the Elysian Fields, and tales of the cannibal prowess of their valiant ances-

Iceland,[23] Greenland,[24] Virginia,[25] Santo Domingo,[26] and Canada[27] had them, and some peoples continued to use them even after the invention of alphabetical writing, as can be seen from the Song of Moses upon the miraculous crossing of the Red Sea.

§33. [CONTINUATION.]

From these first attempts to transmit the memory of events the way to further perfection was taken with slow steps. The picturing of physical objects, which was common among the ancient Egyptians, and which in more recent times has been found among the Mexicans,[28] persisted for a long time before it could be extended to a still imperfect hieroglyphic writing. But since people soon sensed that even these hieroglyphics were not capable of any great perfection, and could not accomplish what was expected of them, given the gradual extension of concepts and the growth of language, they had to make a radical departure from the original path, and seek out another way to attain their goal. At this point they first invented signs for whole words and syllables, and then moved gradually from this word- and syllable-based writing to an alphabetical writing, which is now in general use among the most cultivated of earth's peoples. How much time and effort these grand and important inventions must have cost the human spirit can easily be imagined by anyone who has the least notion of the construction of languages, and realizes that there is no necessary connection between the sound of the words and their arbitrary signs that could have led people easily from one to the other.

That the invention of music notation must have cost the human spirit no less effort and toil can be most easily attested by the millenia required for its

tors. A fourth edition of the Léry (Geneva, 1600) recounts songs dealing with the same subjects (p. 315).

23. *Bibliothèque ancienne et moderne* [29 vols. (Amsterdam, 1714–27)], vol. 2, p. 241. [Au.] Reviewed in this publication is a history of Iceland by Arius, translated into Latin by Torfe (*Historia rerum Norvegicarum*, 4 v. [Copenhagen, 1711]). The review mentions an Icelandic *edde* or ode by one Semund that chronicles deeds of past history.

24. [John Anderson], *Histoire naturelle de l'Islande, [du Groenland, du detroit de Davis, et d'autres pays situés sous le Nord (A Natural History of Iceland, Greenland, the Davis Straits, and Other Countries Situated in the North*), 2 vols.; trans. from the German by Gottfried Sellius (Paris, S. Jorry, 1750)], vol. 2, p. 232. [Au.] Anderson describes a ceremony in which songs about a tribe's past exploits in hunting, fishing, and so on are sung to the beat of a drum.

25. *Journal des sçavans*, March 1681, p. 46. [Au.] This reference has not been identified.

26. [Abbé Prévost, ed.], *Histoire generale des voyages* [64 vols.; Paris: Didot, 1746–89], vol. 12, p. 219. [Au.] The explorer Jean Diaz de Solis tells of Santo Domingan natives whose songs, taking the place of books, "serve as their annals," preserving all their historical knowledge.

27. [Joseph-François Lafitau], *Moeurs des sauvages [ameriquains, comparées aux moeurs des premiers temps*, 2 vols. (Paris, 1724)], vol. 1. p. 519. [Au.] Description of song festivals among Canadian tribes in which the first songs performed chronicle the ancient exploits of the tribe.

28. See *Allgemeine Historie der Reisen zu Wasser und Lande* [21 vols.; 1757], in the description of the conquest of Mexico, where it is alleged that the inhabitants gave Montezuma the news of the landing of Cortez by means of a drawing. [Au.]

development, of which we now avail ourselves. A more detailed history of the matter in the sequel to this work will make it clearer and more vivid.

§34. [WE FIND NO EVIDENCE THAT THE EGYPTIANS HAD A MUSIC NOTATION.]

Now as certain as it is that one can draw conclusions about the cultivation of a people from the quality of its language and writing, it is equally certain that a similar conclusion can be drawn concerning music and notation. But writers of antiquity do not tell us whether the Egyptians had a notation of any kind. If there is not even the smallest suggestion of it, we must be willing to consider what Dionysus[29] says in his treatise on the art of interpretation—that the Egyptians designated the tones of their music by the vowels of their alphabet. But since this is merely a matter of nomenclature, nothing can actually be proven by it.

§35. [THEY MAY HAVE HAD ONE THAT WAS SIMILAR TO THE NOTATION OF THE CHINESE.]

The similarity between the Egyptians and the Chinese in physical form, manners, taste, customary attachments, and so on, and de Guignes's opinion that 1122 years before Christ a colony of Egyptians travelled to China[30] could perhaps suggest some conjectures on this obscure subject. The Chinese actually have a musical notation, although compared to ours it is extremely undeveloped, as is their music in general. Like many peoples, they make use of the letters of their language script for that purpose, and even write them in the same way as in their language, in vertical columns begun on the righthand side.[31] Since not only the letters of the Egyptians but also the way they are written have many similarities with the Chinese method, it could perhaps be conjectured from this correspondence that the Egyptians could also have had a similar notation. But even if they actually did have such a thing, it would not permit us to reach the most favorable conclusions about the perfection of their music, but would rather be proof that among them this art had never emerged from a true state of childhood. With all the praise that has been bestowed on the music of the Chinese, the greatest admirers of Chinese arts and sciences still cannot help but grant that their notation has great inconveniences, and would be of use to no other music but that of the Chinese. If these admirers think that the acknowledged uselessness of Chinese notation for other than

29. Dionysius of Halicarnassus [fl. c. 20 B.C.] was a Greek historian and teacher of rhetoric. His *De compositione verborum* (*On the Arrangement of Words*) is one of the few treatises of antiquity to treat word order and euphony.
30. Joseph de Guignes (1721–1800), *Mémoire dans lequel on prouve, que les chinois sont une colonie egyptienne* (*Memoir in Which It Is Proved that the Chinese Are an Egyptian Colony*), Paris, 1759.
31. A demonstration of this Chinese notation can be found in the *Essai sur la musique ancienne et moderne* by [Jean-Benjamin de] La Borde [4 vols. (Paris, 1780)], vol. 1, p. 144. [Au.]

Chinese styles of music does the music of this country no dishonor, and is, moreover, perfectly consonant with its perfection and intrinsic worth, then they only show that they have not yet received sufficient instruction in these matters. Poverty in signs presupposes poverty in words and concepts, just as too great a variety of the same presupposes disorder and confusion. The Chinese are manifestly in the latter condition regarding the signs of their language, which number 80,000 and are altogether so copious that learning them constitutes the single, lifelong occupation of a scholar among them. Everything we know about their music shows that concerning their notation the former condition prevails.

§36. [BUT THIS IS MERELY AN INSUBSTANTIAL CONJECTURE.]

Nonetheless, the observation of this similarity that obtains between the ancient Egyptians and the Chinese in customs, habits, taste, and other matters justifies only a weak conjecture with regard to the notation of the former people, one that cannot be supported by a single proof. Since the example of countless other nations shows that it is possible to have some sort of music for many centuries without being able to write it down, we may be least liable to error if we make the general assumption that the Egyptians were in no way acquainted with the formidable art of writing music. Not only the erudition of this people, but also its other arts (insofar as their nature is known to us) provide more than one reason to come to such a conclusion, and to accept it as a positive truth, at least as long as no one happens upon the holy book of Mercury, in which the hymns to the Egyptian gods were written down, and by deciphering them convinces us of the contrary view.

26 Johann Friedrich Reichardt

Born at Königsberg in 1752, Johann Friedrich Reichardt began as a student of philosophy and music. He spent the years 1771–74 traveling in Germany and published his impressions in three volumes. In 1775 he became Capellmeister at the court of Frederick the Great, but left this position in 1785 to go to London and Paris; his sympathetic view of the French Revolution undoubtedly had something to do with this. After Frederick's death he returned to Berlin, but was forced to leave again. He died at Halle in 1814.

Reichardt's literary production is a considerable one. He was a man of broad culture who handled his pen with great skill. The books in which he collected his impressions of Germany (1774–76), Paris (1804–5), and Vienna (1810) are valued not only for the information they contain, but also for their pleasant style.

FROM *Personal Letters Written on a Trip to Vienna*
(1810)

ELEVENTH LETTER

[November 30, 1808] I have been anxiously awaiting a wholly free and quiet moment to describe faithfully for you a touching scene which I had with old Haydn. Fräulein von Kurzbeck, whom he loves like a father,[1] and Frau von Pereira, full of admiration for him, as for everything great and beautiful, were my guides. As a fitting overture to the scene, Fraülein von Kurzbeck played for me beforehand on her fortepiano a big and difficult sonata by our late Prince Louis Ferdinand. A pupil of Clementi's, she played it in quite masterly fashion, with delicate expression and equally perfect execution which left nothing whatever to be desired in point of purity and clarity.

In one of the outlying suburbs we had to drive nearly an hour into the remotest alleys and corners. Here, in the small but quite attractive garden house which belongs to him, we found the splendid old man, seated at a table covered with a green cloth. Fully dressed in a simple but neat gray-cloth suit with white buttons and an elegantly groomed and powdered curly wig, he sat there quite stiffly, almost rigid, drawn up close to the table, both hands resting on top of it, not unlike a lifelike wax figure. Fräulein Kurzbeck first explained to him that she would like to introduce me; I was almost afraid he would not know my name, or would perhaps not recall it in this state of apathy, and I was really taken aback and (I may honestly say) ashamed when the old hero opened his eyes wider—they still have an animated sparkle—and said: "Reichardt? A——man! Where is he?" I had just come in, and with outstretched arms he

TEXT: *Vertraute Briefe geschrieben auf einer Reise nach Wien und den österreichischen Staaten zu Ende 1808 und zu Anfang 1809* (Amsterdam, 1810), vol. 1, pp. 161–68, 204–10, 218–22, 231–32, 254–58, 450–54; vol. 2, pp. 138–39, 143–44, 146–50. Translation by Oliver Strunk, with additions by Wye J. Allanbrook.

1. Magdalene von Kurzböck, to whom Haydn dedicated his piano trio in E-flat minor and the Viennese edition of his piano sonata in E-flat (No. 52). Reichardt, who had already met Fräulein von Kurzböck at Baron von Arnsteiner's, has this to say of her (vol. 1, p. 145): "One of the most interesting acquaintances I made was Fräulein von Kurzböck, who was presented to me as the greatest pianist among the ladies of the local musical world, and that is saying a good deal. For a long time I had been hearing about her great talent, and I had just heard about it again in Dresden and Prague; I had thus been looking forward particularly to making her acquaintance. She received me as well and as graciously as if she had been looking forward in the same way to meeting me."

called to me from across the table: "Dearest Reichardt, do come! I must embrace you!" With that he kissed me, pressing my hand tightly and convulsively, then ran his thin hand three or four times over my cheeks, saying to the others: "What pleases me is that the——artist also has such a good honest face." I sat down beside him and retained his hand in mine. He looked at me for a time, deeply affected, then added: "Still so fresh! Alas, I have put too great a strain on my powers—already I am altogether a child"—and wept bitter tears. The ladies were about to interrupt in order to spare him. "No, let me go on, children," the dear old man exclaimed; "this does me good; these are in reality tears of joy over the man beside me; he will fare better." I was seldom able to bring forth a friendly word of gratitude and could only fervently kiss his hand.

Frau von Pereira, whom he had at first not recognized with his feeble memory, reminded him in a childlike, playful way of various jokes, and he presently joined her in this style, of which he is said to have always been very fond. With this the ladies thought we ought to leave the weak old man, lest in the end he be too much affected, and we took our farewell. Scarcely had we gotten out the door, however, when he called us back, exclaiming: "After all, I must show Reichardt my treasures too!" At that a servant girl brought in all sorts of beautiful things, some of them quite valuable. The most interesting among them was a rather large flat box which Princess Esterhazy, the wife of the now reigning prince[2]—the son of the prince who was for the greater part of Haydn's life his master—had had made for him after her own express design. It was of black ebony, heavily mounted in gold and ornamented with a gold bas-relief.[3] On the lid had been painted the beautiful affecting scene in the Akademiesaal, which, on the occasion of the last great performance of Haydn's *Schöpfung,* proved a veritable apotheosis for the composer.[4] (Collin recently recited to me a really beautiful descriptive poem on this scene.[5]) In the box lay a magnificent big autograph album, likewise black and gold, signed on the cover by the Princess, most cordially inscribed within by the whole princely family. I should be the first artist to inscribe myself, the old man said, and he would have the book sent to me. The whole box, incidentally, was filled on either side with the most dainty writing things and with all sorts of pleasant and useful instruments of gold and fine English steelwork.

2. Marie von Lichtenstein, Princess Esterhazy, wife of Prince Nicholas II.
3. For the later history of this box, see Pohl-Botstiber, *Joseph Haydn,* vol. 3 (Leipzig, 1927), pp. 258–59.
4. This miniature, by Balthasar Wigand, is reproduced in many modern sources. The performance in question had taken place on March 27, 1808, some months before Reichardt's arrival in Vienna.
5. Heinrich Josef von Collin (1771–1811), Viennese poet and dramatist and author of the tragedy *Coriolan* for which Beethoven wrote his famous overture. A translation of Collin's encomium to Haydn can be found in *Haydn: Two Contemporary Portraits,* trans. and ed. Vernon Gotwals (Madison: Univ. of Wisconsin Press, 1968), pp. 178–79.

Then he showed me further a great number of gold medals—from the musical society in St. Petersburg, from the Paris concerts, for which he wrote several symphonies expressly, and from many others—also a perfectly magnificent ring from the Russian Czar, a diploma from the National Institute in Paris, another from Vienna, conferring honorary citizenship on him, and many other things of this sort. In them the kind old man seems to live again quite happily.

When after a full hour we took leave in earnest, he detained me alone, holding my hand firmly, and told me, while kissing me repeatedly, that I should visit him at least once a week as long as I remained here. I shall not soil this recital with the little anxious touches of avarice he betrayed, in the midst of treasures he could no longer even use—but they went straight to my heart.

The excellent Beethoven I have also called on, having found him out at last. People here take so little interest in him that no one was able to tell me his address,[6] and it really cost me considerable trouble to locate him. I found him finally in a great deserted and lonely house. At first he looked almost as gloomy as his surroundings, but presently he grew more cheerful and appeared to take quite as much pleasure in seeing me again as I in seeing him, commenting also, openly and cordially, on many things about which I needed information. His is a powerful nature, outwardly Cyclops-like, but in reality sincere, friendly, and kind. He lives much of the time with a Hungarian Countess Erdödy, who occupies the front part of the great house,[7] but he has broken off completely with Prince Lichnowsky, who lives upstairs and with whom for several years he spent all his time. I wanted also to call on the Prince, who is an old acquaintance, and on his wife, a daughter of the excellent Countess von Thun, to whom I owe the greater part of the amenities of my previous stay in Vienna,[8] but I found neither one at home and soon afterwards learned that the Princess lives in virtually complete retirement.

Salieri, who occupies a fine-looking house of his own, I found sitting with a cloth greatcoat over his clothes and frock coat among the music and musical instruments which quite fill his big room, for he never heats it; he wanted me to put on again my own greatcoat, which I had left in the anteroom, but at the moment I was not so chilled, although I cannot ordinarily be as tough as this coarse Italian nature. He has aged, to be sure, since I last saw him, but for all that is still, as he always was, the quite extraordinarily elegant and adroit Italian gentleman in his physiognomy and manner. He too spoke to me in a friendly and confidential way about many things and characterized for me the singers and orchestras of the various theaters with equal frankness and precision. I took leave of him with a sense of pleasure and gratitude.

•   •   •   •   •

6. Krugerstrasse, 1704.
7. To Countess Erdödy, Beethoven dedicated the piano trios, Op. 70, on one of which he was still working at the time of Reichardt's call, also the two sonatas, Op. 102, for cello and piano.
8. During his travels between 1771 and 1774.

THIRTEENTH LETTER

[December 10, 1808] Today I must speak to you about a very fine quartet series that Herr Schuppanzigh, an excellent violinist in the service of Prince von Rasumovsky, the former Russian envoy to the imperial court, has opened by subscription for the winter. The concerts will take place in a private house every Thursday from twelve to two. Last Thursday we heard the first one; there was as yet no great company in attendance, but what there was consisted entirely of ardent and attentive friends of music, precisely the proper public for this most elegant and most congenial of all musical combinations. Had Haydn given us only the quartet, inspiring other genial artists to follow his example, it would already have been enough to make him a great benefactor of the whole world of music. Difficult as it is to bring this sort of music to perfection in performance—for the whole and each of its single parts are heard in their entirety and satisfy only in the most perfect intonation, ensemble, and blending—it is the first variety to be provided wherever good friends of music meet to play together. And since it is charitably rooted in the human makeup that expectation and capacity as a rule keep more or less in step and go hand in hand, each one takes at least some degree of pleasure in the performance, once he has brought to it all that he can offer it individually or through his immediate background. On this account the exacting connoisseur and critic not infrequently finds such groups working away with great enthusiasm, perfectly at home, when he himself, spurred by his overtrained artistic nature, would like to run away.

Here, however, such was not the case. The quartet is on the whole well balanced, although some say that last year, when Herr Kraft[9] played with them, the balance was better. Herr Schuppanzigh himself has an original, piquant style most appropriate to the humorous quartets of Haydn, Mozart, and Beethoven—or, perhaps more accurately, a product of the capricious manner of performance suited to these masterpieces. He plays the most difficult passages clearly, although not always quite in tune, a consideration to which the local virtuosi seem in general to be superior; he also accents very correctly and significantly, and his cantabile, too, is often quite singing and affecting. He is likewise a good leader for his carefully chosen colleagues, who enter admirably into the spirit of the composer, though he disturbed me often with his accursed fashion, generally introduced here, of beating time with his foot, even when there was no need for it, sometimes out of habit alone, at other times only to reinforce the *forte*. Generally speaking, one seldom hears a *forte* here—let alone a *fortissimo*—without the leader's joining in with his foot. For me this ruins the pure free enjoyment, and every such beat interrupts for me the coordinated and perfected performance which it is supposed to help bring about

---

9. The cellist Anton Kraft. Reichardt will have heard the quartet with Joseph Linke as cellist. Kraft subsequently formed a quartet of his own; Reichardt heard their first concert early in 1809 (vol. 1, p. 368).

and which I had expected from this public production. At rehearsal, where one must continue practicing and assist oneself by all possible means of direction until the piece goes together perfectly, there one may beat time and even shout as much as one pleases. At the performance itself, repose in all things is the chief requirement; all preliminary scaffolding must now disappear altogether, and it is far better to let a mistake pass without censure, whether actually committed or only feared, than to try to help matters by using strong measures. Not to mention that the inexperienced and uninformed listener will probably not notice the mistake in any case, while the more competent will notice it no less and be doubly offended. Furthermore, an attentive and conscientious colleague ought never to be disconcerted by such shameful public prompting—it can only disturb his repose and control, on which above all the perfection of the performance depends; an inattentive and sluggish colleague ought not to count on so ordinary a means of assistance and stimulation. Each one must help with all his senses and his entire attention; he who is incapable of this cannot be trained to it by beating time.

At this first quartet morning there was performed—besides a very naïve and charming quartet by Haydn, full of good humor and innocence, and a more powerful, more elaborate one by Mozart—Beethoven's clear and beautiful Sextet with wind instruments, which made a fine vigorous effect.[10] In this a horn player from the orchestra of the Theater an der Wien gave me quite special pleasure, reminding me, with his beautiful tone and accurate, positive intonation of the half tones, of our late excellent Türschmidt.

I shall certainly not willingly neglect this agreeable quartet series, to which Herr Schuppanzigh has given me a ticket.

A few days later, Beethoven gave me the pleasure of inviting this same pleasing quartet to Countess von Erdödy's in order that I might hear something of his new works. He played himself in a brand new trio of considerable force and originality for fortepiano, violin, and violoncello, altogether excellent and resolute.[11]

The quartet played further several of his older and extremely difficult quartets. Herr Schuppanzigh revealed a quite special skill and dexterity in the performance of these difficult Beethoven compositions, in which the violin frequently competes with the piano in the execution of the most difficult keyboard figures, the piano with the violin in singing tone.[12]

The dear Countess, a touchingly cheerful invalid, with a friend of hers, a Hungarian lady also, took such keen and enthusiastic pleasure in each beautiful bold stroke, in each fine well-turned inflection, that the sight of her did me almost as much good as Beethoven's masterly conceptions and performance. Fortunate artist, who can count on such a listener!

10. Op. 81b, an early work not published until 1810.
11. Probably the Trio in D Major, Op. 70, No. 1, the first of the pair to be completed.
12. The works referred to must be Beethoven's early piano quartets, WoO 36, in E-flat major, D major, and C major (composed in 1785 but not published until 1828).

•   •   •   •   •

The Liebhaberkonzerte[13] have begun here for the winter, and the one I have just attended was nearly the death of me, for all that the company was very agreeable. In three rather small rooms, the like of which I have scarcely seen here before, a great crowd of listeners of all classes and an almost equally great one of musicians were so crammed together that I lost both my breath and my hearing. Fortunately, however, I did not also lose my sight, for a part of the company consisted of very attractive fine ladies, some of whom also sang very nicely. But even excellent things by Beethoven, Romberg, Paër, and others could have no effect, since in the narrow space one was quite deafened by the noise of the trumpets, kettledrums, and wind instruments of all sorts. At the same time I was offered something quite perfect to listen to—something that was also thoroughly appropriate here and for this reason did me the more good. It was a Neapolitan guitarist, who played so well that he recalled to me the good old days of the real lute playing; never have I heard anything so perfect from so imperfect an instrument. Two Italians, with agreeable tenor and bass voices, then sang with him a little French romance, "La Sentinelle": facing the enemy in the moonlight, a soldier stands on guard, confiding to the winds for his sweetheart that he watches, lives, fights, and dies for her alone. The elegant Italian, into the bargain a quite handsome young man, a regular Antinoüs, had very cleverly arranged for the guitar a wholly delightful marchlike melody, enriching it with lively interludes. This was perfectly suited to the room and to the company, which was likewise enchanted by it and appeared not to notice that the whole agreeable impression was destroyed again by Beethoven's gigantic and overpowering overture to Collin's *Coriolanus*. In the narrow rooms, my head and heart were nearly burst with the vigorous blows and crackings which each one strained himself to the utmost in augmenting, for the composer himself was present. It gave me great pleasure to see the excellent Beethoven not only on hand but much made of, the more so since he has in mind and heart the fatal hypochondriac delusion that everyone here persecutes and despises him. To be sure, his stubborn outward manner may frighten off some of the jolly good-natured Viennese, and many of those who acknowledge his great talent and merits may perhaps not employ sufficient humanity and delicacy to so offer the sensitive, irritable, distrustful artist the means of enjoying life that he may accept them gladly and also take satisfaction in them as an artist. It often pains me to the quick when I see this altogether excellent and splendid man gloomy and unhappy, although I am at the same time persuaded that it is only in his willful mood of deep discontent that his best and most original works can be produced. Those who are capable of appreciating those works ought never to lose sight of this or to take offense at any of his

13. The orchestra of the Liebhaberkonzerte was made up of amateurs, with a few professional players for the wind instruments.

outward peculiarities or rough corners. Only then are they true, genuine admirers of his.

FOURTEENTH LETTER

[December 16, 1808.] On Sunday[14] I heard that fine quartet again. Three works were played, one by Haydn, then one by Mozart, and finally one by Beethoven; this last was particularly good. It was very interesting to me to observe in this succession how the three true humorists, each according to his individual nature, have further developed the genre. Haydn created it out of the pure, luminous fountain of his charming, original nature. In artlessness and cheerful humor he forever remains unique. Mozart's more robust nature and richer imagination gained further ground, and expressed in many a piece the heights and depths of his inner being. He was himself also more of a virtuoso in performance, and thus expected far more of the performers. In addition, he placed more importance in an artfully developed work, and thus built out of Haydn's charmingly imagined summerhouse his own palace. Beethoven settled down in this palace very early, and thus in order for him too to express his own nature in its own forms, he was left no choice but to build a bold and defiant tower on top of which no one could easily place anything more without breaking his neck. Repeatedly there has occurred to me in this context Michelangelo's proud and daring notion of placing the magnificent Pantheon on his St. Peter's as a dome.

•　•　•　•　•

SEVENTEENTH LETTER

[December 25, 1808] The past week, during which the theaters were closed, the evenings filled with public concerts and musical performances, caused me no little embarrassment in my ardent resolve to hear everything. This applies particularly to the twenty-second, when the local musicians gave the first of this season's great performances at the Burgtheater for their deserving widows' fund, while on the same day Beethoven also gave at the great suburban theater a concert for his benefit, at which only his own works were played. This last I could not conceivably miss; that morning, accordingly, I accepted with many thanks the kind invitation of Prince von Lobkowitz to join him in his box. There we sat, in the most bitter cold, from half past six until half past ten, and confirmed for ourselves the maxim that one may easily have too much of a good thing, still more of a powerful one. Nevertheless—though many a mishap in performance tried our patience to the limit—I was no more willing to leave before the final conclusion of the concert than was the extremely polite and good-natured prince, whose box was in the first balcony, quite near the stage, so that the orchestra, with Beethoven conducting in the midst of it, was almost

14. December 15.

on top of us. Poor Beethoven, who had from this concert his first and only ready profit of the whole year, found considerable hostility and only feeble support in the arrangements and performance. The singers and orchestra were made up of very heterogeneous elements, and it had not even been possible to arrange one full rehearsal of all the pieces on the program, every one of which was filled with the greatest difficulties. How much of the output of this fruitful genius and tireless worker was none the less performed during the four hours will astonish you.

To begin with, a pastoral symphony, or recollections of country life. First movement: Agreeable impressions awakening in man on arrival in the country. Second movement: Scene by the brook. Third movement: Joyous amusements of the country folk. Fourth movement: Thunder and storm. Fifth movement: Benevolent feelings after the storm, joined with thanks to the Divinity. Each number was a very long and fully worked-out movement, filled with the liveliest images and the most brilliant ideas and figures; as a result, this one pastoral symphony alone lasted longer than an entire court concert is allowed to last with us.

Then followed, as the sixth piece, a long Italian scena,[15] sung by Mlle. Killizky, the beautiful Bohemian with the beautiful voice.[16] That today this pretty child rather shivered than sang could not be taken amiss, in view of the bitter cold; in our box near by, we too were shivering, wrapped in our furs and greatcoats.

Seventh piece: A Gloria, with choruses and solos, whose performance, unfortunately, miscarried altogether.[17]

Eighth piece: A new concerto for fortepiano, terribly difficult, which Beethoven played astonishingly well in the fastest possible tempos.[18] The Adagio, a masterpiece of beautiful sustained melody, he actually sang on his instrument with a deep melancholy feeling which awakened its response in me.

Ninth piece: A great symphony,[19] very elaborate and too long. A cavalier sitting near us reported having observed at the rehearsal that the violoncello part, busily occupied, amounted alone to thirty-four sheets. But the copyists here are quite as expert in spreading things out as are at home our lawyer's clerks and court recorders.

Tenth piece: A Sanctus, again with choruses and solos,[20] unfortunately—like the Gloria—a complete failure in performance.

Eleventh piece: A long fantasy, in which Beethoven revealed his full mastery. And finally, by way of conclusion, another fantasy, in which the orchestra

---

15. "Ah, perfido!" Op. 65.
16. Mlle. Killizky (Josephine Killitschgy), Ignaz Schuppanzigh's sister-in-law, was a last-minute substitute.
17. From the Mass in C, Op. 86.
18. The Fourth Piano Concerto, Op. 58.
19. The Fifth Symphony, Op. 67.
20. Again from the Mass in C.

presently came in and was actually followed at the end by the chorus.[21] This strange idea met with disaster in performance as the result of an orchestral confusion so complete that Beethoven, with the inspired ardor of the artist, thinking no longer of his public or of his surroundings, shouted out that one should stop and begin over again. You can imagine how I and all his other friends suffered at this. In that moment, indeed, I wished that I had had the courage to leave earlier after all.[22]

• • • • •

TWENTY-SEVENTH LETTER

[February 25, 1809] Dear father Haydn I am still unable to see again; as often as we send out word to him, asking after his health and for an appointment agreeable to him, we receive from his people the invariable answer that he is very weak and can see no one. Clementi too is most desirous of seeing him again; since his arrival, he has still to succeed in doing so.[23] I fear that his noble spirit will soon depart from us. Although strictly speaking he has for some years been as good as morally dead for the world,[24] one still fears always the final extinguishing of the divine flame which, throughout a half century, has so magnificently lighted the way for us.

Not without being deeply touched can I recall how one of his first "cassations," as he called his cheery, youthful quartets, gave me my earliest artistic joy and was at the same time the chief display piece of my boyish virtuosity;[25] how his quartets, constantly increasing in inner content and character, offered me the best of nourishment and training as well as the most delightful enjoyment; how, on my many visits to England, and especially in France, his superb symphonies were almost everywhere the greatest and the most beautiful that I heard played; how later on his larger choral works for the church and concert hall brought me the keenest and most varied pleasure; and how, after all this, because of a combination of circumstances, I was never able to meet this hero—this patriarch of music—never able to imprint upon his lips or fatherly hand my ardent thanks for all this instruction and enjoyment—until the utmost weakness of mind and body made this for him, as for me, almost a torture.

21. The Choral Fantasy, Op. 80, a work subjected to further revision before its publication in 1811.
22. The announcement of this concert in the *Wiener Zeitung* for December 17 describes the program as consisting entirely of new works, not previously heard in public. With the exception of the scena "Ah, perfido!" and the movements from the Mass in C, which had already been heard in performances away from Vienna, this seems to have been strictly true.
23. Clementi had been in Vienna since the latter part of 1808.
24. In a letter to Breitkopf & Härtel written on June 12, 1799, Haydn himself refers to a falling-off of his mental powers; his last significant work was the "Harmoniemesse," completed during the summer of 1802; his death occurred on May 31, 1809, only a few months after the date of this entry in Reichardt's journal.
25. The Quartet in B-flat, Op. 1, No. 1. In his biography, *Johann Friedrich Reichardt* (Augsburg, 1865; vol. 1, p. 61), H. M. Schletterer reports that Reichardt spoke of this quartet as his boyhood "show piece."

Nearly and deeply affected, I wrote soon after this into his handsome album a choral setting of these magnificent lines from Goethe's "Euphrosyne":[26]

> Cliffs stand firmly based; the water eternally plunges;
>   Down from its cloudy cleft foaming and roaring it falls.
> Ever the pines are green, and even in winter the copses
>   Foster on leafless twigs buds that are hid from the eye.
> Each thing arises and passes by law; a wavering fortune
>   Governs the life of man, treasure of priceless worth.
> Not at the brink of the grave does the father, departing contented,
>   Nod farewell to his son, blooming and splendid heir;
> Nor is the old man's eye closed always by hand of the younger,
>   Willingly parting from light, weak giving place to the strong.
> Ah, more often does fate perversely order man's life-days:
>   Helpless an old man mourns children and grandsons in vain,
> Standing, a desolate tree, round which all shattered the branches
>   Lie upon every side, ravaged by tempest of hail.

To this I added, from the bottom of my heart: "Also to see the shell of the spirit that will live on among us forever and that created for us a new life, rich in joys and destined—so long as harmony shall remain the highest expression of the endless—to outlive all posterity; also to see the shell so soon demolished filled my innermost being with that deep melancholy which sprang from the heart of the poet and which, in memory of a solemn, never-to-be-forgotten hour, I dared to set to music. For I regard myself as fortunate in having gazed deeply into the soul-filled eye—in having pressed passionately to my heart and to my lips the loving, consecrating hand."

THIRTY-SEVENTH LETTER

[April? 1809] For everyone, surely, who can enjoy the good things of life, especially for the artist, perhaps quite especially for the musical artist, Vienna is the richest, happiest, and most agreeable residence in Europe. Vienna has everything that marks a great capital in a quite unusually high degree. It has a great, wealthy, cultivated, art-loving, hospitable, well-mannered, elegant nobility; it has a wealthy, sociable, hospitable middle class and bourgeoisie, as little lacking in cultivated and well-informed gentlemen and gracious families; it has a well-to-do, good-natured, jovial populace. All classes love amusement and good living, and things are so arranged that all classes may find well provided and may enjoy in all convenience and security every amusement that modern society knows and loves.

•   •   •   •   •

In the city and in the suburbs five theaters of the most varied sort give performances all the year round. At the two court theaters in the city itself,

---

26. This is now published in the third number of my *Goethe's Lieder, Oden, Balladen und Romanzen* (Leipzig, 1809). [Au.]

one sees everything outstanding in the way of grand and comic opera, comedy, and tragedy that Germany produces—and, in some measure, Italy and France as well; the same is true of the great suburban Theater an der Wien, where in addition the great romantic magic operas are given with unusual magnificence. At all three theaters, great pantomimic ballets, heroic and comic, are often given also. Two smaller theaters in the Leopoldstadt and Josephstadt play popular dramas of the jolliest kind. On days when no play is scheduled, all these theaters give great concerts and performances of the most important ancient and modern music for church and concert hall. Aside from this, all winter long there are frequent public concerts, by local and visiting musicians, and excellent quartet and amateur concerts by subscription.

For dancing, Vienna makes the greatest and most varied provisions that any city in the world can boast of. The large and small Redoutensaal, the Apollo-saal, the Mehlgrube, the Neue Welt, and countless others are dance halls which offer to all classes the gayest, most elegant, and most convenient resorts. The dance music is everywhere outstanding, the service with everything in the way of food and drink is perfect. And with all these amusements, there prevails the best and most jovial spirit, with never a trace of oppressing distinctions.

• • • • •

Viennese society is, moreover, so rich and so agreeable that, as regards hospitality, good living, freedom, and general merriment, Vienna has no equal in all Europe. He who enjoys the good fortune, in Vienna, of coming to know the societies of the various classes, from the higher nobility down to the petite bourgeoisie, enjoys in the highest degree and in the freest and most agreeable way everything charming, delightful, and satisfying that Europe has to offer. At the same time to have everywhere before one's eyes ladies who are beautiful, cheerful, and merry, who are neither affected nor yet impudently forward, is a pleasure one experiences nowhere in the world to the extent one does in Vienna.

To these countless and inexhaustible attractions of Vienna is further to be reckoned that thousands of strangers from all parts and countries of Europe have residences here and travel constantly back and forth, while some have established themselves with taste and not infrequently on a grand scale and live here in great splendor and hospitality. This applies especially to Russians and Poles, who bring the good sociable spirit with them and amalgamate themselves with the Viennese the more easily. Aside from them, the great Bohemian, Moravian, and Hungarian families, like the Austrians, live regularly all winter long in Vienna, giving it the brilliance and magnificence that make it the great splendid imperial city, for the court itself prefers a retired family life to external pomp and show. Yet the court appears also with great dignity and no little brilliance at the few public festivities which it still maintains. The greatest brilliance consists, however, in the rich background provided by the higher nobility of the crown lands.

In the mild and imperceptible gradations from the higher princely nobility, with an annual income of a million, a half million, or a quarter of a million gulden, to the lesser courtly nobility, with an income of a hundred thousand gulden or over; from thence to the petty new nobility, who not infrequently have and spend as much, if not still more—the bankers and great landowners and manufacturers are included here; and so on through the bourgeoisie proper down to the well-to-do petite bourgeoisie; in the way that all the great public diversions and amusements are enjoyed by all classes without any abrupt divisions or offending distinctions—in these respects, Vienna is again quite alone among the great cities of Europe. If, with respect to the first part of this observation, London shows certain similarities, with respect to the second, it is after all very different. In London, an ordinary citizen does not venture into the parterre of the great Italian opera—the drama of the nobility and the great rich world—without having at least marked himself as an elegant and wealthy gentleman by some outward sign—a fine, expensive ring, or something of the sort—and he can in no way obtain admission to a concert or any other sort of entertainment offered by subscription to the nobility—the Concerts of Ancient Musick, for example—unless he is at least related to the great noble families.

Through the utter banishment of all splendor and affectation in everyday costume, even in the greatest houses and circles, Viennese society has gained still more, and I do not know what one could wish added to it to make it perfectly agreeable.

Thus I had the good fortune to spend in Vienna a whole winter, richer in amusements and pleasures of every kind than any winter I have ever before experienced, for all my good fortune in my many earlier travels. If I have one regret it is that the winter continued severe too long to permit my again enjoying to my heart's content the great public art treasures, which, with the utmost liberality, stand free and open to everyone winter and summer and from which, on my first visit to Vienna, I derived so much pleasure and profit. My own work and the hope of being able to remain in Vienna undisturbed throughout the lovely spring season, so endlessly rich in pleasures here, caused me to put off many things, the more so since the extraordinary hospitality of the highest and most noble as well as greatest and most agreeable houses and families offered me daily so rich a social life.

INDEX

Note: Numbers in boldface refer to pages where definitions for a term are found, or to the source reading passages themselves.